THE GOVERNMENT TAKETH AWAY

AMERICAN GOVERNANCE AND PUBLIC POLICY SERIES

Series Editor: Barry Rabe, University of Michigan

THE GOVERNMENT TAKETH AWAY

THE POLITICS OF PAIN IN THE UNITED STATES AND CANADA

LESLIE A. PAL AND R. KENT WEAVER, EDITORS

GEORGETOWN UNIVERSITY PRESS
WASHINGTON, D.C.

Georgetown University Press, Washington, D.C.
© 2003 by Georgetown University Press. All rights reserved.
Printed in the United States of America

10 9 8 7 6 5 4 3 2 1   2003

This volume is printed on acid-free offset book paper.

Library of Congress Cataloging-in-Publication Data

The government taketh away : the politics of pain in the United States
and Canada / Leslie A. Pal and R. Kent Weaver, editors.
   p. cm. — (American governance and public policy series)
Includes bibliographical references and index.
  ISBN 0-87840-901-7 (hardcover : alk. Paper)—ISBN 0-87840-902-5
(pbk. : alk. paper)
1. United States—Politics and government—1993–2001. 2.
Canada—Politics and government—1980– 3. Comparative government.
I. Pal, Leslie Alexander, 1954– II. Weaver, R. Kent, 1953– III. Series:
American governance and public policy.

JK271.G722 2003

320′.6′0973—dc21

                                                        2002014713

FOR ELLEN AND MARY

CONTENTS

LIST OF TABLES AND FIGURES

TABLES

FIGURES

PREFACE

Writing about political pain and loss imposition has been an oddly pleasurable and rewarding experience. The project had its roots in R. Kent Weaver's work on the differential institutional capacities of presidential and parliamentary systems in the U.S. and Canada to reform their respective countries' pension systems, as well as in theoretical work he had done on credit-claiming and blame-avoiding by politicians. This linked nicely with work that Leslie Pal had done on institutional theory and on some specific cases of what we later termed loss imposition, such as abortion policy in Canada.

The genesis of what eventually became this book was contained in several papers presented over the years. The first was a general overview of the theory and several cases, presented by Weaver at the American and Canadian Political Science Association meetings (CPSA) in 1989. This was followed by a joint paper by Weaver and Pal at the 1997 CPSA meetings in St. John's, Newfoundland. Momentum continued to build as we invited collaborators for panels at the 1999 CPSA meetings in Sherbrooke, Quebec, and the 1999 meetings of the Association for Canadian Studies in the United States in Pittsburgh, Pennsylvania. Other versions were presented in various venues, and we are grateful for the criticisms and suggestions of colleagues: the Cunliffe Centre for the Study of Constitutionalism and National Identity at Sussex University at Brighton (1997); the Brookings Research in Progress seminar (2001); and the Seminar in Economics, Politics and Public Policy at the School of Public Policy and Administration at Carleton University (2002). In particular we would like to thank Henry Jacek (McMaster University) and Richard Simeon (University of Toronto) for their rich and detailed comments at the two CPSA presentations.

This somewhat lengthy gestation was in part a reflection of the conceptual and empirical challenges of studying two examples each of four types of loss imposition in two countries across time. The early fantasy of doing all the cases ourselves quickly evaporated as we realized the enormity of the task. We were extremely fortunate to find contributors of the caliber we did, given the demands of doing effective comparative analysis and the fact that the chapter topics were generated first through our theoretical framework. We are grateful for both the patience and the professionalism of our colleagues in responding to our requests that they engage with that framework in exploring the specifics of their cases. The volume is exceptionally well integrated around key themes thanks in large part to their efforts.

We were also fortunate to have the help of several others in the successful production of this book. Georges Dubé and Richard Lévesque provided indefatigable research assistance. From Georgetown University Press, we are grateful to Barry Rabe, the series editor, who expressed early support and enthusiasm for the project, and to Gail Grella, the Press's associate director, and to the Press staff, for shepherding the manuscript through a bracing editorial process. Their professionalism is inscribed on every page of this book.

As much of a pleasure as it was to collaborate on this project, we must acknowledge that its completion imposed some losses of a different type on those close to us. Manuscripts are beggars and thieves of time, and what we gave up to this book we necessarily had to take from our families. They did not always suffer in silence, but ultimately it was their support for our self-inflicted pain that made this book possible.

1

THE POLITICS OF PAIN

LESLIE A. PAL AND R. KENT WEAVER

DEMOCRATIC POLITICS IS ABOUT MAKING CHOICES, AND SOMETIMES THOSE choices inflict pain. Most western democracies have been through an extremely painful period in the last decade. Across the OECD, there has been a trend of expenditure and program cuts, increased taxes, and downsizing in both the public and private sectors. Yet, the need to make political choices that inflict pain on at least some citizens or organizations is unavoidable. At a minimum, not every tax dollar that citizens pay is returned as a direct benefit to them. Some decisions, like locating a military base or a shipyard, involve benefits that are not easily divisible, and so create winners and losers, at least in relative terms. Implementing new regulatory standards imposes costs either on those who are regulated or on their customers. Pareto optimality (in the sense of increasing total utility without making anyone worse off) is difficult to achieve in practice, and almost any policy initiative will, at least initially, inflict some measure of pain and create a category of those who suffer some loss.

Some decisions impose more visible pain than others, however. Whereas constructing a new military base or awarding a contract to build a new generation of fighter aircraft is likely to create economic gains for communities near the site(s) chosen and deny them to communities who lose out in the competition, closing an existing base creates even more visible losses of jobs and purchasing power in affected communities. Locating nuclear waste sites and other undesirable facilities in any given community arouses so-called "not in my backyard" (NIMBY) concerns. Cutting pensions or unemployment insurance benefits affects constituencies that are geographically more diffuse, but that may nevertheless protest—not least because political competitors to whatever governing party or officeholders who imposed those losses have a strong incentive to mobilize the affected group.

This book is about efforts by democratic governments—or by societal groups using the authority of government—to impose pain. We focus here on the infliction of visible losses—as well as attempts that are made to inflict losses—on groups and communities that are neither so diffuse as to feel no sense of commonality nor so politically and economically marginalized that they are incapable of articulating their pain and trying to exact retribution when it is inflicted. In other words, we focus on loss-imposing initiatives that bear some risk for governments and that require real loss-imposing capacity to succeed.

The politics of pain poses important issues of democratic politics. There is the widely noted negativity bias that has been observed in psychological studies and electoral surveys: Individuals negatively value the loss of a current benefit more than they (positively) value the receipt of a new benefit, even if the two situations have an equal material effect. Individuals facing losses also tend to be relatively easy to mobilize in defense of what they might lose. Thus politicians who impose losses—even losses accompanied by compensating gains—tend to attract blame and lose support.[1] Hence, the politics of loss imposition is very different from that of program expansion, even where some groups receive less additional largesse than others and may thus feel "relatively deprived."

Political systems that are not capable of imposing necessary losses in order to achieve broader benefits suffer paralysis, or at least inflexibility.[2] Of course, an ostensibly democratic political system that concentrates power so effectively that losses can be imposed whenever its leaders desire seems equally undesirable. But no democratic polity can avoid the challenge of loss imposition forever. If we assume that some loss-imposing decisions will inevitably have to be made but that politicians are (equally inevitably) loathe to make them because of the political costs involved, it becomes an empirical question as to how and how often decisions of this type are made and sustained in the face of resistance on the part of potential losers.

Our special interest in this volume is in whether (and if so, how) political institutions affect governmental capacity for loss imposition, and how policymakers and social groups work through and around particular sets of institutions in order to achieve or derail loss-imposing initiatives. Both popular wisdom and political science theorizing suggest that some institutional arrangements facilitate loss imposition more than others. Rational choice theorists, for example, have long argued that majoritarian decision-making rules affect policy outcomes, and may privilege the "default position" (that is, what happens if no action is undertaken—usually the policy status quo) when there is no clear majority preference for a single alternative to the default.[3] André Kaiser argues that the "more veto points in a political system, the more difficult it is to change policies as well as the institutional structure itself."[4] Similarly, George Tsebelis has introduced the related concept of "veto players."[5] A veto player is an individual or collective actor whose agreement is required for a change in policy. Veto players can be political parties, institutional players (courts, or others whose position is determined by law), as well as interest groups. Some systems are more permeable to resistance by potential losers than others.[6]

The institutional literature of most direct concern to us here is that concerning differences in loss-imposing capacity between Westminster-style parliamentary systems (those that have single-member districts with plurality elections, and therefore tend to produce single-party majority governments most of the time) and the U.S. separation-of-powers system. The conventional wisdom is that the concentration of power characteristic of Westminster regimes provides important advantages with respect to loss imposition. Empirical studies produce more nuanced results, however. Most notably, a comparative analysis by Paul Pierson and Kent Weaver of retrenchment initiatives in U.S., Canadian, and British pension policy showed "a decidedly mixed assessment of institutional effects on government capabilities."[7] They found that Westminster institutions provided some advantages with respect to loss imposition, but argued that these advantages are partially offset by concentration of accountability (meaning that governments imposing losses cannot easily avoid blame for their actions). Westminster-presidential differences were by no means decisive in determining policy outcomes; Pierson and Weaver found that other political and institutional factors, such as the proximity of election, the strength of opposition parties, and policy legacies, also come into play.

Edward Lascher, Jr., examines the same issues in his study of automobile insurance reform in the Canadian provinces and U.S. states. Lascher's focus on the subnational level yields many more instances for comparison, and his study combines multiple case studies with aggregate analysis. Lascher examines losses imposed primarily on a professional group—trial lawyers. He finds stronger and more consistent institutional effects than Pierson and Weaver in support of the argument that loss imposition is generally more difficult in the U.S. system. In Canada, he argues, "the provinces' Westminster parliamentary systems made it easier to adopt far-reaching reforms, as well as to reverse such reforms when party leaders' problem diagnosis shifted."[8] In the U.S. state of Rhode Island, on the other hand, "rank-and-file lawyer-lawmakers from both parties formed a solid bulwark of opposition to abandoning traditional tort."[9] Like Pierson and Weaver, Lascher notes that other factors (e.g., Canada–U.S. differences in the strength of interest group opposition and patterns of country-specific policy diffusion) may also account for the differences in outcomes. And he, too, offers caveats to his findings, noting that (1) institutional differences may matter less where executive action alone is sufficient to bring about a loss-imposing change in policy from the default position, and (2) it may be harder for Westminster systems to impose losses when the affected group is a broad middle-class constituency than when it is a relatively small group like trial lawyers.[10]

Pierson and Weaver issue similar cautions in their study, and they call for further research to evaluate the generalizability of their findings. Existing research, for example, alludes to different types of losses (such as symbolic/values-oriented versus material; geographically concentrated versus geographically dispersed but demographically concentrated). But there has been no analysis that we are aware of that has tried to develop an adequate categorization of types of loss imposition and systematically test arguments about the consistency of government's capacity for loss imposition across types of losses. Is a government's capacity for imposing geographically diffuse losses likely to be similar to or different from its capacity to impose losses on geographically concentrated groups like communities affected by a military base closing or the potential opening of a hazardous waste disposal site, for example? Would it be different if the losses were being imposed on corporate interests rather than on individual citizens and communities? Do the dynamics of coalition building and blame generation and the opportunities for governments to impose losses and compensate losers differ if it is not material losses that are being imposed but rather a change in policy away from an individual's or group's preferences on a highly contentious moral issue like abortion, school prayer, or the right to bear arms?

This volume addresses these questions through a series of comparisons between the U.S. and Canada in specific policy sectors. In the concluding chapter, as we look across case studies, we will be asking the following question: Are the differences in capacity to impose losses greater within sector-specific Canada–U.S. pairs of cases or across them? If the differences in outcomes are great across sectors and small within the Canada–U.S. pairs in a single sector, it suggests that the structure of political institutions has little impact on governmental capacity for loss imposition. If the differences between countries are great within each sector and consistent across sectors (e.g., Canada shows greater capacity for loss imposition in every sector), it suggests that differences in political institutions are important.

The first three sections of this introductory chapter develop some preliminary hypotheses about how each of three types of variables—political/institutional arrangements, the type of loss being imposed, and several "confounding" variables—are likely to affect capacity and opportunities for imposing and resisting losses. The fourth section of the chapter outlines several types of strategies that policymakers and social groups may use to impose, and others to resist, loss imposition through government. The final section of the chapter discusses the research design of the study and its limitations.

INSTITUTIONAL INFLUENCES ON GOVERNMENT LOSS-IMPOSITION CAPACITY

A key rule in any democratic system is that governments seek to get re-elected. The political calculus of loss imposition, therefore, is affected by the degree to which potential losers or opponents can, through the rules of the political system, exact some price from politicians in terms of re-election[11] and the pressures that they can bring to bear to reverse or soften the intended loss imposition. Political institutions have an important bearing on this dynamic, since they define the number of access and veto points, the number and role of veto players, accountability relationships (who is likely to be held responsible for decisions and to what degree), and the capacities of decision makers to manage the consequences of loss imposition. If power in a political system is highly concentrated, with few access or veto points and little opportunity for losing groups to exact punishment from officeholders, losses can in principle be easily imposed. Political institutions that maximize access and veto points, however, and whose decision-making rules require consensus or a superma-jority, will face difficulties in loss imposition. Most democratic political systems, of course, lie somewhere between these extremes, and the consequences for loss imposition are accordingly less clear. Table 1-1 outlines a number of effects that specific institutional arrangements are likely to have on governmental capacity for loss imposition and their specific implications for U.S.–Canada differences.

Westminster Parliamentary System vs. Separation-of-Powers Institutions

It is no accident that the contrast between Canada's Westminster parliamentary system and the U.S. separation-of-powers (presidential) system is the central focus of this book. Many authors have argued that the United States, in contrast to Westminster parliamentary systems, is particularly ineffective at making tough decisions like imposing losses.[12] The effect of institutions on decision making is multifold. First, institutional arrangements may affect *who has power and influence* in the political system. Westminster systems, with their emphasis on collective cabinet responsibility and party discipline, tend to concentrate power in the hands of leaders of the governing party or parties and offer fewer veto points to interest groups than does the U.S. system. Institutional arrangements may also affect policy outcomes by establishing *the rules under which alternatives are compared and selected or rejected*. Westminster institutions are usually seen as giving the governing party or parties a substantial advantage over the U.S. system in determining which legislative alternatives are considered, and in what order. Third is *the capacity of opponents to access veto points* in the legislative process itself and to punish the government in the next election. On each of these grounds, we would expect Westminster parliamentary type regimes to be more successful at loss imposition than presidential ones. Westminster institutions generally give governments better control over the legislative agenda and enforce party discipline; presidential systems have less agenda control and are more permeable to outside interests. Finally, political institutions may also affect *the objectives and strategies of policymakers and interest groups*. Institutions that make politicians appear individually accountable for policy decisions, like those in the United States, discourage them from supporting loss-imposing actions for which they may later be blamed. In the Canadian parliamentary system, legislators can afford to impose painful policies, since voters know that they must follow their party whips and are therefore less likely to blame them individually for their votes.[13] Interest groups are unlikely to appeal to backbenchers of the governing party to break with the party on their behalf, because they know that the cost to those legislators of doing so is very high.

These institutional differences can affect a government's capacity to impose losses in a number of ways. Most obviously, fragmentation of power and multiple veto points are generally thought to make it relatively easy for groups in the U.S. to defend status quo policies (or in game theory terms, the "default position") against efforts to impose losses on them. Indeed, the many points of access available to interest groups in the U.S. system mean that organized interests may be

TABLE 1-1

Hypothesized Effects of Institutional Arrangements on Governmental Capacity for Loss Imposition

Theoretical Expectation	U.S.–Canada Application
INSTITUTIONAL ARRANGEMENT	
Presidential vs. Westminster Parliamentary	
Concentration of power in Westminster system creates greater capacity for loss imposition than in separation-of-powers system, all other things being equal	Canadian federal government will be more capable of imposing losses on powerful interests than its U.S. counterpart
Concentration of accountability in Westminster systems partially offsets its advantages in loss imposition, especially as an election nears	Canada–U.S. differential in loss imposition capacity will be greatest immediately after elections; governments in both countries have diminished loss imposition capacity as election nears
Minority government in Westminster system lowers capacity for loss imposition	Governmental capacity for loss imposition in Canada will be lower than usual in periods of divided government
Divided government imposes further veto points and further weakens capacity of separation-of-powers	Governmental capacity for loss imposition in U.S. will be especially low in periods of divided government
Effective Bicameralism	
Effective bicameralism provides additional veto points, making loss-imposing changes from the status quo less likely	Weaker check from Canadian Senate makes Canadian federal government more capable of imposing losses on powerful interests than its U.S. counterpart
Electoral Cycles	
Longer electoral cycles provide greater window for loss imposition by government	Loss imposition in both U.S. and Canada will be concentrated immediately after elections; longer electoral cycles in Canada create greater capacity for loss imposition
Courts	
Nonelected judges will play a substantial role in loss-imposing actions because they do not fear electoral retribution	Lower capacity of U.S. executive and legislative institutions will be partially offset by more activist courts in U.S., but differential will decline in post-Charter era as Canadian courts take a more activist role
Federalism	
Political competition effect: Loss imposition is especially unlikely in cases where jurisdiction is subnational and potential loss sufferers can take valued activities elsewhere	May occur in either country

TABLE 1-1

Hypothesized Effects of Institutional Arrangements on Governmental Capacity for Loss Imposition (continued)

Theoretical Expectation	U.S.–Canada Application
Passing-the-buck effects: (1) Where national government sets broad program parameters and shares funding responsibility with states/provinces, it may be able to force the latter to take blame for loss imposition; (2) Where jurisdiction is unclear, both federal and provincial and state governments may shirk from taking loss-imposing actions	May occur in either country; depends on jurisdictional structure in a particular policy sector
Joint decision trap: Where loss-imposing actions require approval of both federal and provincial governments, capacity for loss imposition diminishes	Canada is likely to encounter difficulties in imposing losses in sectors where joint federal-provincial approval requirements are in effect—a common arrangement there
Emulation effect: When a state or provincial government takes a loss-imposing action and its diffuse benefits become apparent, other states or the federal government may follow its lead	May occur in either country

able to deflect potentially loss-imposing proposals at a very early stage in the policy formulation process. A related criticism of the separation-of-powers system is that it is prone to deadlock in times of crisis: in the aftermath of the 1970s oil shocks, for example, or in face-offs over conflicting budget proposals. Because of the multiple veto points in the system, it is easy for even a small minority of opponents to block bold innovation.[14]

In a Westminster parliamentary system, on the other hand, interest groups have difficulty exercising pressure. Centralization of power in the executive combines with party discipline to insulate decision makers from pressures that might come through political parties, either from the opposition or the government backbenches. And if the government in a parliamentary system is willing to bear the political cost of imposing losses, and is able to reach internal agreement, there is little to stop it from doing so, except in a situation of minority or coalition government. Where party discipline is more tenuous, however, and could even cause a split in the party caucus and the fall of the government (in the case of conscription among Canadian Liberals during World War II, for example, or with respect to European unity issues under the John Major government in the U.K.), the capacity to ignore opposition is diminished.

Another aspect of blocking access or pressure is the speed with which losses can be imposed. Parliamentary systems give governments substantial control over the legislative agenda, with power to limit debates and force votes. This makes it possible, given a commitment to impose certain losses, to move quickly before opposition can effectively mobilize outside the legislature. Indeed, the recent experiences of the Klein and Harris provincial governments in Alberta and Ontario, respectively, in imposing retrenchment and restructuring suggest that, paradoxically, governments may be more successful loss imposers if they act on a wide front of issues almost simultaneously. This destabilizes opposition groups, keeps the mix of issues shifting, and creates a perverse psychology of equal burdens that reduces the intensity of any single group's claim of mistreatment. But these strategies require a substantial capacity to control the legislative agenda.

Parliamentary systems have disadvantages with respect to imposing losses as well, however. Especially in the Westminster variant, they tend to concentrate accountability as well as power, and voters and interest groups who wish to punish the governing party or coalition know very clearly whom to blame: It is much harder to hide who is responsible for the loss imposition. Of course, politicians know this too, and to the extent that they try to anticipate and avoid blame, they will seek to avoid loss-imposing actions. Moreover, opposition politicians in Canada have blame-generating opportunities (notably through a televised Question Period) that have no direct parallel in the United States. Blame can also come from independent bodies such as commissions, task forces, auditors, and commissioners, and these can be more visible and pointed in a parliamentary system because accountability is more concentrated. Thus whether parliamentary or check-and-balance systems have a greater ability to impose losses presumably resolves into an empirical question: Does the "concentration of power" effect outweigh the "concentration of accountability" effect, or vice versa?

Even if parliamentary institutions do in general make the Canadian federal government more effective at imposing losses than the United States government in situations where the distribution of costs and benefits is comparable, this general principle may vary across a variety of governmental situations. Governments differ over time in the cohesion and bargaining position of their executive and legislative branches. In Canada, for example, the federal government is likely to be more effective at imposing losses (1) when a single party holds a majority of seats in the House of Commons, rather than when there is a minority government, and (2) when the Opposition is fractured into several parties rather than one. The logic of this proposition is fairly straightforward. A majority government does not need to gain the support or acquiescence (through abstention) of another party to take loss-imposing actions, and the weaker the Opposition, the less capable it will be of stalling or subverting the government's agenda through procedural tactics, and the less likely the governing party is to fear that it may lose power in the next election if it does something unpopular.

A similar sort of logic can be applied in the United States: The U.S. government is likely to be more effective at imposing losses when control of the executive and legislative branches of government is united in the same party than when it is divided.[15] United government presumably narrows the ideological distance between negotiators from the executive and legislative branches of government, and it lowers incentives to engage in posturing and blame generating to make the other side look bad in ensuing elections.[16] Indeed, even if it is generally true that political executives in Canada are more successful in imposing losses in the face of organized opposition than their counterparts in the United States, this may be not because of differences in Westminster and presidential systems per se, but rather on account of societal and institutional differences that make the U.S. more likely to produce divided government than the Canadian system is to produce minority government.

Effective Bicameralism

Other institutional differences in addition to the Westminster-presidential difference may affect governmental capacity for loss imposition.[17] We cannot give the same attention to these factors that we do to the presidential-Westminster difference; but a brief discussion is necessary, because these institutional differences may reduce, reinforce, or cut across any differential presidential-Westminster institutional effects. Thus an accurate assessment of the latter requires that an effort be made to separate out other institutional and noninstitutional influences on the capacity for loss imposition.

One obvious institutional difference that needs to be considered in a Canada–U.S. comparison is their extent of effective bicameralism, or the degree to which both chambers of the legislature articulate distinctive voices in government and have close to a coequal voice in policymaking.[18] Particularly relevant are differences between the upper chambers of the two federal legislatures. The United-States Senate clearly is on a nearly equal basis with the House of Representatives as a policymaking body, especially as a burial ground for controversial legislation. Provisions of U.S. Senate rules that allow unlimited debate unless a supermajority of senators can be mustered to impose cloture privileges the "default position" vis-à-vis any proposed change in policy, even one that enjoys the support of a majority of senators.[19] It is a particularly effective guardian against loss imposition on less populous states, since these states are dramatically overrepresented in the Senate relative to their share of national population.[20]

The unelected Canadian Senate, on the other hand, is generally regarded more as a national embarrassment than as a powerful policymaking institution. While it is occasionally portrayed as a "lobby from within" for privileged business interests,[21] it is more often seen as simply a toothless institution comprised of the governing party's political faithful. Thus the existence of effective bicameralism in the United States and its absence in Canada should reinforce separation of powers in constraining government loss imposition in the U.S., both absolutely and relative to Canada.

Election Cycles

The scheduling of elections has long been recognized as a potential constraint on and impetus to government action. Edward Tufte explicitly linked electoral cycles to the distribution of costs and benefits: "There is a bias toward policies with immediate, highly visible benefits and deferred, hidden costs—myopic policies for myopic voters. Special interests induce coalition-building politicians to impose small costs on the many to achieve large benefits for the few."[22] Early work on election cycles predicted that governments would impose pain at the beginning of their terms and offer benefits near the end, before the next election.[23] Loss-imposing actions taken early in the electoral cycle are presumably less likely to be remembered by voters in order to punish the government party at the polls than those that occur shortly before the election. This suggests that in both Canada and the United States, loss-imposing actions will be concentrated shortly after an election rather than shortly before an election.[24]

Cross-national differences in the length of electoral cycles also have important implications for loss-imposing capacity. Longer electoral cycles presumably provide a longer window of voter forgetfulness and forgiveness within which loss imposition may occur and a longer period for the more diffuse offsetting effects of any loss-imposing action (e.g., budget cuts that stimulate the economy) to become apparent. The Canada–U.S. comparison on electoral cycle length is not completely straightforward, however, because Canadian electoral cycles at the federal level are not fixed, though they generally average around four years (less when there is a minority government). In the United States, all of the House of Representatives and one-third of the Senate are elected every two years (senators serve six-year terms), while the president serves a four-year term. If we make the plausible assumption that governmental capacity is likely to be determined largely by the shortest electoral cycle of any major institution, it suggests that the federal government in Canada may be more effective in imposing losses than its U.S. counterparts because the period between federal legislative elections is usually longer in Canada than the period between congressional elections in the United States.

"Staggering" of elections may also affect the capacity for loss imposition. The fact that House elections take place in the middle of every presidential term in the United States may both increase the prospects for divided government and undercut public and policymaker perceptions that there is a mandate for policy change in a particular direction.[25] These differences in electoral cycles should be considered as an alternative explanation, besides the difference between parliamentary and presidential systems, for any observed superiority of the Canadian system in loss-imposing capacity. We will see in several of the case studies and in the concluding chapter, however, that other electoral phenomena, notably the staggering of Canadian provincial elections (each province has its own electoral cycle, so multiple elections may occur within a few weeks of each other), and referenda on sovereignty in Quebec, also need to be taken into account in considering the effects of electoral cycles on the federal government's capacity for loss imposition in Canada.

Courts

Although elected politicians are concerned about winning re-election for themselves and their party compatriots, members of the higher federal judiciaries in both Canada and the United States do not have those concerns. This suggests several hypotheses about the role played by courts in the two countries. First, nonelected judges are likely to play a substantial role in loss-imposing actions, because they do not fear electoral retribution. Thus the lower capacity of U.S. executive and legislative institutions with respect to loss-imposing initiatives may be partially offset by more activist courts in the U.S., but this differential between the two countries should decline as Canadian courts have taken on a more active role in policymaking after the embedding of the Charter of Rights in the Canadian constitution in 1982. Second, loss-imposing decisions by courts in the United States will rarely be overturned by legislative action, because multiple veto points in the U.S. system firmly entrench the policy "default position" that has been newly articulated by court decisions. This is likewise the case in Canada and particularly with respect to questions of constitutional rights, even though the Canadian constitution's "Notwithstanding" clause offers the federal and provincial legislatures a mechanism to reinstate even some legislation that the Supreme Court has declared unconstitutional. Governments outside of Quebec have been extremely reluctant to use their "Notwithstanding" legislative powers, even when those court decisions have been extremely controversial.[26] Third, we should see groups that have not been successful in using government to impose losses on others through the legislative route turning to the courts to achieve those objectives—especially in the United States, but increasingly in Canada as well.

Federalism

Federalism describes a very broad array of institutional arrangements between national and subnational governments, ranging from shared and even competitive activities by the two levels of governments to fairly airtight divisions of responsibilities. The implications of federalism for governments' capacity to impose losses are likely to vary greatly depending on arrangements in individual sectors. But existing literature suggests that at least four distinct effects of federalism may exist. First is what can be called a political competition or "race to the bottom" effect, according to which loss imposition by subnational jurisdictions will be especially difficult in cases where potential loss-sufferers can take valued activities elsewhere. Competitive pressure exercised by organized interests, or internalized by politicians and other policymakers themselves, keeps individual provinces or states from imposing losses because they fear that that will drive business, and tax revenue, to other jurisdictions. As Paul Peterson has noted, competition is particularly likely to militate against government policies at the subnational level that involve redistribution of income to the less well off.[27] Even when subnational governments do choose to intervene, their policies are likely to be eroded over time as jurisdictions compete to create a friendlier business climate. This argument has been applied to a variety of policy sectors in the United States, ranging from welfare benefits to environmental regulation.[28]

A second scenario is what can be called the "joint decision trap" effect.[29] Where loss-imposing actions require approval on the part of both federal and all or most state or provincial governments, capacity for loss imposition diminishes. Because a recalcitrant minority of governments can prevent *any* action, the bargaining leverage of potential loss sufferers is maximized and the default situation—the policy status quo—will usually win out.[30] As will be discussed in Kent Weaver's chapter on pensions, the structure of the Canada/Quebec Pension Plan is an example of such a structural relationship.

A third potential impact of federalism is what could be called the "passing the buck effect." Actually, two different such effects are possible, depending on the relationship between the national and subnational governments in a particular sector. If the national government sets broad parameters for an existing program and shares funding responsibility, while subnational governments are responsible for implementation, the national government may be able to cut the funding it commits to the program while the state or provincial government bears the responsibility (and takes the blame) for the resulting cuts in services to affected groups. However, a second and quite different type of "passing the buck" effect has been outlined by Kathryn Harrison, primarily in sectors where neither level of government has yet taken an active role.[31] In this scenario, both the federal and provincial governments may take advantage of shared or unclear jurisdiction in a policy sector to avoid entry into that sector (e.g., regulation of polluters), because they fear that any activity would require imposing losses on some concentrated interest and therefore be politically costly—so the politically wisest course is to do nothing. An "After you, Alphonse" routine develops, perhaps collusively, between the two levels of government. Unitary governments, on the other hand, do not have opportunities to avoid responsibility and may therefore be more willing to undertake loss-imposing actions.

A final potential impact of federalism is what could be called the emulation effect. In this scenario, one or more subnational governments acts as an innovator in imposing losses despite opposition from a concentrated constituency, perhaps because that constituency is unusually weak in that particular state or province. When the more diffuse benefits of these loss-imposing actions become apparent, political entrepreneurs in other jurisdictions (and perhaps eventually the federal government) copy and adapt them. The key is that officials in other governments within the country see political or policy benefits emerging from the loss-imposing action once it is implemented. An oft-cited example of this scenario is the lead taken by the Canadian province of Saskatchewan in developing hospitalization, and later health, insurance over strong opposition from physicians. This action was later copied by several other provinces, and the Canadian government eventually agreed to share the costs of such insurance with provinces that agreed to meet federal guidelines.[32] The leading role of Quebec in establishing pure no-fault auto insurance may have played a similar role with respect to that innovation in Canada.

TYPES OF LOSS

As noted above, there are various hints in the literature that not all losses are the same, and that consequently the political dynamics of loss imposition will vary by type of loss and type of issue.[33] Perhaps the most widely used distinction is between costs or losses that are concentrated versus those that are widely dispersed. Mancur Olson was the first to link concentration of costs and benefits to collective action around public goods.[34] He showed that interest groups were likely to form around concentrated benefits but not around widely dispersed public goods. Olson focused on collective action among interest groups, but the logic can be applied to all policies and programs delivered by political decision makers. More credit comes from concentrated rather than dispersed benefits; more blame comes from concentrated rather than dispersed losses.[35]

A useful application of this simple model was developed by James Q. Wilson in the context of regulatory theory.[36] Wilson was concerned to challenge the prevailing view at the time that all regulation involved capture of agencies by regulated parties. He pointed out that the origins of all major regulatory initiatives in the United States had involved quite broad political coalitions, sometimes including the targets of potential regulatory activity themselves. The challenge was to discern those cases where business influence would be strong and those in which it would be weak. While acknowledging that the political significance of costs and benefits is a function of both their distribution and magnitude, for reasons of simplicity Wilson focused on distributional effects. Both costs and benefits could be either widely distributed or narrowly concentrated, yielding a fourfold classification of political situations.

In *majoritarian* politics, both costs and benefits are widely dispersed, and as a result, there is little incentive for interest groups to form and do battle over policy. Wilson's examples include the Social Security Act of 1935 and the Sherman Antitrust Act of 1890: both were wide in scope (even though Sherman addressed "industry," it did not single out any specific sector). *Interest group* politics, on the other hand, is characterized by concentrated costs (losses) and benefits; this increases incentives to mobilize both for and against the proposed policy. The broad public is largely uninvolved, while battles rage among commercial interests or between business and labor groups. The political result of interest group politics is usually some sort of compromise designed to compensate the losers. When benefits are concentrated within a group or constituency while costs are widely dispersed, we get what Wilson called *client* politics. Potential beneficiaries have high incentives to mobilize but potential losers do not, because costs are either negligible, on a per capita basis, or even invisible. This is the classic pattern for "industry capture" of regulatory agencies. Finally, *entrepreneurial* politics occurs in cases where losses or costs are concentrated but benefits are widely dispersed. Wilson's examples in the regulatory context were antipollution and auto safety legislation, each of which benefited the broad public but also imposed substantial costs on specific industries. Legislation of this type is inherently difficult to pass and requires skilled political entrepreneurs to mobilize the public and politicians, in large part through appeals to their beliefs and values rather than to their interests. This style of politics also relies, however, on the sympathy of third parties: pundits and the media, congressional staff, and the heads of voluntary associations.

Since our discussion in this volume focuses on situations in which costs are concentrated (and benefits are either concentrated or dispersed), we can focus on the second and fourth of Wilson's categories. But Wilson's discussion of costs and benefits contains some often overlooked elements, suggesting that a more complex set of categories may be needed for a systematic evaluation of the politics of pain. First, the "economic interest" focus of Wilson's argument is tempered by several caveats that emphasize the role of argument and persuasion. For example, large coalitions are necessary in regulatory politics because policy "decisions must have justifications."[37] They hinge on arguments and symbols. An assessment of the balance of costs and benefits is itself an expression of a sense of justice and equity, and supporters of what is perceived to be an inequitable policy "must respond by either modifying its terms, changing the perception of its effects, justifying those effects, or inducing (perhaps corruptly) others to ignore those effects."[38] Entrepreneurial politics "requires that attention be paid to beliefs as well as interests."[39]

Second, Wilson touches upon but then ignores several mitigating factors that should make a difference in the dynamics of loss imposition. "These costs and benefits may be monetary or nonmonetary, and the value assigned to them, as well as beliefs about the likelihood of their materializing, can change."[40] This one sentence introduces the issues of (1) symbolic costs and benefits, (2) magnitudes of loss, as opposed to their mere distribution, and (3) assessments of probability. The notion that such assessments can change over time introduces a chronological dimension as well: When an industry is deregulated, for example, some losses probably have a high level of certainty, but others are much less clear.

The many potential variables outlined here for categorizing loss imposition suggest that there is no single typology that is likely to work best or that provides mutually exclusive categories. Four types of losses seem particularly important, however, and sufficiently different in their political dynamics, to deserve separate investigation. (See table 1-2.)

Geographically Diffuse but Group-Specific Losses

A first type of loss imposition is that which is targeted at groups that are geographically diffused across many parts of the country, but that have enough sense of self-identification to potentially protest and organize against losses being imposed. Examples might include senior citizens facing pension cutbacks or recipients of health care services facing declining benefits or increased user fees. This is a somewhat ambiguous category that tries to capture two important dimensions of loss imposition. The first is that if a group is geographically diffuse it is spread out over a large number of electoral constituencies, and hence, if mobilized, has the potential to exact significant retribution on loss-imposing politicians and their political parties. This is a completely different dynamic from that instigated by geographically concentrated losses, which will tend to mobilize either single electoral constituencies (if the loss is something as localized as closing a military base or erecting a waste site) or regional ones.

The second dimension is the nature of group identity and mobilization. Losses that are imposed on a wide and diverse group of citizens often succeed because those citizens find it difficult to mobilize themselves as a distinct group. Taxpayers might be an example, though in recent years antitax campaigns have succeeded in defining "taxpayers" as a distinct group. Another factor is the intensity of the loss. If pensions are cut only minutely, or gradually over time (through changes to inflation indexing, for example), the capacity to mobilize is likewise diminished.

TABLE 1-2
Categories of Loss Imposition

Geographically Diffuse but Group-Specific Losses

Group Interest vs. Group Interest	Group vs. Diffuse Interests
Health care cutbacks	Pension retrenchment

Losses Imposed on Business

Business vs. Business or Other Concentrated Interests	Business vs. Diffuse Interests
Telecommunications deregulation Financial services deregulation Transportation deregulation	Environmental restrictions on air and water pollution, logging, etc. Tobacco control

Geographically Concentrated Losses

Locality-Specific (including NIMBY)	Multiple-Locality	Region-Specific
Highway routing decisions Garbage dumps Hazardous waste dump siting	Military base closings Elimination of government-subsidized rail lines, rail passenger service, or local airline service	Elimination of agricultural subsidies Closing access to a regional fishery

Symbolic Losses

Strong Clientele vs. Weak Clientele	Strong Clientele vs. Strong Clientele
Gun control	Abortion politics Gay rights

Politicians accordingly face an interesting calculus in this type of loss imposition scenario. They must ask themselves whether the loss is being imposed on a group that is sufficiently dispersed geographically and sufficiently specific (or self-aware) that it might generate a backlash and hence punishment at the polls. Some interests are geographically dispersed but not sufficiently well defined to cause trouble—consumers or families, for example. In other instances, loss imposition might itself cause a fuzzy identity to come into focus. Cuts to pensions might lead to the formation of a "seniors lobby," for example.

Westminister systems like Canada's concentrate authority, whereas the U.S. system disperses it. Considering this feature only, we would expect an organized and defined but diverse interest group, such as pensioners, to be better able to mount resistance and block loss-imposing policies in the U.S. There are fewer avenues for opposition in the Canadian system and greater concentration of authority, allowing the executive to carry through a loss-imposing decision even in the face of widespread resistance. Another important variable is the election cycle. If the cycle is short, then the risks are greater that a geographically diffused interest might achieve retribution at the polls. Longer cycles like Canada's make it theoretically more likely that losses can be imposed early in the election cycle, when there can be no effective resistance.

Losses Imposed on Business

Losses imposed on business interests rather than groups of voters are really a special case of the first category. Treating these losses separately recognizes what Lindblom calls the "privileged position of business" in capitalist societies.[41] Not all threatened loss impositions on business are likely to exhibit the same political dynamic, however. While many different permutations are possible (conflicts may pit firm versus firm, for example, or sector versus sector) at least two different overall subcategories seem likely. One is where loss imposition on some sector of business produces diffuse benefits. This would include such cases as increased regulatory burdens (e.g., with respect to pollution control or consumer safety) that threaten profits for some or all firms in a sector, or restrictions on business activity (e.g., reduction in the amount of public lands that can be logged, or requiring more environmentally sound logging techniques). The second category includes conflicts in which losses imposed on some or all firms in a sector may produce concentrated benefits for other segments of the business community (such as loosened entry and pricing regulations in former oligopoly or monopoly markets).

Our theoretical expectation is that losses of the first type (concentrated loss versus diffuse benefits) are going to be difficult to impose in any political system; politicians have to be very creative in order to carry them off. This is because of the hoary maxim that a concentrated loss mobilizes opposition more effectively than a dispersed benefit. Indeed, this is Wilson's point about entrepreneurial politics. Business interests, whether organized as firms or sectors, are well positioned in any political system to resist losses of this type, or indeed of any type, and so the difficulty is in mobilizing support from those who might benefit. Environmental controls, for example, will cost businesses, but the benefits to citizens and consumers are so diffuse in most cases as to be almost invisible.

Potentially counterbalancing this theoretical expectation is the fact that businesses by definition cannot vote—although constituencies associated with those businesses or sectors (e.g., employees or customers) may be mobilized on behalf of particular interests. Business interests may also be able to use lobbying, advertising, and political contributions to defend themselves against government loss imposition initiatives. The empirical issue, therefore, hinges on the reality of the "privileged position" and businesses' capacity to mobilize through political institutions. Once again, we would expect that U.S. institutions will give business interests greater scope and opportunity to resist losses, even when those losses are concentrated and unobjectionable to a silent majority of benefiting electors. Canadian institutions concentrate authority, giving them a capacity to impose losses more easily in favor of benefits to a diffuse public interest.

A second category of business-focused loss imposition involves situations in which some businesses suffer concentrated business losses, which are offset by concentrated gains for other businesses. The telecommunications case in this volume explores the dynamics of this type of loss imposition. As predicted by Wilson, we should observe very intense interest group lobbying in such a situation, wherein concentrated interests on both sides of the issue try to win the day through pressures on politicians and decision makers. But in this case, as opposed to the first category of business losses, electoral considerations (in terms of even diffuse public support) may play a minor role; here the central question is one of the permeability of political institutions. The telecommunications case also brings into play ancillary institutions, such as regulatory agencies, and *their* susceptibility to pressure. The theoretical expectations regarding this type of business-related loss imposition scenario are that conflict is likely to be more visible in the U.S. than in Canada, and that loss imposition decisions will generally be more incremental in the U.S. case, since multiple veto points facilitate resistance to sweeping changes.

Geographically Concentrated Losses

In conflicts where losses are geographically concentrated, the most important dimension of variance is the geographical scope—crudely, narrow, moderate, or wide—of the losses. The narrowest scope results from loss imposition on a single community or constituency. Highway and rapid transit routing decisions along with the siting of garbage dumps are among the clearest cases of decisions likely to be clearly localized to a single community. Other siting decisions are more complex: Nuclear waste storage and hazardous disposal sites are also highly localized, but fears of the long-term and long-range consequences of such sites may spark region-wide resistance. Other decisions are likely to have impacts on multiple communities: decisions to abandon a rail line that serves a number of grain elevators in rural communities, for example, or passenger train routes that likewise serve numerous communities. Examples of region-wide cutbacks include cuts in commodity price supports or transportation subsidies paid to farmers, or the closing of regional fisheries due to a decline in the stock of fish. In each of these cases, there might be long-term benefits to at least some of the farmers and fishermen suffering short-term pain, but the short-term losses are likely to be severe.

Of course, the size of the affected group matters as well as its geographical extent. When a constituency is relatively small (for example, a single trade union representing workers in a few factories), it is probably better off being concentrated in a few localities in order to resist loss imposition; when it is larger (e.g., a union with several locals), it is probably better off being diffused across many electoral districts and regions.

The politics of geographically concentrated loss imposition will also be affected by the kind of precedents that are being set by particular cases of loss imposition—specifically, whether a given case is likely to preclude further loss imposition, to have an uncertain impact, or to lead to *more* loss impositions (a "snowball" or "camel's nose" effect). Establishing a high-level nuclear waste repository is geographically narrow and precluding, for example: If it is placed in Nevada, nobody else is likely to have to have one. Closing a number of military bases is geographically moderate and may have a snowballing effect: If politicians figure out a way to do it without too much pain, they may come back and try it again. The precedent-setting dimension is particularly important in terms of developing a coalition of opposition. In the nuclear waste case, nobody else has an incentive to join, since Nevada's loss is their gain; in the case of base closings, politicians from regions not yet affected may feel that they are likely to be next.

Political institutions may interact with geographically concentrated losses in different ways. One plausible hypothesis is that geographically concentrated losses will be particularly difficult to impose in the United States, because of geographical representation in Congress and the tendency of legislators to self-select onto committees with jurisdiction over issues of particular concern to their constituents (e.g., westerners onto Interior and coastal state representatives onto the now defunct Merchant Marines and Fisheries committee in the House). But again, we should be aware of potential offsetting effects: Canada's Westminster system has long been charged with exacerbating regional tensions (in particular by producing regional underrepresentation in the parliamentary caucus of the national governing party), which can make federal politicians especially sensitive about imposing region-specific losses. Moreover, traditions of regional balancing in the cabinet, and the use of regional ministers to look out for the interests of specific regions, bring such concerns to the center of decision making in Canada. Because regional competition tends to be argued out in cabinet, there is an advantage to proposals that can be divided so as to satisfy regional demands. Bakvis and MacDonald have argued with respect to benefit-engendering policies that "[a] program that provides little opportunity for being divided into discrete, concrete entities suitable for distribution into different locales is not likely to fare very well in cabinet discussion or, alternatively, stands to become radically transformed to make it more acceptable to the regional proclivities of ministers. Overall, this type of distributional politics is not all that dissimilar to what is found in the U.S. congressional system."[42] Initiatives to impose regionally concentrated losses in Canada may also enjoy a fate similar to that of their U.S. counterparts, through mechanisms that are structurally distinctive but produce comparable outcomes.

Symbolic Losses

Some losses are primarily symbolic or value-based rather than material in nature. Material losses (such as jobs) clearly have psychological impacts in terms of self-esteem and self-worth, but there are some political issues about which people feel strongly even if they have no immediate or direct interest. Abortion is perhaps the best example, but a short list of other "hot-button" value issues might include legal recognition of gay and lesbian unions or flag-burning. The loss for those whose values are not validated by policy in such cases is symbolic but nonetheless powerful. It may be perceived as a threat to one's (or a group's) "way of life" and trigger status anxiety over the way in which an issue presents the threat of "real or apparent loss of wealth, power, and prestige by groups."[43]

Symbolic losses, too, have their own distinctive dynamic. Particularly important here are limitations on the ability of governments to compensate losers, to "split the difference," or to "grandfather" some of the persons potentially affected by a policy change in order to weaken opposition to loss-imposing actions. Current retirees may be satisfied if their own pension benefits are protected, and employees of military bases scheduled for closure may be content if they are offered generous buyout and early retirement packages. But opponents of gun control are unlikely to be satisfied if they are personally exempted from registration requirements, and proponents and opponents of abortion rights are both likely to remain dissatisfied at compromise measures such as banning certain types of late-term abortions or limiting teenagers' (but not adults') access to abortions. When opponents of a loss-imposing action believe it to be not only personally inconvenient but morally wrong, the stakes of politics become very high indeed.

Because these are value issues that can be framed in human rights and constitutional terms, the courts often play an important role in making key decisions. (Abortion is the clearest example.) Sometimes this lets governments off the hook; sometimes it complicates their lives, since actions contrary to the legal decision will attract more blame.

Predictions on the institutional interplay with symbolic losses are more difficult to make than in the other cases. Certainly, to the degree that Westminster systems give the legislature (and hence the cabinet) a substantial independence from the judiciary, such systems should be able to better impose symbolic losses that courts might reject on human rights grounds. The Canadian system, however, given the Charter of Rights and Freedoms that was constitutionally entrenched in 1982, is in many respects closer to the U.S. than it is to the United Kingdom, and litigation against symbolic losses or disadvantages on equity and rights grounds is just as plausible in Canada as in the U.S. However, we can still discern loss imposition advantages for the Canadian system even in these cases. First, concentration of authority means that governments can override even the most strident "way of life" objections. We will see in later chapters that the gun control issue demonstrates this in part, whereas in the case of abortion, when the Canadian government allowed a free vote (that is, party discipline was not invoked) in the House of Commons and thereby relinquished its control to individual House members, the result was paralysis. Second, as we discuss below under "confounding variables," the nature of Canadian social cleavages around symbolic issues like gay and lesbian unions, the treatment of criminals, various "unpatriotic" actions, abortion, and gun control is such that governments do not have to fear a concerted backlash among conservative or right-wing groups. The religious right in the U.S., on the other hand, has been a spearhead of resistance to attempts to impose symbolic losses.

These categories of types of loss imposition are not airtight. A good example is the controversy that took place in Canada in the late 1980s over the awarding of a maintenance contract for the Canadian Forces' CF-18 fighter planes. At its base was a conflict between two firms over which would be the lead contractor. But when the federal Cabinet decided to overrule a decision to award the contract to a firm in Winnipeg and award it instead to a company in Montreal, it took on regional overtones, and aroused deep-seated symbolic fears that a government based in the East was once again demonstrating a lack of concern for Canada's western provinces.[44] Similarly, cutting back on government health care expenditures may be predominantly a measure that affects citizens as latent consumers of health care, but it may have other effects as well, depending upon how it is structured: It may, for example, involve cuts in fees to doctors and/or insurance companies (group and business losses), closures of hospitals in some communities (locality-specific or multiple-locality effects), or reductions in subsidies from the central government to subnational governments, accompanied by prohibitions on cuts in services— thereby requiring the subnational governments to absorb the cost of the reductions (losses imposed on governments). Rarely will losses fit neatly in a single category or subcategory. But looking at multiple cases and identifying "category spillovers" where they occur should allow us to make progress in identifying the distinctive political dynamics characteristic of specific types of losses—if such distinctiveness does in fact indeed exist.

THE ROLE OF CONFOUNDING VARIABLES

Complicating any effort to assess governmental capacity to impose losses is the fact that governmental capacity is not something that can be observed directly; it must instead be inferred on the basis of observed outcomes.[45] It is tempting to impute any difference in outcomes to differences in governmental capacity for loss imposition and to impute those differences, in turn, to differences in political institutions, but the real world is far more complicated than that. A number of what can be called "confounding variables" affect each step in the causal chain. Differences in outcomes across countries, for example, may be affected by variations in the organization of a particular sector of the economy. Governmental capacity for imposing losses on particular groups (or in general) may be affected by such factors as the political cleavages in the country, by the relative power of business and labor organizations, or by jurisdictional splits between national and subnational governments. Even political institutions themselves are not sui generis: Both initial choice of institutional arrangements for governing a country and the way that those institutions subsequently function are likely to be influenced by distinctive characteristics of the host society.

A complete untangling of institutional impacts and the impact of confounding variables is obviously impossible, and a comprehensive discussion of confounding variables is beyond the scope of this introductory chapter. It may be helpful, however, to introduce five of the main ones—policy legacies, globalization, emulation, sociopolitical cleavage structures, and political culture and ideas—that appear repeatedly in the case study chapters that follow. (See table 1-3.)

Policy Legacies
Both the capacity of governments to impose losses and their need to do so may be heavily influenced by past policy choices and by the programmatic and institutional

TABLE 1-3
Hypothesized Confounding Variable Effects on Capacity for Loss Imposition

Theoretical Expectation	U.S.–Canada Application
Policy Legacies	
Inherited decision procedures that give government a greater role in decision making in a sector create greater leverage for loss imposition but may also concentrate blame	May occur in either country
Globalization	
Global economic integration makes it more costly to (1) impose losses on mobile capital, and (2) shield domestic social interests from the costs imposed by global trends	Governments in both countries will have weak leverage to impose losses on business or to compensate domestic losers from economic integration, but greater trade dependence means that this will be especially true in Canada
Smaller countries will increasingly find it difficult to pursue policies that deviate from those of their major trading partners	Canadian decisions that impose greater losses on powerful domestic interests than in the U.S. may be the result less of strong political institutions than of stronger pressures for harmonization
Emulation	
Countries emulate policies in other countries, especially neighboring or "peer" countries, that appear to be successful	As a result of emulation, especially on the Canadian side, Canada–U.S. policies will tend toward convergence that masks institutional differences.
Cleavage Structures and Social Organization	
Union organizational strength leads to greater capacity to resist policies that weaken labor rights	Higher union density in Canada leads to lower capacity to impose losses on labor interests in Canada than in the United States
Strong regional cleavages heighten sensitivity to regionally concentrated losses and make imposing them more difficult	Policy actions that have a strong region-specific impact (especially on Quebec) face higher barriers in Canada than in the United States
Governments that lack representation in a particular region are more likely to impose losses there	Regionalization of Canadian parliamentary caucus may facilitate region-specific loss imposition, but concern for national unity makes it less likely
Political Culture and Ideas	
A political culture that is suspicious of governmental intervention provides additional weapons for opponents of governmental loss imposition	Stronger resistance in U.S. to taxation and direct governmental intervention gives additional resources to U.S. interests resisting those sorts of loss imposition mechanisms than in Canada

consequences of those decisions—what can broadly be called *policy legacies* and *path dependence*.[46] These legacies are not merely static results, but ongoing effects that continue to structure choices and decisions in the future. Past choices lead down certain paths, and this path dependency is not easily reversed.

A first type of policy legacy concerns the decision-making mechanisms through which governmental decisions in a sector are (or are not) made. Consider, for example, three regulatory regimes for dealing with unprofitable rail passenger services. Under a purely private sector regime, government merely acquiesces to railway companies' decisions to stop service and the "policy default" is whatever is decided by the companies. Deviation from that default would require deliberate governmental action that would likely be opposed by the railways. In a second scenario, any discontinuance of services by those companies must be approved by a government regulatory commission. In this situation, any discontinuance of service is much more likely to be blamed on government—especially in Canada, where regulatory commissions generally have less autonomy from the executive than in the U.S.

In a third scenario, government operates the service itself, through a government-owned enterprise.[47] Here government itself imposes losses on affected communities when it discontinues a service. All other things being equal, the first of these procedures is most conducive to loss imposition on customers, precisely because customers and others who oppose service cutbacks can't use governmental levers to compel continuation of services. Similarly, a country in which health care expenditures are handled primarily through private sector insurance (with tax subsidies for those expenditures) may find itself having weaker levers for imposing governmental cutbacks than those in which government plays a more direct role. The general point here is that the regulatory regime in effect makes a major difference in the default position, the types of decisions that government is required to make, and the likelihood that it will incur blame for imposing losses.

A second form of path dependence involves specific features of program design that make potential loss imposition more or less visible to those who will be affected. For example, if governments want to cut income transfer programs for equivalent clienteles, it will be harder to do in a program in which benefit levels are indexed for inflation. When benefit levels are not indexed, simple inaction will lead to a decline in the real value of benefits over time. When they *are* indexed, the government will probably have to legislatively change the program, directly incurring opprobrium from affected groups and providing a much more convenient target for opposition politicians.[48]

Policy legacies can influence policy choices and policy outcomes in other ways as well. A government with particularly generous old-age pensions or an especially bloated military infrastructure, for example, may be required to cut more to balance its budget than the government in another country that was less expansive, or expansionist, at the outset. The general point to keep in mind in the following chapters is that differences in policy outcomes between Canada and the United States may reflect differences in previous policy challenges and in path-dependent choices made in the past as much as or more than differences in overall institutional capacity.

Globalization

Globalization is a short-hand term for a variety of technological, economic, and institutional changes that have dramatically transformed the world economy over the past fifty years or so.[49] International capital, product, and labor markets have all become more closely integrated. Multinational corporations have expanded their reach, integrating research, production, marketing, and sales across national boundaries. A revolution in telecommunications has allowed services to be performed in one country and delivered almost instantly in another.

Many of these changes have had important implications for policy outcomes, for governmental capacity to impose losses in general, and for U.S.–Canada comparisons in particular.[50] As Banting, Hoberg, and Simeon have noted:

> On the one side, the need to remain competitive in the global economy
> creates pressures to promote economic adjustment, to reduce detailed
> regulation of economic activity, to lower taxes on corporate activity, and
> to tame large budget deficits. On the other side, increasingly diverse
> social groups demand government action to advance a variety of reform
> agendas and to cushion the impact of dramatic economic change on
> workers and communities.[51]

As a relatively small economy—and one extraordinarily dependent upon its economic relationship with the United States—Canada would, we might expect, be especially affected by globalization. The Canadian government faces increasing pressure, for example, to harmonize its statute of protection of intellectual property with that of the United States, which means changing policies with respect to companies such as Canadian generic pharmaceutical manufacturers that have thrived under a regulatory regime with weaker patent protection and imposing losses on them.[52] In both countries, efforts to impose losses on smokers (and tobacco companies) by increasing taxes on cigarettes are vulnerable to being undercut by smuggling. In general, these considerations suggest that larger changes in policy outcomes in Canada may not necessarily reflect greater capacity for loss imposition on the part of the Canadian government; they may, rather, simply represent greater pressures for change on the Canadian side of the border that offset resistance to loss imposition.

Emulation

As with globalization, explanations of policy choices and outcomes that focus on emulation recognize that policy choices and outcomes occurring in the United States and Canada may not be completely independent phenomena, occurring in hermetically sealed national environments. But whereas globalization explanations focus on economic and social developments that constrain or widen options available to policymakers in the two countries, emulation suggests a more direct transfer of information about the efficacy of policy options in a specific sector from policymakers and societal interests in one country to those in the other. Policymakers in the executive or legislature may, for example, borrow ideas about reorganizing the health care system to cut costs or restructuring public pension programs to make them more sustainable over the long term. Supreme Court justices may borrow legal reasoning across national boundaries about how to balance abortion rights and fetal rights. U.S. and Canadian policymakers may also borrow ideas about *process* as well: A process that successfully insulates elected politicians from the political blame associated with closing military bases or siting nuclear waste repositories in one country, for example, might be copied in the other country. Our general expectation is that policy differences between Canada and the United States will be narrowed by cross-national learning, and that most of the flow of policy lessons will be from the U.S. to Canada, given the greater cross-boundary awareness on the Canadian side of the border.[53]

Cleavage Structures and Social Organization

Policy defaults, loss imposition capacity, and policy outcomes may also be affected by the structure of social divisions and social organization within a country. The percentage of the labor force that is unionized, for example, is more than twice the level in Canada that it is in the United States.[54] Thus Canadian unions might be expected to be better organized to resist proposals to weaken union organizing rights or other policies inimical to the interests of organized labor.

Of even greater importance are differences in the dominant social cleavages dividing the two countries. In Canada, the intertwined divisions of language, ethnicity, religion, and culture that divide French-speaking from English-speaking, Quebec from the rest of Canada, Catholics from Protestants (decreasingly), and aboriginal peoples from others (increasingly) have exerted a powerful influence on virtually all spheres of public life. Region—especially the Central Canadian heartland of Quebec and Ontario versus "Outer Canada"—is also a powerful symbol and factor in political organization. Loss impositions that have (or are perceived to have) differential impacts across these divides are likely to be more difficult to get on the agenda, let alone win adoption, because the governing party in Ottawa is likely to fear that advancing them will spark a wider reaction against their party. In particular, fears that significant losses (or perceived losses) imposed on Quebec may boost the cause of pro-sovereignty forces in that province acts as a strong constraint.

However, the fact that Canada's Westminster system sometimes leads to a situation in which one region is severely underrepresented in the governing party caucus in the House of Commons (e.g., Western Canada in later Trudeau governments),[55] combined with the concentration of power in a Westminster system, means that a Canadian federal government *can* in fact impose quite severe regionally concentrated pain if it is willing to bear the political cost of doing so—if party leaders calculate that they can win re-election without winning more seats in that region in the future, for example, or that they are unlikely to increase their support in that region no matter what they do. The classic example is the Trudeau government's imposition of the National Energy Program on Western Canada in

1980—an action that the Conservative Party under Brian Mulroney promptly reversed when it took power in 1984.

In the United States, region is a much weaker force (at least since the easing of "Southern exceptionalism" since the 1950s), and language hardly ever figures as an issue in political life. In the United States, it is race—sometimes muted, sometimes unstated—that casts a shadow over many aspects of politics, even on issues far away from the obvious ones such as affirmative action. In both countries, though, the "confounding effect" is the same: What may appear to be weaknesses in governmental capacity to impose losses may result more from political divisions that raise the political costs of loss imposition than from weaknesses in political institutions themselves.

Political Culture and Ideas

A fourth cluster of variables that clearly may affect both governmental capacity for loss imposition and policy choices and outcomes is the realm of political culture, ideas, and public opinion. Ideas define the realm of what is politically legitimate for both government and private actors to do. And observers have long noted that while the two countries share most elements of a modern, liberal, and secular culture, there are nevertheless important differences between Canada and the United States in the world of ideas.[56] Most commonly cited are a stronger preference in Canada for social order and a greater tolerance of governmental intervention as a vehicle for securing it, although recent comparative empirical evidence is mixed.[57] Resentment against taxation also appears less dramatic in Canada, at least until the victory of the Progressive Conservative Party and its "Common Sense Revolution" in the 1995 provincial election in Ontario. Thus Canadian groups that want to avoid having losses imposed on themselves are less able to draw upon latent antitax sentiment by claiming that such an action would constitute a "hidden tax." The general point that needs to be made here is the (confounding) effect of cultural and public opinion factors on efforts to assess the relationship between political institutions and governmental capacity to impose losses: If that capacity appears greater in Canada than in the United States, it may be not because Canadian institutions facilitate loss imposition by government, but because Canadian *values* facilitate it.

STRATEGIES FOR IMPOSING AND RESISTING LOSS IMPOSITION

Thus far, this chapter has focused on the relationship between several types of variables—notably political institutions, but also factors such as the geographical distribution of losses and the role of policy legacies—in determining governmental capacity for loss imposition. Implicit in much of this analysis, however, is the notion that success or failure at loss imposition also involves a set of "intermediate variables": strategic choices made by proponents and opponents of loss-imposing actions. The institutional and other variables outlined earlier in this chapter shape both the strategic choices made by political actors in an effort to impose or avoid losses and the probability that specific strategies will succeed.

A growing body of social science literature addresses the efforts of politicians to reconcile their electoral interests with the inevitability of imposing losses. Politicians, of course, seek credit for policies that provide benefits and try to avoid blame for policies that impose losses; Anand has, from a game-theoretic point of view, argued that "the manipulation of blame can play a major role in the design and success of economic policy."[58] And prudent political actors design policy in anticipation of complaints, even if those complaints never materialize. Weaver outlines several strategies for escaping blame.[59] One such strategy is delegation to an agent empowered to make choices on behalf of the legislature. Unpleasant decisions can therefore be blamed on others.[60] Another is to distribute losses over time.[61] Similarly, political psychologists have explored the roles of rhetoric and argument in the context of "blame management strategies" whereby representatives have to "explain the vote" on legislation that has negatively affected their constituents.[62]

Michael Prince has recently developed an elaborate model of what he calls the "stealth style" of policymaking in connection with cuts to Canadian social programs. In the face of public opposition to such cuts, both the Mulroney and Chrétien governments relied on stealth: the introduction of changes without consultation, largely through technical measures announced in budgets, such as partial deindexation of benefits, targeting benefits, and supplementary conditions attached to tax changes.[63] Robert Behn explores similar themes in his analysis of the dynamics of policy and program termination, something that is likely to be resisted by the policy's or program's beneficiaries.[64] Behn offered strategic hints to enable policymakers to successfully implement termination: Losses are most likely to succeed, for example, when they can be imposed by surprise; when the potential group of beneficiaries of replacement policies is expanded; when opportunities for compromise and delay are minimized; when outsiders who have no stake in building a career in the sector are brought in as terminators; when legislatures are not engaged in voting on termination; and when opponents can be financially compensated for their loss.[65]

This disparate literature illustrates both the salience of loss imposition and the danger it poses to politicians seeking re-election. From a strategic perspective, assuming that a decision has been taken to impose a loss and that, in general, the imposition of loss generates blame, politicians do what they can to (1) effectively manage the impact of that loss, and (2) protect themselves from blame. Opponents of a particular loss imposition initiative, on the other hand, may want to generate blame against proponents of a loss-imposing initiative and manipulate payoffs in a way that minimizes their loss or holds it to tolerable levels.

Strategies for imposing and avoiding loss imposition can be divided into three broad categories: manipulating procedures, manipulating perceptions, and manipulating payoffs.[66] Equally important to understand are the conditions under which these strategies are more or less likely to succeed or fail. The "opportunity structures" for many loss-imposing and loss-avoiding strategies are heavily affected both by political institutions and by the type of loss that is involved. A capsule summary of these strategies and opportunity structures is provided in table 1-4.

Manipulating Procedures

Efforts to manipulate procedures flow from a recognition that the decision-making processes used to bring about a potentially controversial policy decision can affect both the opportunities available to opponents of a loss-imposing action to block that decision and their opportunities to generate blame against those involved in making a decision to impose losses. *Insulation* tactics involve delegating loss imposition decisions to bodies such as regulatory agencies or the courts that will not face electoral consequences. In theory, politicians in both the United States and Canada can attempt to avoid blame for loss imposition by delegating power over politically ticklish decisions to autonomous bodies such as regulatory commissions. In practice, however, notions of collective Cabinet responsibility in Westminster-style systems have made such arrangements less common under Westminster systems, or made them subject to Cabinet override rather than appeal to the courts, as is more common in the United States.[67]

A variant of this strategy is what could be called *passing the buck*. Here discretion over detailed policymaking is delegated to another body, but that body's options are limited in such a fashion that it has to impose losses—preferably shouldering all the blame for doing so. For example, a federal government could dramatically cut its financing for a shared cost program delivered by its states or provinces, leaving it up to them to decide what specific services or beneficiaries will be cut.

Agenda limitation strategies constitute another mechanism for maximizing the probability that loss-imposing actions will succeed, but they involve efforts to lower the political visibility of such actions (and thus decrease opportunities for generating blame) and minimize veto points within existing institutions rather than shift decision making to other institutions. For example, decisions may be made in large bundles (e.g., budget votes in Canada or votes on budget reconciliation packages in the U.S. Congress), so that legislators do not have to take separate, highly visible votes on contentious issues. Manipulating the order in which various alternatives are voted on and limiting roll call voting in legislatures may also be used to maximize the probability that a loss-imposing initiative will be approved while lowering the probability that those voting to approve it will incur blame for their actions.

Political forces seeking to block a loss-imposing action are likely to pursue a parallel set of policies for opposite ends. They may try to force *venue shifting* to decision-making bodies whose decision makers are perceived to be less favorable to a loss-imposing initiative, or in which the hurdles to change of any sort are higher. Challenging loss-imposing initiatives in the courts is a common technique—especially in the United States, where both the overall legal culture and many specific statutes encourage such challenges. Where such challenges fail to block a loss-imposing initiative, opponents may seek to have implementation of

TABLE 1-4
Loss-Imposing and Loss-Avoiding Strategies

Loss-Imposing Strategies	Loss-Avoiding Strategies	Factors Influencing Strategic Opportunities for Imposing and Avoiding Losses
Manipulating Procedures		
INSULATION: Delegate decision-making power to another body (e.g., court, regulatory agency) that is less sensitive to blame-generating pressures	VENUE SHIFTING: Seek to shift decision making to more favorable or multiple venues, where loss-imposing actions (1) are less likely to be taken; (2) can be more easily be blocked; or (3) can be weakened in implementation	Structure of decision-making institutions, notably the number of potential veto points, requirements for supermajority approval and open voting, and opportunities for venue shifting that characterize a specific level of government and/or policy sector.
PASSING THE BUCK: Delegate detailed decision-making power to another body, but constrain its options so that it will have to impose losses while shouldering the blame for doing so	MAXIMIZING ACCOUNTABILITY: Require that loss-imposing actions be taken in open venues with individual accountability	
AGENDA LIMITATION: Keep loss-imposing actions from being taken openly (e.g., by bundling them with other legislation) so as to limit blame-generating activity by opponents		
Manipulating Perceptions		
OBFUSCATION: Use technical changes or other mechanisms to lower visibility of loss-imposing actions	CONCENTRATING BLAME: Generate blame against the politically most vulnerable decision makers and those least likely to be viewed sympathetically, to make loss-imposing action seem unnecessary and/or capricious	General favorable or unfavorable public perceptions of the issue and of decision makers; technical nature of the policy sector
FINDING A SCAPEGOAT: Blame loss-imposing action on another actor (e.g., courts, a previous government) to make it seem inevitable and/or necessary		

TABLE 1-4
Loss-Imposing and Loss-Avoiding Strategies *(continued)*

Loss-Imposing Strategies	Loss-Avoiding Strategies	Enabling/Constraining Conditions
CIRCLING THE WAGONS: Achieve a consensus among all major policymakers before a loss-imposing initiative is announced, to make that initiative seem inevitable and necessary		
REDEFINING THE ISSUE: Portray loss-imposing action in a new way that mobilizes previously unmobilized beneficiaries of that action and/or those with no direct stake in it	REDEFINING THE ISSUE: Portray loss imposing action in a way that mobilizes potential losers or those with no direct stake to oppose it	Presence or absence of spillover effects

Manipulating Payoffs

Loss-Imposing Strategies	Loss-Avoiding Strategies	Enabling/Constraining Conditions
DISPERSION: Keep level of losses low and broad enough or disperse over a long time period, so that opposition lacks incentives to mobilize	COMPENSATION: Seek sufficient compensation for potential losers so that loss becomes minimal, while costs of compensation are broadly distributed	Availability of resources to compensate opponents of loss-imposing action Presence or absence of potential differing interests among opponents of loss-imposing actions
COMPENSATION: Provide sufficient compensation to specific categories of potential losers so as to mitigate or dispel their opposition	CUTTING OFF THE CAMEL'S NOSE: Oppose any compromise or compensation cheme that is likely to split opponents of loss imposition and weaken their political clout	Degree to which loss is all-or-nothing or subject to gradation Extent to which loss-imposing action is seen as precedent-setting or as preventing further losses
EXEMPTION: Exempt enough specific categories of opponents of loss-imposing action to split and weaken opposition coalition		
CONCENTRATION: Impose losses on groups that are politically weakest or viewed least sympathetically by others and, thus, unlikely to build a broad coalition against loss-imposing action	DEFECTION: Agree not to oppose a loss-imposing initiative that protects one's own group against losses while imposing them on others	

that initiative shifted to bodies believed to be sympathetic to their views, in hopes that it can be watered down if not stymied entirely. Parallel to the agenda limitation strategy, opponents of a loss-imposing initiative may try to *maximize accountability* by making sure that unpopular actions are taken openly and separately and by threatening to publicize the relevant votes.

As this discussion suggests, the structure of political institutions (both generally and in particular sectors) is likely to weigh heavily in whether forces favoring and opposing particular loss-imposing initiatives utilize procedure manipulation strategies, and in whether those strategies succeed. In general, Canadian institutions allow governing parties greater control over the policy agenda and offer fewer opportunities to opponents of a loss-imposing initiative to try to block those changes in multiple venues. However, there are also fewer truly independent policymaking bodies in Canada to which policy decisions can be delegated (hence insulating elected officials).

Manipulating Perceptions

In addition to manipulating procedures, politicians can try to manipulate *perceptions* so as to avoid blame, or, more precisely, the negative political consequences of blame. Again, several tactics are possible for both the proponents and opponents of a loss-imposing action. Perhaps the most common strategy for the former is what can be called *obfuscation:* hiding or obscuring losses, often by burying them in a swamp of technical details. Detailed provisions of the tax code are an example, as are technical changes in the reimbursement of health care providers that cause those reimbursements to gradually erode over time. Another strategic option is *finding a scapegoat*: trying to create the impression that a loss imposition was directly or indirectly caused by others, leaving the political incumbent(s) no choice. Scapegoats may include powerful but anonymous forces—globalization, for example—or more identifiable political opponents, such as previous officeholders who, it is argued, left the budget in terrible shape. A third perception-oriented strategy, *circling the wagons*, tries not to redirect blame entirely to others but rather to diffuse it, by getting as many policymakers as possible to agree to a loss-imposing action before it is publicly announced. In so doing, decision makers hope to increase the likelihood that the public will see the action as both necessary and inevitable, and hence weaken the likelihood that the issue will become the subject of partisan debate.

Opponents of blame, on the other hand, may try to *concentrate blame* by making loss-imposing actions seem unnecessary or even capricious, and by focusing on those political actors who are most vulnerable politically. Finally, both those trying to impose and those trying to block loss-imposing actions are likely to *redefine the issue* in an effort to mobilize potential supporters for their side and to demobilize potential foes. Opponents of polluting industries, for example, may seek to redefine their opposition to particular industries as the pursuit of "environmental justice"—resistance to the allegedly differential placement of environmentally hazardous sites in poor communities and communities of color—in order to build coalitions with civil rights and liberal advocacy groups.[68] As Wilson noted, the imposition of concentrated loss-imposing actions, such as automobile safety regulations and environmental legislation, requires changing perceptions about the salience of relatively diffuse interests.

Efforts to manipulate perceptions about the incidence of loss and who is to blame for past or potential loss-imposing actions clearly depend both on political institutions and on other factors. Political systems where power is concentrated, for example, may make it more difficult to engage in "circling the wagons" across party lines. Both checks and balances and federalism may encourage scapegoating another branch or level of government. In Canada, "Ottawa-bashing" by provincial premiers is a particularly common manifestation of scapegoating, with Quebec premiers particularly likely to indulge.

Past policy choices are especially likely to increase or decrease opportunities to obfuscate loss-imposing actions. Specific attributes of a policy sector and loss-imposing action, notably the geographical incidence of losses and whether there are identifiable "spillover" effects that may allow the mobilization of tangentially affected clienteles, can also have an important impact on the utilization, and the success or failure, of perception-manipulating strategies. Finally, general perceptions of the actors on whom loss avoiders are trying to pin blame may affect the probability that such blame will stick: If targeted politicians are generally mistrusted (by the public as a whole or by some subset), efforts to concentrate blame may be more successful than with respect to politicians who are generally trusted and held in high regard. Similarly, efforts by targeted politicians to scapegoat others and avoid having blame attach to themselves are more likely to succeed if the potential scapegoats are held in low esteem by the public.

Manipulating Payoffs

Politicians or others trying to use government to impose losses may also try to maximize their probability of success by manipulating the magnitude and incidence of "payoffs"—gains and losses—that different groups will experience. Proponents of loss imposition may employ several tactics, alone or together. First, *dispersion tactics* try to spread the pain in various ways so as to reduce its incidence. Dispersion of costs over time, for example, means that losses can be gradually phased in; this would include cases such as graduated fees or incrementally expanding the target population for a less-imposing action over time. Dispersion can also occur by spreading the costs over as wide a population as possible. This may seem counterintuitive, but insofar as wide dispersion of a loss reduces the unit cost per member of the population, it actually lowers the incidence of perceived pain. When the Mulroney government in Canada instituted the Canadian Goods and Services Tax (a national sales tax), for example, the government resisted demands to exempt certain categories of goods on the basis that this would mean a higher rate of tax overall: the more universal the tax, the lower the rate. Such dispersion also has the effect of avoiding invidious comparisons between groups that lose and groups that do not; it fosters the resignation that comes with "being in the same boat."

Concentration tactics are the opposite of dispersion: They deliberately target losses on small groups. These may be geographically concentrated, as in the case of siting waste dumps, or more spatially diffuse, as in the case of controls on gun owners. In the first case, the electoral damage of imposing losses can, in principle, be contained. In the second the challenge is a bit trickier, and politicians will have to calculate whether the affected subgroup has pockets of regional concentration: in the case of guns, for example, the U.S. West and the Canadian North. Loss-imposing politicians may also concentrate losses when the affected subgroup is publicly disfavored or politically weak. Immigrants, racial minorities, criminals, questionable companies, or business sectors such as cigarette manufacturers are all examples.

Compensation tactics involve partially offsetting losses by means of accompanying benefits, either now or in the future. When the Canadian Atlantic fisheries were closed, for example, the government established an adjustment program that provided temporary income to unemployed fishermen. And *exemption tactics* remove particularly troublesome subcategories—notably those who are most likely to mobilize or who are most likely to be viewed sympathetically by other members of the public—from the losing target population. Grandfathering is a species of this strategy, in that current members of the target population are exempted from the loss.

A variety of payoff manipulation strategies are used by opponents of loss imposition initiatives—some of which mirror strategies used by proponents, while others are quite different. Clearly opponents of loss imposition may seek compensation for most or all the losses that are imposed upon them, with the costs of compensation being diffused among the broader public. They may employ more specific strategies to respond to exemption and concentration strategies employed by loss imposers. For example, if loss imposers try to exempt major sectors of a constituency from loss-imposing action—by restricting access to abortion only for teens, for example, or restricting ownership only of handguns, or cutting future pensions only for those under age 55—leaders of affected constituencies may try to maintain unity by arguing that such initiatives represent "the camel's nose inside the tent," which will quickly be followed by the rest of the camel (i.e., wider cutbacks) unless they are resisted. Only by "cutting off the camel's nose," it is argued—intransigently resisting any cutbacks and remaining united in opposition—can wider and deeper cutbacks be avoided. Some elements of a constituency, however, may be tempted to pursue a defection strategy, either supporting or acquiescing in a loss imposition initiative if they are guaranteed exemption from all or most of its effects. This is particularly true in situations where there is strong reason to believe that concentration of loss imposition lowers rather than raises the probability that they themselves will suffer losses in the future (e.g., in the case of the creation of a single nuclear waste repository).

Clearly, the probability that any one of these strategies will be employed, and that it will either succeed or fail, depends on a variety of factors. Compensation strategies are more likely to be employed, for example, if resources to pay compensation are relatively plentiful. Specific characteristics of a policy sector are also likely to affect strategic choices and their success or failure. If there are potential differences of interests among potential victims of loss imposition (e.g., between current and future recipients of benefits) that make concentration and exemption strategies easier to employ, they are more likely to be used. If, on the other hand, those constituencies are united by strong moral beliefs (opponents of gun control or abortion rights, for example), a "cutting off the camel's nose" strategy of resistance is more likely to succeed. And as noted above, defection is more likely to occur when potential targets of loss imposition believe that agreeing to impose losses on others now lowers the probability that they themselves will be subjected to losses in the future—as opposed to cases where they believe it will set a snowballing precedent.

For our purposes, outlining this inventory of potential loss-imposing and loss-avoiding strategies is useful for thinking more systematically about how as well as how much loss imposition occurs in the U.S. separation-of-powers and the Canadian Westminster parliamentary systems. Do certain strategies tend to be used repeatedly in one system or the other? Are some strategies not available, or unsuccessful when they are attempted, in one of the two countries but not the other? Focusing on the strategic choices of loss imposers and their opponents can help to deepen our understanding of how political institutions affect the loss-imposition capacity of different institutional arrangements.

A COMPARATIVE CASE STUDY APPROACH

The chapters that follow immediately after this one provide comparative case studies of policymaking involving actual or attempted loss imposition in eight sectors of U.S. and Canadian society. The cases have been selected to provide diversity both within and across the four types of losses outlined earlier in this chapter. The first two chapters, for example, focus on a geographically diffuse clientele, the elderly, and initiatives to cut back on public pension and health care services to this group. But even within these cases there is diversity: In health care, far more than in pensions, there are a number of other concentrated interests (notably health care providers) whose views and interests cannot be ignored. The next two chapters focus on the imposition of losses on two sectors of the business community: telecommunications and tobacco. Here again, the telecommunications industry features a greater array of concentrated interests in potential opposition to one another than does the tobacco industry. Chapters 6 and 7 focus on two cases of geographically concentrated losses: location of nuclear waste storage sites and military base closings. As suggested earlier, neither case is unambiguous. Nuclear waste storage is, as Barry Rabe puts it "the ultimate NIMBY," because of the extraordinary toxicity and longevity of the material involved. But that means that its politics are not entirely "locality-specific": Fear of accidents and contamination spark fears far away from the actual site where storage is to take place, as well as along the routes to be traveled to get the material there. Individual military base closings, on the other hand, are locality-specific in their effects, but they have frequently been considered together, in large groups that increase the potential for wider coalitions of opposition among affected communities. Finally, there is diversity in the two cases of symbolic losses considered in chapters 8 and 9. Abortion pits two large and well-organized coalitions against each other: the so-called "pro-life" and "pro-choice" coalitions. Gun control, on the other hand, is more one-sided. Groups defending citizens' right to own guns have long been larger and better organized than pro–gun control groups, although the balance has shifted over the past thirty years.

The final chapter of this volume attempts to draw conclusions and generalizations across these cases. We address the questions raised in this introductory chapter. Do Canada's Westminster parliamentary system and the U.S. presidential system differ consistently across sectors in their capacity to impose concentrated losses on powerful groups within society, or are sectoral politics (and policy outcomes) more powerful than national differences? What other differences, both institutional (e.g., electoral cycles and federalism) and noninstitutional, affect governmental capacity for loss imposition? Do governments in the two countries use similar strategies in seeking to impose losses, or are there national differences here as well?

Using a comparative case study approach that focuses on two countries, and specifically on Canada and the United States, has both advantages and pitfalls with respect to assessing potential institutional differences in governmental capacity for loss imposition. The two countries have many similarities that lessen the confusion introduced by "confounding variables" in trying to isolate institutional impacts on governmental capacity and on outcomes. Both countries are geographically immense, and both are federations. Their political cultures are relatively similar, and so is their level of economic development. And unlike most countries in Western Europe, where the European Union has taken over or at least required some level of harmonization of whole swaths of domestic policymaking, both Canada and the United States have surrendered relatively little domestic policymaking to supranational bodies. Yet, as noted earlier, important differences remain—in policy legacies, in social organization, in political culture, and in relative size. An ideal research design would include more sectors and more countries. But that would demand multiple volumes rather than a single book. Social science has to start somewhere, and the Canada–U.S. comparison is better than most.

The potential pitfalls in our research design have played an important role in our selection of specific sectors to include in this volume and the way that they are presented. First, issues that appear to be comparable may be of very different salience, interact differently with major social divisions, or feature different allocations of losses in the two countries. An obvious example is the Canada–U.S. Free Trade Agreement, which involved potential job losses on both sides of the border, but with proportionately much greater effects—both on employment and on less tangible factors, such as national identity—north of the 49th parallel. In sectors like language policy, differences both in issue salience and in the way those differences interact with major social divisions are likely to overwhelm any potential institutional effects and make policy choices less comparable. The political dynamics are also quite different with respect to the cross-national movement of acid rain: In this case, Canada is generally the recipient of costs exported from the U.S., and interregional tensions within Canada are relatively weak, while interregional tensions in the U.S. between pollution-generating regions (primarily in the Midwest) and recipient, cost-bearing regions (largely in the Northeast) have been intense. We have tried to select cases where the issues were of comparable if not precisely equal salience, and where the losses being discussed were of the same magnitude and similarly distributed.

A second problem that arises in a comparative case study approach is deciding what unit of analysis to use. In the Canadian case, the obvious approach is to examine governmental proposals and whether they succeed or fail to be implemented. But such an approach may seriously overestimate loss-imposing capacity, because it excludes initiatives that never become public because of opposition within the Cabinet or the governmental caucus, or because of interest group opposition raised in quiet consultations. The American process is inevitably noisier, and the prospects for executive initiatives being passed without revision by the legislature are much lower. But that does not necessarily mean that the American system is less effective at imposing losses. In our case studies, we have tried to be sensitive to how these differences in process affect the "look" of policymaking, without assuming that those differences translate into differences in governmental capacity or outcomes.

A third problem that arises in case selection is controlling for policy legacies that may make it easier for one government or another to lower the costs of a given loss-imposing action (e.g., regulatory regimes for cutting rail passenger service or the presence or absence of indexation in income transfer programs). To minimize the problem of differing opportunities provided by existing program structures, we have attempted to choose cases where the policy status quo at the beginning of the period we investigate was reasonably comparable in the two countries.

Finally, it is important to be wary, in selecting cases, of the contaminating effects of cross-national pressures for harmonization—especially from the United States vis-à-vis its much less populous neighbor. In cases where two countries have highly interdependent economies, successful loss imposition on a powerful group may have very little to do with one government's capacity to impose losses; rather, it may, in fact, simply be a byproduct of actions taken by the other government. In the integrated North American automobile industry, for example, the movement in Canada toward provision of passive restraints to protect against injuries in automobile crashes had much less to do with actions taken in Ottawa than with actions taken in Washington. For Ottawa to have taken such actions independently—or even to have imposed a different standard, such as a lower airbag deployment speed more appropriate to the Canadian public (which has a higher percentage of seat belt wearers)—would have imposed very high costs on Canadian auto purchasers. To minimize the contamination effects of cross-border loss imposition on our analysis, we have attempted to choose cases where governments retained substantial autonomy in their policy choices. We have not attempted, however, to omit cases where cross-border learning was possible or did occur.

In the chapters that follow, authors were asked to work within this framework with respect to the politics of loss imposition—with all of its nuances and caveats.

We also encouraged them to explore the framework in their particular cases—and to be alert to any factors or forces that we might have missed. Indeed, the case studies provide many analytical insights and several surprises. We return to these in the concluding chapter.

NOTES

1. R. Kent Weaver, "The Politics of Blame Avoidance," *Journal of Public Policy* 6 (1986): 382. See also Paul Pierson, "The New Politics of the Welfare State," *World Politics* 48 (January 1996): 144, 145.
2. See, for example, Samuel P. Huntington, Michel Crozier, and Joji Watanuki, *The Crisis of Democracy* (New York: New York University Press, 1975).
3. See, for example, Thomas Flanagan, "The Staying Power of the Legislative Status Quo: Collective Choice in Canada's Parliament and *Morgentaler*," *Canadian Journal of Political Science* 30 (March 1997): 31–53.
4. André Kaiser, "Types of Democracy: From Classical to New Institutionalism," *Journal of Theoretical Politics* 9 (1997): 419–44, at 436.
5. George Tsebelis, "Decision Making in Political Systems: Veto Players in Presidentialism, Parliamentarism, Multicameralism and Multipartyism," *British Journal of Political Science* 25 (1995): 289–325.
6. This bears some resemblance to the notion of "political opportunity structures" developed to explain the success and failure of social movements. See Hanspeter Kriesi et al., "New Social Movements and Political Opportunities in Western Europe," *European Journal of Political Research* 22 (August 1992): 219–44.
7. Paul D. Pierson and R. Kent Weaver, "Imposing Losses in Pension Policy," in R. Kent Weaver and Bert A. Rockman, eds., *Do Institutions Matter?: Government Capabilities in the United States and Abroad* (Washington, D.C.: Brookings Institution Press, 1993), p. 140.
8. Edward L. Lascher, Jr., *The Politics of Automobile Insurance Reform: Ideas, Institutions and Public Policy in North America* (Washington, D.C.: Georgetown University Press, 1999), p. 106. See also Lascher, "Loss Imposition and Institutional Characteristics: Learning from Automobile Insurance Reform in North America," *Canadian Journal of Political Science* 31 (March 1998): 143–64.
9. Lascher, *The Politics of Automobile Insurance Reform*, 106.
10. Ibid., 124.
11. For a similar argument made in terms of the capacity of state actors to effect change, see Andrew P. Cortell and Susan Peterson, "Altered States: Explaining Domestic Institutional Change," *British Journal of Political Science* 29 (January 1999): 177–203.
12. For American views on this subject, see Lloyd Cutler, "To Form a Government," *Foreign Affairs* 59 (fall 1980): 126–43; Donald L. Robinson, ed., *Reforming American Government: The Bicentennial Papers of the Committee on the Constitutional System* (Boulder, Colo.: Westview Press, 1985); James L. Sundquist, *Constitutional Reform and Effective Government* (Washington, D.C.: Brookings Institution Press, 1986), chap. 1; and James MacGregor Burns, *The Deadlock of Democracy* (Englewood Cliffs, N.J.: Prentice Hall, 1963).
13. Voters may still be less disposed to vote for them because of the party leadership's actions, however.
14. See, for example, David W. Brady, *Critical Elections and Congressional Policy Making* (Stanford, Calif.: Stanford University Press, 1988). Brady argues that nonincre-

mental change is possible, however, after "critical elections" that alter the distribution of power within Congress.

15. The leading work on divided government, David Mayhew's *Divided We Govern* (New Haven, Conn.: Yale University Press, 1991), finds no important differences between periods of united and divided government in the number of pieces of important legislation enacted. But a recent study by Sarah Binder suggests that legislative productivity is lower relative to agenda size during periods of divided government, and that intrabranch disagreement between chambers of Congress (see the discussion of bicameralism below) is an important contributor to gridlock. See Sarah A. Binder, "The Dynamics of Legislative Gridlock, 1947–1996," *American Political Science Review* 93 (September 1999): 519–33.

16. On divided versus united government, see James Sundquist, "Needed: A Political Theory for the New Era of Coalition Government in the United States," *Political Science Quarterly* 103 (1988): 613–35.

17. For a parallel discussion, see R. Kent Weaver and Bert A. Rockman, "Assessing the Effects of Institutions," pp. 1–41 in Weaver and Rockman, eds., *Do Institutions Matter?: Government Capabilities in the U.S. and Abroad* (Washington, D.C.: Brookings Institution Press, 1993). Weaver and Rockman note that other factors, such as electoral rules that lower the probability of single-party majority governments in parliamentary systems, may also have an impact on loss-imposing capacity. Since this study includes data from only two countries, however, both of which use single-member electoral districts for legislative elections, it is not possible to test for the effects of electoral rules.

18. For general discussions, see George Tsebelis and Jeanette Money, *Bicameralism* (Cambridge: Cambridge University Press, 1997), and Samuel C. Patterson and Anthony Mughan, eds., *Senates: Bicameralism in the Contemporary World* (Columbus: Ohio State University Press, 1999).

19. For a comparison of the Canadian and U.S. Senates, see Roger Gibbins, *Regionalism: Territorial Politics in Canada and the United States* (Toronto: Butterworths, 1982), chap. 3. On the filibuster and cloture, see Sarah A. Binder and Steven S. Smith, *Politics or Principle? Filibustering in the United States Senate* (Washington, D.C.: Brookings Institution Press, 1997).

20. On the consequences of equal representation of states in the U.S. Senate, see Frances E. Lee and Bruce I. Oppenheimer, *Sizing Up the Senate: The Consequences of Equal Representation* (Chicago: University of Chicago Press, 1999).

21. Colin Campbell, *The Canadian Senate: A Lobby from Within* (Toronto: Macmillan, 1978).

22. Edward R. Tufte, *Political Control of the Economy* (Princeton, N.J.: Princeton University Press, 1978), p. 143.

23. William D. Nordhaus, "The Political Business Cycle," *The Review of Economic Studies* 42 (1975): 169–90; Anthony Downs presents another theory of cycles in "Up and Down with Ecology: The Issue Attention Cycle," *Public Interest* 28 (1972): 38–50.

24. For Canadian evidence, see Francois Petry, Louis M. Imbeau, Jean Crête, and Michel Clavet, "Electoral and Partisan Cycles in the Canadian Provinces," *Canadian Journal of Political Science* 32 (June 1999): 273–92.

25. See Matthew Soberg Shugart, "Presidentialism, Parliamentarism, and the Provision of Collective Goods in Less-Developed Societies," *Constitutional Political Economy* 10 (1988): 53–88.

26. For example, conservative governments in Alberta and Ontario have announced that they will, despite misgivings, introduce legislation making provincial laws consistent with a May 1999 Supreme Court of Canada decision requiring that same-sex couples be treated the same under family law as heterosexual common-law couples. See James McCarten, "Ontario Extends Legal Rights to Same-Sex Couples," *National Post*, October 26, 1999.

27. Paul E. Peterson, *City Limits* (Chicago: University of Chicago Press, 1981).
28. See, for example, Paul Peterson and Mark Rom, *Welfare Magnets: A New Case for a National Welfare Standard* (Washington, D.C: Brookings Institution Press, 1990).
29. See the discussion in Fritz Scharpf, "The Joint-Decision Trap: Lessons from West German Federalism and European Integration," *Public Administration* 66 (1988): 239–78.
30. There are, however, program structures that can be used to avoid joint decision traps, such as allowing the federal government and individual provincial governments to engage in bilateral agreements, or allowing reluctant provincial governments to opt out of national programs.
31. Kathryn Harrison, *Passing the Buck: Federalism and Canadian Environmental Policy* (Cambridge: Cambridge University Press, 1996).
32. See Malcolm G. Taylor, *Health Insurance and Canadian Public Policy: The Seven Decisions That Created the Canadian Health Insurance System and Their Outcomes*, 2d ed. (Kingston and Montreal: McGill-Queen's University Press, 1987).
33. This is similar to Lowi's notion that types of policies determine distinctive types of political relationships. See Theodore J. Lowi, "American Business, Public Policy, Case-Studies, and Political Theory," *World Politics* 16 (July 1964): 667–715. For an updated and revised version of this schema, see Theodore J. Lowi, "Forward: New Dimensions of Policy and Politics," in Raymond Tatalovitch and Byron W. Davies, eds., *Moral Controversies in American Politics: Cases in Social Regulatory Policy* (Armonk, N.Y.: M. E. Sharpe, 1998), pp. xiii–xxvii.
34. Mancur Olson, *The Logic of Collective Action: Public Goods and the Theory of Groups* (Cambridge, Mass.: Harvard University Press, 1965).
35. Hoberg and Harrison, for example, explain the array of instrument choice in the Canadian Green Plan by this logic. George Hoberg and Kathryn Harrison, "It's Not Easy Being Green: The Politics of Canada's Green Plan," *Canadian Public Policy* 20 (June 1994): 119–37. Another example is Canadian Employment Insurance revisions in the mid-1990s. Hale shows that the greatest stumbling block to the changes was resistance by MPs and Cabinet ministers from Atlantic Canada, a region that, as a result of the changes, would suffer a 20 percent reduction in EI transfers under the program. Despite changes designed to address some of these regional concerns, the minister responsible for EI (Doug Young) lost his Atlantic Canada seat in the 1997 election. See Geoffrey E. Hale, "Reforming Employment Insurance: Transcending the Politics of the Status Quo," *Canadian Public Policy* 24 (December 1998): 429–51.
36. James Q. Wilson, "The Politics of Regulation," in James Q. Wilson, ed., *The Politics of Regulation* (New York: Basic Books, 1980), pp. 357–94. Wilson has published two other versions of the same argument: James Q. Wilson, "The Politics of Regulation," in James W. McKie, ed., *Social Responsibility and the Business Predicament* (Washington, D.C.: Brookings Institution Press, 1974), pp. 135–68, and James Q. Wilson, *Bureaucracy: What Government Agencies Do and Why They Do It* (New York: Basic Books, 1989), pp. 76–79.
37. James Q. Wilson, "The Politics of Regulation," in Wilson, *The Politics of Regulation*, 365.
38. Ibid., 367.
39. Ibid., 372.
40. Ibid., 366.
41. Charles E. Lindblom, *Politics and Markets: The World's Political-Economic Systems* (New York: Basic Books, 1977), chap. 13.
42. Herman Bakvis and David MacDonald, "The Canadian Cabinet: Organization, Decision-Rules, and Policy Impact," in Michael M. Atkinson, ed., *Governing Canada: Institutions and Public Policy* (Toronto: Harcourt Brace Jovanovitch, 1993), pp. 47–80, quote at p. 75.
43. Raymond Tatalovich and Byron W. Davies, "Introduction: Social Regulation and Moral Conflict," in Raymond Tatalovich and Byron W. Davies, eds., *Moral Controversies in*

American Politics: Cases in Social Regulatory Policy (Armonk, N.Y.: M. E. Sharpe, 1998), pp. xxx–xxxi.

44. See "The CF-18 Affair," pp. 19–52, in Robert M. Campbell and Leslie A. Pal, *The Real Worlds of Canadian Politics*, 1st ed. (Peterborough, Ontario: Broadview Press, 1989).

45. Weaver and Rockman, "Assessing the Effects of Institutions."

46. See Paul Pierson, *Dismantling the Welfare State?* (Cambridge: Cambridge University Press, 1994), and "Increasing Returns, Path Dependence and the Study of Politics," *American Political Science Review* 94, no. 2 (June 2000): 251–67; and Carolyn Hughes Tuohy, *Accidental Logics: The Dynamics of Change in the Health Care Arena in Britain, the United States and Canada* (New York: Oxford University Press, 1999).

47. These three scenarios, in that order, roughly approximate the evolution of regulation of rail passenger service regulation in Canada. See R. Kent Weaver, *The Politics of Industrial Change: Railway Policy in North America* (Washington, D.C.: Brookings Institution Press, 1985).

48. For a detailed discussion, see R. Kent Weaver, *Automatic Government: The Politics of Indexation* (Washington, D.C.: Brookings Institution Press, 1988).

49. See, for example, Keith Banting and Richard Simeon, "Changing Economies, Changing Societies," pp. 23–70, in Keith Banting, George Hoberg, and Richard Simeon, *Degrees of Freedom: Canada and the United States in a Changing World* (Kingston and Montreal: McGill-Queen's University Press, 1997).

50. For a discussion of the impact of globalization on policymaking in the U.S. and Canada, see G. Bruce Doern, Leslie A. Pal, and Brian W. Tomlin, "The Internationalization of Canadian Public Policy," pp. 1–26, in G. Bruce Doern, Leslie A. Pal, and Brian Tomlin, eds., *Border Crossings: The Internationalization of Canadian Public Policy* (Toronto: Oxford University Press, 1996), and the introductory chapters in Banting, Hoberg, and Simeon, *Degrees of Freedom*.

51. Keith Banting, George Hoberg, and Richard Simeon, "Introduction," pp. 3–4, in Banting, Hoberg, and Simeon, *Degrees of Freedom*.

52. See "Drug Deals: Globalization and the Politics of Patents," pp. 27–65, in Campbell and Pal, *The Real Worlds of Canadian Politics*, 3d ed. (Peterborough, Ontario: Broadview Press, 1994).

53. On cross-border learning between Canada and the United States, see, for example, George Hoberg, "Sleeping with an Elephant: The American Influence on Canadian Environmental Regulation," *Journal of Public Policy* 11 (1990): 107–31.

54. Banting and Simeon, "Changing Economies, Changing Societies," pp. 39–42, in Banting, Hoberg, and Simeon, *Degrees of Freedom*.

55. See, for example, Alan Cairns, "The Electoral System and the Party System in Canada," *Canadian Journal of Political Science* 1, no. 1 (March 1968): 55–80; and R. Kent Weaver, "Electoral Reform for the Canadian House of Commons," *Canadian Journal of Political Science* 33, no. 3 (September 1997): pp. 473–512.

56. See Seymour Martin Lipset, *Continental Divide: The Values and Institutions of the United States and Canada* (New York: Routledge, 1990); and George Perlin, "The Constraints of Public Opinion: Diverging or Converging Paths," pp. 71–149, in Banting, Hoberg, and Simeon, *Degrees of Freedom*. For earlier discussions focusing more broadly on the role of political culture, see Kenneth McRae, "The Structure of Canadian History," in Louis Hartz, ed., *The Founding of New Societies* (New York: Harcourt Brace, 1964), pp. 219–74; Gad Horowitz, *Canadian Labour in Politics* (Toronto and Buffalo: University of Toronto Press, 1968), pp. 3–57; Donald Forbes, "Hartz-Horowitz at Twenty: Nationalism, Toryism and Socialism in Canada," *Canadian Journal of Political Science* 20 (June 1987): 287–315; Nelson Wiseman, "A Note on 'Hartz-Horowitz at Twenty': The Case of French Canada," and rejoinder by Forbes, *Canadian Journal of Political Science* 21 (1988): 795–811; and David Bell, *The Roots of Disunity: A Look at Canadian Political Culture*, 2d ed. (Toronto: Oxford University Press, 1992).

57. See Perlin, "The Constraints of Public Opinion," 86–88.
58. Paul Anand, "Research Note: Blame, Game Theory and Economic Policy: The Cases of Health and Public Finance," *Journal of Theoretical Politics* 10 (1998): 111–23, quote at 111.
59. R. Kent Weaver, "The Politics of Blame Avoidance," *Journal of Public Policy* 6 (1986): 371–98; see also his "Setting and Firing Policy Triggers," *Journal of Public Policy* 9 (1989): 307–36.
60. See Melissa P. Collie, "The Legislature and Distributive Policy Making in Formal Perspective," *Legislative Studies Quarterly* 13 (1988): 427–58, and Morris P. Fiorina, "Legislative Choice of Regulatory Forms: Legal Process or Administrative Process," *Public Choice* 39 (1982): 33–66. Delegation can be made for efficiency as well as blame-avoidance reasons: See D. Roderick Kiewiet and Matthew D. McCubbins, *The Logic of Delegation: Congressional Parties and the Appropriations Process* (Chicago: University of Chicago Press, 1991). For an empirical case study of delegation and blame avoidance, see Kenneth R. Mayer, "Closing Military Bases (Finally): Solving Collective Action Dilemmas Through Delegation," *Legislative Studies Quarterly* 20 (August 1995): 393–413.
61. Michael J. Trebilcock, Robert Prichard, Douglas Hartle, and Donald Dewees, *The Choice of Governing Instrument* (Ottawa: Minister of Supply and Services, 1982), pp. 33–34.
62. Kathleen M. McGraw, Samuel Best, and Richard Timpone, "'What They Say or What They Do?" *American Journal of Political Science* 39 (February 1995): 53–74.
63. Michael J. Prince, "Canadian Social Policy: From Health and Welfare to Stealth and Farewell," in Leslie A. Pal, ed., *How Ottawa Spends 1999–2000: Shape Shifting: Canadian Governance toward the Twenty-first Century* (Toronto: Oxford University Press, 1999), pp. 151–96. The concept of "policymaking by stealth" was introduced by Ken Battle in 1986.
64. Peter de Leon focused attention on the obstacles facing policy termination in terms similar to our notion of loss imposition. See his "Public Policy Termination: An End and a Beginning," *Policy Analysis* 4 (1978): 369–92; "A Theory of Policy Termination," in J. W. May and A. B. Wildavsky, eds., *The Policy Cycle* (Beverly Hills, Calif.: Sage, 1978), pp. 279–300; "New Perspectives on Program Termination," *Journal of Policy Analysis and Management* 2 (1982): 108–11; "Policy Evaluation and Program Evaluation," *Policy Studies Review* 2 (1983): 631–47; and "Policy Termination as a Political Phenomenon," in D. Palumbo, ed., *The Politics of Program Evaluation* (Newbury Park, Calif.: Sage, 1987), pp. 173–99.
65. R. D. Behn, "How to Terminate a Public Policy: A Dozen Hints for the Would-be Terminator," *Policy Analysis* 4 (1978): 393–413. For an empirical application of Behn's dozen hints, see Mark R. Daniels, "Implementing Policy Termination: Health Care Reform in Tennessee," *Policy Studies Review* 14 (winter 1995/1996): 353–74.
66. For a full discussion, see R. Kent Weaver, "The Politics of Blame Avoidance." In this section, we assume, notwithstanding the Weaver article, that losses must be or have been imposed. The question, then, is how to avoid blame for an action taken, as opposed to avoiding blame by not taking the action in the first place.
67. The Charter of Rights and Freedoms has changed this in Canada, giving opponents of loss imposition a legal avenue to claim that their losses constitute a contravention of Charter rights.
68. Christopher Foreman, Jr., *The Promise and Peril of Environmental Justice* (Washington, D.C.: Brookings Institution Press, 1998).

2

CUTTING OLD-AGE PENSIONS

R. KENT WEAVER

Cutting pensions for the elderly is a difficult task for any government.[1] The elderly are a large, politically active group, and they are viewed sympathetically by the rest of the electorate. In pension programs that are based on a system of contributory social insurance, a sense that benefits have been "earned" adds to recipients' perception of entitlement and of the inviolability of prior commitments. Moreover, even those who are too young to receive old-age pensions currently may view themselves as being indirectly hurt by cutbacks, either because it will lower their benefits in the future or because it will force them to give additional help to elderly relatives. Yet reform of public pensions has been on the agenda in both Canada and the United States—more frequently in the former—over the past two decades.

The first section of this paper outlines common pressures for austerity that have given rise to pension reform initiatives in the U.S. and Canada and discusses differences in political institutions and policy legacies that might lead to different policy outcomes in the two countries. The middle two sections review the experiences of the two countries with pension reform. The final section reflects on and tries to draw lessons from these experiences with respect to the political limits on pension reform in particular and on loss imposition in general in the two political systems.

PRESSURES FOR CHANGE

The enormous blame-generating potential of pension-cutting initiatives suggests that politicians will undertake such initiatives only with great reluctance. Yet, although their pension systems are structured differently, the Canadian and U.S. governments, along with governments in most other Western industrialized countries, confront countervailing pressures that have placed reform of public pensions—including reductions in benefits and eligibility—on the agenda in recent years. First, aging populations have caused both governments to face rapidly increasing pension expenditures. This pressure has been exacerbated by the maturation of contributory pension programs (Social Security in the United States, the Canada/Quebec Pension Plan in Canada), which caused a larger share of both populations to become eligible for payments from inadequately funded contributory pension systems.

A second and closely related pressure faced by governments in both countries for most of the past twenty-five years has been high budget deficits and tremendous resistance to increased taxes, which together limit alternatives to expenditure reductions in pension programs. At the end of the 1990s, budget deficits were briefly supplanted by budget surpluses, which changed the short-term pension policymaking calculus yet again. But throughout most of this period, the huge size of pension expenditures made these programs a tempting target for budget cutters.

A third source of pressure is more long term: The aging of the "baby boom" generation means that pension systems will undergo even more strain after 2010 as baby boomers begin to retire.

Fourth, the increasing generosity of pension programs in both Canada and the United States since the 1970s has contributed to a situation in which overall poverty rates among the elderly are as low as or lower than those rates among the general population.[2] Indeed, the growth of contributory, earnings-related public pensions in both countries—along with a near-universal Old Age Security program in Canada—has meant that substantial pension benefits are received by persons who are relatively well off and do not "need" them.

Fifth, conservative groups in both countries increasingly criticized contributory pension schemes as inefficient mechanisms that subsidize government deficits (by allowing governments to borrow money cheaply), while stifling investment and providing an inadequate return on workers' contributions. The perception that workers could do better if their pension contributions were invested in equities rather than lent to government was also fueled by an enormous run-up in stock prices on North American markets in the 1990s. Conservatives have called for at least partial replacement of government-run contributory pension systems by personal pensions, in which individuals rather than governments make investment decisions and benefits are determined by the return on those investments rather than a collective "defined benefit" based on earnings history. Both countries already have large private pension sectors, and the growth of individually managed, tax-subsidized retirement savings programs (Individual Retirement Accounts and 401(k) plans in the United States; Registered Retirement Savings Plans in Canada) helped to legitimize "individual account" plans as an alternative to the government-managed, historically pay-as-you-go contributory pension systems operating in Canada and the U.S.[3]

Options for Change

Politicians have, in short, faced strong pressures to impose some pain austerity on pension recipients and/or taxpayers. As shown in table 2-1, the repertoire of potential responses to these pressures for pension change in the two countries has three broad components, each presenting distinctive political dynamics and distinct challenges for policymakers concerned with avoiding blame. A first possible response is *retrenchment* with respect to benefits and/or eligibility, such as increases in the retirement age, cuts in indexation of benefits for inflation, or targeted reductions in benefits to upper-income recipients. Because these changes are most clearly targeted at a particular group (namely, present or future pensioners), they have the greatest potential to spark opposition and political retribution. Thus we would

TABLE 2-1
Responses to Pressures for Pension Reform

Approach to Pension Reform	Examples of Specific Reforms	Blame-Reduction Strategies
Retrenchment: Cut pension benefits or eligibility	Reduce initial pension benefits of retirees Reduce inflation adjustments in pension benefits of existing retirees Raise "normal retirement age" for receipt of full pension benefits Increase penalties for early retirement Increase years of employment history (or residency) used in calculating initial pension benefit Reduce benefits for upper-income retirees	Delay onset of cuts until after next election (or longer) Phase in pension cuts gradually and/or disguise them by manipulating indexation formula Disguise pension cuts as adjustments in arcane program formulas Target cuts at politically weak or disorganized groups
Refinancing: Increase revenue inputs to pension system	Increase payroll tax rates or tax base Inject general government revenues into contributory pension system Include groups who were previously exempt from pension payroll taxes (e.g., civil servants)	Delay onset of initial payroll tax increases until after next election (or longer) Phase in payroll tax increases gradually Impose payroll tax increases on employers rather than employees, thereby weakening public awareness of tax increases
Restructuring: Restructure existing pension programs	Eliminate universal pension tiers Mandate employer-provided pensions as partial or full replacement for government-provided pension tiers	Grandfather current retirees and the near-elderly into current system, or allow them to choose

expect to see policymakers resort to some of the strategies outlined in chapter 1 in an attempt to minimize blame. (See especially table 1-4.) They may, for example, delay the onset of such changes for several years, phase them in gradually, or target them at politically weak constituencies, such as noncitizens. Existing beneficiaries may also be "grandfathered"—that is, protected from any cutbacks.

Governments may also seek to *refinance* pensions by injecting more revenue into the pension system. For example, both payroll tax rates and the tax base (the share of payroll that is subject to taxation) may be increased. This diffuses rising pension costs more broadly across the population—a potential advantage if the tax increases are low but a potent liability if they are not, or if opposition to any tax increase is high. Again, we would expect policymakers concerned with minimizing the political costs of imposing pain to try to make such effects more obscure by delaying them, phasing them in, etc.

A third family of pension reforms consists of broader efforts to restructure existing tiers of pension programs, by effecting major changes in their structure—e.g., by turning tax deductions for pension contributions into tax credits, by adding a new individual account tier, or by merging or eliminating existing tiers. For example, governments might, as we have noted, replace a country-wide "defined benefit" pension, in which benefits are based on workers' earnings history, with a "defined contribution" pension, in which workers each have their own individual pension account and final benefits depend on the return over time on investments made with that account's funds. Such a change will limit the government's future pension expenditure liability. As with other cuts, politicians may try to make any pain associated with those changes less noticeable by phasing changes in slowly (e.g., by phasing out an existing tier over time) or applying them only to future beneficiaries.

Constraints on Change

Common pressures may nevertheless have differential effects cross-nationally if the balance of those pressures is different, or if those pressures are mediated by different program structures, political institutions, political cultures, or political forces. One important mediating factor, particularly relevant for this volume, is the role of political institutions. In particular, we might expect that Canada, with its concentration of power in the executive, would enjoy more success with respect to pension retrenchment initiatives than the United States, with its separation-of-powers system—at least during periods when there is a single-party majority government in the Canadian House of Commons. This difference is likely to be reinforced by strong party discipline in Canada, which may give an individual MP protection from his or her constituents when voting for unpopular measures, because voters know that an MP cannot vote against the party position without incurring severe consequences. Party discipline also encourages voters to consider a party's entire record in voting decisions. In the U.S., on the other hand, candidate-centered elections discourage legislators from casting any votes that may come back to haunt them later—a tendency reinforced by negative, so-called sound-bite advertising. As Pierson and Weaver noted in an earlier, three-nation study of pension retrenchment, however, the advantage that Westminster-style parliamentary systems enjoy in concentration of power may be at least partially offset by concentration of accountability: Voters know that it is the governing party that is imposing losses and those in power know that they know it—and may therefore be reluctant to undertake initiatives that are very likely to incur retribution at the next election.[4]

A second institutional difference that might lead to Canada–U.S. differences concerns the electoral cycle. In the United States, all members of the House of Representatives and one-third of all senators are elected every two years. Thus voters have to have very short memories if a loss-imposing action is going to be adopted by Congress without incurring any retribution at the polls. In Canada, on the other hand, general elections for the House of Commons must be called only once every five years, although by tradition they occur about every four years. This should afford a greater window of opportunity for loss imposition—in pension retrenchment or other sectors.

A third institutional difference concerns federalism. Both the U.S. and Canada are federal states, but they are structured very differently: Canada has fewer first-level subnational units and these have broader and more constitutionally protected jurisdiction; their leaders are also much more active on the national political stage. Overall, the political science literature suggests that federalism tends to inhibit welfare state growth,[5] but the effects are clearly not unidirectional and depend on the specifics of both program structure and federal arrangements. Three specific hypotheses about federalism in mature welfare states seem appropriate. First, pension programs that fall entirely under provincial jurisdiction and are entirely financed by provinces or states are likely to be especially meager and subject to retrenchment initiatives as subnational governments seek to avoid becoming "welfare magnets," in a process that leads to a "race to the bottom." Second, programs that are primarily financed by one level of government but delivered by the other are also likely to be especially vulnerable to cuts, as the financing level of government may feel, if it is pressed by high budget deficits, that it can cut expenditures knowing that the level of government delivering the benefits is likely to incur most of the blame. Finally, pension programs that require any changes to be approved by both levels of government are likely to encounter what Fritz Scharpf has labeled the "joint decision trap" and thus be especially impervious to change, especially to retrenchment.

The introductory chapter to this volume outlined several noninstitutional "confounding" variables that may also affect prospects for loss imposition. One important potential noninstitutional set of influences on the prospects for pension reform is what Paul Pierson has called "policy feedbacks"—the policies already in place and the political support coalitions that tend to grow up around and defend them.[6] Some scholars have argued that universal pension programs are likely to be more resistant to cutbacks than means-tested programs because they benefit a broader constituency. And Pierson has shown in the case of the U.K., for example, that contributory pension systems are more likely to be highly resistant to cutbacks after large numbers of pensioners have begun to draw significant benefits from them than be-forehand. Programs in which benefits are indexed for inflation are harder to cut than unindexed programs, in which benefits can be eroded over time simply by doing nothing. And pension programs that are funded exclusively by payroll taxes may be-come more susceptible to cutbacks when expenditures in that program exceed pay-roll tax revenues: If injecting general revenues to sustain the program is not an op-tion, there is an action-forcing mechanism demanding either benefit and eligibility cuts or payroll tax increases.

Differences in interest group structure and strength are another potential source of difference in governmental capacity to enact loss-imposing change. In the United States, the AARP (formerly the American Association of Retired Persons) has long been seen as one of the biggest and most powerful lobbies in Washington—at least in terms of blocking changes that its members do not like. In addition to a huge membership of almost 35 million, AARP also has a large research and lobbying staff that gives it enormous clout. It is joined by a number of other seniors organizations that have, for the most part, also been resistant to substantial changes in the Social Security program. In Canada, on the other hand, seniors organizations have been relatively weak. The Canadian Association of Retired Persons, for example, claims a membership of close to 400,000, but its focus has been more on providing dis-counts and information for members than on issue advocacy. Thus we might ex-pect that differences in interest group strength would reinforce presidential/parlia-mentary and electoral cycle differences and lead to greater loss imposition capacity in Canada than in the United States.

PENSION REFORM IN THE UNITED STATES

The United States has a two-tiered system of public old-age pensions for its resi-dents. By far the larger of the two is Old Age and Survivors Insurance (OASI), more commonly known as Social Security. Social Security is a contributory system fi-nanced entirely by payroll taxes, paid equally by employers and employees (the self-employed pay both employer and employee contributions). Any excess of rev-enue over contributions is held in a "trust fund" that invests only in U.S. govern-ment securities. Benefits are loosely linked to a worker's earnings (and, therefore, contributions) history, with low-wage workers receiving a higher return on their contributions than high-wage workers.

Social Security depends entirely on payroll tax contributions and interest earned on trust fund surpluses to finance benefits: With a few exceptions, general govern-ment revenues are not used to pay benefits and cannot be injected into the system to pay for any spending shortfalls without changing the basic Social Security legis-lation. Social Security has historically operated on a "pay-as-you-go" basis—under which current workers' contributions are used to pay the benefits of current bene-ficiaries—rather than building up, as most private-sector pension plans do, ade-quate reserves to pay the expected pension liabilities of current workers. This fund-ing mechanism has meant that Social Security is vulnerable to potential funding crises—shortfalls of revenue relative to current expenditure requirements—that serve as "action-forcing mechanisms," putting expenditure reductions or tax increases (or both) on government's agenda and giving proponents of expenditure reductions critical leverage to force spending cutbacks.

In addition to Social Security, old-age pensions in the United States are funded by a means-tested program, Supplemental Security Income (SSI), which also provides benefits to low-income, disabled, and blind persons. SSI is financed from general government revenues. The federal government provides a basic benefit, which some states supplement. Benefit levels for both Social Security and SSI have been indexed for inflation since 1975. In 2000 almost $275 billion was paid to retired workers and their dependents (and another $78 billion to the survivors of insured workers) under the Social Security Old Age and Survivors Insurance program, compared to only $4.8 billion paid to the aged under the SSI program.[7] Because SSI earnings and asset tests are quite severe, and benefits are quite low, the number of aged SSI recipients is only 3.3 percent of the number of OASI recipients.[8]

In addition to the legacy of past policy structures, the possibilities of pension reform in the United States over the past quarter-century have also been heavily constrained by specific political configurations: Divided government (a majority of seats held in at least one chamber of Congress by a political party different from that of the president) has been in effect for all but a little over six years of the period from 1975 to 2002 (1997–80 under Carter; 1993–94 under Clinton; three months under George W. Bush). At least some degree of bipartisanship is needed to enact any major pension reform proposal—but pension reform is an issue on which the gulf between the parties has generally been quite wide. Equally important, it is an issue that has enormous potential for generating blame against any politician who is seen as favoring benefit cuts.

Initial Retrenchment Efforts in the United States

Repeated crises with regard to the Social Security trust fund along with overall budgetary pressures led to numerous attempts to introduce Social Security cutbacks beginning in the late 1970s.[9] Political struggles over pension cutbacks in the United States have been more frequent than in Canada—where the centralization of political authority means that battles over pensions have stemmed from a few clear governmental initiatives—and have emerged from a variety of sources in Congress and the executive branch, but they have enjoyed a lower success rate. The most important Social Security cutback initiatives took place in 1977, 1981, and 1983; only the first and last of these resulted in major changes. There were also abortive initiatives in 1979, 1981, 1985, and 1987.

An impending Social Security trust fund crisis prompted the Carter administration's initial Social Security initiative, in the fall of 1977. This crisis resulted from a combination of stagflation, which lowered revenue inflow to the fund, and a faulty indexation mechanism that gave newly retiring workers unexpected windfalls. Although there was strong agreement that some changes needed to be made, neither the administration nor the Congress was willing to impose substantial short-term losses on persons already receiving benefits. Instead, policymakers relied almost exclusively on injecting new revenues into the system to produce short-term improvements in the program's financial status. These revenues came in the form of increases both in payroll taxes and in the wage base (the amount of wages subject to the Social Security tax); they were phased in after the next election in order to minimize political blame.[10] Long-term savings were produced largely by reducing the initial benefit of most future beneficiaries.

The reforms were not widely perceived as imposing losses because they were portrayed by sponsors as restoring the always-intended benefit levels. But policymakers did not attempt to retroactively lower the real purchasing power of workers who had already retired or who were about to become eligible to retire. Instead, policymakers attempted to lower the visibility of the benefit cuts by phasing in the corrected formula for initial benefits over five years, beginning with workers who would turn 62 in 1979. In short, Congress attempted to correct a serious program flaw in a way that minimized blame by not cutting the benefits of those who were most likely to notice and by delaying almost all benefit cuts until after the next election.

When the Reagan administration came into office in 1981, it sought further cuts in OASI. However, President Reagan had promised in the 1980 presidential campaign that Social Security would be exempt from cuts, so the new administration initially proposed only minor changes in Social Security. But in the spring of 1981, Office of Management and Budget (OMB) Director David Stockman, desperate to find immediate spending cuts to diminish spiraling deficit forecasts, sold a Social Security reform package to the president that contained a large dose of immediate political pain. Proposed cuts included a three-month delay in cost-of-living adjustments, a change in calculating future retirees' initial benefits that would eventually lower the percentage of a retiree's prior earnings that would be replaced by Social Security benefits, and a severe and almost immediate cut in benefits for future early retirees. The package immediately generated enormous criticism from congressional Democrats, the American Association of Retired Persons, and other groups in the "seniors lobby." The White House quickly backed away from the proposals.

While the political dangers of proposing Social Security benefit cuts were evident, however, awareness of looming trust fund deficits forced a response. Both sides in the dispute eventually agreed to entrust Social Security's financial problems to a bipartisan commission, which was to report after the 1982 elections. Although the commission almost came to an impasse, it did provide political cover, allowing negotiators for the president and congressional Democrats to come to an agreement that was eventually approved, with some additions, by Congress in 1983.[11] Because both parties shared responsibility for the agreement the potential for blame was minimized, and thus the ability of the various participants to stick to the agreement was maximized.

The 1983 legislation made major changes in Social Security on both the tax and benefit sides. But again a lot of attention was paid to minimizing blame. In the short term, the most important change was a six-month "delay" in inflation adjustments for benefits, which really amounted in a permanent benefit cut for current recipients. In addition, the legislation imposed a gradual increase in the standard retirement age (the age at which full Social Security retirement benefits are received) from 65 to 67. This increase was phased in gradually, beginning in the year 2000 and ending in the year 2021. Workers can continue to retire at age 62, with a greater actuarial reduction in their benefits. However, the long delay between the 1983 passage of the Social Security rescue package and its initial "bite," along with its gradual phase-in, lessened near-term blame associated with the cuts.

The 1983 Social Security rescue package dramatically altered the short- and medium-term financial condition of OASI. The trust funds are currently generating surpluses, making it politically very difficult to either raise Social Security taxes or cut benefits in the short term. Continued concern over the budget deficit and the recognition that large expenditure reductions were unlikely without a contribution from Social Security led Republican politicians to repeatedly propose pension cutbacks in the final years of the Reagan and George H. W. Bush administrations, but each attempt fizzled, reconfirming Social Security's reputation as the "third rail" of American politics.[12]

Several lessons emerge from these initial rounds of retrenchment. First, politicians are well aware of the blame-generating potential associated with Social Security retrenchment and do their best to avoid it. Social Security cutback initiatives have been most successful when they occur in the context of an imminent trust fund crisis, when they gain the support both of the president and of key congressional leaders, and when they are directed at narrow and politically weak clienteles rather than all retirees. Efforts to use cuts in Social Security benefits and eligibility in the battle to shrink the federal deficit in the absence of a looming trust fund crisis are almost certain to fail, and long-term trust fund shortfalls can be addressed successfully only in the context of a short-term funding crisis.

Reforming U.S. Pensions in the Clinton Years

The 1983 Social Security rescue package, combined with generally positive economic performance and favorable demographic trends (the baby boom generation began entering its peak earning years) meant that there was no short-term funding crisis in the Social Security program in the 1990s to act as an action-forcing mechanism for retrenchment initiatives.[13] Thus the decade after passage of the 1983 Social Security rescue package saw virtually no legislation on the issue. The only significant exception was a provision adopted as part of President Clinton's 1993 budget package that made 85 percent of benefits taxable for beneficiaries at the upper end of the income scale. But this provision affected relatively few Social Security recipients.[14]

The story was initially the same after Republicans gained control of Congress in 1994. House Republicans, having learned from the Reagan experience with Social Security retrenchment initiatives and seeking to avoid proposals that did not enjoy popular support, explicitly excluded Social Security cutbacks from their "Contract with America" campaign pledge in the 1994 congressional election.[15] Even when congressional Republicans endorsed very unpopular (and ultimately unsuccessful) Medicare and Medicaid cuts in the fall of 1995 in an effort to make their deficit and tax reduction promises "add up," they resisted Social Security cuts. The Clinton-Republican budget agreement of 1997 also excluded Social Security cuts.

The major Republican initiative on retirement benefits during the 1995–96 "Gingrich Revolution" concerned benefits received by noncitizens under the relatively small and heretofore largely uncontroversial SSI program. There is little dispute that noncitizens who are legal permanent residents and contribute to social insurance programs such as Social Security, Medicare, and Unemployment Insurance should be eligible for benefits on the same basis as citizens.[16] Controversy over the means-tested SSI program increased in the early 1990s, however, as solid quantitative evidence began to emerge in government studies that noncitizens, especially refugees and elderly persons admitted to the United States as part of family reunification policies, were heavy users of means-tested benefits. In the Supplemental Security Income program, noncitizens increased from 7 percent of aged recipients in 1983 to 30.2 percent of recipients in 1994.[17]

The political calculus for politicians who consider cutting benefits to aged immigrants is a tricky one, however. On the surface, cutting benefits to noncitizens seems like a politically easy decision. Noncitizens can't vote, so they can't electorally punish politicians who cut their benefits. But the situation is more complicated in two ways. First, most noncitizens are related to persons who *are* citizens of the United States and therefore *can* vote. Second, many persons who receive means-tested benefits or may receive them in the future are *eligible* to become citizens and will do so if they have incentives to do it. The new Republican majority that took over control of Congress in 1995 passed legislation that barred most noncitizens from receiving Supplemental Security Income and Food Stamps until they became citizens. Moreover, the bill's SSI retrenchment provisions took effect almost immediately and did not exempt current recipients. These provisions proved to be highly controversial. The Balanced Budget Act of 1997 restored SSI benefits to those who had been receiving them when the 1996 welfare law was passed—a limited backtracking on SSI consistent with the blame-avoiding principle that taking benefits away from those who already have them is most likely to spark retribution.[18]

Toward Fundamental Reform?

Controversy continues in the U.S. over a complex set of more fundamental Social Security reform proposals (1) involving investment of Social Security trust funds in the stock market and/or (2) allowing individuals increased control over their retirement incomes through a set of individual accounts embedded within the Social Security system.[19] Democratic politicians have generally been more sympathetic to the former, while many Republicans and conservative think tanks like the Cato Institute and Heritage Foundation have called for varying degrees of "privatization" of Social Security through mandatory or optional contributions to personal pensions.[20]

Disagreements about which approach to pursue reflect not only different values but different assessments of risk and differential willingness to accept that risk—or to assign it to individual Social Security recipients. Can decision making on "collective" investment of Social Security funds be protected from political interference? What would happen to retirees who lost money on investments in their personal accounts, and what safeguards should be put in place to minimize those losses? How would the creation of individualized Social Security accounts financed by a payroll tax increase affect individuals' other savings? The uncertainties posed by these issues translate into big political risks for politicians.

In the debate over Social Security privatization, conflict has centered in part on the distributional consequences of the proposed reforms for particular groups. Privatizers have in particular focused on the lower returns to contributions that younger workers will receive relative to their parents, arguing that Social Security is a bad deal for this group. Critics of individual accounts, on the other hand, have argued that because of stock market volatility, individuals who retire a few years apart after contributing over their working lives to a broad stock index fund could end up with dramatically different earnings replacement rates—and those who pulled out their funds in a stock market trough would end up with very inadequate benefits.[21]

The course of the debates in the late 1990s over equities investment and creation of personal accounts for Social Security was heavily influenced by the political maneuverings of Bill Clinton. President Clinton clearly saw a long-term solution to Social Security financing as one of the few issues on which he could leave a positive legacy to dispel his impeachment-tarnished image. In his January 1999 State of the Union address, Clinton proposed to devote 62 percent of the budget surplus anticipated over the next fifteen years to bolstering the Social Security (Old Age and Survivors Insurance) trust fund.[22] Approximately one-fifth of this amount would be invested in equities—collectively rather than individually—through a mechanism insulated from government influence. Thus returns on trust fund revenues would be raised at least modestly, but the size of the investment would also be modest enough to lessen fears about government control of the economy. In addition, another 11 percent of the surplus was to be reserved for governmental subsidies to new "Universal Savings (USA) Accounts"—new retirement savings accounts through which the federal government would match individual retirement savings accounts, with extra benefits for low-income workers. These accounts would help individuals prepare for retirement based on personal choice and individual accounts, as privatizers prefer. They have one fundamental difference from privatizers' plans, however: They would not take money out of existing payroll taxes or be part of the basic OASI system. Thus they would not require cutting the existing "defined benefits" of the OASI system, and government commitments could be scaled back when government budget surpluses shrink.

Also influencing the course of the debate were changing projections about when the OASI funding crisis would hit. For most of the last quarter of the twentieth century, the Social Security Administration's projections of when the OASI trust fund would run out of money had proven too optimistic. After each legislative change, the date when the OASI trust fund was expected to be empty would quickly begin moving forward. But in 1997, this began to reverse: With a better than expected economy, the anticipated trust fund crisis moved further way (from 2029 in 1997 to 2034 in 1999 and

2041 in 2002), lessening the already weak sense of systemic crisis. Although President Clinton sought to maintain sufficient flexibility that he could sign almost any piece of legislation, the positions of congressional Republicans and Democrats remained far apart, leading Republicans to fear that any Social Security initiative on their part could lead them into a political trap. The idea that individual accounts invested in the stock market could constitute a "free lunch" for politicians partially dissipated.

The option of investment of Social Security trust funds in the stock market has been blocked by strong opposition from congressional Republicans. Alan Greenspan, the powerful and widely respected chairman of the Federal Reserve Board, has also been a highly vocal critic of government investment in equities markets. Greenspan argues that no mechanisms to insulate investment managers from political pressures would be adequate.[23] Critics of privatization have challenged this position, citing the experience of the Thrift Savings Plan (for federal employees) and of state employee plans.[24]

How and how much to restructure Social Security was an important issue in the 2000 presidential election campaign in the United States. Republican candidate George W. Bush proposed allowing workers to divert part of their Social Security payroll taxes to individual accounts, while his Democratic opponent, Al Gore, argued that doing so would further weaken the viability of the current Social Security system.[25] After the election, the new president decided to wait on Social Security until after his top priority, a tax cut, had made it through Congress. Instead, President Bush decided to appoint a commission on how best to implement an opt-out plan.[26] The commission eventually decided to present a menu of policy options rather than a single plan, in part to shield the administration from criticism over the benefit cuts that would be required to fund a Social Security opt-out. Numerous news stories about retirees needing to return to work after the post September 11 stock market declines as well as Enron and other corporate scandals regarding management of 401(k) accounts have also dampened, at least temporarily, support for partial privatization of Social Security.[27] Thus, while Social Security privatization is clearly now on the public agenda, it is likely far from enactment.

PENSION REFORM IN CANADA

Canada currently has a public pension system comprising three main tiers of cash benefits, rather than the two-tier system in effect in the United States. Moreover, the history of its pension system—and therefore the legacy of that history with respect to future choices—is quite different. Canada began with federal subsidies to the provinces for means-tested pensions in 1927. This was supplanted in 1951 by Old Age Security (OAS), which, until changes made in 1989, was a universal program providing a flat amount to all Canadians aged 65 and over. The 1989 changes reduced, and in some cases eliminated, OAS benefits to upper-income Canadians.

A second, income-tested tier is made up of the Guaranteed Income Supplement (GIS), created in 1965, and the Spouses Allowance (SPA), created in 1975. (There is no asset test for any of these programs, however, as there is for SSI in the United

States.) These programs supplement OAS payments to low-income senior citizens and their near-senior spouses. OAS, GIS, and SPA are all financed out of general revenues and together provide an income guarantee higher than the Supplemental Security Income floor in the United States. As of 1999, about 37 percent of OAS pensioners also received at least some GIS payments.

The third major cash tier in Canada's retirement income system is the Canada Pension Plan (CPP), a contributory social insurance plan that, like Social Security in the U.S., pays benefits linked to an individual's contribution history. The normal retirement age for CPP pensions is 65, but early retirement (with a reduction in benefits) is available from age 60 on.[28]

While both OAS and GIS are entirely under federal jurisdiction, Ottawa does not have exclusive decision-making authority over the CPP. Changes in the Canada Pension Plan require approval of a "supermajority" of the Canadian provinces, making it a more difficult target for either expansion or contraction than the programs under federal jurisdiction.[29] Provinces can also opt out of the CPP to establish their own plans. Only Quebec has chosen to do so, and a separate Quebec Pension Plan, with contribution and benefit policies generally identical to those of the CPP, operates in Quebec. (Quebec is included in the formula necessary for amending the CPP, however.) Moreover, as part of the federal-provincial bargaining that allowed Ottawa to establish the CPP in 1966, Ottawa agreed to allow the provinces to borrow CPP surpluses as they accrued in the early years of the program at Ottawa's borrowing rate—generally better than most provinces could get on their own in financial markets.[30] Thus the provinces had both a veto power over change in the CPP and a substantive stake in policy: maintaining their privileged access to low-cost capital and delaying as long as possible the need to pay back the money they had borrowed.

As in the U.S., benefits are also delivered to seniors through the tax system—both directly through the Age Credit and Pension Credit (both were tax exemptions, and therefore regressive in their impact, until 1988), and indirectly, through tax subsidies for contributions to employment-based (Registered Retirement Plans or RRPs) and personal pension plans (Registered Retirement Savings Plans, or RRSPs). RRPs and RRSPs, as in the United States, allow contributors to defer taxation on income until they retire. They primarily benefit middle- and upper-income Canadians, who are more likely to have employer-provided pensions and to be able to save for retirement.[31]

Initial Retrenchment Initiatives

Several efforts to reduce pension costs in Canada were made in the 1980s.[32] In 1982, the Trudeau government put a cap on cost-of-living adjustments in Old Age Security, as well as on previously negotiated public-sector wage increases, as part of a two-year inflation-fighting package. However, increases in the income-tested Guaranteed Income Supplement were "super-indexed"—i.e., increased more than inflation—to ensure that those at the very bottom of the income scale kept up with inflation. The cap ended up having little effect, since inflation declined to levels close to the government's inflation guidelines.[33]

A more dramatic initiative occurred as part of attempts by the Progressive Conservative government headed by Brian Mulroney to reduce the federal deficit shortly after it came into office with a huge House of Commons majority in 1984. Prime Minister Mulroney was trying to fashion a sustained political realignment favoring the perennial also-ran Conservatives; attacking popular pension programs did not seem like an auspicious beginning. But Canada's huge federal budget deficit pushed the new government to consider pension cuts. News leaked in late 1984 that the government was considering cutting both Old Age Security and the popular Family Allowances program as a way to reduce the deficit and channel resources to the needy. The government ultimately retreated from an attack on universality without ever articulating a clear proposal. Indeed, Mulroney backed himself further into a fiscal corner by pledging to *maintain* universality.

Budget pressures remained strong, however, and the following spring Finance Minister Michael Wilson won cabinet approval for cutting social spending through an attack on indexing rather than on universality. Under the government's proposal, adjustments would be made in Old Age Security (as well as in Family Allowances and income tax brackets) only for inflation in excess of 3 percent. Full indexing of the Guaranteed Income Supplement was to be maintained; but since the latter is an add-on to OAS, poor seniors would also have their benefits cut.

The government's proposal would have affected all recipients from the first dollar of inflation, because it did not protect the poorest elderly from cutbacks by "super-indexing" the Guaranteed Income Supplement. Moreover, the government's move contradicted Mulroney's campaign pledge to retain full indexation of Old Age Security, leaving him open to criticism not only on the substance of the policy change, but with respect to his honesty and trustworthiness as well. The proposal sparked intense protests from opposition parties, senior citizens organizations, several provincial governments (including Quebec), and even the business community. Within a month, the Mulroney government retreated completely, announcing that full indexation of Old Age Security (but not of Family Allowances or the personal income tax system) would be continued.

The humiliating retreat on Old Age Security in 1985 led the Conservatives to leave OAS alone until after they won re-election in 1988. But persistent federal budget deficits led Finance Minister Wilson to announce in his April 1989 budget that there would be a special tax (known as a "clawback") of 15 percent on Canada's universal demogrants (OAS payments and Family Allowances) for upper-income families and individuals. This tax was to be phased in over three years. The OAS clawback, when fully phased in, would initially affect only 4.3 percent of the elderly population, with 1.8 percent of OAS recipients losing their OAS benefit entirely. But since the thresholds at which the clawback began were only partially indexed (to inflation over 3 percent, with the potential for additional adjustments to be added on an ad hoc basis), the clawback gradually affected more pensioners. Moreover, the clawback contained a serious inequity: Because it was calculated on an individual basis, couples each of whom had an income just below the $50,000 phase-in point could escape the clawback entirely, while those with the same total income contributed by just one of the partners would lose that person's OAS benefit entirely.[34]

Social policy advocates strongly criticized the erosion of universality implicit in the clawback, but this time the finance minister did not back down. There was little public protest, and both major opposition parties, the Liberals and the New Democrats, were in the midst of searches for new leaders. In addition, the government's proposals were so complicated, so selective in their short-term impact, and so gradual and uncertain in their long-term effect that it was difficult for the media or interest groups to present them in a way that was intelligible to the public.[35]

Pension Reform in the Chrétien Years

The Liberal government headed by Prime Minister Jean Chrétien that came to power after the crushing defeat of the Conservatives in the 1993 election was elected on a platform that stressed job creation and made no mention of pension retrenchment. Once elected, however, the new government devoted most of its attention to deficit reduction, propelled toward acting quickly in part by the future liabilities represented by pension commitments, but even more by a tremendous fear that without major deficit reduction, the financial markets would effectively declare Canada bankrupt.[36] Much of the burden was to be borne by transfers to the provinces in the areas of post-secondary education, social assistance to the poor, and (especially) health: sectors where the provinces actually delivered services and hence would have to make the tough decisions—and presumably incur most of the political blame—resulting from federal budget cuts.[37] But this option was not available in the pensions sector, where the federal government financed and administered benefits directly (except for the Quebec Pension Plan).

Government initiatives were heavily constrained by the political calendar, however. A Quebec provincial election was anticipated in the fall of 1994, and if (as expected) the Parti Québécois won, a referendum on Quebec sovereignty would follow within a year—and another federal election, presumably, in 1997. That left a very narrow window of opportunity—after the Quebec referendum but as far away as possible from the next federal election—for any pension retrenchment initiative.

THE SENIORS BENEFIT: AN ABORTIVE INITIATIVE

As part of their drive to reduce deficits, Finance Minister Paul Martin and Finance Department officials led an effort to win the approval of Prime Minister Chrétien and the Liberal cabinet for a restructuring of OAS and GIS that would reduce pensions to middle- and upper-income recipients, while leaving lower-income recipients slightly better off.[38] Ultimately, Prime Minister Chrétien forced the finance minister to back down on including pension reform in his 1995 budget—just half a year before the expected Quebec referendum—but promised that he would include it the following year.[39]

The pension reform announced in the 1996 budget constituted a major restructuring of OAS and GIS. The two programs were to be replaced in the year 2001 by a single, integrated "Seniors Benefit"; pension and old-age tax credits were to be eliminated at the same time. The basic effect of the changes would have been to start phasing out pension benefits (except the CPP/QPP) at lower income levels, and at a faster rate, than under the current system.[40] The outcome would be particularly noticeable for couples, since the Seniors Benefit would be calculated on the basis of family income rather than individual income. The result was to be lower pension benefits for middle- and upper-income seniors and elimination of those benefits for a larger group than those affected by the current OAS clawback.

The changes were supposed to produce substantial savings for the federal government—$200 million in the first year and $2.1 a year by 2011.[41] By the year 2030, the new Seniors Benefit was expected to save 10 percent (about $7 billion) vis-à-vis the cost of the existing programs.[42] The political palatability of the proposal was increased by changes made in the plan in the weeks before it was unveiled: Existing senior citizens—and those over age 60 as well—would remain under the existing system as long as they lived if they chose not to switch to the new system. The government claimed that 75 percent of senior citizens (and 90 percent of single senior women, who tend to have the lowest incomes) would be as well off or better off than under the old system.[43] Thus the government sacrificed immediate budget savings for the sake of increased political viability for the proposals and with an eye to their long-term savings.

In short, the Seniors Benefit proposal contained numerous elements—significant lead time before going into effect, a lengthy phase-in, "grandfathering" of the aged and near-aged, and minimal sweetening of benefits for the lowest-income seniors—designed to diffuse opposition and political blame. The Liberals' proposed changes to old-age pensions also relied on several elements of what Canadian social policy critic Ken Battle has called "the politics of stealth," begun under the Mulroney government, to increase their political viability. First, they were announced not in "election campaigns or in public discussion papers where they would be subject to scrutiny and debate, but rather in . . . budgets as part of a long list of policy measures that were imposed largely without debate."[44] Inclusion in the budget both lowered their visibility and made them almost immune from procedural attack or amendment. Second, the amendments were highly technical and complex, involving the interacting effects of several programs and making it impossible for the average voter to understand.[45]

The measures nevertheless did prove very controversial, and the Chrétien government did not take the opportunity to impose the measures immediately, as part of its 1996 budget legislation. Action was first postponed until after the spring 1997 federal election.[46] The long delay after announcement of the Seniors Benefit gave ample opportunity for interest group opposition to emerge. Women's groups criticized the fact that benefits were to be based on family income rather than individual income, resulting in steep cuts in benefits for women whose husbands had substantial income but who had little of their own. Business groups, retirement planners, and even the Canadian Institute of Actuaries argued that the Seniors Benefit contained severe disincentives with respect to retirement savings.[47]

Even more important than interest group opposition was growing public awareness that the federal budget was headed toward a surplus. Polls conducted for the government showed that there was little public support for cutting pension benefits in the absence of a budget crisis.[48] A deal with the provinces to stabilize the financing of the Canada Pension Plan (discussed below) also undercut the financial urgency of implementing the Seniors Benefit. The political ambitions of Finance Minister Paul Martin did not bode well for the proposed reform, either: Martin was widely seen as the leading candidate to succeed Jean Chrétien as leader of the Liberal Party, and offending senior citizens and other groups arrayed against the Seniors Benefit was not a very good way to boost his prospects. By spring of 1998, the Finance Ministry was outlining for Martin alternatives to the Seniors Benefit;[49] at the end of July, he announced that he was simply canceling it altogether.[50]

REFORMING THE CPP

Throughout each of these rounds of retrenchment in the universal Old Age Security program, the Canada/Quebec Pension Plan remained largely off politicians' agenda, despite the fact that the CPP shared with the U.S. Social Security system a deteriorating financial condition, shaped in part by declining economic and demographic conditions, a number of benefit enhancements enacted in the 1970s, and a dramatic increase in take-up of disability benefits in the 1980s and 1990s.[51] As a result, cash flow from contributions (i.e., contributions minus expenditures) turned consistently negative beginning in 1983. In 1993, overall CPP cash flow began to turn negative (that is, contributions plus interest payments were no longer adequate to pay benefits), meaning that the provinces were beginning to have to repay the principal that they had borrowed from the CPP at favorable rates.[52]

Despite these financial problems, the difficulty of securing provincial assent helped to keep CPP cutbacks from even getting on the agenda. It doesn't pay for a Canadian politician to go out in front on an issue when resolution in the absence of a crisis is very doubtful and when it is almost certain that at least some provincial ministers as well as the federal opposition parties will use the occasion to denounce the federal government in a high-profile setting.[53] Getting agreement on payroll tax increases was difficult, too: They remained flat at 3.6 percent (shared equally by employers and employees) from 1966 through 1986, when they began a steady but slight increase of roughly 0.2 percent per year (figure 2-1). Moreover, things were expected to grow steadily worse in the future: The CPP's chief actuary estimated in 1995 that the CPP trust fund would be exhausted by the year 2015, and that with an empty trust fund, the contribution rate needed to finance contributions on a pay-as-you-go basis would have to reach 14.2 percent by the year 2030.[54] As in the United States, critics also warned that the CPP, as currently constituted, was also grossly unfair to younger workers and thus ultimately politically unsustainable.[55] Projections for the Quebec Pension Plan were similarly bleak.[56]

Declining trust fund balances, eroding public confidence in the CPP, and growing awareness that a failure to address the CPP's problems quickly would lead to soaring contribution rates in the future finally led to an initiative by Ottawa in 1995 to alter the program.[57] Initially, much of the effort was devoted to a behind-the-scenes effort led by the federal Finance Ministry to bring its counterparts in the provincial capitals on board with respect to the need for change.

Ottawa and eight of the ten provinces reached agreement in 1997 on a package of CPP changes that distributed pain among all parties.[58] (The provinces of British

FIGURE 2-1

Canada Pension Plan and OASDI Employee Payroll Tax Rates

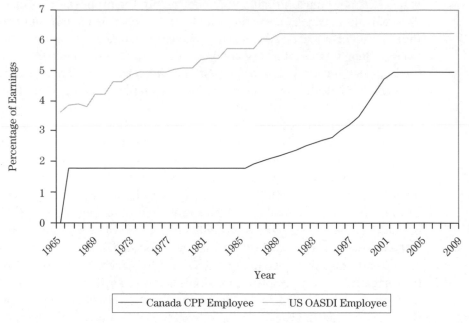

Canada CPP Employee   US OASDI Employee

Columbia and Saskatchewan, both governed by the left-of-center New Democratic Party, backed an alternative proposal that would have raised the ceiling on the CPP tax base, resulting in a substantial tax increase for middle- and upper-income workers.[59]) The Liberal government did not back off from these changes (as happened with the planned Seniors Benefit), and they went into effect in 1998.[60]

The most visible change in the CPP rescue package—and the one with the biggest fiscal impact—was with respect to payroll taxes.[61] Tax rates on employers and employees are scheduled to rise from 5.85 percent to 9.90 percent (shared equally between the two) over a six-year period, to finance a move away from pay-as-you-go toward partial advance funding of the CPP (figure 2-1). As critics on the political right pointed out, this represents a 70 percent increase in the tax rate. In exchange, Ottawa bowed to provincial demands for a cut in the Unemployment Insurance payroll tax, which was running large surpluses.[62]

The CPP payroll tax increase was more rapid than the increases already scheduled under the statute then in effect, but politicians sold it as a measure that would prevent payroll taxes from having to go as high as previously projected if the CPP contribution rate was not quickly changed; moreover, the initial tax increase was not scheduled to be felt until 1998—after the next federal election.[63] In addition, the amount of earnings of low-income workers that is exempt from the CPP payroll tax was frozen at the 1997 level ($3,500), rather than being indexed for inflation, as was the previous practice. As a result, the real subsidy to low-wage-earning Canadians will gradually decline, and contributions to the CPP trust fund will grow.

Cuts in CPP retirement benefits were, not surprisingly, made much harder for beneficiaries to discern and understand. In consultation documents, bureaucrats suggested a number of options for cutbacks, including an explicit 10 percent cut (from 25 to 22.5 percent) in replacement rates and increases in the normal and earliest retirement ages.[64] But most of these highly visible cuts, enabling the largest potential savings—including retirement age increases, cuts in the replacement rate, and cuts in indexation—were rejected by the Quebec government in a 1996 discussion paper.[65] Thus the scope for change on the benefit side was dramatically reduced. Benefit cuts in the CPP were, therefore, made largely through technical changes to formulas that are almost incomprehensible to most beneficiaries, such as increasing from three to five the years of (unindexed) earnings prior to retirement on which initial retirement benefits are calculated.[66] Reflecting the familiar principle of "grandfathering" current retirees in order to reduce political opposition from the group with the most intense negative interest, this group was protected from CPP benefit cuts.

Little noticed at the time the legislation was passed, but potentially of great importance in the longer run, the new CPP legislation also put in place a new "default" or fail-safe procedure for ensuring the long-term financial viability of the CPP. In the future, the chief actuary for the CPP was to prepare estimates of the long-term financial sustainability of the plan. Over the next year, ministers from Ottawa and the provinces are supposed to agree on any needed changes to keep the plan viable; if they do not agree, contribution rates will automatically increase (phased in over three years) to meet half of the anticipated deficiency, and indexation of the CPP will be frozen for the next three years.[67] This procedure can be overridden by cabinet order, but it would take affirmative action to do so.

In short, the new statute influenced the future direction of CPP changes in five critical ways. First, it created a strong procedural presumption, and sent a strong signal to beneficiaries and contributors, that the CPP would be kept fiscally sound: Its fail-safe trigger kicks in when the long-term viability of the plan is in question, not (as in the 1983 U.S. law) when the plan is in immediate danger of not being able to pay out benefits. Second, unlike in the United States, where contribution increases were essentially banished from the agenda, contribution increases are likely to play a major role in any future CPP "fix" unless federal and provincial finance ministers can agree on an alternative. Third, it sets up a procedure for sharing the pain of a future CPP fix by dividing it between taxpayers (through contribution rate increases) and beneficiaries (through benefit freezes). Fourth, the new statute sets up a "clean hands" default procedure that allows losses to be imposed on beneficiaries and contributors without politicians having to do anything—although the concentration of accountability in Canada's Westminster political system means a future cabinet will still be tempted to avoid blame by canceling contribution increases and indexation freezes. Finally, by turning the highly inexact science of long-term actuarial projections into a policy trigger for prescribing loss-imposing actions, it makes it very likely that those projections will be the subject of future political conflict.

The CPP reform also contained some modest elements of restructuring. CPP investment practices are being changed. Provinces will eventually have to pay higher rates on borrowings;[68] more importantly, CPP funds will be invested in a broader range of securities, including equities, with these investments being managed by an independent twelve-person board. But like Canadian pension funds eligible for RRSP tax treatment, 70 percent of CPP investments will have to be located in Canada.

Political conservatives in Canada remain dissatisfied with the 1997 CPP reform package, arguing that it will produce an inadequate return on investment for future generations of contributors. Pressure for additional CPP changes has also come from the Reform Party (renamed the Canadian Alliance since 2000), the official opposition in the federal House of Commons. Reform/Alliance has called for replacing the CPP with mandatory private pensions, and more recently for an opt-out from the CPP to individual pensions on the British model.[69] But Reform/Alliance has not spelled out how it would handle the "double payment problem" if younger workers withdrew in large numbers from the CPP. Nor does it have strong leverage to get its proposals on the agenda.

REFLECTIONS ON PENSION REFORM POLICYMAKING

This review of pension reform policy in the U.S. and Canada over the last twenty years suggests both cross-national similarities and differences in pensions policy processes and outcomes. It also suggests some interesting conclusions with respect to the role of political institutions, policy legacies, and other factors in shaping these patterns.

Processes

There have clearly been differences in the political processes through which pension reforms were considered in the two countries. Retrenchment initiatives in the United States came onto the "action agenda" of changes given serious consideration by policymakers more frequently than in Canada, and they originated from a greater variety of sources. However, those initiatives had a lower success rate than in Canada. Even in Canada, however, the success rate for pension reform initiatives was hardly consistent with the image of an omnipotent government that could impose losses at will.

Outcomes

Pension policy outcomes can be divided into three broad categories: retrenchment, financing, and programmatic restructuring.

RETRENCHMENT

There are striking similarities between Canada and the United States in the level and incidence of pension retrenchment and in the repertoire of techniques used by politicians in the two countries to avoid accountability and blame when they did cut pension expenditures.[70] Cost savings in both countries were achieved through highly technical changes to benefit formulas that were hard for beneficiaries to understand. Grandfathering current beneficiaries, who were most likely to notice and mobilize against losses, was used in both Canada and the United States. In both countries, tinkering with benefit indexation mechanisms proved politically risky, and indexation mechanisms for persons who had already retired survived multiple rounds of retrenchment largely intact in both countries. Trust fund crises served as an "action-forcing mechanism" that put retrenchment on the agenda with respect to contributory pension plans in both countries, although those crises were more immediate in the U.S. than in Canada. Trust funds also helped to define the range of acceptable solutions in both countries: Changes had to be made that experts would certify as moving funds close to actuarial balance in both the short and long terms.

There have also been important similarities with respect to the *targets* of cutbacks. Cuts in cash pension benefits in both countries have been targeted especially (through taxation of OASI benefits in the U.S. and the OAS clawback in Canada), although not exclusively, at upper-income beneficiaries. In both countries, changes targeted at higher-income retirees were partially offset by changes in tax subsidies for retirement savings that primarily benefit people with higher incomes. In Canada, efforts to impose across-the-board cuts (notably through indexation changes) were defeated, while some broad-based cuts in the U.S., notably a long-term increase in the normal retirement age, were adopted. Both the GIS in Canada and SSI in the United States, have, with the exception of benefits for immigrants, been very resilient in avoiding retrenchment initiatives; such initiatives have rarely even made it to the agenda. Indeed, the rank ordering of vulnerability to cutbacks appears to be, in declining order of vulnerability, universal pensions (Canada only), contributory pensions, and income-tested pensions (except for immigrants).[71] The two countries' experience appears to reverse the conventional wisdom that income- or means-tested welfare state programs are more resistant to retrenchment initiatives than universal ones. The lesson appears to be that the public and politicians in both countries feel a commitment to preventing severe poverty among a group, the elder poor, that is seen as deserving and is not expected to work

Finally, there have also been some important differences in pension retrenchment *outcomes*. In particular, Canadian officials have been able to enact significant retrenchment in the absence of an immediate trust fund crisis, while U.S. officials—with the exception of the cuts to upper-income Social Security recipients enacted in 1993 and to noncitizen SSI recipients in 1996—have not.

PENSION FINANCING

Differences between the two countries with respect to financing pension systems have been much more evident than those for retrenchment (figure 2-1). Taking into account the fact that both the quasi-universal Old Age Security and income-tested Guaranteed Income Supplement in Canada are financed from general revenues rather than payroll taxes, the major difference between the two countries appears to be one of timing: Major increases in the payroll tax occurred much earlier in the U.S. than in Canada. Increases in the CPP contribution rate were enacted in Canada in 1997, albeit from a lower base than in the U.S. Payroll tax increases have been virtually banished from the agenda in the United States since the early 1980s, although payroll tax increases enacted in earlier years with lagged implementation continued to come into effect for another decade. While the need to secure intergovernmental agreement long served to prevent changes in CPP tax rates, once an agreement was reached, there was little public protest or mobilization against the agreement—it was treated as a fait accompli.

These national differences on the revenue side have several roots. One is certainly the immediacy of a CPP funding crisis in Canada in the late 1990s; in the United States, that crisis occurred in 1977 and 1981–1983. A second reason is the Republican control of the congressional policymaking process in the U.S.: With opposition to any tax increase a bedrock issue for most Republicans, there was little incentive for any political actor to suffer the political costs of proposing a Social Security payroll tax increase when there was virtually no chance that it would be adopted. A third difference is that the intergovernmental bargaining process in Canada provided both a "backroom" process for negotiating such an agreement and a mechanism for legitimizing it. Canada's parliamentary institutions meant that a federal-provincial pact on CPP financing was almost certain to be adopted once an agreement was reached.

RESTRUCTURING

There are also some differences between the two countries in the extent to which their pension systems have been restructured. In both countries, the basic structure of cash pension tiers has remained intact. The weight of past programmatic choices makes it politically almost impossible for countries to start afresh with a dramatically different system and almost as hard to delete existing tiers of pensions. In the United States, very heavy reliance on a single system of contributory Old Age and Survivors Insurance has reinforced the initial decision to provide higher replacement rates to those with lower earnings histories; failure to do so would put very heavy pressure on the SSI system. Canada has ended the universality of Old Age Security by income-testing it at the upper end of the income scale, a move that mirrors the actions of many European countries as their contributory pension schemes have matured.

Canada has enjoyed greater success than the U.S. in a second element of restructuring: moving from lending solely to governments toward collective investment of public pension funds in equities markets. Both governments were attracted to equities investment for essentially the same reason: It appeared to offer a "free lunch" of higher returns on trust fund balances, and thereby less need to incur blame by cutting benefits or raising payroll taxes. In Canada, however, the Chrétien government's decision to invest a modest share of CPP funds in the stock market was undertaken with relatively little controversy. In the United States, on the other hand, whether to allow collective investment has been a major divisive issue and is unlikely to occur so long as Republicans control al least one chamber of Congress or the presidency. On the other hand, partial conversion of Social Security into individual accounts remains much more of an option than in Canada, a fact that has more to do with the strength of political ideologies in the two countries than with their institutions.

EXPLANATIONS

Some of the patterns outlined above are consistent with the hypotheses outlined at the beginning of this chapter about the politics of concentrated loss imposition vis-à-vis a specific, geographically diffused group, while others are not. With respect to retrenchment in eligibility and benefits, for example, the larger number of retrenchment initiatives in the U.S., the greater variety of sources for such initiatives, and their lower success rate all reflect the greater diffusion of power in U.S. political institutions. But the fact that even in Canada the federal government has backed down from pension retrenchment initiatives suggests that there is indeed a significant gap between the theoretical capacity of Westminster-style parliamentary systems to impose losses and the political practicality of reelection-seeking governments in those systems actually doing so. The results also cast doubt on the suggestion that Canada's federal government will enjoy greater loss-imposition capacity because of the longer electoral cycle there. The reason seems fairly straightforward: It is not just elections where MPs' own seats are at stake that are relevant to policy decision making in Canada. Looming provincial elections (especially those in Quebec) and referenda on Quebec sovereignty also cast long shadows on pension policy and on many other policy sectors.

The effects of federalism on pension policy are quite complex. The fact that most major pension programs are run by the federal governments in both countries has almost certainly helped to prevent a race to the bottom and helped to protect these programs against the cuts made in other sectors (notably, in Canada, cuts to health spending throughout the Canadian Health and Social Transfer) in which the federal government cuts transfers to subnational governments who actually deliver benefits, assuming that the latter will bear the brunt of the blame for those cutbacks. Canada's peculiar system of governance for the CPP/QPP, on the other hand, is more mixed. It almost certainly helped delay agreement on cutbacks and contribution increases until the late 1990s. But, as noted earlier, once an agreement *was* reached—between governments, behind closed doors—it both legitimized that agreement and made it almost impossible to overturn.

A third and quite different effect of federalism can be seen in comparing Canadian and U.S. policies toward collective investment in equities markets. Here, the experience of the Quebec Pension Plan in investing in equities markets appears to be somewhat analogous to that of Saskatchewan in health insurance innovation. In both cases, a provincial government acted as an innovator for reasons idiosyncratic to that province (a social democratic concern for universal health care in Saskatchewan, a commitment to promoting Quebec business in Quebec for pensions), but those innovations were ultimately emulated by the federal government. In short, federalism can bequeath a more varied set of policy legacies from which policymakers can learn than in a more centralized system—especially where underlying patterns of political cleavage also encourage differences in policy choices across states or provinces.

Policy feedbacks are at least as important as political institutions in explaining both cross-national similarities and cross-national differences in pension reform choices, however. These take several forms, and are sometimes intertwined with institutional effects. Clearly, as Paul Pierson has suggested, mature contributory pension schemes are extremely difficult to dislodge. Only the most radical of pension reformers have favored actually phasing out Social Security in the United States, although many favor lowering its role relative to that of individual portable pensions. But mature contributory public pension schemes are also vulnerable to trust fund crises unless there is a mechanism for injecting general revenues into those funds. Universal pensions, both Canada's OAS and those in other major countries, have become more vulnerable to cutbacks as contributory earnings–related pensions have become more ubiquitous, the phenomenon of the affluent elderly becomes more common, and high marginal tax rates on those with high incomes have been scaled back in many nations.

The ubiquity of indexation in cash pension programs, both immediately before the onset of huge pressures for retrenchment and at the end of the century, undercut our ability to draw conclusions about the relative hardiness of indexed and unindexed benefits. But they do suggest quite clearly that once indexation of benefits to retirees has begun, it is almost impossible to undo. Indexation is both less inevitable and less impregnable, however, when its effects are less visible—for example, with respect to the income limits for taxation of Social Security or the Year's Basic exemption for onset of Canada Pension Plan contributions.

The intertwining of institutional and policy feedback effects is clearly evident in the role that the Quebec Pension Plan's experience with investment in equities markets has played in making that issue less sensitive in Canada than in the United States. Indeed, Finance Minister Paul Martin explicitly acknowledged the Quebec Pension Plan's investment policies as constituting a positive model for the CPP.[72] In the U.S., on the other hand, resistance to collective investment of Social Security funds in equities markets was enhanced by both (1) the hopes of advocates that they could enact a greater transformation of the system in the direction of individual accounts, and (2) the opposition of a powerful political actor, Federal Reserve Board chairman Alan Greenspan, to such investments.

A final explanatory factor that appears to be important in explaining Canada–U.S. differences in outcomes is the ideology of governmental elites—in particular, the role of Republicans in the U.S. in banishing Social Security payroll tax increases from the U.S. agenda and in creating a much higher level of controversy over government investment in equities markets. The ability of conservatives in the U.S. to do both, however, has almost as much to do with institutions as it does with ideology: The greater institutional leverage they have enjoyed within the U.S. system of checks and balances has been fundamental to their success. The United States may eventually follow Canada toward collective equity investment, especially if conservatives in the U.S. decide that moving to individual accounts is not politically feasible and can be reassured about insulation of collective investment funds from government interference. But the road to that decision will have been much more rocky. Conservative proponents of partial privatization of Social Security in the United

States confront the same institutional obstacles to fundamental restructuring as do those favoring collective equity investment.

Techniques and Strategies of Loss Imposition

As suggested above, the type of strategies used to facilitate loss imposition in pension policy (see the discussion in chapter 1) were strikingly similar in the two countries. For example, near-term cuts in pension benefits were concentrated on relatively small groups of well-off recipients (in both countries), or on nonvoting immigrants (in the United States). In both countries, obfuscation through technical changes was used heavily for benefit cuts. Time lags and grandfathering were invoked in connection with both benefit cuts and payroll tax increases to lessen their political impact, while impersonal "scapegoating" of demographic change—the need to respond to population aging—was used to justify those measures. In Canada, insulation through use of the CPP/QPP intergovernmental mechanism was clearly critical to the success of the 1997 CPP reform, but this mechanism is a two-edged sword, since fears that no change would be possible (and that any government proposing painful changes would be blasted by one or more provinces for having done so) had helped to block change in prior years. "Passing the buck" to a bipartisan commission in 1981–83 in the United States had helped to "circle the wagons" around a Social Security rescue package combining benefit cuts and revenue increases, but it is unlikely that this would have been sufficient without the impetus of a trust fund crisis.

Strategic options for those seeking to avoid losses were fairly limited in both countries. Well-established legislative procedures for altering public pension programs meant that opponents of loss imposition could not hope to venue-shift to the courts or to another, friendlier decision-making arena. Nor were there major opportunities for redefining the issue in a way that would enlist new allies. But no such redefinition was needed: Public pensions already enjoyed a passionate constituency among the elderly and near-elderly in both countries and at least passive support among most younger citizens. Even in Canada, where seniors organizations are relatively weak, concentrating blame on proponents of austerity measures—or the threat of doing so—has generally been a successful strategy in preventing all but incremental change.

NOTES

The research reported herein was partially funded pursuant to a grant from the U.S. Social Security Administration (SSA), funded as part of the Retirement Research Consortium at Boston College. The opinions and conclusions are solely those of the author and should not be construed as representing the opinions or policy of SSA or any agency of the federal government.

1. See John Myles and Jill Quadagno, "Recent Trends in Public Pension Reform: A Comparative View," pp. 247–71, and Paul D. Pierson, "The Politics of Pension Reform," pp. 273–93, in Keith G. Banting and Robin Boadway, eds., *Reform of Retirement Income*

Policy: International and Canadian Perspectives (Kingston, Ontario: Queens University School of Policy Studies, 1997); R. Kent Weaver, "The Politics of Pension Reform: Lessons from Abroad," in R. Douglas Arnold, Michael Graetz, and Alicia Munnell, eds., *Framing the Social Security Debate: Values, Politics and Economics* (Washington, D.C.: Brookings Institution Press, 1998), pp. 183–229.

2. On declining poverty rates among the elderly in Canada, see Keith G. Banting and Robin Boadway, "Reforming Retirement Income Policy: The Issues," pp. 1–26, in Banting and Boadway, eds., *Reform of Retirement Income Policy*.

3. On this point, see, in particular, Steven M. Teles, "The Dialectics of Trust: Ideas, Finance and Pension Privatization in the US and the UK" (paper presented at the Annual Research Conference on the Association for Public Policy Analysis and Management, New York, October 29–31, 1998).

4. Paul D. Pierson and R. Kent Weaver, "Imposing Losses in Pension Policy," pp. 110–50, in R. Kent Weaver and Bert A. Rockman, eds., *Do Institutions Matter? Government Capabilities in the U.S. and Abroad* (Washington, D.C.: Brookings Institution Press, 1993).

5. See, for example, Keith G. Banting, *The Welfare State and Canadian Federalism*, 2d ed. (Kingston and Montreal: McGill-Queen's University Press, 1987).

6. Paul Pierson, *Dismantling the Welfare State? Reagan, Thatcher and the Politics of Retrenchment* (Cambridge: Cambridge University Press, 1994).

7. The SSI figure includes state supplementation. Social Security Administration, *Annual Statistical Supplement, 2001* (Washington, D.C.: SSA, 2000), pp. 155, 277.

8. The OASI figure used in this calculation includes retired workers and their spouses and surviving nondisabled spouses of retired workers, but excludes children of retired and deceased workers. Social Security Administration, *Annual Statistical Supplement, 2001* (Washington, D.C.: SSA, 2000), pp. 189, 276.

9. On this period in both the United States and Canada, see Pierson and Weaver, "Imposing Losses in Pension Policy," and Paul Pierson and Miriam Smith, "Shifting Fortunes of the Elderly: The Comparative Politics of Retrenchment," pp. 21–59, in Theodore R. Marmor, Timothy M. Smeeding, and Vernon L. Greene, eds., *Economic Security and Intergenerational Justice: A Look at North America* (Washington, D.C.: Urban Institute Press, 1994). On the United States, see Paul Light, *Still Artful Work: The Continuing Politics of Social Security Reform* (New York: McGraw-Hill, 1995).

10. For a detailed description of the 1977 legislation, see John Snee and Mary Ross, "Social Security Amendments of 1977: Legislative History and Summary of Provisions," *Social Security Bulletin* 41 (March 1978).

11. For a detailed discussion, see Light, *Still Artful Work*.

12. For a description of these episodes, see Pierson and Weaver, "Imposing Losses in Pension Policy."

13. See R. Douglas Arnold, "The Politics of Social Security," *Political Science Quarterly* 111, no. 2 (1998): 213–40.

14. For details, see House Ways and Means Committee, *1994 Green Book: Overview of Entitlement Programs: Background Material and Data on Programs within the Jurisdiction of the Committee on Ways and Means*, WMCP 103–27 (Washington, D.C: GPO, 1994), pp. 30–34.

15. Dan Balz and Ronald Brownstein, *Storming the Gates: Protest Politics and the Republican Revival* (Boston: Little, Brown, 1996).

16. Illegal aliens are, with very few exceptions, barred from receiving federally financed benefits (see House Ways and Means Committee, *1996 Green Book* (Washington, D.C.: GPO, Committee Print 104-14), November 4, 1996, pp. 1301–2, 1353–59), although the courts have ruled that they cannot be barred from most *state*-financed programs, most importantly public education.

17. House Ways and Means Committee, *1996 Green Book*, 1305.

18. For a review of legislative changes in SSI made between 1993 and 1997, see House Ways and Means Committee, *1998 Green Book* (Washington, D.C.: GPO, Committee Print 105-7, May 19, 1998), pp. 318–25.

19. 1994–96 Advisory Council on Social Security, *Report*, vol. 1, *Findings and Recommendations* (Washington, D.C.: The Council, 1997).

20. See for example, Peter J. Ferrara and Michael Tanner, *A New Deal for Social Security* (Washinton, D.C.: Cato Institute, 1998).

21. See Gary Burtless, *How Would Financial Risk Affect Retirement Income under Individual Accounts?* Center for Retirement Research at Boston College, Issue Brief No. 5, October 2000.

22. See Executive Office of the President, *Budget of the United States Government, Fiscal Year 2000*, 41.

23. For Greenspan's views, see Richard W. Stevenson, "Fed Chief Warns of Painful Choices on Social Security," *New York Times*, January 29, 1999.

24. For a review of the literature concluding that government investment of Social Security funds could be adequately shielded from political interference, see Alicia H. Munnell and Annika Sunden, "Investment Practices of State and Local Pension Funds: Implications for Social Security Reform" (paper presented at the first annual conference of the Retirement Research Consortium, Washington, D.C., May 20–21, 1999).

25. See Kevin Sack, "Gore and Bush Trade Jabs on Pensions and Spending; Vice President Sees Threat to Future of Social Security," *New York Times*, November 2, 2000. p. A1.

26. For a discussion, see Amy Goldstein, "Bush Plans Panel to Study Overhaul of Social Security," *Washington Post*, February 27, 2001, p. A1, and Sara Fritz, "Proof of Bush's Social Security Intentions Will Be in the Panel," *St. Petersburg Times*, April 2, 2001, p. 3A.

27. See for example, Richard Morin and Claudia Deane, "Poll Shows New Doubts on Economy; President's Tax Cut, Policy Are Questioned," *Washington Post*, March 27, 2001, p. A1; Christine Dugas, "Retirement Crisis Looms as Many Come Up Short," *USA Today*, July 19, 2002, p. 1A; Dee DePass, "Job Obstruction," *Minneapolis Star-Tribune*, August 26, 2002, p. 1A; Damian Paletta and Robert Johnson, "Dow's Drop Dashes Dreams," *Orlando Sentinel*, July 26, 2002, p. A1; Glenn Kessler, "Democrats View Social Security as Election Issue," *Washington Post*, February 23, 2002, p. A2; William O'Rourke, "GOP Shifts Course on Social Security," *Chicago Sun-Times*, August 20, 2002, p. 27.

28. There is a 6 percent reduction of benefits for each year below age 65 at which a person elects early retirement. Individuals can also elect to delay CPP benefits to any point up to age 70, with a bonus of 6 percent for each year of postponement. Like Social Security in the United States, the CPP provides a higher return to low wage workers, but it uses a different mechanism: Contributions are not paid on an initial amount of yearly earnings—the year's basic exemption, or YBE—but those earnings are counted toward benefit entitlement.

29. Changes in the CPP must be approved by the governments of two-thirds of Canadian provinces having two-thirds of the Canadian population. This means that any four provinces have a veto, as does Ontario alone. In practice, Quebec has a veto over major changes as well, since policymakers want to keep the Ontario and Quebec plans closely integrated. See Keith Banting, "Institutional Conservatism: Federalism and Pension Reform," in Jacqueline Ismael, ed., *Canadian Social Welfare Policy: Federal and Provincial Dimensions* (Kingston and Montreal: McGill-Queens University Press, 1985), pp. 48–74, esp. pp. 56–57.

30. Negotiation with the provinces was required because supplementary benefits (e.g., for widows and survivors) fall under exclusive provincial jurisdiction, and thus federal entry required provincial assent to an amendment to the British North America Act. On the negotiations surrounding creation of the Canada Pension Plan, see Richard Simeon, *Federal-Provincial Diplomacy: The Making of Recent Policy in Canada* (Toronto: University of Toronto Press, 1972), chap. 3, and Kenneth A. Bryden, *Old Age Pensions*

and Policy-Making in Canada (Kingston and Montreal: McGill-Queens University Press, 1974), chap. 8.

31. For general background on government pensions in Canada, see National Council of Welfare, *A Pension Primer* (Ottawa: Supply and Services, summer 1996), and Banting, *The Welfare State and Canadian Federalism.* On the origins of Canadian pension policies, see Bryden, *Old Age Pensions and Policy-Making in Canada.*

32. For an overview of changes in Canadian pension programs, see Ken Battle, "A New Old Age Pension," pp. 135–90, in Keith G. Banting and Robin Boadway, eds., *Reform of Retirement Income Policy: International and Canadian Perspectives* (Kingston, Ontario: Queens University School of Policy Studies, 1997), pp. 135–90, and Michael J. Prince, "Lowering the Boom on the Boomers: Replacing Old Age Security with the New Seniors Benefit and Reforming the Canada Pension Plan," pp. 211–34, in Gene Swimmer, ed., *How Ottawa Spends, 1997–98, Seeing Red: A Liberal Report Card* (Ottawa: Carleton University Press, 1997).

33. See Ken Battle, "Indexation and Social Policy," *Canadian Review of Social Policy,* Issue No. 16/17 (October 1986 and January 1987): 1–20.

34. Prince, "Lowering the Boom on the Boomers," 215.

35. See Ken Battle (Grattan Gray, pseud.), "Social Policy by Stealth," *Policy Options* 11 (March 1990): 17–29, and "A New Old Age Pension," pp. 146–47.

36 On this period, see Edward Greenspon and Anthony Wilson-Smith, *Double Vision: The Inside Story of the Liberals in Power* (Toronto: Doubleday Canada, 1996).

37. See Leon Muszynski, "Social Policy and Canadian Federalism: What Are the Pressures for Change?" pp. 288–318, and Miriam Smith, "Retrenching the Sacred Trust: Medicare and Canadian Federalism," pp. 319–37, in François Rocher and Miriam Smith, eds., *New Trends in Canadian Federalism* (Peterborough, Ontario: Broadview, 1995), and Allan M. Maslove, "The Canadian Health and Social Transfer: Forcing Issues," pp. 283–301, in Gene Swimmer, ed., *How Ottawa Spends, 1996–1997: Life under the Knife* (Ottawa: Carleton University Press, 1996).

38. See Prince, "Lowering the Boom on the Boomers," and Greenspon and Wilson-Smith, *Double Vision,* esp. chap. 16.

39. Edward Greenspon, "Martin Chose Lesser of Two Evils," *Globe and Mail* (Toronto), July 29, 1998, p. A4. The 1995 budget did enunciate a set of five principles to be followed in pension reform initiatives, however: maintenance of benefits for low-income seniors, full indexation of benefits, using family income in income testing for OAS, increased benefit progressivity, and cost control. See Battle, "A New Old Age Pension," pp. 151–71.

40. For an overview, see National Council of Welfare, *A Guide to the Proposed Seniors Benefit* (Ottawa: Supply and Services, summer 1996).

41. Ibid., 23.

42. Shawn McCarthy, "Martin Backs Off Seniors Plan," *Globe and Mail* (Toronto), July 29, 1998, p. A1.

43. Government of Canada, *Budget Plan 1997: Building a Future for Canadians,* February 18, 1997, p. 117.

44. See, for example, Ken Battle, "The Politics of Stealth: Child Benefits under the Tories," pp. 417–48 in Susan D. Phillips, ed., *How Ottawa Spends, 1993–1994: A More Democratic Canada . . . ?* (Ottawa: Carleton University Press, 1993), at p. 439.

45. A third element of the "politics of stealth," manipulation of indexation mechanisms, was not used in this case: The level at which "clawback" of the Seniors Benefit begins is more fully protected from inflation than the OAS clawback phase-in under the current system.

46. See Shawn McCarthy and Edward Greenspon, "Ottawa Girds for Pension War," *Globe and Mail* (Toronto), September 8, 1997; Laura Eggertson, "Martin Defends Premium Hike for CPP Security," *Toronto Star,* October 29, 1997.

47. Because middle-income seniors would lose twenty cents of Seniors Benefit for every dollar of income that they pulled from Registered Retirement Savings Plans in addition to paying income tax on that RRSP income, senior citizens could end up with higher marginal tax rates after retirement than before—rates over 70 percent. Shawn McCarthy, "Martin Backs Off Seniors Plan"; Alan Toulin, "Martin Scraps Seniors Benefit Plan," *National Post*, July 29, 1998, p. A1; Sean Durkan, "Martin Kills Plan to Cut Pensions," *Edmonton Sun*, July 29, 1998, p. 24. See also Prince, "Lowering the Boom on the Boomers," pp. 226–29.

48. Shawn McCarthy, "Ottawa Finds Little Support for New Seniors Plan," *Globe and Mail* (Toronto) June 30, 1998, p. A3.

49. See Eric Beauchesne, "Martin Ignored Bureaucrats' Advice on Adjusting Pension Plans," *National Post*, May 17, 1999.

50. Shawn McCarthy, "Martin Backs Off Seniors Plan."

51. Benefit enhancements included full indexation of benefits rather than just for inflation over 2 percent in 1975, dropping retirement and earnings tests for persons aged 65 to 69 in 1975, and addition of child-rearing drop-out provisions in 1987. Overall, these benefit enhancements were estimated to add costs amounting to 2.4 percent of contributory earnings to the program. Federal/Provincial/Territorial CPP Consultations Secretariat, *An Information Paper for Consultations on the Canada Pension Plan* (Ottawa: Department of Finance, February 1996), chap. 3.

52. Assets in the trust fund continued to increase through the end of 1992 because of investment earnings and fell each year after that. See Office of the Superintendent of Financial Institutions, Chief Actuary, *Canada Pension Plan, Seventeenth Actuarial Report as at 31 December, 1997* (Ottawa: Office of the Superintendent of Financial Institutions, December 31, 1998), Table II.1.

53. On Ottawa's reluctance to proceed in the face of opposition from provincial governments in the 1996–97 round of CPP reform, see Edward Greenspon, "Martin Won't Push Changes to Pension Plan," *Globe and Mail* (Toronto), October 3, 1996, p. A4.

54. See the discussion in Office of the Superintendent of Financial Institutions, Chief Actuary, *Canada Pension Plan, Sixteenth Actuarial Report, September 1997* (Ottawa: Office of the Superintendent of Financial Institutions, September 24, 1997).

55. See, for example, William Robson, "The Coming Revolt against the CPP," *Globe and Mail* (Toronto), December 6, 1996, p. A23. See also Robson, "Ponzi's Pawns: Young Canadians and the Canada Pension Plan," in J. Burbidge, *When We're 65: Reforming Canada's Retirement Income System* (Toronto: C. D. Howe Institute, 1996).

56. The Quebec Pension Plan's actuary estimated that to maintain its current benefits, the contribution rate would have to rise 0.4 percent per year from 1997 to 2001 and 0.25 percent per year thereafter until it reached a stable rate of 13 percent in the year 2023. Régie des rentes du Québec, *For You and Your Children: Guaranteeing the Future of the Québec Pension Plan* (Sainte-Foy, Quebec: Régie des rentes du Québec, 1996), p. 21 and Appendix 2.

57. Federal/Provincial/Territorial CPP Consultations Secretariat, *An Information Paper for Consultations on the Canada Pension Plan*, p. 17.

58. Human Resources Development Canada and Finance Canada, *Securing the Canada Pension Plan: Agreement on Proposed Changes to the CPP*, February 1997.

59. On the British Columbia government's proposal for an increase in the tax base, see Andrew Petter, "How to Save the Canada Pension Plan," *Globe and Mail* (Toronto), October 3, 1996, and Barrie McKenna, "Provinces Block CPP Reform," *Globe and Mail* (Toronto), October 5, 1996. Petter was then the finance minister of British Columbia.

60. The CPP legislation did run into opposition in Canada's unelected (and therefore usually docile) second chamber, the Senate. Conservative Senators threatened to delay consideration of the bill past the end of 1997, meaning that payroll tax increases scheduled for January 1, 1998, could not be implemented as scheduled. In exchange for

securing speedy passage of the legislation, Finance Minister Paul Martin agreed to delay implementation of provisions of the new legislation dealing with the CPP Investment Board until March 31, 1998, giving the Senate Committee on Banking, Trade and Commerce an opportunity to hold a series of hearings on the CPP Investment Board, the proposed Seniors Benefit, and RRSPs and issue a report on the Investment Board. See Laura Eggertson, "Pension Changes Pass Hurdle in Senate," *Toronto Star*, December 17, 1997.

61. On the fiscal impact of the 1997 changes, see David W. Slater and William B. P. Robson, *Building a Stronger Pillar: The Changing Shape of the Canada Pension Plan* (Toronto: C. D. Howe Institute, March 1999).

62. See McKenna, "Provinces Block CPP Reform."

63. In fact, the initial tax increase—from 5.85 to 6.0 percent of payroll—was retroactive to January 1997, but was not scheduled to be paid until income tax time in the spring of 1998. Derek Ferguson, "73% Premium Increases to Save Pensions: Martin," *Toronto Star*, September 26, 1997. For a schedule of prior and revised payroll tax rates, see Human Resources Development Canada and Finance Canada, *Securing the Canada Pension Plan*, p. 7.

64. For a list of proposals and estimates of their likely savings see Federal/Provincial/Territorial CPP Consultations Secretariat, *An Information Paper for Consultations on the Canada Pension Plan*, p. 43.

65. The Quebec government announced its opposition to these changes being applied to the Quebec Pension Plan. In theory, Ottawa could have implemented major benefit cuts in the CPP anyway if Quebec either went along or was outvoted by other provinces. But a strong desire on the part of all participants to keep the CPP and QPP closely integrated meant that the benefit cuts opposed by Quebec were effectively off the table for both the CPP and QPP once Quebec decided to oppose them. Régie des rentes du Québec, *For You and Your Children*.

66. If this policy had been in effect in 1997, the maximum pension benefit would have been twelve dollars a month lower. Human Resources Development Canada and Finance Canada, *Securing the Canada Pension Plan*, p. 10. Cuts were also made in disability benefits.

67. See Canada Pension Plan, Chapter C-8, *Consolidated Statutes of Canada*, sections 113–15; *Statutes of Canada*, Chapter C-40 (Bill C-2), sections 94–96; and Slater and Robson, *Building a Stronger Pillar*, pp. 6–7.

68. Provinces will have to pay their own market rate of interest rather than Ottawa's—but they were given the option of rolling over their current CPP borrowings for another twenty-year term.

69. Reform Party of Canada, *Blue Sheet: Principles and Policies of the Reform Party of Canada, 1998–99*; Neville Nankivell, "Reform's New Strategy Reopens Serious Debate about CPP's Future," *Financial Post*, June 6, 1998, p. 21.

70. On techniques for obfuscating losses in entitlement programs, see R. Kent Weaver, "Controlling Entitlements," pp. 307–41, in John E. Chubb and Paul E. Peterson, eds., *The New Direction in American Politics* (Washington, D.C.: Brookings Institution Press, 1985), and Pierson, *Dismantling the Welfare State?*, chap. 1.

71. See the discussion and data in Banting, "The Social Policy Divide," pp. 267–309, in Keith G. Banting, George Hoberg, and Richard Simeon, eds., *Degrees of Freedom: Canada and the United States in a Changing World* (Montreal and Kingston: McGill-Queens University Press, 1997).

72. Martin said, "I have always been an apostle of the Caisse de depot [the Quebec agency that invests QPP and Quebec civil service pension funds] and I think having a Canadian Caisse de depot to manage the savings of Canadians is very important." Ferguson, "73% Premium Increases to Save Pensions: Martin."

3

CONTROLLING HEALTH CARE COSTS FOR THE AGED

CAROLYN HUGHES TUOHY

Over the course of the 1980s and 1990s, governments in Canada and the U.S. adopted a number of measures directed at holding down the rate of increase in health care costs borne by the public treasury. In both countries, these measures focused primarily on controlling payments to providers rather than reducing eligibility or scope of coverage. The two countries' rates of increase in nominal health care expenditures in both public and private sectors had paralleled each other at double-digit values in the 1980s. In the 1990s the rates of increase began to slow in both countries and both sectors. But interestingly, the pattern of change in public and private finance diverged in this period. In Canada, the rate of increase in public spending was sharply constrained. As for private finance, however, although the rate of increase declined, it more than kept pace with general inflation. In the U.S., just the reverse was true: Public expenditure was constrained less tightly than was private expenditure. Toward the end of the decade, however, both public and private spending rebounded in both countries, and rates of increase began to converge.

While the restraint measures undertaken by public payers in the 1990s had effects on the availability of health care services, they were targeted in the first instance at providers. Because health care providers—particularly physicians and hospitals—are hardly without political resources, these instances of loss imposition beg to be explained. Indeed, the health care arenas of Canada and the U.S., densely populated with interests and accounting for a substantial proportion of public budgets, provide fertile ground for an exploration of the politics of loss imposition in an era of fiscal constraint. These arenas exemplify a rich range of variation with respect to both dependent and independent variables. The dependent variable, the type of loss involved, falls into a number of analytical categories. The first concerns the *incidence* of loss. To the extent that losses are concentrated, at least in the first instance, on providers of health care, they fall into the category of "industry-focused" losses. This is an "industry," however, that is highly decentralized by point of delivery. Hence losses may be geographically diffused if they are imposed on the industry as a whole, but geographically concentrated if they are targeted at particular facilities, such as hospitals. The second set of categories concerns the nature of the *value* involved in the loss. Reductions in payments to providers or in services provided to beneficiaries, for example, are clearly tangible losses. But tangible losses do not exhaust the range of possibilities: Changes in decision-making structures may involve "positional" losses (or gains) in influence for particular groups. And because there may be trade-offs between tangible and positional gains, the calculus of advantage or disadvantage is quite complex.

Canada and the U.S. also offer a range of variation along the relevant explanatory variables. As we shall see, the key variables in this regard relate to political institutions and policy design. The contrast between the Canadian Westminster model of cabinet-dominated parliamentary government and the U.S. congressional system of checks and balances is one that is explored throughout this book. In the health care arena, these differences are compounded by differences in policy design: The respective systems of governmental coverage for health services to the elderly are embedded in broader systems of health care financing and delivery that have diverged sharply over the last three decades.

PUBLIC HEALTH CARE INSURANCE FOR THE ELDERLY: CANADA VS. THE UNITED STATES

The Context

At first blush, a comparison of the politics of retrenchment in the U.S. and Canadian health care arenas, within the framework that informs this book, might appear to be misconceived. After all, one of the criteria that the editors asked contributors to observe was that the baselines in the two arenas to be compared should be roughly similar. Students of comparative health policy are accustomed to treating the single-payer universal Canadian system and the U.S. mixed market system essentially as foils for each other. A "similar systems" approach to Canadian and U.S. health care in the 1990s, then, is unusual to say the least.

On closer examination, however, the two systems do present important dimensions of similarity in one subarena—that of health care for the elderly. In both countries, the balance of financing for services for those over sixty-five years of age is predominantly public: In the U.S. the public share is about two-thirds;[1] in Canada it is about 79 percent.[2] (In fact, the two-thirds share of public finance in this subarena in the U.S. is just slightly less than the public share in the Canadian health care arena as a whole.) Hence the political constituency of beneficiaries is similar in the two nations. Governmental plans in both systems, moreover, rely primarily upon fee-for-service payment of physicians and prospective payment of hospitals. These gross similarities mask important differences, and recent policy changes in the U.S. are widening these differences. But it is nonetheless fair to say that the world of health care financing and delivery experienced by the elderly in the U.S. is more similar to that experienced by their Canadian counterparts than it is to the world experienced by their younger American compatriots.

The Canadian and American subarenas of health care for the elderly are, of course, embedded in broader national health care arenas, and any comparison regarding health care for the elderly needs to take account of these broader contexts. The two health care systems have been driven in very different directions from a common point in the late 1950s and early 1960s as a result of policy decisions taken at that time. Policymakers in each nation, in their own distinctive ways, took an incremental approach to the achievement of universal health insurance. Canadians took a sector-based approach, adopting first universal hospital insurance at the federal level in 1958, followed by universal medical care insurance in 1966.[3] American policymakers proceeded in increments defined by population groups, adopting government-sponsored hospital and medical care insurance for the elderly (through Medicare) and the indigent (through Medicaid) in 1965. Despite the expectations of strategists within the Democratic party that additional population categories would be added until universal eligibility was achieved, only one such addition was made—when, in 1973, Medicare eligibility was extended to the disabled.[4] Medicare currently covers about 14 percent of the population: About 87 percent of Medicare beneficiaries are sixty-five and over, while 13 percent are under sixty-five and disabled. About 20 percent of Medicaid beneficiaries, most of them aged sixty-five and over, are also eligible for Medicare and are dually enrolled in both programs.

As a result of these different strategies, the boundary between public and private financing of health care services is defined in very different ways in the two nations. In Canada, the world of hospital and medical services is almost entirely publicly financed. Each province operates a universal hospital and medical insurance plan ("medicare"), within the framework of federal legislation (the Canada Health Act) that establishes the fundamental principles with which provincial plans must comply in order to be eligible for federal transfer payments. Within the Canadian medicare world, providers are bound into a close, if often tense, accommodation with the state, as will be discussed further below. For patients in this world, health care services are free at the point of service, although access to certain specialized procedures may involve waiting time. As patients move out of hospitals, and to health care providers other than physicians,[5] however, they move into a world not governed by the Canada Health Act, a world in which the basis of financing is a complex mix of public finance, out-of-pocket payments, and private insurance. In contrast, in the U.S., where the distinction between public and private financing is based on population groups, it is providers who move from one world of finance to another as they move from patient to patient. This model, as we shall see, provides a much slimmer basis for a political and economic accommodation between

providers and the state than exists in Canada, as well as a narrower base of beneficiaries of public finance within the population. These differences have profoundly
shaped the politics of public-sector retrenchment in each nation.

American and Canadian "Medicare": Similarities and Differences

Under the model that predominates in both systems, elderly patients have free
choice among physicians in fee-for-service private practice and are treated in hospitals through the referral and affiliation networks of those physicians. In Canada, this
is the model that prevails throughout the health care arena; in the U.S. it contrasts
with the broader health care arena, which is characterized by a plethora of organizational and contractual arrangements linking providers, insurers, and payers in a
great variety of forms of "managed care" and "preferred provider" networks, to be
discussed below.

Beyond this important similarity, however, the Canadian and American systems
for the elderly have several important differences. Public financing arrangements
differ markedly. Whereas Canada funds its medicare program from general revenue,[6] U.S. Medicare is financed through a more complex system. "Part A" of
Medicare, covering largely institutional services, is financed through a "trust fund"
funded primarily by payroll taxation. This financing arrangement creates a situation in which the "solvency" of the fund is strongly related to the dependency
ratio—that is, the ratio of the population of Medicare beneficiaries to the employed
workforce. This has allowed for a uniquely American projection of financial "crisis" in the public health care program as the aging of the population leads to the
insolvency of the trust fund. "Part B" of Medicare, largely related to physician services, is funded through a combination of general revenues and premiums. (Premiums are set according to a formula established in legislation and intended to ensure that 25 percent of Part B costs are funded through premiums. The premium
rate has, however, been subject to periodic modification by Congress.)

In addition to these differences in methods of public finance, American seniors
bear a larger proportion of health care expenditures privately, largely as a result of
copayments, deductibles, and ceilings and limitations on coverage. These private
expenses are borne either out of pocket or through private "Medigap" insurance for
expenses not covered by Medicare. Private insurance for long-term care is rare,
however. Hence, ceilings on long-term care coverage drive many middle-income
beneficiaries to draw down or transfer their assets (including the family home) in
order to qualify for Medicaid coverage for nursing home care. In Canada, in contrast, basic nursing home charges are set at a level that can be met by the universal old-age pension, minus a "comfort allowance," which varies by province. Above
the basic minimum, most provinces apply income-tested copayments. In five
provinces (Ontario and the western provinces) assets are not taken into account;
in Quebec and the Atlantic provinces, some assets are considered, though most ex-
clude the principal residence.[7] Affluent seniors, as in the U.S., may opt for private
alternatives.

As for limitations in the scope of benefits, the most significant differences between the U.S. and Canada pertain to prescription drugs and home care. Prescription drug coverage outside hospitals is not required under the terms of the Canada
Health Act. Nonetheless, all Canadian provinces provide prescription drug coverage to at least some population groups. Seniors are eligible for prescription drug
coverage in all provinces, although in most there are income-related terms and conditions. In some cases, eligibility for coverage is income-related; in other cases,
there are income-related copayments and/or deductibles. This range of coverage
contrasts with U.S. Medicare, which has very limited coverage for prescription
drugs (although low-income seniors may qualify for such coverage under Medicaid). On the other hand, U.S. Medicare coverage of home care services is more generous than is public coverage in Canada. The universal, first-dollar, unlimited coverage of home care in the U.S. contrasts with the variety of income-related terms
and conditions surrounding provincial home care plans in Canada.

Despite these differences, Canadian medicare and U.S. Medicare have one final
important similarity: They have been extraordinarily popular social programs.
Canadian medicare has become a veritable defining element of national identity,
and fiscal constraint on medicare expenditures in the 1990s led to rising levels of
public concern and anxiety, as well as support for increased public expenditure on
health.[8] U.S. Medicare may not quite enjoy the iconic status of Canadian universal
health insurance; but, like the Social Security program of which it is part, it has
been consistently ranked at or near the top of the list of programs to be protected
from spending cuts.[9] In both countries, indeed, support for increased public expenditures spans all age categories. This public popularity means that expenditure
restraint in each of these programs has carried great political risk.

Cost Control in the 1980s and 1990s

As noted at the outset of this paper, experience with expenditure restraint in the
public and private sectors differed in intriguing ways between Canada and the U.S.
in the 1990s. The trends are illustrated in figure 3-1. In Canada, public-sector constraint was for most of the decade more severe than that in the private sector, while
in the U.S., it was the private sector that drove expenditure restraint.

The explanation for these differences lies both in the characteristics of political
institutions and in the consequences of policy design. In both Canada and the U.S.,
episodes of "big" policy change in the health care arena (that is, changes in the parameters that govern the balance of influence among key actors and the mix of policy instruments) are very rare, and their timing is dependent on confluences of factors in the broad political arena.[10] This phenomenon is not unique to Canada and the
U.S.,[11] but it is exacerbated in those two countries by distinctive institutional characteristics. The multiple veto points inherent in the U.S. congressional model make
major policy change notoriously difficult. And in Canada, where the Constitution as-
cribes most authority over social programs to the provinces while ascribing an implicit broad "spending power" to the federal government, major policy change in
most social policy areas has required federal-provincial negotiation and agreement.

FIGURE 3-1

Annual Percentage Change in Health Care Expenditures (Current Dollars), Public and Private, Canada and the U.S., 1990–99

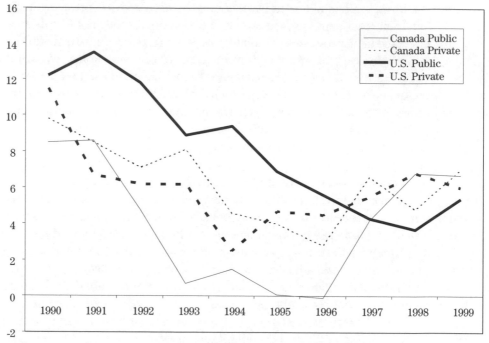

Sources: Canadian Institute for Health Information, *National Health Expenditures— Summary, 1975–2000* (Ottawa: Canadian Institute for Health Information, 2001), www.cihi.ca/facts/nhex/nhex2001/B.3.2.shtml (Accessed February 21, 2002); Health Care Financing Administration website, www.hcfa.gov/stats/nhe-oact/tables/nhe00.csv (Accessed February 19, 2002).

Indeed, only once in each country in the past four decades has major change in the financing of health care delivery been brought about by policy change: namely, through the establishment of Canadian medicare and American Medicare and Medicaid in the 1960s. At that time, a rare conjunction of conditions in each country made these changes possible. First, a consolidation of authority on the scale necessary to overcome institutional barriers was brought about—in the United States by the 1964 landslide election that gave the Democrats control of the White House in addition to supermajorities in both houses of Congress, and in Canada by the dawning of an era of "cooperative federalism" in the interlude between the beginning of Quebec's "quiet revolution" of modernization and the rise of a Quebec separatist party as a strong political force. Second, key political actors mobilized the political will to bring about changes in health policy as part of a broad agenda of social policy development in an era of economic and fiscal buoyancy. A similar conjunction of forces would not occur for the rest of the twentieth century.

As a result, when public expenditure restraint took hold in the 1990s it occurred through ordinary political processes, within the parameters of the programs established in the 1960s. In the U.S., this has meant that the primary vehicle for restraint has been the congressional budgetary process. In that process, congressional decision makers have sought, through a budgetary process that is inherently intensely political, to establish payment formulas that substitute technical analysis for politics. This process has generated geometric increases in complexity as fragmented politics intersected with technical arcana, both in the budgetary arena and at the implementation stage. In Canada, in contrast, because of differences both in the nature of political institutions and in the design of the policy framework adopted in the 1960s, expenditure restraint has been accomplished largely through blunt budgetary limits at both federal and provincial levels and implemented through centralized negotiations between provincial governments and health care providers, as well as though unilateral government action.

IN THE UNITED STATES

Budgetary Politics, 1982–95: Hospital and Physician Payment Formulas

Although a variety of attempts were made to restrain Medicare expenditures in the 1970s, a true watershed was reached in 1982, when as part of the Tax Equity and Fiscal Responsibility Act (TEFRA), Congress mandated a shift from a cost reimbursement to a prospective payment system for hospitals. Unlike earlier attempts at cost control, this measure was clearly part of broad budgetary politics—marked, in the first Reagan administration, by tax reductions, increased defense spending, large budget deficits, and a relentless search for reductions in nondefense areas. As an indication of the intimate relationship of Medicare payment reform to broad budgetary strategy, the mandating of hospital cost control was a key priority for the chairman of the Senate Finance Committee, Bob Dole, who in the judgment of one well-informed observer at the time "reign[ed] as the single most influential legislator in matters of health-financing policy."[12]

The new hospital reimbursement formula imposed by TEFRA was the first of the major technical fixes aimed at controlling Medicare spending. Payments per case were to be determined up front, according to a formula essentially geared toward determining the average cost of treating cases with similar diagnoses (the so-called diagnosis-related group or DRG methodology, developed by academic health services researchers and economists). But notwithstanding this seemingly technical solution, congressional budgetary politics continued to shape the hospital reimbursement process. Here is a pithy assessment from a former administrator of the Health Care Financing Administration (HCFA), which administered Medicare and Medicaid:

> Medicare spends so much money on hospitals . . . that at the highest
> levels of aggregation, hospital politics becomes indistinguishable from
> macrobudgetary politics, to the disadvantage of the hospital community.
> But most hospital politics around Medicare occurs at levels lower than
> that of the hospital community as a whole. . . . [A] large part of HCFA's

administrative resources are devoted to evaluating claims on behalf of
particular hospitals, or small groups of hospitals, advanced by individual
members of Congress. With every passing year, the prospective payment
system (PPS), which was touted by some of its initiators as a model of
uniform, "scientific" national policy, looks less like a theoretical exercise
in health economics and more like the Internal Revenue Code.[13]

The effects of the shift to prospective payment were nonetheless profound. In
response, hospital providers sought to control costs, but they also sought to *shift*
some costs from public to private payers—largely private insurers and employers.
The evidence for such shifts having actually occurred has been a matter of considerable academic debate. Broad aggregate trends, however, suggest that charges to
privately insured patients were raised to compensate for the tightening of reimbursement policies under Medicare and Medicaid, until the resistance of private
payers forced a tempering of this strategy in the early 1990s.[14]

Faced with increasing costs, private payers were jolted out of what had been
their essentially passive roles. A number of economic factors combined to raise the
price consciousness of private payers, but the adoption of Medicare prospective
payment arguably catalyzed this development. And it produced the first crack in the
alignment of incentives between professionals and entrepreneurs in the health care
arena. Under an open-ended system of third-party payment in which financing was
diffused across employers, employees, individual consumers, and taxpayers, both
professionals and entrepreneurs had an incentive to maximize the exploitation of
technology and the generation of revenue. Under a system of prospective payment
per case, however, the route to profit maximization for entrepreneurs became the
minimization of costs per case. This dynamic fueled the development of intermediate "managed care organizations" (MCOs) to control costs borne by third-party
payers. The rise of a proliferating variety of MCOs was to be the most significant
development in the American health care arena of the 1990s.

These developments had their political analogues. Rapid organizational change
created what Allen Schick has called "hyper-pluralism" in the health care arena[15]—
the fracturing of once broadly based alliances and coalitions of physicians, hospitals,
insurance companies, and business interests into diverse constituencies—as well as
the rise of new constituencies of interest created as a result of economic and technological change. As I have described it elsewhere, "the political fissioning of the
dominant alliance mirrors the fracturing of the symmetry of objectives of physicians,
institutional providers and insurance companies" that accompanied the demise of
the traditional system of open-ended third-party payment.[16] Of 121 major interest
groups active in the health care arena in 1992, 50 (41 percent) had not been in existence when Medicare and Medicaid were established in 1965.[17] Furthermore, the
breaking up of established coalitions created a much more fluid political dynamic.

While hospitals were subject to the DRG-based formula, physicians, as well as
nursing homes, home care agencies, and other nonhospital providers continued to
be reimbursed on the basis of "reasonable costs" or, in the case of physicians,
"reasonable charges." Congressional attention soon turned, however, to the next

largest category of expenditures after hospitals, physician services. Another piece of major budget legislation, the Consolidated Omnibus Budget Reconciliation Act (COBRA) of 1985, established the Physician Payment Review Commission, with a mandate to develop a modified payment mechanism. Again, Congress drew attention to technical work being done by health economists in this regard—in this case, the so-called Resource-Based Relative Value Scale (RBRVS), which related fees for particular services to the inputs necessary to provide those services, including the physician's own labor and that of other providers, the costs of training the labor inputs, and other practice costs.

As in the case of the development of the DRG system, the development of RBRVS involved intense negotiation between providers and the administering agency, further complicated by interventions from members of Congress. Just as the DRG methodology created both winners and losers within the hospital community, so, too, the design of the RBRVS pitted the interests of different groups of physicians (urban vs. rural, specialty vs. specialty) against each other. In this process, organized medical associations, and particularly the American Medical Association, became deeply implicated in the design process and in the process of political mediation.[18] By 1989, this process was sufficiently advanced that Congress included a provision for the RBRVS, to be implemented by 1992, in the 1989 Omnibus Budget Reconciliation Act (OBRA 89). This methodology produced a schedule of fees in the form of "units," to which a "conversion factor" would be applied annually through the budget process to translate these unit values into dollar values.

This assignment of "unit" values to particular services, based on an assessment of the time, training, and skill necessary to perform a given service, required the balancing of the interests of various specialty groups against each other. In the event, the adoption of the RBRVS led, at least in the first instance, to a relative enhancement of the remuneration of "primary care" practitioners, such as internists and family physicians, at the expense of specialists, such as general surgeons and radiologists. The "conversion factor," on the other hand, ostensibly took account of economic factors: not only the overall fiscal situation but also differences in input costs in different regions of the country. And the changes resulting from *this* methodology were more favorable to rural than to urban physicians. These intersecting axes of conflict—specialty-based and geographical—greatly complicated the process of mobilizing physicians and effectively splintered medical influence.[19]

OBRA 89 also contained other provisions relating to physician payment. The adoption of RBRVS did not in itself change the open-endedness of the fee-for-service payment system. Hence the changes implemented in 1992 also included Volume Performance Standards (VPS)—essentially utilization targets that, if exceeded in a given year, would lead to a reduction in the rate of fee increases in subsequent years. Finally, it increased the incentives for physicians to participate in Medicare and to accept Medicare payment as payment in full, by tightening the limits on the amounts that nonparticipating physicians could charge their patients.

The period surrounding the introduction of the RBRVS-VPS system, from 1991 to 1993, was one of historically low rates of increase in payments to physicians.[20] Shortly thereafter, however, payments began to climb again, at rates well exceeding those for privately financed medical services. Under the variety of contractual and organizational arrangements for privately financed services noted above, managed care organizations, other insurers, and employers held down the rate of increase in expenditures for physician services through aggressive bargaining for price discounts as well as through utilization review and control. These private mechanisms, then, yielded a greater degree of success in holding down expenditure increases than was possible under the budgetary politics of Medicare, for reasons to be elaborated below.

Changes in Eligibility, Coverage, and Contributions for Beneficiaries

Throughout the 1980s and 1990s, Congress chose not to seek to reduce Medicare expenditures by reducing the scope of eligibility or benefits. Indeed, essentially the only changes in this regard until 1996 involved the *expansion* of eligibility and/or benefits. Notably, in 1988, the Medicare Catastrophic Coverage Act (MCCA) placed a $2,000 per year limit on the expenses that individuals would be expected to bear for a range of Medicare-covered services, in addition to adding benefits, such as coverage for prescription drugs outside hospitals. The MCCA was, however, repealed the following year.

The rise and fall of the MCCA illustrates the intricacies and complexities of Medicare politics. Bound up as it was with the budget process, legislative decision making about Medicare had come to be characterized by "insider politics,"[21] a pattern that carried over into the development of the MCCA. The process was driven by a dedicated policy entrepreneur, the secretary of Health and Human Services in the Reagan administration, Otis R. Bowen. The legislation that resulted bore the hallmarks of the bipartisanship that characterized the 100th Congress, elected in 1986: It expanded benefits while also providing that those benefits would be financed by increased contributions and, hence, would be revenue-neutral vis-à-vis the government. It was to be financed through an increase in the Medicare Part B premium and a new income-related "supplementary" premium attached to the mandatory Part A coverage. In effect, it universalized a form of "Medigap" coverage under public auspices, at comparable or lower premium rates.[22]

The fate of the MCCA, however, demonstrates the dangers of a disjunction between the logic of insider politics and public perception. Certain key benefits—notably long-term care, which was of primary concern to many middle-class beneficiaries—were not included. For upper-income beneficiaries, moreover, the new arrangements did little more than replace their existing Medigap coverage, with less choice of plan. And, possibly most important, the new income-related premium made the financing of the program more progressive, and did so in an explicit way. Wealthier beneficiaries saw themselves as paying more in order to subsidize benefits for lower-income groups. In the face of the furious backlash that ensued, Congress repealed all the Medicare-related provisions of the Act (leaving in place some provisions related to Medicaid) in 1989.

Some expansion of Medicare benefits nonetheless occurred. In 1989, eligibility for home health care under Medicare was effectively expanded—not through legislative action, but rather through an administrative "clarification" in the form of a revised HCFA payment manual. A similar "clarification" expanded eligibility for nursing home care. As a result, expenditures in each of these categories increased exponentially, albeit from a very small base.

The Clinton Proposal and the Medicare Program

An analysis of the Clinton health care reform episode of 1993–94 is well beyond the scope of this chapter and has indeed been the subject of numerous treatises. Clinton's proposals on Medicare, however, warrant some mention here. Medicare might have provided a model for a universal health care plan covering the entire population, as its proponents in the 1960s had believed it would. Following this path, as championed by some Democratic politicians in the early 1990s, would have led to a single-payer governmental system on the Canadian model. But this was a route to universality that was inconsistent with the neoliberal "New Democrat" agenda espoused by Clinton, who chose instead to "harness market forces to the liberal ideal of universal coverage."[23] Clinton's model was based on "managed competition" among insurance plans in an employer-based system enhanced by regional purchasing alliances organized by state governments. But if Medicare was not a model from which Clinton and his advisors wanted to extrapolate, neither was it one that they wished to tamper with. Under the Clinton proposals, Medicare would remain much as it was, although states would have the option of allowing Medicare recipients to transfer their entitlement to obtain equal or better coverage through a regional alliance.

Clinton's relatively weak position as president (having entered office with only a 43 percent plurality of the popular vote and with a Democratic majority in the Senate less than the 60 percent necessary to prevent effective Republican vetoes through procedural maneuvering) meant that he could succeed in a major initiative such as health care reform only through bipartisan compromise or by creating a "bandwagon" momentum that would draw supporters to a winning cause. Strategic judgments made by the Clinton administration, however, militated against either of these outcomes; and the Clinton proposals, including their implications for Medicare, went down to spectacular defeat.

Budgetary Politics in the 104th and 105th Congresses: The Politics of the BBAs

With the failure of the Clinton health care proposal, Medicare politics reverted to the budgetary arena. But that failure had contributed to a fundamental reshaping of the partisan landscape on which those budgetary politics would be played out. The shifting of momentum from the advocates to the opponents of the Clinton plan had arguably catalyzed the coalescence of the neoconservative forces that gained ascendancy in the 1994 congressional elections.[24] In any event, those elections brought about a circumstance that had not existed since 1946: a divided government in which both houses of Congress were controlled by the Republicans, while the White House was controlled by the Democrats. Indeed, the Republicans had not constituted a majority in the House of Representatives since 1954.

In general, conditions of divided government increase the likelihood of bipartisan compromise, since both sides can then claim credit for policy outcomes.[25] But in this case, conditions were ripe for stalemate. None of the House Republicans had had experience in the majority—nor, accordingly, had any served as chair of a committee or subcommittee.[26] An unprecedented proportion of majority party members were freshmen. The leadership was in the hands of a strongly ideological group committed to lowering taxes, reducing government spending, and balancing the federal budget. Prospects for bipartisan compromise, then, were dim, and they were rendered even dimmer by tactical decisions made by the House leadership.

Given the centrality of a balanced budget to the Republican agenda, it was inevitable that budgetary politics would loom large in the battles between the House and the president. Medicare was inexorably drawn into the politics of developing a Balanced Budget Act. The Republicans followed a highly unusual procedure to develop their Medicare proposals, working not through the relevant House committees but rather through a task force chaired by the Speaker of the House himself and including the relevant committee and subcommittee chairs plus selected other members. The product of the task force was then ratified, with party-line votes, by the relevant House committees.[27]

The Balanced Budget Act of 1995, incorporating the Republicans' Medicare provisions, would have reduced Medicare expenditures by $270 million below what they would otherwise have been by 2002, according to Congressional Budget Office projections. These reductions would be accomplished largely by reducing rates of increase in payments to providers and by introducing more "choice" into the program by facilitating the option for beneficiaries to be covered by managed care organizations, who would receive prepaid payments from Medicare, determined by discounting average expenditures for Medicare patients to reflect the presumed greater efficiency of managed care. In order to satisfy the Congressional Budget Office, moreover, a "fail-safe" provision had to be included capping the Medicare budget, both overall and within each of nine categories of expenditure.

The Balanced Budget Act of 1995, however, crashed on the rocks of the governmental shutdown resulting from the stalemate between the House and the president in November 1995. The president vetoed the Balanced Budget Act on December 6, 1995, and the budgetary stalemate continued throughout the rest of the 104th Congress and shaped the landscape on which the 1996 presidential and congressional elections were contested. That election, in turn, reshaped the partisan landscape in Washington, along lines that boded somewhat better for bipartisan budgetary compromise. House Republicans remained in the majority but the leadership was somewhat chastened by the net loss of three seats and by the recognition of the extent to which that result could be attributed to negative public reaction to their role in the budget stalemate. The dynamics of the 105th Congress, then, were more typical of situations of divided government than those of its predecessor had been: Both parties now wished to find a bipartisan consensus for which each could claim credit.[28]

In this they were greatly aided by new CBO projections, based on the continued strengthening of the economy, that reduced the targets for Medicare savings. These new projections greatly reduced the major obstacle to bipartisan consensus—the magnitude of the savings to be achieved—and allowed some of the most contentious features of the 1995 BBA, such as budget caps, to be removed. The Balanced Budget Act that emerged in 1997 extended coverage to seven new areas of service while instituting greater reductions in payments to providers than the 1995 BBA would have done. These greater reductions were to be accomplished by slowing the "update" to payments to hospitals, moving to prospective payment for outpatient and rehabilitation services (as well as for nursing homes and home care agencies, as contemplated in the 1995 BBA), adopting more stringent eligibility criteria and utilization controls for home care, and reducing payments to teaching hospitals.

Savings were also to be achieved by expanding the participation of managed care organizations by formally establishing a "Part C" of the Medicare program, named "Medicare+Choice," similar to what had been proposed in the 1995 BBA. Once again, Congress made a leap of faith into the arms of health service researchers, by calling for the development of a risk adjustment formula to govern the capitation payments made to private insurers on behalf of beneficiaries under this option. Such a formula would adjust the payment upwards for beneficiaries who presented a greater risk of incurring health care costs, and downwards for healthier, less risky beneficiaries. Such adjustments are essential to remove incentives for "cream skimming" on the part of insurers—that is, recruiting relatively healthy, less risky clients and leaving the poorer risks to Medicare itself. An effective risk adjustment formula is, however, the Holy Grail of health care financing reform cross-nationally; and a number of reforms, such as those in the Netherlands, have foundered on the imperfections of real-life models.

In summary, the budgetary politics of Medicare in the 105th Congress led to a focus on reducing payments to providers as the common denominator of a bipartisan consensus. In simplest terms, Republicans opposed increases in expenditures; Democrats opposed reductions in benefits or a shifting of the financial burden onto beneficiaries other than through a more progressive premium structure. Only a reduction in payments to providers could satisfy both of these criteria. Those who supported the traditional single-payer Medicare model, moreover, saw it preserved for the majority of beneficiaries; those who wanted to open up Medicare further to private insurers got Part C, on the condition that those insurers would accept discounted payments.

Providers, however, are not without political resources. Why were they not more effective in fending off these provisions for budgetary restraint? Why, indeed, did the American Medical Association actively endorse this legislation? There are several complementary answers to this question. First, the 1997 BBA, like its 1995 predecessor, contained a number of compensatory gains for providers. Second, providers continued to exert their influence within the Byzantine arena of the technical design and computation of payment formulas; and in that arena they tended to fragment into discrete groups—and, indeed, individual institutions, in pressing their own interests. But third, and perhaps most important, providers in the late 1990s were operating in an economic context in which private payments were more tightly constrained than were those in the public sector, as will be recalled from figure 3-1. They thus faced a delicate calculus: Opposing too vigorously a general constraint on provider payments under fee-for-service and prospective payment could lead Congress to place even greater emphasis on encouraging the shift to private, managed care organizations under the Medicare umbrella. Such a shift, experience under private insurance suggested, could well lead to even greater constraints on payments to service providers.

Sure enough, when the threat of restraint in the private sector began to recede in the late 1990s as the potential for price discounting was exhausted, providers intensified their pressure on Congress to reverse the BBA 1997 cuts in Medicare payments. In November 1999 Congress passed the Balanced Budget Refinement Act (BBRA), which raised payments (or delayed or reduced reductions) for various nursing home, home care, and hospital services.[29]

The Impact of Budget Changes

The effects of the budgetary changes of the 1980s and 1990s on expenditures in various categories are shown in table 3-1. Consistent with the overall pattern observed in figure 3.1, we see that each of these categories—hospitals, physicians, prescription drugs,[30] home care, and nursing homes—experienced sharper fiscal constraints from private payers than under Medicare in the 1990s. In 1998 and 1999, however, the effects of the BBA of 1997 are dramatically apparent in the hospital, home care, and nursing home sectors. In the hospital sector, not only did the rate of increase in Medicare expenditures sharply contract, but also the rate of increase in private expenditures on hospital services outpaced Medicare for the first time since the early 1990s. This suggests a degree of cost-shifting onto private payers similar to that which occurred after the introduction of the Medicare PPS system in the mid-1980s.

In the home care sector, the decline in Medicare expenditures began with administrative tightening in 1997 and accelerated under BBA in 1998, following a decade of very large annual rates of increase under Medicare's generous home care provisions. Growth in the average number of visits per person served accounted for about half the growth in spending from 1990 to 1997; conversely, about three-fourths of the decline in spending in 1998 can be attributed to a reduction in the number of visits per person served under the tighter utilization controls of the 1997 BBA.[31] Reflecting the impact of the BBRA of 1999, however, the downward trend in Medicare spending on hospitals, home care, and nursing homes was reversed, and these expenditures began to increase in 2000. Finally, it is worthy to note that, of all categories of providers, physicians fared best under the 1997 BBA, at least as indicated by these initial data. Only in the area of physician services did Medicare expenditures growth continue to outpace that in the private sector, a point to which I shall return below.

TABLE 3-1

Annual Percentage Change in Private and Medicare Expenditures, by Category of Service, for Selected Years, 1980–2000

	Hospitals		Physicians		Prescription Drugs		Home Care		Nursing Homes	
	Private	Medicare	Private	Medicare	Private	Medicare	Private	Medicare	Private	Medicare[a]
	%		%		%		%		%	
2000	5.0	5.0	4.9	9.1	16.6	7.5	−1.9	0.8	−1.9	7.2
1999	4.5	0	4.0	7.8	18.9	20.2	−1.9	−11.9	0.5	−0.2
1998	6.2	−0.8	6.1	8.5	14.5	28.1	8.8	−20.8	8.2	2.4
1997	3.6	5.2	5.1	6.8	12.6	27.5	14.7	−9.6	5.9	7.0
1996	2.2	7.5	4.0	4.8	9.9	39.7	15.2	7.3	5.2	8.5
1995	1.5	8.1	3.4	10.5	10.7	50.0	17.9	20.2	13.8	6.3
1994	−0.7	10.0	3.5	8.6	5.3	36.8	11.8	31.5	−3.9	9.6
1993	4.6	7.1	6.8	6.1	5.3	22.6	14.9	30.6	0.0	10.3
1992	3.2	13.5	8.2	3.1	6.5	24.0	12.1	41.4	0.7	12.2
1991	6.8	8.8	11.9	6.7	10.4	25.0	8.2	41.7	3.4	18.5
1990	10.3	9.7	9.0	11.1	14.7	33.3	13.0	49.2	21.3	9.7
1985	7.0	6.5	18.4	13.3	11.2	400.0	13.9	2.6	12.8	7.2
1980	15.0	18.2	15.7	22.4	10.8	–	29.1	18.6	17.4	15.0

Note: Calculated from Health Care Financing Administration, *National Health Expenditures* HCFA website, www.hcfa.gov/stat/nheoact/tables/nhe00.csv.

[a] Includes Medicaid.

IN CANADA

Federal-Provincial Politics in the 1980s and 1990s

The politics of fiscal retrenchment under Canadian medicare occurred in two intersecting arenas: federal-provincial relations, and relations between provincial governments and health care providers. Let us consider each of these in turn. Canadian medicare was first established as a federal-provincial cost-shared program, with the federal government paying approximately 50 percent of the cost. After the late 1970s, however, federal policy was essentially to reduce, on a gradual and essentially unilateral basis, the share of its financial contributions to provincial health insurance programs, while retaining sufficient fiscal leverage to ensure provincial compliance with the five "principles" of medicare: universality, comprehensiveness, access on "uniform terms and conditions," portability, and public administration. The reduction of the federal share occurred over time through the operation of a highly arcane formula, modified over time either through federal-provincial negotiations or unilaterally by the federal government.[32] After the mid-1980s, these changes were made through the federal budgetary process as part of a deficit-reduction agenda.

Then, in its 1995 budget, driven entirely by a deficit-reduction agenda, the federal Liberal government consolidated transfers for social assistance with transfers for health and post-secondary education transfers to create a new "Canada Health and Social Transfer" (CHST) and set out a new schedule for the reduction of those transfers over time. The budget set out a schedule of reductions until 1997–98, subsequently modified to provide for a guaranteed "cash floor." The shift to the CHST decreased by one-third the federal government's total cash transfers for health, post-secondary education, and social assistance;[33] but it made the total transfer amount available to enforce the principles of medicare, and thus potentially increased federal fiscal leverage in the health care field.

In the wake of the establishment of the CHST, federal-provincial politics in the last half of the 1990s was marked by provincial demands that federal funding be restored to at least its pre-1995 level; federal insistence that any increase in federal funding would be made only on the basis of an agreed-upon plan of health care reform that would govern its expenditure; and periodic incremental increases in federal transfers through the federal budgetary process, as negotiations lurched and sputtered. Throughout this period, governments at both levels engaged in a remarkably blatant politics of blame shifting. In the period leading up to the first ministers' meeting of September 2000, for example, the Ontario government took the unprecedented step of commissioning a series of television advertisements blaming the federal government for reducing the federal share of health expenditures in the province. In fact, however, provincial reductions did not closely track reductions in federal transfers: The rate of increase in federal transfers was considerably below the rate of increase in provincial spending from 1986 onward. It was only in the mid-1990s that restraint took hold at the provincial level, and in most provinces real reductions preceded the adoption of the CHST.

Finally, at the September 2000 meeting of first ministers a resolution appeared to be reached. The federal government agreed to an annual base CHST transfer of $15.5 billion through 2005–6 and committed an additional $20 billion to the CHST (including $2 billion earmarked for Early Childhood Development) spread over the 2001–2 to 2005–6 period. In addition to these CHST transfers, the federal government established a $1 billion fund for medical equipment, another of $500 million for health information technology, and an $800 million "Health Transition Fund" over four years to finance pilot projects in primary care reform. In return, the provinces agreed to an eight-point "Action Plan for Health System Renewal,"[34] a separate action plan related to early childhood development, and to the development and public reporting of measures of health system performance.

These agreements firmly established an era of reinvestment in health care after the severe constraints of the mid-1990s and signaled that this reinvestment was likely to occur without major change to the overall sectorally based single-payer design of the Canadian system. But they did not lay to rest provincial demands for increases to the CHST. Led by Ontario Premier Mike Harris and Alberta Premier Ralph Klein, the provinces continued to draw attention to the gap between the rate of increase in federal transfers and the rate of increase in provincial health care costs.[35] Harris and Klein threatened that unless the federal share was increased the provinces would have no alternative other than to consider private supplements, such as copayments. Premiers' Conferences in September 2001 and January 2002 could agree only on common denominators. They united behind a demand for an increase of $7 billion in the base CHST transfer (based on provincial calculations as to what was necessary to bring the federal share of health expenditures back to its pre-1995 level).[36] All continued to profess allegiance to the five principles of the Canada Health Act—but provinces that wished to test the limits of the interpretation of the Act insisted upon a deadline for the establishment of a federal-provincial dispute resolution mechanism. Recognizing the importance of pharmaceuticals as the most rapidly escalating driver of health costs, and possibly wishing to forestall federal initiatives regarding coverage of pharmaceuticals, the provinces agreed to establish a common review process for pharmaceuticals to be added to provincial formularies.

Developments at the Provincial Level

While this federal-provincial wrangling was taking place, provinces were taking their own fiscal actions: Across provinces, the fiscal agenda of the 1990s was dominated by deficit reduction. In 1993, combined federal and provincial deficits in Canada peaked at over $65 billion. By 2000, the combined total of provincial and federal budgets was back in the black, with a surplus of over $16 billion. Throughout this period, program spending had to compete not only with deficit reduction but also with tax cuts at both levels of government. But as budgets turned around, the first priority for program spending in all provinces was health care.[37]

The effects of the rapid contraction and equally rapid rebounding of public spending on health care in Canada were highly disruptive. Across-the-board cuts to hospital and physician services budgets left little "redundancy" in the system to allow for planned reorganization. The rapidity of contraction, moreover, meant that when reinvestment began, providers were almost entirely focused on demands for "catch-up." And although the limited evidence available suggests that restraint measures such as the restructuring of hospitals did not have a negative impact on health outcomes,[38] they created an atmosphere of crisis that shook public confidence in the health care system and in the ability of governments to manage it. As a dramatic illustration of this effect, the proportion of Canadians in a cross-national survey reporting that the health care system needed "only minor change" plunged from 56 percent to 20 percent between 1988 and 1998 and remained at that level in 2001 despite increased public investment.[39]

The process through which cuts were made and restored in Canada stands in some contrast to the U.S.. Throughout the life of Canadian medicare, provincial governments had exercised their fiscal authority over health expenditures through fairly blunt instruments. In contrast to the complex formulas embedded in budget legislation to fund Medicare in the U.S., Canadian provincial governments relied upon negotiations with providers over overall rates of change and, increasingly, upon budgetary caps.

The hospital sector functioned under a global budgeting strategy adopted by provincial governments in the 1970s to replace the earlier system of per diem payments. These budgets were essentially historically based, with across-the-board percentage increases each year, based ostensibly on some consideration of economic factors but effectively on the fiscal considerations of provincial governments. This strategy proved effective in containing hospital expenditures, relative to other sectors of the health care system, in the 1970s and 1980s.[40]

In the 1990s, constraints on hospital budgets increased dramatically. Global budgets were reduced in real terms; and some provinces, notably Ontario and Alberta, began to experiment with case-based funding formulas in establishing hospital budgets.[41] These formulas, developed with the collaboration and support of provincial hospital associations, sought to reward hospitals for efficiency. But these experiments were overshadowed in the mid-1990s by the wave of hospital restructuring that swept through all provinces, aimed at increasing horizontal integration, reducing the number of acute care beds, and to some extent building up capacity for community-based care.

The mechanisms through which these changes were accomplished varied across provinces. In all provinces except Ontario, regional boards for the management of the hospital sector were established, although the organization and the mandate of these boards varied widely. All of the boards had the authority to allocate budgets across institutions and agencies in their region. No province, however, granted the boards revenue-raising authority: All received global budgets from the province. These global budgets were initially determined on a historical basis, although in each province the development of a needs-based allocation formula was on the agenda and in one province—Saskatchewan—considerable progress was made in this regard. In two provinces the scope of the boards' authority was restricted to institutional services; others embraced some community-based services as well. In some cases, the mandate of regional boards extended to the direct management and operation of the institutions under their purview. In British Columbia, Alberta, and Saskatchewan the regional boards replaced the boards of individual institutions, and the assets of the institutions were transferred to the regional boards. In no case, significantly, did the mandate of regional boards extend to physicians' services, although some maintained various types of medical liaison committees.

In contrast to the 1970s and 1980s, when it had appeared that the local economic and symbolic significance of hospitals combined with an area-based legislative system made it practically impossible for a provincial government to close a hospital, in the 1990s provincial governments of all partisan complexions showed a remarkable determination to stay the course toward closures. Different strategies for hospital restructuring through regional boards were pursued in different provinces. In Saskatchewan, a substantial amount of downsizing—the closing of fifty-two small rural hospitals (representing about 200 beds in total)—was accomplished by the provincial government before regional boards were established, so as to avoid encumbering the boards with such politically difficult tasks at their inception.[42] The boards were nonetheless expected to continue restructuring over time. Newfoundland and Manitoba followed similar strategies. In Alberta and New Brunswick, by contrast, an important part of the mandate of the newly created regional boards was to accomplish a significant reduction of the system themselves. And in Quebec, the task of allocating budget cuts to institutions was implemented through a regional board structure that was established in the 1970s and revitalized in the 1990s.

Ontario was the exception to this strategy of regionalization. In Ontario, regional bodies—the district health councils, remained advisory only and had no budgetary authority. In the early 1990s, each council was charged by the New Democratic Party (NDP) government of Ontario with developing a hospital restructuring plan for its region. The Conservative government that succeeded the NDP in 1995 established a Health Services Restructuring Commission (HSRC) with a four-year mandate to make binding decisions about hospital restructuring. This dramatic attempt to distance the government from decisions about hospital closures was put to the test when the HSRC indicated its intention to direct the closure of the sites of the sole francophone-only teaching hospital in Ottawa (the Montfort Hospital) and of two teaching hospitals in Toronto, one with a long history of providing a professional venue for women physicians and a focus on "women's health" and the other with a more recent history of service to the gay community and the homeless in a downtown area of the city. The institutions themselves were to be acquired by or merged with other hospitals in their respective cities. Intense lobbying campaigns on behalf of the two Toronto hospitals did not bear fruit: The commission's final report for Toronto directed the closure of their sites, although it provided for the new merged or amalgamated institutions to operate ambulatory care centers in those locations.

In the Montfort case, however, the HSRC bowed to political pressure and revised its decision. This being Canada, the perceived threat to "national unity" posed by the commission's original "notice of intent" directing the closing of the Montfort Hospital site proved to be its Achilles' heel: The notice became the subject of a furious lobbying campaign and provoked unprecedented public interventions from the prime minister and the Québec premier in support of maintaining the hospital. In its response to the HSRC report, the Ministry of Health (represented by the deputy minister, not the minister, in keeping with the depoliticization of the process) stated only that it wished to see the francophone services offered by the Montfort survive. Subsequent to the issuing of the notice, three new members, including one francophone, were added to the commission. In its final report for Ottawa, the HSRC relented somewhat, allowing the Montfort to continue to exist on a substantially reduced scale.

Several hospitals took HSRC directives to judicial review; but the legislation under which the commission had been established left very few grounds for challenging its decisions, and the courts in all cases but one deferred to the government's authority to make policy judgments. Again, however, the Montfort case stood apart. In November 1999, in a remarkable decision with potential ramifications well beyond the health care arena, the Ontario Divisional Court overturned the HSRC decision on Montfort and the hospital was allowed to remain as it was. The Court found that the HSRC decision constituted governmental action that contravened constitutional protections for minority rights. Indeed, it went beyond the rights specifically protected in the written constitution to find a broad "constitutional imperative for the protection and preservation of francophone minority rights—including, in our view, the right to have at least minimal institutions necessary to feed and nurture the continued existence and vitality of their language and culture."[43] This court decision was highly controversial and was immediately appealed by the provincial government. It was upheld by the Ontario Court of Appeal, however, and the government declined to pursue the case further to the Supreme Court of Canada. This remarkable case by its very aberrance testifies to the great difficulty that hospitals faced in using the courts to challenge restructuring decisions. Only by appealing to what is arguably the most politically sensitive dimension of Canada's constitution could hospitals gain any ground in such challenges.

The process of restructuring involved a greater degree of state activism in the exercise of the state's regulatory authority and monopsony power than had been typical in the relationship between provincial governments and hospitals, and thus arguably involved a degree of "positional" as well as tangible losses for hospitals. In those provinces in which provincially appointed (or directly elected) regional boards replaced the governing structures of individual institutions and took over their assets, there was a permanent expansion in the scope of formal state authority in the hospital sector. The effective degree of expansion was open to question: De facto, the provincial government had previously had control of the hospital sector through its budgetary and regulatory authority, and provincial appointment of boards with managerial authority promised to give the provincial government access to finer levers of control. Arguably, regionalization amounted in effect to a reorganization within the state (as regional bodies took on functions previously performed at the center), rather than a redefinition of the state-hospital relationship. By the late 1990s, the regional boards were not mature enough to allow for an assessment of the extent to which they would in fact lead to increased provincial governmental intervention or would function, in effect, merely as local institutional boards on a larger scale.[44]

In Ontario, the exception to the strategy of regionalization (albeit an important exception, constituting about 40 percent of the Canadian health system), the formal expansion of state authority necessary to achieve restructuring, was purported to be temporary. The HSRC was established for a four-year period under an extremely controversial piece of omnibus legislation passed in 1996, empowering the cabinet and in some cases individual ministers with a set of "tools" to achieve reductions in spending—tools that in some cases involved unprecedented levels of discretion. Prior to the passage of that legislation, there had been no legislative head of authority under which the cabinet or an individual minister could order the closing or merger of hospitals, although the legislature could, of course, do so through the passage of specific legislation. By adopting the HSRC mechanism, the state effectively enhanced its capacity to act expeditiously.[45] The ongoing result in Ontario was not, however, to change the relationship between the state and the hospital sector. Hospitals continued as self-governing bodies receiving global budgets from the provincial government, although the determination of those budgets began to move away from its traditional historical basis toward formulas designed to reward efficiency.

In summary, the experience of the 1990s refuted the conventional wisdom that geographically concentrated losses such as hospital closings could not be accomplished through a governmental structure based on a legislature comprising representatives of local districts. At least three factors can be adduced to explain this result. First, the firming of political will: Under the unprecedented fiscal constraint of deficit reduction agendas, combined with technological changes impelling reduced hospital utilization as discussed below, all provincial governments responded to the imperative (or at least the *perceived* imperative[46]) to reduce the supply of the most costly component of the health care system—the acute-care hospital infrastructure. (In this they were not alone. The proportion of expenditures on acute care hospitals amongst total public spending on health care declined in most OECD nations in the 1980s and 1990s.[47]) Second, the instrument of implementation: Most provinces accomplished hospital restructuring by establishing intermediate agencies between the provincial government and the locality affected. And third, the policy design: Restructuring hospitals rather than imposing across-the-board budget reductions created a dynamic of winners and losers that defused the potential for a coalescence of opposition. The restructuring process, while often extremely controversial at the local level, was carried out without strong opposition from, and in some cases with the cautious endorsement and collaboration of, provincial hospital associations. One notable exception, the Montfort case, proves the rule: Only when the highly politically freighted issue of national unity was invoked could opposition be effectively mobilized.

Capping Budgets for Physician Services

While the hospital share of total public expenditures on health care declined slowly from 1970 to 1990 and more sharply in the 1990s, the share of total expenditures going to physicians' services remained essentially constant until the mid-1990s, when it declined only slightly.[48] Throughout the 1970s and 1980s, however, physicians had maintained a constant share of an expanding pie. As governments sought to constrain the expansion of the pie (or at least the public portion thereof), the contrast between the globally budgeted hospital sector and the open-ended physician services sector was not lost on them. The most important development in the physician services sector in the 1990s, not only in terms of its direct effects on expenditures but because its broader policy ramifications and implications for profession-state relations, was the decision by provincial governments to cap their budgets for physician services.

Understanding the significance of this development requires some historical context. As noted above, under Canadian medicare, governments initially underwrote the costs of a fee-for-service system of private medical practice. But rather than paying medical fees that were "usual and customary" for a given locality, as did U.S. Medicare, Canadian provincial governments followed the model of the physician-sponsored insurance plans that had predated medicare and paid physicians on the basis of fee schedules set by the provincial medical associations, prorated by a given percentage (usually 15 percent). After the first few years, governments insisted that any increases in the fee schedule be negotiated. It is important to note that in almost all provinces (the notable exception being Quebec), what was negotiated was the overall rate of increase; the determination of the relative value of particular items was accomplished entirely through the committee structures of the provincial medical associations.

For a time, individual physicians could escape the constraints of this regime by "extra-billing," billing their patients a discretionary amount above that covered by the government plan. Again, this practice continued the model that had been established by the physician-sponsored insurance plans, under which "participating" physicians agreed to accept prorated payment directly from the plan, while "nonparticipating" physicians charged fees at their discretion and were responsible for collecting fees from their patients, who were reimbursed by the plan at the prorated level. Extra-billing was of economic significance for only a small minority of physicians, albeit "clustered" in certain specialties and localities.[49] But it was of great symbolic significance for both governments and physicians. On the one hand, it flew in the face of one of the fundamental principles underlying Canadian medicare: the removal of financial barriers to access to medical and hospital care. But it had also come to symbolize the preservation and legitimization of private, individualistic, entrepreneurial medical practice even in the context of a largely state-funded system.[50]

In 1984, the federal Liberal government introduced legislation, the Canada Health Act, that incorporated and clarified the principles of universality, accessibility, comprehensiveness, public administration, and portability and prescribed "dollar-for-dollar" reductions in federal transfers for provinces that allowed extra-billing or other user charges for physician and hospital services. The legislation passed with the support of all parties in Parliament, and within the three-year deadline imposed by the Act, all provinces came into compliance. They did so, with one exception, by elaborating their respective accommodations with organized medicine so as to compensate the profession for the loss of the extra-billing option. Hence, although the passage of the Canada Health Act constituted an undeniable symbolic defeat for the medical profession, there were significant tangible and positional gains for the profession as a result of the legislation. (The exceptional case was Ontario, where for reasons that I have discussed more fully elsewhere,[51] the profession became locked in a losing battle of wills with the provincial government.)

The regime of negotiated prices constrained the rate of increase in medical fees (to different degrees across provinces, reflecting the different accommodations made between the medical associations and provincial governments). A contrast with the United States starkly demonstrates this point. Between 1971 and 1985, real physician fees declined 18 percent in Canada and rose 22 percent in the U.S.[52] The impact on physicians' net incomes was less dramatic, however. Changes in "utilization" factors, involving the volume and mix of services rendered, to some extent blunted the impact on medical incomes of real reductions in fees. Utilization tended to increase faster in provinces that experienced the greatest degree of fee level constraint, with the result that cross-provincial differences in incomes were considerably smaller than were differences in fee schedules.[53]

In effect, then, the constraint on price-per-service was essentially the only one that physicians faced. Although provincial governments expressed growing concern over increases in the volume and mix of services billed to their plans, mechanisms of utilization review were very modest, generally established under the aegis of professional bodies rather than governments, and limited to the investigation of extreme cases of billings greatly beyond the norm for a given specialty.[54] In effect,

Canadian physicians traded discretion regarding price for the preservation of autonomy over all other aspects of their practices.

In the 1980s, provincial governments sought to limit the open-endedness of the physician remuneration model. Quebec had led the way: Beginning in 1976 and 1977, the Quebec government negotiated separate capped annual budgets for general practitioners and specialists. Individual billing caps, above which payments were reduced on a prorated basis, were also adopted for general practitioners in 1976. Over the course of the 1980s a number of other provincial governments began to move in this direction.[55] Most adopted mechanisms for factoring utilization increases into the negotiation of fee schedule increases, as U.S. Medicare was to do with the introduction of Volume Performance Standards in the 1990s. Manitoba, British Columbia, and Saskatchewan capped their physician expenditure budgets at fixed rates of escalation (although the Manitoba cap was in place for only a brief period). These budgetary limits were of varying degrees of firmness: They allowed for a variety of factors that might justify exceeding the limits, and they did not always require that excess expenditures be fully recovered. No province other than Quebec, moreover, established individual billing thresholds.

In the 1990s, however, all provincial governments acted to cap their physician services budgets, and in most cases to cap them more firmly than had been done in the past. A variety of mechanisms for recapturing excess expenditures were adopted, including "clawbacks" (fee adjustments in the year following the overrun to recover the excess), "holdbacks" (holding back a portion of payments, to be released after a year-end reconciliation), and "paybacks" (repayment of excesses, determined by a year-end reconciliation, through some mechanism other than fee adjustments).[56] In addition, five provinces negotiated (or at times imposed) individual billing thresholds, above which payments were prorated, usually on a sliding scale; and Quebec added billing thresholds for specialists to the GP thresholds that had been in place since the 1970s. The provinces varied in the degree to which they discriminated across specialties in the establishment of individual billing thresholds: Some discriminated only between general or family practitioners and all other specialists, while others divided specialists into two or more subgroups—and the categories chosen varied not only across but within provinces over time.[57]

The adoption of global expenditure limits for physician services placed an enormous strain on the structures of organized medicine. As Hurley and his colleagues have noted, global caps in a fee-for-service system create "common-property resource" problems: Individual physicians had no incentive to restrain their billings, since the penalty for exceeding the budget cap would be equally shared by all.[58] The management of these incentive problems was left to provincial medical associations, whose role proved crucial and whose success in dealing with them varied considerably across provinces.[59]

The tensions associated with the introduction of capped physician services budgets signaled the beginning of a new era in profession-state relations in Canada. As medical associations and governments sought ways to ease the pressure of fee-for-service billings against the budget cap, the policy agenda expanded to include issues that had long simmered in the background of profession-state relations:

issues of supply control, the scope of public coverage, alternative payment mechanisms, and clinical protocols. To deal with this expanding agenda, the structures of accommodation between profession and state were elaborated. By the mid-1990s, bipartite joint management committees, with equal representation from government (including, in most cases, a representative of the Finance Ministry) and the provincial medical association, had been established in seven provinces. (A functionally equivalent arrangement had existed in Quebec since the early 1980s.) These arrangements formalized and arguably increased the influence of the medical profession; but they also involved the medical associations in controversial decisions that led to fissurous tendencies within their memberships.[60]

Delisting, Copayments, and "Passive Privatization"

The implications that these constraints on payments to providers had for recipients of health care cannot be ignored; but the lack of systematic data over the course of the 1980s and 1990s makes investigating these implications a very difficult exercise. There is some evidence, indeed, that hospital restructuring in at least one major metropolitan area did not adversely affect either access to or quality of hospital services.[61] Beyond these effects, Canadian governments generally avoided explicit reductions in eligibility for or scope of benefits under government programs in their pursuit of fiscal restraint.

In a few respects, however, patients did experience changes in public coverage, either de jure or de facto. Most provinces, largely through joint mechanisms with the medical profession, reviewed the range of publicly covered services, and some services were accordingly "delisted." By the late 1990s some services had been identified under government-profession agreements as "medically unnecessary" and accordingly removed from coverage under the public plan in eight provinces; and the issue continued to be under active negotiation between governments and professional bodies in at least five of these provinces.[62] The first round of delisting tended to concentrate on cosmetic and reproductive procedures; and the impact on physician services and on governmental budgets (particularly with regard to the elderly) was marginal. Subsequent rounds pruned away various services that had been incorporated into the universal coverage provisions of various provincial plans over time beyond the requirement to insure "medically necessary" physician and hospital services—specifically, certain services provided by nonmedical personnel, such as physiotherapists, unless under the direct supervision of a physician or in a hospital setting.

Meanwhile, charges were shifted to elderly patients through increases in copayments for publicly covered services not under the umbrella of the Canada Health Act, notably pharmaceuticals. There was considerable convergence across provinces in the 1990s on a model of coverage for prescription drugs for those over sixty-five, requiring income-related copayments up to an annual maximum. In the late 1980s and 1990s, copayments were introduced in five provinces (three of these on an income-scaled basis) that had previously had first-dollar coverage; and existing provisions for copayment were increased in four other provinces.[63]

It must be noted, moreover, that costs were also shifted to patients, including elderly patients, not as a matter of deliberate policy but as a result of the unique sectoral design of the Canadian public/private boundary. In the Canadian system, when technological change drives services out of hospitals, the effect is to shift services from a fully public sector to a sector in which private finance plays a large role. This "passive privatization" process, together with fiscal constraint, is largely responsible for the shrinkage of the public share of total health expenditures in Canada from 74.2 percent in 1990 to 70.6 percent in 2000.[64]

Provider Demands for "Catch-up"

Much concern has been expressed in Canada that increased funding for health care is largely going toward "catch-up" increases in pay for health care personnel rather than toward planned health care priorities, and that provinces are engaging in "beggar-thy-neighbor" bidding wars for personnel in key areas of perceived shortage.[65] Evidence bearing on these concerns for the 1997–2000 period is mixed, but suggests at most a limited "catch-up" effect.[66] In 2001 and 2002, however, a number of high-profile settlements fueled fears of large catch-up increases and competitive bidding. In January 2001, the Alberta government agreed to a 22 percent increase in the medical fee schedule over two years and later agreed to similar rates of increase for nurses and other health care workers; Saskatchewan nurses, demanding parity, gained a 20 percent increase over three years in April 2002. In August 2001, bitter labor disputes led to an arbitrated settlement of 17 percent over three years for nurses in Nova Scotia and an imposed settlement of 23.5 percent over three years for nurses in British Columbia. And in the first half of 2002, B.C. physicians became embroiled in a protracted and acrimonious dispute with the provincial government, during which the government passed legislation to repudiate an arbitrator's award that had relied heavily on comparisons with Alberta, until a settlement was reached in July 2002.

The Pattern of Expenditure Restraint

The effects of the restraint policies of the 1990s on public expenditures are shown in table 3-2. For purposes of comparison with the U.S., table 3-2 also incorporates data regarding changes in Medicare expenditures from table 3-1. It is apparent that in the 1990s both countries entered into periods of constraint on public payments to providers—at different times and to different degrees for various categories of providers. Canadian governments constrained payments in all categories to a greater degree than did public payers in the U.S., although home care was subject to greater fiscal swings in the U.S. as the very generous provisions of the early 1990s were rolled back beginning in 1997. (Indeed, a comparison with table 3-1 shows that constraint in the public sector in Canada was greater than that in the private sector in the U.S. over the course of the decade.) Hospitals and other institutions (including nursing homes) were the categories most constrained in Canada, reflecting both the restructuring and downsizing of acute care hospitals and the lag in putting in place alternative facilities. As in the United States, however, physicians were more

TABLE 3-2

Annual Percentage Change in Public Health Care Expenditures, U.S. and Canada, by Category of Service, for Those Sixty- five and Older, for Selected Years, 1980–2000

	Hospitals		Physicians		Prescription Drugs		Home Care		Nursing Homes	
	Canada %	U.S.	Canada %	U.S.	Canada %	U.S.	Canada %	U.S.	Canada %	U.S.[a]
2000	7.9	5.0	6.3	9.1	6.0	7.5	5.1	0.8	14.4	7.2
1999	3.9	0	4.7	7.8	6.6	20.2	9.2	−11.9	10.2	−0.2
1998	8.8	−0.8	6.1	8.5	5.5	28.1	10.2	−20.8	13.0	2.4
1997	5.3	5.2	7.6	6.8	5.2	27.5	15.8	−9.6	−3.3	7.0
1996	−0.3	7.5	5.7	4.8	1.3	39.7	7.2	7.3	−7.3	8.5
1995	0.2	8.1	0.6	10.5	5.5	50.0	8.7	20.2	10.5	6.3
1994	−6.9	10.0	3.9	8.6	5.0	36.8	9.5	31.5	−0.6	9.6
1993	1.6	7.1	3.0	6.1	−3.5	22.6	8.0	30.6	−1.1	10.3
1992	4.7	13.5	1.1	3.1	3.0	24.0	8.6	41.4	3.4	12.2
1991	10.6	8.8	12.7	6.7	12.9	25.0	18.5	41.7	14.5	18.5
1990	6.6	9.7	10.8	11.1	7.0	33.3	17.2	49.2	16.3	9.7
1985	9.9	6.5	12.7	13.3	7.4	400.0	19.4	2.6	19.7	7.2
1980[b]	22.6	18.2	19.0	22.4	14.4	NA	27.9	18.6	24.0	15.0

Sources: For Canada: Health Canada, *National Health Care Expenditures by Age and Sex, 1980–81 to 2000–2001*, www.hcsc.gc.ca/english/pdf/health_care/age_sex_annex-tabes.pdf, tables 7A, 17A, 18A, 19A, 21A, 22A.
For U.S.: See table 3-1.
[a] includes Medicaid.
[b]Canada 1981.

buffered against fiscal swings than were providers in any other category. Notwithstanding the imposition of expenditure caps on physician services budgets, with all the attendant conflict between profession and state and within the profession itself, profession-state accommodations modulated the effects of fiscal constraint.[67] Table 3-2 also demonstrates the greater constraint on pharmaceutical costs escalation in public programs in Canada relative to the U.S., but again it must be remembered that the base of expenditure in the U.S. is proportionately much smaller.

LOOKING TO THE FUTURE

Both of these national systems are vulnerable to change in the future as a result of the experience of the 1990s—and the positions of influence of various actors will be important in shaping these changes. In the U.S., the BBA of 1997 did not mark the end of the debate about the fiscal viability of Medicare; on the contrary, it marked the beginning of a new wave of debate about the transformation of Medicare through the adoption of some form of "voucher" system. Such a system would enhance the role of private finance by essentially providing beneficiaries with "premium support" toward the selection of a private policy offered within a regime of managed competition. The

BBA of 1997 itself established a Bipartisan Commission on the Future of Medicare, which explored a voucher-style system but disbanded without coming to a consensus. In the wake of the commission's failure, voucher-type models of "premium support" gained popularity, particularly among Republicans, and indeed formed the basis of George W. Bush's approach to Medicare in his 2000 presidential campaign.

The regulatory frameworks put forward by voucher proponents to deal with problems such as "cream-skimming" and adverse selection in private insurance markets are exquisite in their complexity. As new data suggest that the apparent advantage of private insurers in constraining costs may have been a temporary phenomenon due to aggressive price discounting, and as private insurers increasingly exit the Medicare+Choice market, the "premium support" option appears less salable.[68] But if such a system *were* to be adopted, providers would find themselves dealing, across the full spectrum of their practices, with private payers. And experience suggests that these private payers are more likely to constrain both the economic discretion and the clinical autonomy of physicians and other providers than is Medicare in its traditional form. In recognition of this threat, the American Medical Association has focused its lobbying efforts on the maintenance of the fee-for-service sector and on attempts to reduce the role of private insurance, and, in particular, on limiting the role of managed care models under Medicare.

In Canada, the abrupt fiscal swings of the 1990s had important implications for the dynamics of health care policymaking. They further exacerbated the growing acrimony between federal and provincial governments and reduced the possibility of achieving intergovernmental agreement on either the reinforcement of the system or its modification. They fueled conflict between provincial governments and health care providers over resources and placed provider organizations, especially medical and hospital associations, under extreme pressure to manage internal conflicts, fueled demands for "catch-up" increases as the first call on any new investment in health care. They reduced redundancy in the system, thus reducing an essential condition for phasing in reforms in health care delivery. And they created an atmosphere of crisis that shook public confidence in the health care system and in the ability of governments to manage it.

On the other hand, the disruption of the system also laid the groundwork for change. Health policy has now come to define the climate of federal-provincial relations rather than being constrained by that climate, as in the past. As for relations between provincial governments and medical and hospital providers, fissures that deepened within both medical and hospital communities under the pressure of constraint have created some footholds for support of reform, especially among primary care providers. And finally, growing public concern may lead politicians to assess the risks of *in*action on health care as higher than the risks of action.

In the period from 2000 to early 2002, a number of reports were issued by governmentally appointed commissions at both federal and provincial levels, as various governments sought to shape the agenda for health care reform. The proposals made are in almost all cases consistent with the Canadian model of universal, first-dollar, single-payer coverage for core health services, although they leave open the question as to what should be *in* that core. While a number of reports have raised as "options for consideration" some changes that would be incompatible with this model—including the possibility of a broad imposition of copayments and/or of permitting privately financed services to compete with those in the publicly financed core—most have either explicitly or implicitly rejected these options. It is nonetheless clear that the menu of possibilities for health policy being publicly debated in Canada now is broader than it has been for three decades.[69] Medical associations, for their part, displayed considerable ambivalence as to the proper course to be taken. While maintaining their commitment to a universal system of coverage for health care services and arguing strongly for increases in public funding, the Canadian Medical Association and a number of provincial medical associations also at various times called for a public "debate" or "discussion" of options providing for a larger role for private finance.

In both Canada and the United States, then, the experience of the 1990s brought fundamental issues regarding the design of programs of public coverage for health care to the center of the political agenda. It also left health care providers in the two countries differently positioned to shape the policy response. In Canada, the design of political institutions and of the public health care program continued to concentrate authority and influence on both governmental and provider sides, and to bind governments and medical and hospital interests to a process of mutual accommodation. Strategic judgments on each side will determine the ongoing viability of this accommodation and, hence, the maintenance of the universal single-payer model. In the U.S., the design of both political institutions and the public program made for a much more fragmented politics. At the end of the 1990s, the political dynamics of an arena populated by a variety of governmental actors, types of providers, and private financial interests raised the prospect of a significant transformation of the Medicare program and a continuing augmentation of the role of private insurers.

CANADA AND THE U.S.: COMPARATIVE LESSONS

The experiences of Canada and the U.S. with regard to constraining payments to providers of health care to the elderly show some broad similarities. In both countries, fiscal pressures led to an increased focus on holding down public health care expenditures in the mid-1990s. In both, the popularity of the respective government programs made direct cuts in benefits highly risky politically, so attempts at restraint focused largely on reducing payments to providers. In both countries, moreover, providers and governments negotiated these payments within well-established processes. In both countries physicians fared relatively better than other health care providers in this process. And in both, public payments began to increase again after a period of restraint. Beyond these similarities, however, lie important differences. The public payer in the U.S. was less able to impose *tangible* losses on providers in the form of reduced payments than were public payers in Canada. Yet Canadian providers, especially physicians, emerged from this era better *positioned* to shape the agenda of reform than did their American counterparts.

In short, we have here a case in which similar policy choices (constraining payments to providers), driven by similar concerns (fiscal pressures), and using similar instruments at the level of the federal government (budget legislation) led to
different outcomes. We can now return to the proposition asserted at the beginning of this paper: This contrast between Canada and the U.S. can be attributed in
large part to differences in political institutions and broad policy design. Consider
the differences in political institutions—both the difference between parliamentary and congressional systems and the different roles of the respective federal
governments vis-à-vis Canadian and American Medicare. Primary authority for
health care in Canada rests with provincial governments, who deal with health
care providers from a position of considerable consolidated authority, by virtue of
a Westminster parliamentary model that concentrates power within the cabinet. As
Pierson and Weaver have argued, however, the Westminster model concentrates
not only authority but also accountability.[70] Governments must, therefore, mobilize the will to take the political risks of imposing losses in the health care arena.
For the first two decades of the existence of Canadian medicare, no government
would take the political risk of making real cuts to health care expenditures;
indeed, per capita spending continued to outpace inflation.

In the 1990s, however, the federal government and all provincial governments
entered into a sustained period of real fiscal constraint in health care, whose phases
varied only slightly by province. Two factors combined to firm the political will for
restraint in health care expenditures at this time: first, the diffusion of a broad
agenda of debt and deficit reduction across provinces and at the federal level; and
second, the opportunity for a dispersion of blame for spending reductions. In the
context of a deficit reduction agenda, no provincial government could ignore the
sector that, on average, accounted for 30 percent to 40 percent of provincial budgets. Furthermore, the federal government's ongoing reductions in transfer payments as part of its own deficit reduction agenda—which, in the first instance,
shifted the brunt of responsibility for spending cuts to the provincial government—
in turn provided provincial governments with the possibility of deflecting some of
the blame for spending cuts back to the federal level. The blame-shifting dynamics
of Canadian federalism, then, provided political cover, while the consolidated authority of the parliamentary system allowed governments to act decisively.

In the U.S. congressional system, by contrast, no such consolidation of governmental authority was possible; furthermore, responsibility for Medicare rested
with the federal government, limiting its capacity to deflect blame. The multiple
veto points of the U.S. budgetary process tend to generate intricately crafted trade-
offs and compromises and militate against significant change, such as dramatic
constraints on health care expenditures. In the health care field, this dynamic generated highly complex reimbursement formulas embedded in legislation. Furthermore, the 1980s and 1990s were characterized by situations of divided government in which the presidency and at least one house of Congress were in
different partisan hands. Under such circumstances, three dynamics are possible:
bipartisan compromise; stalemate; or, on rare occasions, a "bandwagon" momentum that leads all actors to support a popular proposal. For a time, it appeared

that a bandwagon might build to carry President Clinton's proposals for health care reform to fruition; but that process fell prey to the delay resulting from strategic misjudgments and from Clinton's need to deploy his limited political capital in other arenas as well, and a brief window of opportunity for major change closed.[71] In the wake of that failure, attention reverted to Medicare, but partisan stalemate in the mid-1990s meant that the payment formulas devised in the 1980s and early 1990s could not be changed. It was not until 1997, in the wake of a chastening election and in the context of an increasingly robust economy, that conditions allowed for bipartisan compromise on an again complex set of changes entailing reductions in payments to providers.

Political institutions, then, *strengthened* the state in dealing with health care providers in Canada but *weakened* the state in the U.S. The design of the respective government health care programs, moreover, provided a very different context for negotiations in the two nations. As in other systems of public finance, providers of health care services, especially physicians and hospitals, are deeply involved not only in the negotiation but in the administration of public payments in both Canada and the U.S. Under both Canadian and American versions of Medicare, providers are bound into an accommodation with the state. But the context, and therefore the dynamics, of that accommodation vary greatly between the two countries.

The universal, single-payer system in Canada made provincial governments monopsonists with regard to medical and hospital services; whereas providers in the U.S. negotiated with (and shifted costs across) a wide variety of payers. Medicare is the single largest payer for hospital and medical services in the U.S.; but it is far from having monopsony power. At first blush, this would appear to strengthen the position of providers in negotiations with the state—an impression borne out by the higher rates of increase in public payments to physicians and hospitals under U.S. Medicare than in Canada. But this impression may belie the long-term dynamics of the two systems. Bound as it is into an accommodation with the state, the Canadian medical profession occupies a central position of influence over the design of the system. As I have argued at length elsewhere, the Canadian profession, like its counterparts in other nations such as Britain and Germany, has traded off entrepreneurial discretion and economic gain for professional autonomy and influence, and it continued to do so during the period of tight fiscal constraint in the 1990s.[72]

American physicians, on the other hand, now find their conditions of work and the terms of their remuneration increasingly set out in contracts with payers, large-scale provider networks, and intermediary organizations; and their medical organizations now face a political landscape transformed by the fragmentation of previous coalitions and the emergence of new actors as a result of turbulent, market-driven change in the American health care arena in the 1980s and 1990s. While not as tangible as the economic restraints imposed upon their Canadian counterparts, these "positional" losses for American medicine have important implications for the future.

In the end, we are brought back to the original insight of Pierson and Weaver. Because a Westminster parliamentary system concentrates accountability as well as authority, it does not necessarily enhance the likelihood that a government will initiate and implement loss imposition strategies. Governments in Westminster systems, as in other institutional regimes, need to adopt strategies to mitigate the political costs of loss imposition. In the case of health care in Canada, two additional institutional features were important in shaping these strategies. First, the federal-provincial division of authority in Canada afforded governments at both levels the opportunity to deflect blame to the other. Second, the design of the Canadian medicare program, which bound medical and hospital providers into an accommodation with the state, allowed for tangible losses to be partially offset by gains in influence over the broad design of the system. The implications of the latter contrast and were not lost on providers and governmental actors on either side of the border; and it continues to fuel debate about the tradeoffs to be made in the future.

NOTES

1. Victor Fuchs, "Health Care for the Elderly: How Much? Who Will Pay for It?" *Health Affairs* 18, no. 3 (January/February 1999): 11.
2. Calculated from Health Canada, *National Health Care Expenditures by Age and Sex, 1980–81 to 2000–01*, www.hcsc.gc.ca/english/pdf/health_care/age_sex_annex-tabes.pdf, Tables 1A, 7A.
3. Later, in response to criticisms that federal cost-sharing for hospital care but not long-term and home care was creating incentives toward overutilization of hospital services, the federal government introduced a per-capita grant to provincial governments in support of home care in 1977. Unlike federal funding for hospital and medical services, however, this "extended care" grant carried no conditions with respect to the design of provincial programs.
4. Included were patients with end-stage renal disease (ESRD) as an identified category.
5. Coverage for the services of nonmedical health care practitioners varies across provinces. All cover dental surgery, with some limitations. Seven provinces cover optometric services, with some limitations, for all beneficiaries, and one other includes such coverage for seniors. Six cover chiropractic services and three cover physiotherapy, again subject to limitations.
6. Alberta and British Columbia have income-related premium systems, from which seniors and certain other groups are exempt. The premium functions essentially as an earmarked tax, since eligibility for benefits is not linked to payments of the premium.
7. Quebec places a maximum on the value of the principal residence to be excluded, and Nova Scotia exempts the principal residence only if it is designated to another person. For an excellent review of cross-provincial variation in copayments for services to the elderly outside the scope of the Canada Health Act, see National Advisory Council on Aging, *The NACA Position on Enhancing the Canadian Health Care System* (Ottawa: Minister of Public Works and Government Services Canada, 2000).
8. See, for example, Frank L. Graves, "Rethinking Government as if People Mattered: From 'Reaganomics' to 'Humanomics,'" in Leslie A. Pal, ed., *How Ottawa Spends, 1999–2000* (Toronto: Oxford University Press, 2000), 59–63; Edward Greenspon and Hugh Winsor, "Spending Increase Favoured, Poll Finds," *Globe and Mail* (Toronto), January 13, 1997, A1, A8; Edward Greenspon, "Health Care Tops List of Concerns," *Globe and Mail* (Toronto), July 11, 1998, A1; Angus Reid, "17 Country Poll Shows 72% Say Taxes Too High," March 16, 2000, www.ipsosreid.com/search/pdf/media/mr000316_1.pdf (accessed February 21, 2002).

9. Robert J. Blendon, "Public Opinion and Medicare Restructuring," in Robert D. Reischauer, Stuart Butler, and Judith R. Lave, eds., *Medicare: Preparing for the Challenges of the Twenty-first Century* (Washington, D.C.: National Academy of Social Insurance, 1998), pp. 288–93.

10. Carolyn Hughes Tuohy, *Accidental Logics: The Dynamics of Change in the Health Care Arena in the United States, Britain and France* (New York: Oxford University Press, 1999).

11. David Wilsford, "Path Dependency, or Why History Makes It Difficult but Not Impossible to Reform Health Care Systems in a Big Way," *Journal of Public Policy* 14, no. 3 (fall 1994): 251–83.

12. John K. Iglehart, "The New Era of Prospective Payment for Hospitals," *New England Journal of Medicine* 307, no. 20 (November 11, 1982): 1288.

13. Bruce C. Vladek, "The Political Economy of Medicare," *Health Affairs* 18, no.1 (January/February 1999): 27.

14. Michael A. Morrisey, *Cost Shifting in Health Care: Separating Evidence from Rhetoric* (Washington, D.C.: AEI Press, 1994); Eric Weissenstein, "Managed Care Eats at Hospital Cost Shifts," *Modern Healthcare* (April 24, 1995): 3.

15. Allen Schick, "How a Bill Did Not Become Law," in Thomas E. Mann and Norman J. Ornstein, eds., *Intensive Care: How Congress Shapes Health Policy* (Washington, D.C.: AEI/Brookings, 1995), pp. 227–72.

16. Tuohy, *Accidental Logics*, 153.

17. Ibid., pp. 81–82.

18. Vladek, "The Political Economy of Medicare," 28.

19. Keith J. Mueller, *Health Care Policy in the United States* (Lincoln: University of Nebraska Press, 1993), pp. 94–95.

20. Margaret H. Davis and Sally T. Burner, "Three Decades of Medicare: What the Numbers Tell Us," *Health Affairs* 14, no. 4 (winter 1994): 240–41; see also table 3-1.

21. Joe White, "Budgeting and Health Policymaking," in Mann and Ornstein, *Intensive Care*, pp. 53–78; Theodore R. Marmor, *The Politics of Medicare*, 2d ed. (New York: Aldine de Gruyter, 2000), pp. 175–76.

22. Julie Rovner, "Congress's 'Catastrophic' Attempt to Fix Medicare," in Mann and Ornstein, *Intensive Care*, 166.

23. Jacob S. Hacker, *The Road to Nowhere: The Genesis of President Clinton's Plan for Health Security* (Princeton, N.J.: Princeton University Press, 1997), p. 12.

24. Theda Skocpol, *Boomerang: Clinton's Health Security Effort and the Turn against Government in U.S. Politics* (New York: W. W. Norton, 1996).

25. Schick, "How a Bill Did Not Become Law," pp. 227–72.

26. Charles N. Kahn III and Hanns Kuttner, "Budget Bills and Medicare Policy: The Politics of the BBA," *Health Affairs* 18, no. 1 (January/February 1999): 38.

27. Ibid., 39.

28. Marmor, *The Politics of Medicare*, 146–48.

29. Katharine Levit et al., "Inflation Spurs Health Spending in 2000," *Health Affairs* 21, no. 1 (January/February 2002): 172–81.

30. Rates of increase in Medicare expenditures on prescription drugs are large, but coverage is limited and hence the base is very small—accounting for about 1 percent of Medicare spending.

31. Katharine Levit et al., "Health Spending in 1998: Signals of Change," *Health Affairs* 19, no. 1 (January/February 2000): 128.

32. These changes are described in Tuohy, *Accidental Logics*, 90–93.

33. Department of Finance, *Budget Plan* (Ottawa: Department of Finance, 1995), Table 4.4.

34. The eight areas were access to care, health promotion, primary health care, supply of health personnel, home care and community care, pharmaceuticals management (i.e., strategies for assessing the cost effectiveness of prescription drugs), health informa-

tion and communications technology, and health equipment and infrastructure. No specific commitments were made regarding actions to be taken in these areas.

35. Provincial and Territorial Ministers of Health, *Understanding Canada's Health Care Costs: Final Report*, August 2000.

36. The poorer provinces insisted upon coupling this demand to a demand for an additional $4 billion in "equalization" payments.

37. Conference Board of Canada, *Performance and Potential, 2001–2* (Ottawa: Conference Board of Canada, 2001), pp. 85–95.

38. See, for example, Marni D. Brownell, Noralou P. Roos, and Charles A. Burchill, *Monitoring the Winnipeg Hospital System: 1990/91 through 1996/97* (Winnipeg: Manitoba Centre for Health Policy and Evaluation, University of Manitoba, March 1999).

39. Robert J. Blendon, Cathy Schoen, Catherine M. DesRoches, Robin Osborn, Kimberly L. Scoles, "Trends: Inequities in Health Care: A Five-Country Survey," *Health Affairs* 21, no. 3 (May–June 2002): 182–91.

40. Real per capita spending increased by 26.6 percent in the hospital sector and by 48.9 percent in the physician services sector between 1975 and 1990. Health Canada, *National Health Expenditures in Canada, 1975–96* (Ottawa: Health Canada, 1997), Table 5.

41. V. Bhatia, S. West, and M. Giacomini, "Equity in Case-Based Funding: A Case Study of Meanings and Messages in Hospital Funding Policy," Working Paper No. 96-13 (Hamilton, Ontario: McMaster University, Centre for Health Economics and Policy Analysis, 1996); Dominic S. Haazen, "Redefining the Globe: Recent Changes in the Financing of British Columbia Hospitals," in Raisa B. Deber and Gail G. Thompson, eds., *Restructuring Canada's Health Services System: How Do We Get There from Here?* (Toronto: University of Toronto Press, 1992), pp. 73–84.

42. Steven Lewis, "Issues in the Evolution of Decision-Making at Regional Levels" (paper presented at the symposium *Reorganizing Canadian Health Care: Global Pressures/New Institutional Realities*, Robarts Centre for Canadian Studies and the Centre for Health Studies, York University, Toronto, April 1–2, 1996).

43. *Lalonde v Ontario*, 48 O.R. (3d) 50, [1999] O.J. No. 4488 (div. Ct.).

44. Jonathan Lomas, Gerry Veenstra, and John Woods, "Devolving Authority for Health in Canada's Provinces: III. Motivations, Approaches and Attitudes of Board Members." Working Paper 96-4 (Hamilton, Ontario: McMaster University Centre for Health Economics and Policy Analysis, 1996).

45. For a telling critique of the omnibus legislation under which the HSRC was appointed as having adopted an "autocratic, centralized" mode of government in the interests of streamlining and efficiency, see Lorraine Weinrib, "The Exercise of Public Power under the Savings and Restructuring Act, 1995 (Bill 26)," *CanadaWatch* 4, no. 3 (January/February 1996): 62.

46. Uwe Reinhardt, "Spending More through 'Cost Control': Our Obsessive Quest to Gut the Hospital," *Health Affairs* 15, no. 2 (summer 1996): 145–54.

47. Organization for Economic Cooperation and Development, *Internal Markets in the Making: Health Systems in Canada, Iceland and the United Kingdom* (Paris: Organization for Economic Cooperation and Development, 1995), pp. 99–106; Gerald F. Anderson and Jean-Pierre Poullier, "Health Spending, Access and Outcomes: Trends in Industrialized Countries," *Health Affairs* 18, no. 3 (May/June 1999): 182–85.

48. The hospital share of total health expenditures declined from 44.7 percent in 1975 to 31.8 percent in 2000. The physician share declined from 15.1 percent to 13.5 percent over the same period. Canadian Institute for Health Information, *Health Care in Canada, 2001* (Ottawa: Canadian Institute for Health Information, 2001), p. 75.

49. Carolyn Hughes Tuohy, "Medicine and the State in Canada: The Extra-billing Issue in Perspective," *Canadian Journal of Political Science* 21 (June 1988): 268.

50. Marc A. Baltzan, "Why C.M.A. Opposes Canada Health Act." *Ontario Medical Review* (July 1983): 347.

51. Tuohy, "Medicine and the State in Canada," 267–96.
52. General Accounting Office, *Canadian Health Insurance: Lessons for the United States* (Report to the Chairman, Committee on Government Operations, House of Representatives) (Washington, D.C.: United States General Accounting Office, June 1991), p. 35.
53. Morris Barer and Robert G. Evans, "Riding North on a South-Bound Horse: Expenditures, Prices, Utilization and Incomes in the Canadian Health Care System," in Robert G. Evans and Greg L. Stoddart, eds., *Medicare at Maturity* (Calgary: University of Calgary Press, 1996), pp. 78–96.
54. Carolyn J. Tuohy, *Policy and Politics in Canada: Institutionalized Ambivalence* (Philadelphia: Temple University Press, 1992), p. 127.
55. Jonathan Lomas et al., "Paying Physicians in Canada: Minding Our P's and Q's," *Health Affairs* 8, no. 1 (spring 1989): 80–102; Jeremiah Hurley, Robert Card, and Laurie Goldsmith, "Physician Expenditure Cap Policies in Canada: Development, Design and Implications for Analysing Their Effects," final report submitted to the National Health Research and Development Program (Hamilton, Ontario: McMaster University Centre for Health Economics and Policy Analysis, 1997, mimeographed).
56. Jeremiah Hurley and Robert Card, "Global Physician Budgets as Common-Property Resources: Some Implications for Physicians and Medical Associations," *Canadian Medical Association Journal* 154, no. 8 (April 15, 1996): 1161–68.
57. These thresholds were established at relatively generous levels. In Ontario, for example, thresholds imposed during a stalemate in negotiations in 1996 were calculated at 40 percent above the median billings in each of thirty-two groups. This yielded thresholds roughly comparable to those that were previously and subsequently negotiated in Ontario and in other provinces. Across those provinces with individual billing thresholds in the mid-1990s, payments to GPs began to be prorated at about C$250,000–300,000 and payments to specialists at about C$350,000–400,000. See Hurley, Card, and Goldsmith, "Physician Expenditure Cap Policies in Canada," table 2.
58. Hurley and Card, "Global Physician Budgets as Common-Property Resources," 1161–68.
59. Jeremiah Hurley et al., "A Tale of Two Provinces: A Case Study of Physicians' Expenditure Caps as Financial Incentives," Working Paper No. 96-12 (Hamilton, Ontario: McMaster University, Centre for Health Economics and Policy Analysis, 1996).
60. Steven J. Katz, Cathy Charles, Jonathan Lomas, and H. Gilbert Welch, "Physician Relations in Canada: Shooting Inward as the Circle Closes," *Journal of Health Politics, Policy and Law* 22, no. 6 (1997): 1413–32.
61. Marni D. Brownell, Noralou P. Roos, and Charles A. Burchill, *Monitoring the Winnipeg Hospital System: 1990/91 through 1996/97* (Winnipeg: Manitoba Centre for Health Policy and Evaluation, University of Manitoba, March 1999).
62. Hurley, Card, and Goldsmith, "Physician Expenditure Cap Policies in Canada."
63. Compiled from Paul Grootendorst, "Beneficiary Cost Sharing under Canadian Provincial Drug Benefit Programs: History and Assessment," Working Paper No. 99-10 (Hamilton, Ontario: McMaster University, Centre for Health Economics and Policy Analysis, 1999).
64. Health Canada, *National Health Care Expenditures by Age and Sex, 1980–81 to 2000–2001*, www.hcsc.gc.ca/english/pdf/health_care/age_sex_annex-tabes.pdf, tables 1A, 7A. The public share of total health care expenditures on those sixty-five years of age and older declined, proportionately, from 82.7 percent to 78.6 percent in the same period.
65. A background paper on health human resources, prepared for the Premier's Conference in August 2001, makes both of these arguments strongly. See Shawn McCarthy, "Wage Offers Threaten Health Care, Report Says," *Globe and Mail* (Toronto), July 28, 2001; Patrick Sullivan, "Large Fee Increase in Hand, Alberta Goes Courting Canada's MDs," *Canadian Medical Association Journal* 164, no. 11 (May 29, 2001): 1607.
66. Carolyn Hughes Tuohy, "The Costs of Constraint and the Prospects for Health Care Reform In Canada," *Health Affairs* 21, no. 3 (May/June 2002): 32–46.

67. Table 3-2, like table 3-1 and figure 3-1, reports changes in nominal expenditures, adjusted neither for inflation nor for changes in the age-sex composition of the population. This methodology allows for comparisons across types of providers and across public and private payers with regard to expenditures for care given to the elderly. But it neglects the effects of population aging, which shifts more beneficiaries into the sixty-five-years-and-older category. *Per capita* public expenditures on the elderly in Canada increased in nominal terms by 27 percent between 1990 and 2000, as opposed to a 56 percent increase in nominal *total* expenditures on the elderly. These comparisons, therefore, understate the constraints on payments to providers under universal programs in Canada.

68. Jonathan Oberlander, "Is Premium Support the Right Medicine for Medicare?" *Health Affairs* 19, no. 5 (September/October 2000): 84–99.

69. Tuohy, "The Costs of Constraint," 32.

70. Paul D. Pierson and R. Kent Weaver, "Political Institutions and Loss Imposition: The Case of Pensions," in R. Kent Weaver and Bert A. Rockman, eds., *Do Institutions Matter?* (Washington, D.C.: The Brookings Institution, 1993), pp. 110–50.

71. Tuohy, *Accidental Logics*, 73–85.

72. Tuohy, *Accidental Logics*. See also Marian Döhler, "Physicians' Professional Autonomy in the Welfare State: Endangered or Preserved?" in Giorgio Freddi and James Warner Bjorkman, eds., *Controlling Medical Professionals: The Comparative Politics of Health Governance* (London: Sage, 1989), pp. 178–244.

4

TELECOMMUNICATIONS DEREGULATION

RICHARD J. SCHULTZ AND ANDREW RICH

Loss, even pain, is too antiseptic a word to describe the trauma-inducing changes that public authorities have imposed on incumbent telecommunications firms in North America over the past three decades. In the United States, where the restructuring process began, AT&T, then the largest corporation in the world, fought vigorously, but to no avail, as public authorities in incremental stages chipped and stripped away the protective domains of whole sections of its monopoly operations. The process culminated in AT&T "consenting" to the corporate amputation of its local operating companies in 1982, the most consequential American antitrust settlement since the settlements involving American Tobacco and Standard Oil in 1911. In Canada, although a similar restructuring process began a decade later, it progressed much more quickly. What had taken three decades in the United States was completed in almost half that time—although Bell Canada, then Canada's largest corporation, was spared the pain of state-imposed amputation or divestiture.[1] In both cases, not only did the most fundamental preferences of these two corporate entities carry very little weight in the restructuring process, but the outcomes imposed an onerous set of costs—economic, organizational, and indeed psychic—on the two firms.[2]

Many reasons account for the restructuring of telecommunications from monopoly to competitive provisioning of services and equipment in both the United States and Canada. A full explanation must acknowledge the role of technological changes, ideological reformulation, and economic entrepreneurialism, not to mention strong doses of opportunism. Notwithstanding the multicausal nature of the changes and the consequent difficulty in disentangling their effects, the premise of this chapter is that telecommunications restructuring, and the concomitant imposition of loss and pain, were the products of political processes, albeit ones fought out not in primary, or first-level, political forums, such as Congress in the United States or the cabinet in Canada, but in third-level agencies, specifically regulatory agencies and courts. What is striking about the restructuring processes in both countries is how similar they were in outcomes, despite the institutional differences. The only major difference was a temporal one, in that the American process began before the Canadian and there was, until recently, almost a decade lag between the two countries.

The specific purpose of this chapter is to attempt to explain, in the first instance, why similar processes and outcomes of loss imposition occurred in the two countries despite the fundamental institutional differences between them—differences that are elaborated in other chapters in this book, particularly in the overview chapter by Pal and Weaver. The second purpose is to attempt to determine if at least the temporal divergences can be explained by the two countries' different institutional profiles.

Loss imposition such as that applied to AT&T and Bell Canada challenges conventional understandings of both corporate power and the role of institutions. AT&T should have been able to exploit its unquestionably formidable political resources within the American Congress, with its multiple veto points, so as to protect its interests. Conversely, in Canada, with its centralization of power in the cabinet, Bell Canada should have been able to exploit similar political resources to deflect demands for change. The opposite occurred in both cases, however, as neither corporation was able to defend the status quo. In fact, the politics of loss imposition in the telecommunications sector in Canada and the United States was remarkably similar.

Macroinstitutional political forces were largely, although not wholly, irrelevant to both outcomes. Elected political actors, whom one would have expected to be primary players in such a conflict-ridden process when the stakes were so substantial, played strictly secondary roles, and had little direct impact on the overall process. This was true even in Canada, where the nature of the regulatory system gives the cabinet an opportunity to exercise considerable direct leverage. Moreover, as our analysis suggests, in letting regulatory agencies and courts take responsibility, politicians were not simply engaged in blame avoidance. In the case of the United States, members of Congress and the president were simply unable to control the process of restructuring, despite their attempts to do so. In the case of Canada, there may initially have been some effort at blame avoidance, but as the process of restructuring proceeded, conflicts within the cabinet and among their departmental advisors inhibited any attempt to impose control.

The structure of institutional arrangements did matter, but not in the ways predicted by most existing institutional analyses. Radical change in the telecommunications sectors was, in both countries, the product of a polycentric, multiorganizational policy system characterized by institutions with limited jurisdictions, overlapping responsibilities, and relative autonomy. In both countries, "divided government" at the microagency level was the norm, with lower-level institutions sometimes engaging in competition for influence and control and sometimes coalescing to thwart potential rivals. The decision points were consequently multiple, but, surprisingly, the corresponding veto points that *should* have been a force were either unavailable or were unused by those empowered to use them in order to prevent losses.

Furthermore, despite the magnitude of the losses involved, loss imposition was not the product of a conscious, coherent policy design by any particular set of actors. The outcomes were not preordained, because the loss imposition processes were episodic and halting. They followed multiple paths with significant discontinuities, not to mention occasional reversals and stalemates. Despite the stakes, especially for the companies involved, no single political actor was willing or able to assume control. Institutions with limited jurisdictions and relative autonomy from effective hierarchical control—through processes best characterized, in most instances, as disjointed, discontinuous incrementalism—produced a cumulative result that inflicted pain not simply at the margins but at the very core of the affected corporations.

The chapter proceeds through three stages. In the first section, we develop some introductory points pertinent to the general themes of political institutions and loss imposition from the perspective of telecommunications restructuring. In particular, we seek to provide a general description of the restructuring that occurred and to clarify the nature of the losses involved from a conceptual perspective. The second section of the chapter consists of a narrative describing two of the three major stages of telecommunications restructuring in both countries between 1968 and 1992, specifically those involving the terminal or customer equipment market and the vastly more important long distance services market.[3] In the final section, we develop conclusions about the specific cases described and their general relevance to larger concerns about the importance of different institutional structures and systems for the politics of loss imposition.

SETTING THE SECTORAL AND CONCEPTUAL STAGE

The Specifics of Telecommunications Restructuring

Historically, AT&T and Bell Canada had monopolies to provide customer premises equipment (CPE) or terminal equipment to their respective countries. This equipment included telephones, modems, faxes, answering equipment, and private branch exchanges (PBXs) found in large offices. Both AT&T and Bell Canada rigorously policed their monopolies for providing these goods, and their monopolies were reinforced by the incentives flowing from a vertically integrated service structure. Restructuring transformed the equipment market into a highly competitive market, with the incumbent firms very quickly losing a significant proportion of their market share; and it facilitated a flood of new entrants into both countries—

including, not insignificantly, the entry of Bell Canada's equipment subsidiary into the American market.

The long distance telephone service market was the second segment of the market to be restructured. Again, long distance had been provided exclusively by AT&T and Bell Canada within their operating territories for almost seven decades, but after a series of steps toward restructuring that involved first, private, and subsequently, and more importantly, public long distance, both companies lost significant market share. AT&T's market share fell from approximately 85 percent in 1984, when the restructuring went into effect, to little more than 50 percent in 1996. Bell Canada's loss was less substantial, from 100 percent to less than 65 percent, but this was even more dramatic, in that the loss occurred in less than six years.[4] The liberalization of this market segment was accompanied by the divestiture by AT&T of its local operating companies in 1982–84 as a structural reform intended to protect new competitors from anticompetitive behavior by AT&T.

Winners and Losers

Obviously, the primary losers in this restructuring were the incumbent telephone companies. Thus, these developments in telecommunications should be classified as a case of business-focused concentrated loss. This is too narrow a conception, however, of the losses affected by, or at least presumed to be affected by, the restructuring. From the outset in both countries, the incumbent telecommunications companies sought, with only a limited degree of success, to have the debates and conflicts cast as risking the imposition of loss on telephone *subscribers*. The companies emphasized that low-income subscribers in particular, along with all subscribers in rural and remote areas—that is, a geographically diffuse constituency—would be the "real" losers. Another more concentrated set of losers in the United States would be state regulators, who were faced with significant reduction in their authority and in their power to subsidize local rates with long distance revenues.

Identifying who would benefit from restructuring is no less complex. One view was that the beneficiaries were highly concentrated—namely, the firms that sought to enter the various market segments either as long distance competitors or as equipment manufacturers. Another was that restructuring and the introduction of long distance competition might result in a substantial regressive redistribution, with large corporations or upper-income users of long distance as the primary beneficiaries.[5] In both cases, the presumed beneficiaries, while concentrated in specific sectors of society, were geographically diffused. In short, the complex composition of the costs and benefits of telecommunications restructuring, and of the attendant winners and losers, cautions one to be wary of the Wilsonian matrix, with its relatively straightforward two-by-two categorization.

Institutional Aspects and the Loss Imposition Process

Analyzing the process of loss imposition requires an understanding of the institutional complex within which it occurs. Other chapters in this book discuss major features of the institutional configurations in the United States and Canada and their possible implications for loss imposition or its prevention. We limit our discussion to the different role of federalism with respect to the telecommunications systems in the two countries and some of the pertinent specifics for telecommunications of the two national regulatory systems.

In the United States, as a result of the 1934 Communications Act, individual telecommunications companies were made subject to two-tier regulation—with AT&T, for example, subject to both Federal Communications Commission (FCC) regulation with respect to interstate long distance and to state regulation for intrastate long distance and local service. In the event of interjurisdictional conflict, the FCC preempts state regulation. In Canada, federalism has played a somewhat different role in telecommunications restructuring. For most of the twentieth century, the jurisdictional split between the federal and provincial governments, while never constitutionally or judicially authorized, was taken for granted and resulted in a company-specific allocation of responsibilities between governments. The federal government had exclusive regulatory responsibility for two companies: Bell Canada, operating in Ontario and Quebec, and British Columbia Telephone Company (BC Tel), operating solely in that province. The complete range of telephone services provided by companies operating in the remaining seven provinces—intraprovincial, interprovincial, and international—were regulated exclusively by the individual provinces. Complicating this allocation of authority was an interregional cross-subsidy system, similar in purpose if not in substance to that found in the United States. This subsidy system was not a product of governmental or regulatory action but rather resulted from what Lederman labeled "private sector cooperative federalism."[6] In 1931, the major telephone companies, without any direct governmental involvement, formed a consortium to provide a nationally integrated telephone system based in part on revenue-sharing.

Federalism plays out differently in Canada than in the United States because of the more powerful salience of intergovernmental conflicts in Canada, whatever the issue area. This has been particularly true over the past thirty years, characterized as they have been by "megaconstitutional conflicts."[7] Given the traditional allocation of responsibilities in the telecommunications industry, it was inevitable that the threat of loss imposition occasioned by telecommunications restructuring would become inextricably embedded within the larger set of constitutional political dynamics in Canada.

The regulatory arena was central to the process of loss imposition in telecommunications in Canada and the U.S., and the two countries' regulatory agencies had substantial similarities. There is a common belief that regulatory agencies in a parliamentary system such as Canada's are less independent than those found in a congressional system such as that in the United States.[8] This assumption is premised on the belief that a centralization of power over regulatory agencies accompanies a system with parliamentary supremacy. It is indeed the case that decisions of the Canadian telecommunications regulator, the Canadian Radio-television and Telecommunications Commission (CRTC), are subject to review by the cabinet when appealed by affected parties. Moreover, in telecommunications decisions, the cabinet can send a regulatory decision back for reconsideration, veto it outright, or change it in whole or in part, which can include turning a negative decision into a positive one. That it has such power has led some to question the claim that Canadian regulatory agencies are independent at all, especially in comparison with their American counterparts, such as the FCC.

But notwithstanding this political appeal mechanism, Canadian politicians cannot interfere with agency discretion during the course of its decision making. Indeed, ministerial contact with an agency on a quasi-judicial matter is expected to lead to resignation from the cabinet. This provides a regulatory agency with considerable latitude during decision making and permits the agency to write decisions that impose possible constraints concerning the range of alternative actions available to the cabinet. Cabinet-level political intervention is also discouraged by the public process of hearings and evaluation of evidence that regulatory agencies normally undertake. In the end, the mere presence of a cabinet-level override power should not lead one to conclude that Canadian agencies lack independence in their decision making.

Similarly, one should beware of overstating the relative independence of American regulatory agencies. While there is nothing comparable to the Canadian political appeal mechanism, in many important ways American regulatory agencies are subject to greater political constraints, and more possible interference, than their Canadian counterparts. The system of congressional oversight in the United States brings regulators into much more routine contact with politicians and their staffs, for example, than is true in Canada. Personal intervention by members of Congress, despite the presumed prohibitions against contact with commissioners and staff on quasi-judicial decisions, is reportedly common. Likewise, the president apparently can, and often seeks to, use indirect means to influence specific decisions on cases with policy or political significance. Moreover, that the chairs of independent regulatory agencies serve at the pleasure of the president, who can use such appointments to define policy mandates and the approaches taken by agencies, is a lever of power that Canadian cabinet ministers can only envy. In Canada, agency chairs serve for a stipulated term notwithstanding changes in government, a rule that has caused distress for both Conservative and Liberal governments over the past fifteen years. In sum, the "independence" governing the two regulatory systems is something to be investigated rather than assumed, particularly when developing comparative explanations of the loss imposition process in the two countries.

While it is a source of frustration at times for politicians, the structural position of regulatory agencies vis-à-vis telecommunications policy within both the Canadian and American systems reduced the potential for exploiting these agencies in order to "pass the buck" and avoid responsibility for loss imposition, compared to what can ensue, for example, when the courts administer policy disputes. The cabinet override, or Canadian "political appeal," discussed above, attenuates the possibility of blame avoidance in the Canadian system, as affected parties can directly appeal to the cabinet to override adverse decisions, and members of Parliament can challenge the government about its use, or nonuse, of the override power. In the United States, the absence of a comparable explicit "veto" power on the part of either the executive or the legislature does not necessarily mean that politicians can hide behind regulatory independence in order to shift responsibility. Historically, presidents and members of Congress, when sufficiently motivated, can find a way to effectively make their preferences known to regulators—thereby, if not denying politicians a "blame avoidance" strategy, at least rendering it less plausible.[9]

UNRAVELING THE FIBERS OF TELECOMMUNICATIONS MARKETS

Canada and the United States stand out in relation to the rest of the world in the extent to which both countries adopted private ownership with public regulation as the means to control and develop telecommunications systems. The evolution of their respective regulatory regimes, and the system of ideas, institutions, and policies that helped define them, created the context for sectoral restructuring in the two countries. In both countries, the regulatory regime was introduced following a series of interrelated developments: the expiration of the original telephone patents granted to Bell Canada and its American parent, AT&T; the subsequent emergence of competitive local telephone companies; aggressive, even ruthless, corporate behavior to overcome such competition; and corporate, subscriber, and general political discontent.[10]

Regulation by an independent agency was introduced in Canada in 1906, when jurisdiction for telephones was added to the responsibilities of the railway regulator. As Armstrong and Nelles note, the Bell Telephone Company (as Bell Canada was then known) "did not seek regulation but certainly sought to shape it once public pressure made it inevitable."[11] Regulation was limited to rates that had to be "just and reasonable" and to noncompetitive system interconnection. The alternative to regulation was public ownership, which had some public and political advocates and was introduced almost simultaneously in the three Canadian prairie provinces.[12]

In 1908, Theodore Vail embraced public regulation as AT&T's preferred alternative in the United States. This reflected essentially a north-to-south learning process, as Vail and his colleagues, with ownership control of Bell Canada, followed Canadian developments very carefully and quickly came to appreciate that regulation was not the threat they once feared and was not necessarily hostile to corporate interests. Rather, the limited degree of public control that regulation entailed was more than compensated for by the stability and legitimacy that regulation generated for the firm.

One reason for telecommunications' embrace of regulation was that the policies and practices of the regulators in both countries were relatively benign. In Canada, the regulator from the outset adopted what has been described as a "policing" role by confining its activities to those prescribed by the narrowest possible interpretation of its statutory responsibilities.[13] The agency insisted that it had only a remedial and reactive role in disputes rather than an initiating one, and it disclaimed any responsibility for monitoring corporate decision making, except insofar as a decision constituted a (narrowly defined) abuse. The result was that while rates were regulated, the actual design of rate structures remained a corporate prerogative. The regulator was also not responsible for intercorporate relations, such as those between the operating company and its equipment manufacturer.

In the United States, the regulator's role and behavior were comparable, if not even more benign. Beginning in 1910, regulation by the Interstate Commerce Commission (ICC) was nominal at best, and after 1934, when the Federal Communications Commission took over, regulation was essentially passive, at the federal level at least, and was characterized as "continuing surveillance" rather than policing, aggressive or otherwise. The only major differences between Canada and the United States during this period, and they were not insubstantial, were the role of antitrust authorities in the U.S., which resulted in major regulatory interventions in 1913 and 1956, and the imposition by the U.S. Supreme Court in 1930 of a rate-setting approach that favored local subscribers whose rates were determined by state regulators.[14]

One of the most important consequences of the policy of regulatory "benign neglect" in both countries was that the telephone "system" as it developed in North America was primarily the product of corporate, rather than governmental, design. The system rested on several basic principles. The first was the preservation of territorial monopolies for individual companies for both local and long distance service, a principle that was taken for granted but was not explicitly authorized in either country by legislation. The second was the concept of "end-to-end" service, which meant that the transmission and receiving equipment attached to the telephone network was considered an intrinsic part of the monopoly and, therefore, subject to exclusive control by the telephone companies. This subsequently came to include any equipment attached to the network, such as faxes and answering machines. The third essential principle was value-of-service pricing, which meant that the price of an individual service, such as local or long distance, was based not on its intrinsic costs but on its value to the customer. The result of this pricing system was a series of cross-subsidies between residential and business service, between urban and rural subscribers, and, ultimately and most significantly, between local and long distance service.

These were principles established by corporate rather than governmental efforts, a point often misunderstood. Many commentators have argued, or assumed, that the system of cross-subsidization that results from value-of-service pricing is the product of regulatory design and the cornerstone for the public policy known as "universal service." State regulators in the United States did play more of a role in specifying these policies than their counterparts in Canada. But in establishing the details of how to use long distance revenues to cover a larger portion of the cost of local service, regulators, supported by the Supreme Court's decision in 1930, were simply extending a practice that already had been developed and employed by the telephone industry. In Canada, the interregional dimension of the cross-subsidy system, designed to support the creation and extension of a nationally integrated system, was introduced and refined without any political or regulatory role whatsoever.

It is often assumed that value-of-service pricing and the concomitant cross-subsidization to keep local rates low were intended by both the telephone companies and their regulators in both countries to serve a "social mission"—namely, to provide telephone service universally and at affordable rates.[15] But both Mueller and Schultz argue that the conventional wisdom in both countries is wrong.[16] Mueller describes universal service as "a concept in search of a history." In both countries, "an entire mythological history has evolved around the concept."[17]

Yet, if the material pains imposed on telephone companies were complex, so, too, were the psychic or symbolic costs they weathered. For most of this century, telephone executives in both countries defined their role and responsibility as going beyond mere profit-making. To be sure, they were concerned with profit—but notwithstanding our comments above about the supposedly "social mission" of universal service, industry executives perceived their role in society to constitute, in the words of one of AT&T's chairmen, "an unusual obligation." In 1927, AT&T president Walter Gifford stated that AT&T had a responsibility "to see to it that the service shall be at all times adequate, dependable, and satisfactory to the user. Obviously, the only sound policy that will meet these obligations is to continue to furnish the best possible telephone service at the lowest cost consistent with financial surety."[18] These words and commitments would have been equally acceptable to Gifford's Canadian counterpart. They reflected a deeply ingrained, self-conscious corporate culture, and indeed an ideology, that shaped managerial philosophy and behavior at all levels of the firm. As Temin notes, this "holy mission of service . . . was as deeply rooted and as well integrated with the corporation as any such belief system in the history of this nation's business."[19] To give effect to this culture—and to implement this privately developed yet quasi-public policy so as to create the most technologically advanced, most efficient, and most widely available telephone service in the world—telephone executives in both countries were willing to strike what Temin described, in the case of AT&T, as a "variety of bargains" with different governments and agencies.[20] To see, in the 1970s and 1980s, the bargains challenged and then renounced, their motives questioned and indeed ridiculed, their "system" torn asunder and radically, profoundly recast, was to cause executives of the traditional telephone industry perhaps greater pain than that occasioned by restructuring itself. The pain was only heightened by the fact that they went from a position where they had been in control for most of the century to one where no one appeared to be in control.

Loss Imposition in the Terminal Equipment Market

IN THE UNITED STATES

Beginning with the introduction of telephone service in the 1880s, AT&T imposed severe restrictions on the attachment of customer-owned equipment to its network. After the beginnings of regulation in 1910, provisions in customer-company contracts began to take the form of ICC-approved tariffs. In 1913, the equipment tariff stated: "No equipment, apparatus, circuit or device not furnished by the telephone company shall be attached to or connected with the facilities furnished by the telephone company, whether physically, by induction, or otherwise."[21]

The first major challenge to this prohibition came in 1948, when the Hush-a-Phone company sought permission to attach a rubber cup device to the telephone handset to facilitate conversations in busy offices. When AT&T denied permission, the company turned to the FCC for redress. After seven years, the commission ruled in favor of AT&T, on the grounds that unrestricted use of the device "could result in a general deterioration of the quality of interstate and foreign telephone service."[22] Hush-a-Phone was not prepared to accept the FCC decision, however, and sought relief elsewhere. Its refusal to accept AT&T's prerogatives on equipment attachment marked the beginning of the erosion of AT&T's role as primary policy-maker in this area. It began a fundamental recasting of terminal equipment policies and paved the way for the imposition of direct financial losses on AT&T.

AT&T's policy dominance, and the role of the FCC as the enforcer of that dominance, was directly challenged when Hush-a-Phone turned to the courts for relief. In less than one year, the courts overturned the AT&T/FCC decision on the grounds that neither AT&T nor the FCC had established that harm to the system would indeed occur. Notably, the decision came in 1956, the same year that AT&T agreed to an antitrust consent decree that seriously restricted its corporate mandate. AT&T accepted the consent decree in the hope that by revising its restrictive tariffs in small ways, it might restrict the challenges to its hegemony from other companies. This, however, was not to be.

The next, far more influential, challenge came from Carter Electronics, manufacturer of the "Carterphone," which wanted the right to connect its telephones to the AT&T network. Specifically, the case revolved around who would provide telephone service to the lucrative offshore drilling industry in Texas. The more general issue was whether customers had a right to attach their own equipment to the network, and whether there was a corresponding right on the part of manufacturers to make equipment that could access the network directly.[23] Establishing these rights would have introduced competition into the provisioning of equipment and further eroded AT&T's policymaking monopoly.

The Carterphone challenge elicited a wide range of support, support that represented a fundamental break with the past. Encouragement came from a large number of parties with direct and immediate financial stakes in opening up the equipment market. Not only did independent equipment manufacturers individually and through their trade association (the Electronics Industries Association) desire to breach AT&T's monopoly, but large corporate users joined the fray. These included the American Newspaper Publishers Association, the National Retail Dry Goods Association, the American Petroleum Institute, and the Automobile Manufacturers Association, among others.[24] The entry of large business interests, both competitors and users, into telecommunications policy disputes was new in the political dynamic of the issue. These groups had considerable resources to engage AT&T in battle, both before regulators and in more high-profile political venues.

In addition to new interests advocating competition, changes in personnel within government created a less friendly regulatory environment for AT&T. The

FCC shared jurisdiction over the Carterphone issue with the Antitrust Division of the Department of Justice. In this instance, the Antitrust Division's initial action was to advise the FCC of its concerns about AT&T's anticompetitive practices. Carter Electronics, in the meantime, had also filed an antitrust suit in court. Like the Antitrust Division, the court remanded the issue to the FCC for resolution. Making the FCC resolve the issue would appear to have favored AT&T, given the commission's track record, but in the ten years between Hush-a-Phone and the Carterphone challenge, the FCC had changed considerably. In particular, the FCC bureau responsible for advising commissioners, the Common Carrier Bureau, was now headed by Bernard Strassberg, who, according to Temin, "had a healthy suspicion of big business . . . [and] seized the opportunity presented by his bureaucratic position and set out to test his beliefs in the marketplace."[25] The FCC ruled in 1968 that AT&T's traditional tariff restrictions were unreasonable and had to be removed so as to permit customers to attach their own equipment to the network, provided they did no harm. Recognizing the threat posed by the ruling, AT&T struck back. It revised its tariffs to comply with the FCC's decision, but it simultaneously imposed protective coupling devices at the interface between its network and its customers' equipment. Justice Department and other officials interpreted the high standards required of these devices to be little more than an attempt to do indirectly what the FCC had ruled AT&T could not do directly.

In a second and more important response, AT&T sought to broaden public debate over the issue in an attempt to exploit the support of its traditional allies. The company sought to emphasize the substantial losses that might ensue should unrestricted terminal attachment policies be adopted and the likely detrimental effects on consumers. AT&T attempted to persuade the FCC, courts, and the general public that the integrity of its network would be undermined and the quality of telecommunications in the United States debased if liberalization of equipment attachment proceeded. More importantly, it sought to frame the debate in terms of the economic harm that would result. AT&T contended that there would be two major casualties: state regulatory commissions and residential telephone subscribers. AT&T officials argued that the company could lose its terminal business completely as a result of open competition, which would cause a revenue loss of $6 billion. They claimed that most of this loss would be absorbed by cuts in the subsidies that kept residential rates low. The chairman of AT&T stated this position clearly in a 1973 speech before the annual conference of the National Association of Regulatory Utility Commissioners, an association dominated by state regulators and one of AT&T's staunchest supporters:

> we cannot live with the deterioration of network performance that would be the inevitable consequence of "certification" and the proliferation of customer-provided terminals that would ensue from it. No system of certification we can envision—and no interface requirement—can provide a fully adequate alternative to the unequivocal and undivided responsibility for service that the common carrier principle imposes. . . . For where will the burden of increasing interconnection fall? . . . the

> burden will fall on the average customer, the users [sic] of basic services
> that it has been regulatory policy from time immemorial to keep as
> inexpensive as possible. . . . The ultimate effect of this shift is not hard to
> see—a shutoff of service to people with marginal resources.[26]

Encouraged by the Common Carrier Bureau, and goaded by the Justice Department's Antitrust Division, which reminded the FCC that it could take action on its own, the FCC rejected AT&T's arguments and its preferred solution of a protective coupling and ordered the creation of a neutral equipment certification system. Having lost before the FCC, AT&T sought redress in both the courts and through state regulators. But in a court challenge to the FCC's jurisdiction, the commission's authority was upheld, and its rulings immediately preempted state regulation of terminal equipment. Not willing to concede defeat, AT&T sought to appeal the issue to the Supreme Court, where it was once again rebuffed.

While it was fighting in the courts, AT&T also sought legislative protection in its attempt to forestall equipment competition. In 1976, AT&T persuaded 175 members of the House of Representatives and sixteen senators to cosponsor a sympathetic bill, the "Consumer Communications Reform Act," drafted by AT&T with the support of state regulators and its major unions. The legislation would have required the FCC to end its "experiment" in long distance competition, reaffirm AT&T's monopoly, and transfer the issue of terminal attachment policy to individual state regulatory commissions, which had established that they shared AT&T's position. The bill was never passed, but not simply because politicians wanted to buck responsibility to regulators. Rather, and despite initial support from some, the "Bell Bill" aroused considerable congressional opposition, especially from key committee chairs and senior members of Congress. Congress was divided over the issue of competition, with respect to both terminal equipment and long distance service, and so proved incapable of imposing a decision on the FCC.[27]

If Congress was too divided to impose a decision on the FCC, the president was too preoccupied. The debates over the FCC certification program and the subsequent preemption of state commissions were unfolding just as then-Vice President Agnew and then-President Nixon were forced to resign. The institutional chaos at this time reinforced the FCC's autonomy to act, but as Temin notes, this instance of presidential deference to the FCC was part of a new pattern of loss imposition in both the terminal equipment and long distance services arenas. "Executive authority went into retreat," he points out, "and departmental and agency power increased. Even a strong president would have been hard-pressed to keep control of the many power centers in the federal government in these circumstances."[28]

Rebuffed by both the FCC and the courts, unable to persuade Congress to intervene, and with its traditional monopoly in tatters, AT&T sought to cut its losses. It asked the FCC to require telephone subscribers to obtain their primary telephone instrument from AT&T, thereby confining the liberalization process to the extension portion of the marketplace. Even this concession, however, was unacceptable to corporate users, manufacturers, and, most importantly, the FCC, which responded by imposing a neutral certification program for all customer equipment, including residential and business telephone sets, answering machines, and, most significantly, the private branch exchanges used in corporate offices. In a final attack on its equipment monopoly, in 1983 the FCC ruled that AT&T could no longer provide terminal equipment directly to its customers but would henceforth have to provide it through a highly regulated and structurally separate company.

In short, AT&T had lost not only its preferred policy outcome but also the right to structure its own corporate activities and operations without regulatory approval. In addition, AT&T would no longer be able to use its equipment leasing business for regulatory rate-making purposes, as it had since the introduction of regulation. Where once AT&T exercised monopoly power in the terminal attachment field, the FCC was now giving its competitors an advantage, at least for the short term, while new organizational structures and accounting systems were established and gaining regulatory approval.

IN CANADA

Bell Canada, like its American counterpart, also had long-standing contractual restrictions prohibiting the attachment of non-Bell-owned or -authorized equipment to its network. In 1953, Bell's regulator, then the Board of Transport Commissioners, approved regulations giving legal effect to those restrictions. Two years later, a conflict similar to the Hush-a-Phone controversy erupted in Bell Canada's territory. In this case, however, rather than the manufacturer of the device suing Bell Canada or seeking regulatory relief, as had occurred in the United States, Bell Canada successfully sued the manufacturer, seeking to prohibit its use of the device.

The issue reappeared in 1968—coinciding with the American Carterphone dispute—when a witness in a parliamentary proceeding complained that he had been harassed by Bell Canada following his disclosure that he had attached a non-Bell telephone at his residence.[29] Parliament amended Bell Canada's authorizing statute, permitting it to prescribe regulations for the attachment of terminal equipment but only subject to regulatory assessment of the "reasonableness" of the regulations. In 1975, this reasonableness was challenged after Bell ordered a subscriber to remove an automatic dialing device or risk termination of service. The subscriber sought relief from the regulatory agency, now renamed the Canadian Transport Commission (CTC); but, as in the Hush-a-Phone case, the agency ruled in favor of Bell. Bell argued effectively that the statutory amendments permitted but did not require Bell to issue regulations; since Bell did not have any such regulations, their order to the subscriber could not be ruled as unreasonable. The CTC ruled that it lacked jurisdiction, which "thus rendered the amendments to the [Bell] Act meaningless."[30] These events reinforced the conventional perception of the relatively benign character of Canadian telecommunications regulation and strengthened the argument being advanced, particularly from the recently created Department of Communications, that responsibility for telecommunications should be transferred from the transport regulator to the broadcasting regulator.

In the same period, a manufacturer brought another application to the CTC requesting authorization to attach to the telephone system a device that would divert calls from one office to another, which was particularly valuable to companies operating in several time zones. The regulator once again claimed that it lacked jurisdiction over the matter in the absence of Bell regulations. In this case, however, the company was unwilling to accept the regulatory verdict and sought relief in the courts, on the grounds that Bell was wrongly interfering with its business and engaging in wrongful discrimination. It also sought an injunction restraining Bell Canada from any further interference. Bell contended that the regulatory agency, not the courts, had jurisdiction, but the court disagreed, ruling that it had jurisdiction and granting the injunction. The decision was upheld on appeal, and Bell's request to appeal to the Supreme Court was denied in 1978.

These cases were unfolding during a period of major discontent with the Canadian Transport Commission as telecommunications regulator, which appeared to exhibit either the classic characteristics of "capture" of a regulatory agency by the regulated or simple incompetence. For several years, the federal government had indicated its intention to enact new telecommunications legislation that would transfer responsibility for telecommunications away from the transport regulator, which had exercised jurisdiction since 1906, and set forth a new statement of telecommunications policy. Provincial governments, including British Columbia, Ontario, and Quebec, opposed such actions—in part because they did not want to cede jurisdiction to the federal government and in part because they objected to the federal government's specific policy objectives, which included the introduction of competition and the liberalization of the terminal equipment restrictions.[31] The provincial demand was to transfer almost all responsibility for telecommunications regulation from the federal government to the provinces, which did not have significant jurisdiction at the time, a position remarkably similar to that which was being promoted by AT&T in the same period.

Unable to come to any agreement with the provinces and anxious to avoid another major federal–provincial conflict, the federal government opted to proceed in two stages, the first being the transfer of regulatory responsibility and the second being the passage of new policy legislation. In early 1976, in an act described as "simple housekeeping," Parliament legislated the transfer of telecommunications regulation to the Canadian Radio and Television Commission, which was renamed the Canadian Radio-television and Telecommunications Commission, thus keeping the initials CRTC.

Far from being "simple housekeeping," however, the move was a watershed in the development of telecommunications regulation in Canada generally and with respect to the terminal attachment issue in particular. A very intelligent and ambitious lawyer, Charles Dalfen, who had previously taught law and been a senior advisor to the deputy minister of the Department of Communications, headed the telecommunications side of the CRTC. Both the department and, subsequently, the commission and its young staff were eager to put their mark on the telecommunications sector, in order to distinguish themselves from predecessors. Within three months of the jurisdictional transfer, the CRTC renounced the narrow interpretation that its predecessor had given to its mandate. Although there was no statutory change to that mandate accompanying the transfer, the CRTC proclaimed that a new era had arrived:

> The principle of "just and reasonable" rates is neither a narrow nor a static concept. As our society has evolved, the idea of what is just and reasonable has also changed, and now takes into account many considerations that would have been thought irrelevant 70 years ago, when regulatory review was first instituted. Indeed, the Commission views this principle in the widest possible terms and considers itself obliged to continually review the level and structure of carrier rates to ensure that telecommunications services are fully responsive to the public interest.[32]

This new era would have immediate and comprehensive consequences with regard to consumer representation, long distance competition, and terminal attachment. One year after receiving jurisdiction, the CRTC received an application for relief similar to that of Carterphone a decade earlier in the United States. Challenge Communications, a manufacturer and distributor of automatic mobile radio telephones, which could access the telephone system without going through an operator, charged that Bell's regulations were invalid and sought relief from the CRTC. Bell Canada made arguments remarkably similar to those offered by AT&T, to the effect that customer ownership would cause harm to the network, undermine the company's research program, and have a negative impact on the system of cross-subsidies and, therefore, on universal service.

In response to the former claim, Canada's antitrust or competition authority, the Director of Investigation and Research, Combines Investigation Act, intervened and called as witnesses Canadian manufacturers of similar equipment.[33] Witnesses testified that customer ownership posed no such problems and that Bell was only seeking to stifle or preclude competition to its own manufacturing subsidiary, then Northern Electric (subsequently renamed Northern Telecom and then Nortel). In the same period, the Canadian competition authorities issued a report highly critical of the Bell–Northern Electric linkage and recommended divestiture as the appropriate solution. Subsequently, the Restrictive Trade Practices Commission ordered a public inquiry to determine if Bell Canada's corporate structure was in the public interest, an inquiry begun during the CRTC's hearing. Neither the commission nor consumer groups believed the dire threats of economic consequences for subscribers invoked by Bell. In both Canada and the United States, in fact, the fear-mongering by telephone companies on the equipment issue appeared to significantly erode their overall credibility, a factor that influenced subsequent regulatory behavior.

The CRTC was not impressed either by the arguments Bell Canada made in defense of its traditional position or by what it regarded as the company's high-handed behavior toward both its putative competitors and the commission itself.[34] It suspended Bell's tariff regulations; and furthermore, it opted not to confine its decision to the case before it, but instead issued what was immediately labeled as "a competitor's Bill of Rights."[35] It did so by revising the interpretation of the statutory prohibition against "undue discrimination," which had previously meant that the company could not discriminate between customers, to mean that it could not discriminate against its *competitors*. The commission ruled that the law did not permit Bell to confer on itself an undue advantage in relation to its competitors, and it put the onus on the company to justify any attempt to give itself a preference. Moreover, to indicate how displeased the commission was with what it considered to be arrogant behavior by Bell, the CRTC imposed a comprehensive remedial action that in some respects was also punitive. It ordered Bell Canada to provide, not simply the applicant, Challenge Communications, but all competitors, the specifications for mobile telephone equipment that Bell intended to offer its customers.

Subsequent developments illustrate that the political appeal mechanism is often not as available as institutional alignments might make it appear to be. Bell Canada could have appealed the decision to the cabinet but chose instead to launch a judicial appeal against the recasting of the "undue discrimination" prohibition. One reason for not seeking political relief was that Bell and other telephone companies had only recently asked the cabinet to overturn the CRTC's rejection of an application from Canada's domestic satellite company, Telesat, to join the consortium of Canadian telephone companies and thus limit itself to being a "carrier's carrier." The CRTC, in August 1977, four months before its Challenge decision, had rejected the application on the grounds that the agreement was anticompetitive and therefore not in the public interest. This was the first time it had considered competition in its decisions. The decision infuriated both the telephone companies and the Department of Communications, which had received cabinet authorization, prior to the application, for the agreement. The minister and Department of Communications, the cabinet generally, and presumably Bell Canada were all cognizant of the political constraints that existed with respect to the use of the political appeal power, especially under the circumstances of the commission's having so recently being granted jurisdiction. To intervene again would have been seen as undermining the legitimacy of the transfer of jurisdiction, and of the agency itself. Consequently, Bell Canada chose to confine itself to the judicial appeal route, which turned out to be not particularly hospitable. The Federal Court of Appeal, demonstrating institutional deference to specialized agencies on issues of fact and policy—deference that was traditional for Canadian courts—upheld the commission's interpretation and rejected the appeal. And the Supreme Court subsequently refused to allow Bell Canada to appeal the decision.

Even if it had wanted to employ the political appeal mechanism, Bell realized that by the time the judicial appeals had run their course, too much time had passed. Moreover, recognizing that its monopoly over terminal equipment had been seriously breached and that its counterpart, AT&T, was having no greater success in the United States in preventing the introduction of competition in the terminal equipment market, Bell decided to pursue a revised strategy. It initiated in 1978 an application to amend its existing regulations—proposing to permit, on an interim basis while the commission was examining the question, customer attachment of any equipment, except for the primary telephone set, which would have to be leased from Bell. In addition it proposed that the CRTC establish an equipment approval process. The commission, for its part, accepted the first proposal but refused to be involved in approving equipment, which would become the responsibility of the Department of Communications.[36] Moreover, as far as it was concerned, "interim" would be for a very short period indeed; for in 1982 the commission established permanent rules that granted subscribers the right to attach any equipment that satisfied certification requirements, including a primary telephone set. Although Bell Canada's monopoly power over terminal equipment had lasted for close to a century, it had taken a regulator only five years to dismantle it.

Loss Imposition in the Long Distance Market

IN THE UNITED STATES

As with the equipment market, the restructuring of the long distance market, which saw AT&T stripped of its traditional monopoly, was not the result of a coherent, integrated plan imposed on the industry by legislative and executive authorities. Rather, it was a disjointed, incremental process characterized by interorganizational conflicts, competition, and coalitions including regulatory agencies, departmental subunits, and courts, over which elected authorities, in both branches, were unable to impose control. As Brock has noted, over the twenty-five-year period from 1959 to 1984, "at no time was there a comprehensive plan for the phased introduction of competition to long distance."[37] In the battles over competition in the long distance market, however, political authorities, who had not sought to play a major role in the terminal equipment restructuring process, did seek to control the process and its outcomes. But they were unable to do so. This was a case where the multiple veto points available as a result of the American separation of powers worked *against* the defenders of the status quo.

The path toward competition in long distance began in 1959 when the FCC, in response to demands from large corporate users of long distance services and from equipment manufacturers, authorized the former to provide strictly intracorporate microwave long distance service where such service was not generally available.[38] Within three years, a new entrant, MCI, petitioned the FCC for permission to provide a microwave service for corporate clients but only for their private use, on the grounds that such a service would differ from, and therefore not compete with, that currently offered by AT&T. In both proceedings, AT&T, its local operating companies, and state regulators opposed the applications.

Between 1962 and 1967, the FCC deliberated on the MCI application. Commissioners were not initially predisposed to accept it, but, encouraged by Bernard Strassberg, then chief of the Common Carrier Bureau, who narrowly framed the issue as being more of an experiment than a radical new policy on competition, the commission voted 4–3 in favor. Not surprisingly, this led to additional applications to provide similar services. The result was the generalization of the MCI decision in the Specialized Common Carrier Decision in 1971, whereby the FCC explicitly adopted a new policy that permitted private-line long distance systems to connect, by right, to individual customer locations by means of local public systems. What was not permitted, however, was competition in the public long distance market, which was to continue to be AT&T's monopoly.

Having unsuccessfully fought the introduction of competition in the federal regulatory process, AT&T and its allies opted to seek redress in other venues. They initially sought to have responsibility for the issue assigned to state regulatory commissions, which were much more sympathetic to the maintenance of the AT&T monopoly, but the FCC rejected that alternative. AT&T then petitioned Congress to order the FCC to reverse its pro-competitive policies. The result, discussed already, was the "Consumer Communications Reform Act" of 1976. Despite initial political encouragement, after the House Subcommittee on Communications held hearings it was clear that AT&T lacked sufficient political support to stop, let alone reverse, the FCC's "experiment" with long distance competition.

It is often assumed that the multiple veto points of the American system protect the status quo. In the case of long distance competition, however, the status quo had already been overturned by the Federal Communications Commission, supported by both the Antitrust Division of the Department of Justice and by congressional opponents, and Congress was not able to impose a return to the previous status quo. The fragmentation of power within Congress *prevented* action of any kind.

While the FCC "experiment" was under challenge from AT&T, it was also—and surprisingly—contested by one of its primary beneficiaries, MCI. In the mid-1970s, while seeking support from the FCC for its entry into the private service market, MCI developed a service named Execunet, which was essentially a public long distance message toll service. The FCC upheld an AT&T complaint and ordered MCI to cease offering the service, on the grounds that it was contrary to FCC policy. Even MCI's primary ally in the FCC, Bernard Strassberg, supported AT&T's petition. MCI was not prepared to simply comply, however, and was able to use the courts to overrule the FCC. The Appeals Court ruled that the FCC action was procedurally flawed because it had not explicitly stated that AT&T's monopoly in public long distance or MCI's restriction to private service was in the public interest. Consequently, the court ruled that the FCC was not empowered retroactively to so restrict MCI—and the Supreme Court refused to hear the FCC's appeal on the matter. In a related case, and over the objections of both AT&T and the FCC, the courts ordered AT&T to provide MCI with the necessary technical interconnection to provide its new service.

In addition to congress, regulatory agencies, and appellate courts, the battle to end AT&T's monopoly was being fought out in the Department of Justice. In 1974, MCI had filed a private antitrust suit against AT&T and had aggressively lobbied the Antitrust Division in the Department of Justice to file a public suit. The Antitrust Division did file the suit, with AT&T unable to persuade the Watergate-plagued President Nixon to overturn the Justice Department's decision. While the other battles were being fought, the case was being prepared for trial. That trial finally began in 1981.

The suit is revealing about the politics of loss imposition, in that it illustrates how institutional independence can flow not simply from statutory relations but from happenstance. When the Reagan administration took office in 1981, there was considerable pressure from senior administration officials who had been lobbied by AT&T, including the secretaries of Commerce and Defense, to have the president order Justice to drop the suit.[39] The case for continuing with the suit was made by a relatively junior member of the administration, William Baxter, the head of the

Antitrust Division, a "mere assistant attorney general";[40] both the attorney general and his deputy had to recuse themselves from the issue because of prior relationships with AT&T affiliates. Without taking a clear position, President Reagan expressed interest only in seeing whether a compromise solution could be worked out.

The resolution of the antitrust suit resulted from defective hierarchical relations within the Reagan administration and brilliant bureaucratic maneuvering. Pressured by senior White House personnel and officials from other departments, Baxter agreed to join with AT&T to ask the presiding judge to suspend the court case for approximately one year to see if a legislative solution could be developed. Baxter, who did not support the legislative proposal before Congress at the time, was confident that this request would be denied. He believed that the court would feel that its institutional prerogatives were being challenged; moreover, he was certain that when knowledge of this approach became public there would be a political backlash within Congress from those who supported the suit. He was not disappointed. Judge Harold Greene, apparently "appalled and angered" by the request, dismissed it out of hand, stating that "the court has an obligation to deal with this lawsuit under existing antitrust laws, and it will do so irrespective of speculation outside the judicial arena."[41] Greene was backed up by strident political opposition to delay.

Having successfully outmaneuvered external and internal pressures to drop the suit against AT&T, Baxter and the Antitrust Division returned to their preferred option: to litigate AT&T, in Baxter's words, "to the eyeballs."[42] Baxter was now free to do so in reasonable confidence that there would be no further attempt to pressure him to drop the case. His position was strengthened even further when, in September 1981, Judge Greene rejected AT&T's request that the suit be dismissed and did so in a manner that suggested that the government had made a persuasive case that AT&T had indeed violated the antitrust laws. Faced with the court's apparent hostility and their own repeated failure to persuade the Reagan administration to drop the case, AT&T concluded within a few months that it was in "an endless and unwinnable war with Washington."[43] They sought to make peace—which, one year later, took the form of the radical divestiture of their local operating companies from their long distance system. Having fought the introduction and spread of competition in long distance service for over twenty years, AT&T, in a word, surrendered.

IN CANADA

Unlike in the United States, in Canada, beginning in the late 1960s, political authorities, including the prime minister, spoke of imposing "a national communications plan and a national communications policy to integrate and rationalize all systems of competition, whether those of today . . . or those of tomorrow."[44] This plan was to include some provision for competition in both the equipment and long distance markets. The "plan" was never developed, however, because of internal conflicts over its substance and because of serious intergovernmental conflicts when those provinces, which had traditionally regulated and, in three cases, owned their telecommunications systems, engaged in a vigorous battle to protect their jurisdiction.[45] Developing a plan that was premised, at least in part, on the introduction of competition faced formidable obstacles because some in Ottawa, including senior officials in the Department of Communications, preferred to treat Bell Canada, the company that would be most adversely affected by such competition, as a "chosen instrument" for the attainment of public policy objectives.[46]

When a variant of the "plan" emerged in legislation tabled in 1977, competition was not even mentioned as a policy objective. The fact that neither this legislative proposal, nor two reiterations introduced the following year, proceeded beyond first reading was an indication of the government's unwillingness, despite its majority position, to proceed to impose its plan on the telecommunications sector—reflecting, in part, both the unresolved internal conflicts and the continuing intergovernmental disputes over telecommunications policy.

Despite the absence of authoritative legislative guidance, the entrenched opposition from provincial governments and the telephone companies, and the limited executive commitment to the introduction of competition, in 1976 the process of transforming the Canadian long distance market began. Within sixteen years, the same length of time that it had taken in the United States, competition in long distance telecommunications had become the fundamental policy of Canada. As in the United States, though the process was somewhat less Byzantine, the explanation for the imposition of this policy on the telephone companies lies in the relative autonomy of lower-level institutions, encouraged and buttressed by intragovernmental conflicts and coalitions. Not surprisingly, the loss imposition process did not occur without setbacks and stalemates; nevertheless, by 1992, the process of stripping Bell Canada of its long distance monopoly was complete. Throughout this period, despite its status as the "chosen instrument" for the attainment of national policy goals and its presumed political and regulatory clout in Ottawa and in the provincial capitals of Ontario and Quebec, Bell Canada was, with one partial exception, unable to marshal the political support necessary to prevent the loss of its monopoly.

The loss imposition process began almost immediately after the CRTC gained jurisdiction over telecommunications. The commission set out to establish its independent authority vis-à-vis both the government and Bell Canada, through its rejection of the cabinet-approved application of Telesat Canada to join the Trans-Canada Telephone System, of which Bell was the dominant member. The cabinet had to use its appeal power to overturn this decision. In addition, the CRTC radically reinterpreted the statutory prohibition against "unjust discrimination" so as to prohibit Bell from discriminating against its competitors as opposed to its subscribers; Bell was, as we have seen, unable to persuade the courts to overrule the commission on this decision. The CRTC also put everyone on notice that, notwithstanding federal-provincial tensions, it was prepared to regulate Bell Canada's rate agreements with the other members of the TransCanada Telephone System, something that had hitherto been beyond federal regulatory scrutiny. Finally, over the objections of Bell Canada, the CRTC reversed the regulatory policy of refusing to reimburse consumer groups for their regulatory interventions, a policy that had been reaffirmed by its predecessor only two years earlier. Bell was unable to persuade either the cabinet or the courts to overturn that action. Whatever its intrinsic merits, the larger purpose of the policy was to assist the CRTC to develop external support sources in its forthcoming regulatory battles.[47]

The first major challenge to Bell Canada's long distance monopoly came two months after the CRTC acquired its telecommunications responsibilities. CNCP, a joint venture of the two major railroads, Canadian National and Candian Pacific, which offered a private long distance data communications service, asked the CRTC to order Bell Canada to interconnect its local lines to CNCP's private long distance system. (This was the service for which MCI had received regulatory approval in the U.S. in 1968.) CNCP had engaged in private negotiations with Bell Canada for several years; it waited until the CRTC had acquired its new responsibilities because it was confident that its predecessor would have rejected the application out of hand.[48]

Bell Canada, supported by its provincial counterparts, vigorously opposed the application, going so far as to intimidate one of the major banks into withdrawing support for the application. Although it had received no direct policy guidance from political authorities on the question of competition, the CRTC ruled in 1979 in favor of the application, giving the applicant "everything [it] asked for."[49] Although still acting under the 1905 Railway Act, the CRTC based its decision on a very expansive definition of the public interest—although there was no mention of the public interest in its statute, the Railway Act. In making its decision, the commission received strong support from Canadian competition policy authorities, who had simultaneously initiated a separate investigation into the anticompetitive consequences of Bell Canada's relationship with Northern Electric, its equipment arm. The 1979 CRTC decision applied only to the two federally regulated telephone companies and not to the provincially regulated or owned companies.

The cabinet turned down Bell Canada's appeal of the decision. While this could easily be interpreted as passing the buck to the regulatory agency, the decision also reflects the first tentative support of competition at the time. The appeal was filed three weeks after the Conservative government of Joe Clark was sworn into office and then rejected two days later.[50] Given the government's minority position in Parliament, the rejection was surprising, because Bell Canada and its allies were thought to have political strength in their fight against loss imposition. And not only did the government reject the appeal: It indicated, through the new minister of communications, approval of the limited introduction of competition. Bell Canada, despite the support it received from the provincial telephone companies for its appeal, clearly had little political capital within the new government.

Cognizant of MCI's subterfuge, which had undermined the Federal Communication Commission's restricted embrace of competition, the CRTC was adamant in its decision that it had approved only private-line long distance competition; public toll service was to remain a monopoly. When CNCP applied for permission to enter this market in 1983 its application was rejected, and the rationale offered by the CRTC offers an important insight into the institutional aspects of loss imposition. In its decision in 1985, the CRTC concluded that public long distance competition was indeed in the public interest, based on the test it had employed in the earlier decision. It ruled against the application (which, again, was supported by the Canadian competition authorities) on extremely narrow grounds: namely, what it perceived to be the inadequacy of CNCP's financial plan, which, it concluded, was not sustainable in a competitive market.

Although it is possible that the commission was showing deference to political pressure in this decision, evidence suggests that the commissioners were acting solely on their own preferences. Unlike the commissioners who made the 1979 decision, the current set of regulators were far less sympathetic in principle to competition. More importantly, perhaps, they were heavily influenced by what appeared to be the highly negative consequences flowing from the divestiture of AT&T in the United States in 1984. There were widespread complaints in the U.S. of deteriorating service and of significant rate increases for local service. Consumer advocates from the United States, brought as witnesses before the CRTC by the Consumers Association of Canada, which opposed the CNCP application, claimed that universal service was being threatened by the adoption and spread of telephone competition in the United States.[51] They warned, as did the telephone companies, that similar adverse consequences faced Canada if it approved CNCP's application. According to CRTC staff members, who had written a preliminary decision approving the application, the commissioners were "paralyzed with fear" over the potential negative consequences that could flow from approval. So, in order to protect the commission from charges that it was responsible for any such negative consequences, they ordered staff to write a new decision denying the application.[52]

Although we argue that the CRTC rejection of the application to enable public long distance competition reflected the independent preferences of the CRTC commissioners who heard the application, this is not to suggest that there was no political activity relevant to the issue. Immediately prior to the release of the decision, but after it had been written, the Conservative minister of communications warned that the recently elected Conservative government would not tolerate what he characterized as the American style of brutal deregulation of telecommunications.[53] In many respects this was surprising, since the government was at that time engaged in the deregulation of the energy, rail, and airline sectors, mimicking what had occurred in the United States over the previous decade.[54]

Despite the trauma of the 1985 CRTC decision, however, within seven years the commission reversed itself—and in a manner that was as revolutionary as its 1985 decision had been conservative. In 1992, the commission effectively opened up the public long distance telecommunications sector to unlimited competition, a change that illustrates well the role of institutions in the political process.[55] And by 1992, the federally regulated sector had come to include all but two of the provincially owned telephone companies.

The road to open competition between 1985 and 1992 was not one-directional. In fact, for most of the rest of the 1980s, following the CNCP rejection, it appeared that the forces opposed to competition were dominant, and that Bell Canada and the other regional monopolies had successfully overcome any further inroads into their markets. In 1985, the same year as the CRTC decision, the federal minister of communications forged an agreement with his provincial counterparts on a set of principles to govern telecommunications: Notably absent from these principles was a commitment to public long distance competition. No provincial government in this period was strongly in favor of telecommunications competition, and the overwhelming majority were adamantly opposed—as were the telephone companies, their unions, and consumer groups. As a result, the federal Department of Communications sought to remove the dispute from the table. Their inability to do so was a consequence of changes in the institutional structure of decision making within Ottawa along with other institutional factors.

The cabinet decision-making process had changed significantly in the years immediately preceding this period. Beginning with the Trudeau government of 1968, Canada had moved from what Stefan Dupré called a departmental to an institutionalized cabinet system.[56] For our purposes, the most significant aspect of this move was the relative decline in departmental autonomy and the corresponding growth in influence on the part of other departments and governmental units that claimed a stake or interest in individual departmental decisions. Whenever a department had to go to the cabinet for a decision, the affected actors had an opportunity to push their positions; consequently, intragovernmental negotiations became a far more central aspect of the decision-making system in Ottawa. Although the Mulroney governments from 1984 to 1993 were less inclined to follow the more formal decision-making strictures of the Trudeau era, there was no return to the practice of departmental autonomy.

The decision-making system affected the loss imposition process in telecommunications in a number of instances. While agreement was being sought with the provinces on telecommunications matters, for example, the federal government was simultaneously pursuing the Free Trade Agreement with the United States. This provided an opportunity for those within the federal government who favored competition in telecommunications, such as the Competition Bureau and the Office of Privatization and Regulatory Affairs, to urge Canada's negotiators, who were outside the Department of Communications, to adopt a more liberal approach. Similarly, when the minister of communications went to the cabinet in 1987 with a more formal federal–provincial agreement that was not sympathetic to competition, critics were able to lobby other departments, such as External Affairs, Industry, and, especially, Finance, to reject the agreement.[57]

Perhaps the most significant setback for the Communications Department and the CRTC in their opposition to competition came in an extended conflict over competition in the resale of public long distance services, as opposed to the facilities-based competition that had been the core of the 1985 CNCP decision. As part of that decision, the CRTC had concluded that there would be no resale of basic public long distance service; provision of enhanced services, however, was to be permitted. Subsequently, Bell Canada applied to the CRTC for permission, which was granted, to disconnect a service reseller on the grounds that it was offering a service in contravention of the CRTC policy.

Unlike CNCP, however, which accepted its fate, the reseller, CallNet Communications, launched a political campaign against the order by appealing to the cabinet.[58] The subsequent process revealed not only the impact of the institutionalized cabinet system on departmental powers but also some of the weaknesses of the cabinet appeal process as a means of controlling regulatory outcomes. The Department of Communications completely supported the CRTC decision in the appeal; but CallNet, through extensive lobbying efforts, was able to marshal considerable internal political and bureaucratic support on its behalf. Although the Department of Communications was the lead agency in writing the memorandum to the cabinet advising that the appeal should be rejected and the company disconnected, officials in the other federal units and agencies who had been battling the Communications Department successfully persuaded the full cabinet that the recommended course of action was in conflict with other governmental policies and initiatives, such as favoring small business, alleviating regulation, and promoting freer trade. This internal coalition, although not able to win outright, was successful enough to frustrate Bell Canada and its governmental advocates by winning a series of delays for the reseller. After three years, recognizing the potency of the internal opposition, the CRTC reversed itself, over the opposition of Bell Canada, and permitted the resale of public long distance services.[59] In short, rather than the concentration of power we associate with the parliamentary system, it was the internal dissension, and the bureaucratic politics that resulted, which produced the additional losses imposed on Bell Canada.

While these internal battles were being waged, the fight over telecommunications competition was being fought in the courts as well, and the outcome of this conflict would have major implications for the loss imposition process. The courts became a major player because CNCP had applied to the CRTC in 1982 for an order against Alberta Government Telephones (AGT) enabling it to impose the same private-line interconnection that the CRTC had granted it in 1979 with respect to the two federally regulated telephone companies. For the previous eighty years, the question of the extent of federal vis-à-vis provincial jurisdiction over telecommunications had never been tested, particularly since the governments involved preferred, in the words of two commentators, "to let sleeping dogs lie."[60]

AGT's refusal led CNCP to try to wake the "sleeping dogs," which it did with the tacit support of the federal minister of communications of the day, Francis Fox. Fox was angry with the provinces over their obstinacy on communications matters in intergovernmental negotiations over the previous decade. Apparently unable or unwilling to persuade his cabinet colleagues to directly challenge the jurisdictional stalemate, Fox encouraged CNCP to litigate the matter.[61] CNCP was preempted, however, by AGT, which directly challenged, before the Federal Court of Canada, the authority of the CRTC to hear CNCP's application. Two years later the Court ruled that the federal government had exclusive jurisdiction over the intraprovincial as well as interprovincial services of all the major telephone companies, because they constituted interprovincial undertakings. The effect of the ruling was somewhat mitigated because it also provided that such federal jurisdiction did not extend to the three prairie provincial telephone companies until the federal government legislatively removed their crown immunity. The Supreme Court upheld the lower court's decision in 1989, with the result that, after almost two decades of federal–provincial conflicts over jurisdictional issues, private action had radically extended the jurisdiction of the federal government.[62]

The 1992 CRTC decision to permit unlimited public long distance competition was almost a foregone conclusion, albeit one that came about as a result of a wide range of institutional battles. Intergovernmental conflict had lost its salience, since the provinces had largely been stripped of their jurisdiction and therefore would not bear the responsibility for any negative consequences flowing from competition. Moreover, the much anticipated adverse consequences expected to flow from pro-competition decisions in the United States did not materialize, thus removing another obstacle. For its part, the CRTC, having been rebuffed repeatedly by the cabinet in its attempts to shut down a reseller as a result of intragovernmental conflict, decided to give up the battle on that aspect of competition by announcing in 1991 that it would permit unlimited reselling of public long distance voice service. The CRTC commissioners were all new, and they did not regard the 1985 decision as a binding precedent. Consequently, although Bell Canada and the other telephone companies maintained their opposition to competition, there were no significant political forces that could be marshaled to forestall it. By 1992, although the actual scope of permitted competition was unexpected, especially insofar as the successful primary applicant was concerned, there was almost an air of easy predictability as to the decision the CRTC would make. The telephone companies were stripped of their long distance monopoly—a loss made possible by a succession of institutional forces, and the battles they waged, over the previous seven years.

CONCLUSIONS

The processes of loss imposition in telecommunications were remarkably similar in Canada and the United States. Despite the obvious differences in the two countries' institutional and political configurations, decision making on telecommunications matters in both countries fell largely to lower-level bureaucratic actors (especially regulatory agencies) and courts, rather than elected officials: members of Congress in the United States and cabinet officers in Canada. While there was a temporal difference in how the two countries handled deregulation, with the American process beginning first and Canadian decisions lagging behind American ones by almost a decade until recently, elected political actors in both countries played strictly secondary roles in these conflict-ridden processes and had little direct impact on their outcomes. In both countries the loss imposition process was episodic and halting. Decisions were made in multiple lower-level institutions, and, despite the size of the losses involved, they were not the product of a conscious, coherent policy design on the part of any particular set of actors.

The result of restructuring in both the terminal equipment and long distance markets was, at least initially, great losses and considerable pain for the telecommunications companies involved, AT&T and Bell Canada. The losses were economic in that both companies lost considerable market share in both segments; and both companies were also stripped of their long-standing institutional dominance as de facto policymakers for their respective telecommunications systems. Where once, like Caesar, they did "bestride the narrow world like a Colossus," in a few short years they were progressively humbled, and deprived of stature and status in the policymaking arena. Moreover, their losses were not time-specific but cumulative and ongoing, as they had to develop, learn, and inculcate radically new approaches to cost management, marketing, and customer relations. The relatively short tenure of the most senior management in both companies over the past two decades is one indication of how difficult and painful this learning experience has been and, perhaps, continues to be.

The pain imposed was also psychological, because the two companies' seemingly deeply rooted corporate missions were dismissed as self-serving or no longer relevant and ultimately cast aside, like any other consumer good that had lost its value or its novelty. Although they tried repeatedly, ultimately the companies failed to redefine the stakes and the stakeholders so as to either preempt or minimize their losses.

Again, in the end, the processes by which losses were imposed and the consequences for the incumbent telecommunications companies were remarkably similar. Distractions and fragmented authority in both countries kept politicians from controlling the processes of restructuring. Reforms emerged, instead, from microinstitutions with limited jurisdictions, overlapping responsibilities, and relative autonomy. In both cases, the core preferences of the major corporate entities carried little weight, while far smaller competitors manipulated their entry into new markets.

In light of the similarities in processes and losses in the two countries, can we conclude that macroinstitutional differences—at least with respect to the telecommunications sector and the specific set of losses analyzed—have little impact? One possibility that must be considered, given the temporal difference in the loss imposition processes between the two countries, is that the telecommunications sector exhibited a transnational learning process, whereby Canada simply emulated the American example. This hypothesis is not without some attractiveness, particularly given the fact that the two telecommunications systems are perhaps the most integrated in the world—sharing, for example, a common numbering system and common backup transmission capacities. The large presence of American corporations in the Canadian economy and the often ritualistic desire on the part of some Americans to export that which they think is wise and admirable reinforce the potential power of such an explanation.

Nevertheless, the American model in fact had little direct impact on the Canadian process.[63] Since the American restructuring and loss imposition started first, it did make contestable, as it were, in both countries and elsewhere, assumptions, practices, and policies that had long been *un*contested—indeed, accepted as articles of faith. But there was much more than policy emulation at work in Canada. In fact, at particular stages, the American example was invoked in terms of what *not* to do—and this led to dilution or suspension of the change process.

In the process of loss imposition, institutions both did and did not matter. They mattered in that they established the battlefields and the contours for the conflicts and influenced the strategies and tactics of the combatants. They did not matter at the level of macro–political institutions, however, in ways that were hypothesized. Pal and Weaver refer to the conventional assumption that the "fragmentation of power and multiple veto points are generally thought to make it relatively easy for groups in the United States to defend status quo policies against efforts to impose losses."[64] This was not the result with regard to telecommunications reform in the United States, however, inasmuch as the then-largest corporation in the United States was unable to prevent, or even significantly slow or dilute, the process of having fundamental, long-term losses imposed on it.

In both Canada and the United States, public decision makers were able to impose what we have described as maximum pain because of the microinstitutional similarities the countries shared, despite the macroinstitutional differences between them. The loss imposition process in both countries was characterized by the inability of those threatened with loss to employ access to either concentrated power centers or multiple veto points. Politicians were not simply engaged in blame avoidance by letting regulatory agencies and courts take responsibility; rather, as AT&T and Bell Canada discovered, institutional power was widely dispersed and diffused. Multiple veto points—long assumed to be effective, particularly in the U.S.—lost their potency. The loss imposition process in both countries resulted from actors with limited jurisdictions, most notably regulatory agencies and courts, that nonetheless proved capable of having significant impact. There were overlapping jurisdictions, competitive battles and coalitions, displacement and transference.

In many respects, the institutions that mattered in the telecommunications loss imposition process reflected the characteristics of the telecommunications system itself in the "age of the Internet." The effective institutions in both countries typified a "network of networks": highly differentiated, nonhierarchically organized, responsive to multiple mandates, and bordering on the anarchic. In telecommunications today—and, we would suggest, in the telecommunications loss imposition process as it unfolded—the institutional center does not, and cannot, "hold," because there is no center. The telecommunications loss process was characterized by a "centerless institutional system"—a system in which there is not one but many centers of power.[65] Sometimes such centers collaborate; sometimes they compete. Unhappy with the results in one place, participants turn to other venues. And so the process of loss imposition in telecommunications policy, characterized as it was by significant losses imposed on traditionally powerful actors, may reflect the fundamental convergence of microinstitutional aspects of the Canadian (Westminster) parliamentary and the U.S. congressional models and may suggest a value to focusing on these areas of convergence in order to understand loss imposition not just in telecommunications policy but in other cases where concentrated business interests are at stake.

NOTES

1. The corporate structures of the Canadian and U.S. telecommunications systems differed in that Canada lacked a corporate equivalent of AT&T Long Lines, and Bell Canada was confined to operating in only two provinces, Ontario and Quebec. The discussion of telecommunications restructuring in Canada in this chapter is limited to how it affected Bell Canada, which traditionally accounted for more than 50 percent of overall national telecommunications revenues. For a description of the structure of the Canadian telecommunications industry as it began the restructuring process, see

Richard Schultz and Alan Alexandroff, *Economic Regulation and the Federal System* (Toronto: University of Toronto Press, 1985), chap. 3.

2. After the restructuring process had been largely completed, the overall profitability of the incumbent individual firms in both countries grew rather than decreased. This growth does not undermine our claim, however, that restructuring entailed painful costs for some and an apprehension of costs on the part of others.

3. The third market segment, and the one most recently opened to competition, is local telephone service, not discussed in this chapter.

4. Neither firm had 100 percent market share prior to restructuring, because in both countries there were independent telephone companies with territorial monopolies providing local service with which AT&T and Bell Canada had interconnecting agreements to provide long distance service. These companies did not compete, however, with either of the dominant firms.

5. This latter possibility was the central thesis, for example, of Dan Schiller, *Telematics and Government* (Norwood, NJ: Ablex Publishing, 1982), and, to a lesser extent, Robert Horwitz, *The Irony of Regulatory Reform: The Deregulation of American Comunications* (New York: Oxford University Press, 1989).

6. William R. Lederman, "Telecommunications and the Federal Constitution of Canada," in H. Edward English, ed., *Telecommunications for Canada: An Interface of Business and Government* (Agincourt, ON: Methuen, 1973), pp. 339–87.

7. For an excellent overview of these conflicts, see Peter Russell, *Constitutional Odyssey: Can Canadians Become a Sovereign People?* 2d ed. (Toronto: University of Toronto Press, 1993).

8. See Hudson Janisch and B. Romaniuk, "Canada," in Eli Noam, Seisuke Komatsuzaki, and Douglas A. Conn, eds., *Telecommunications in the Pacific Basin: An Evolutionary Approach* (New York: Oxford University Press, 1994).

9. An excellent example of congressional action to force a regulatory reversal was the FCC's response to congressional opposition to its initial subscriber line charge in the early 1980s. See Richard Vietor, *Contrived Competition: Regulation and Deregulation in America* (Cambridge, MA: Harvard University Press, 1994), pp. 215–17.

10. Christopher Armstrong and H. V. Nelles, *Monopoly's Moment: The Organization and Regulation of Canadian Utilities, 1830–1930* (Philadelphia: Temple University Press, 1986); Gerald W. Brock, *The Telecommunications Industry: The Dynamics of Market Structure* (Cambridge, MA: Harvard University Press, 1981); Vietor, *Contrived Competition*.

11. Armstrong and Nelles, *Monopoly's Moment*, 185.

12. Robert E. Babe, *Telecommunications in Canada: Technology, Industry and Government* (Toronto: University of Toronto Press, 1990).

13. Schultz and Alexandroff, *Economic Regulation and the Federal System*.

14. Gerald W. Brock, *Telecommunications Policy for the Information Age* (Cambridge, MA: Harvard University Press, 1994); Vietor, *Contrived Competition*.

15. Elizabeth E. Bailey, "The Evolving Politics of Telecommunications Regulation," in Noll and Price, eds., *A Communications Cornucopia: Markle Foundation Essays on Information Policy* (Washington, D.C.: Brookings Institution Press, 1998).

16. Milton Mueller, *Universal Service: Competition, Interconnection and Monopoly in the Making of the American Telephone System* (Boston, MA: MIT Press, 1997); Richard Schultz, "Old Whine in New Bottle: The Politics of Cross Subsidization in Canadian Telecommunications," in Globerman et al., eds., *The Future of Telecommunications Policy in Canada* (University of Toronto, Institute for Policy Analysis, 1995); Richard Schultz, "Universal Service/Universal Subsidies: The Tangled Web," in David Conklin, ed., *Adapting to New Realities* (Ivey School of Business, University of Western Ontario, 1998).

17. Mueller, *Universal Service*, 150.

18. Quoted in Alvin von Auw, *Heritage and Destiny: Reflections on the Bell System in Transition* (New York: Praeger, 1983), p. 45.

19. Peter Temin, *The Fall of the Bell System: A Study in Prices and Politics* (Cambridge, MA: Cambridge University Press, 1987), p. 59.

20. Temin, *The Fall of the Bell System*, 7.

21. Quoted in Brock, *Telecommunications Policy for the Information Age*, 83.

22. Vietor, *Contrived Competition*, 191.

23. Richard E. Wiley, "The End of Monopoly: Regulatory Change and the Promotion of Competition," in Harry M. Shooshan III, ed., *Disconnecting Bell: The Impact of the AT&T Divestiture* (New York: Pergamon Press, 1984), p. 28.

24. Horwitz, *The Irony of Regulatory Reform*.

25. Temin, *The Fall of the Bell System*, 41.

26. Quoted in Brock, *Telecommunications Policy for the Information Age*, 89.

27. For a more detailed discussion of the congressional battles and of Congress's inability to pass new telecommunications legislation in this period, see Georgia Persons, *The Making of Energy and Telecommunications Policy* (New York: Praeger, 1995).

28. Temin, *The Fall of the Bell System*, 108.

29. Lawrence Surtees, *Pa Bell: A. Jean de Grandpre and the Meteoric Rise of Bell Canada Enterprises* (New York: Random House, 1992), p. 114.

30. Gordon Kaiser, "Competition in Telecommunications: Refusal to Supply Facilities by Regulated Common Carriers," *Ottawa Law Review* 13 (1981).

31. Canada Minister of Communications, "Proposals for a Communications Policy for Canada: A Position Paper of the Government of Canada" (Information Canada, 1973), p. 14. The intergovernmental conflicts are described in Schultz and Alexandroff, *Economic Regulation and the Federal System*, and Richard Schultz, "Partners in a Game without Masters," in Robert Buchan et al., eds., *Telecommunications Regulation and the Constitution* (Montreal: Institute for Research on Public Policy, 1982).

32. Canadian Radio-television and Telecommunications Commission (CRTC), "Telecommunications Regulation—Procedures and Practices" (July 20, 1976), p. 3.

33. Kaiser, "Competition in Telecommunications," 430.

34. CRTC, "*Challenge Communications v Bell Canada*," Telecom Decision CRTC 77-16.

35. Kaiser, "Competition in Telecommunications," 97.

36. CRTC, "Bell Canada—Interim Requirements Regarding the Attachment of Subscriber-Provided Equipment," Telecom Decision CRTC 80-13.

37. Brock, *Telecommunications Policy for the Information Age*, 103.

38. Horwitz, *The Irony of Regulatory Reform*; Temin, *The Fall of the Bell System*; Schiller, *Telematics and Government*.

39. Perhaps one of the best narratives on this episode is found in Steve Coll, *The Deal of the Century: The Breakup of AT&T* (New York: Atheneum, 1986), pp. 211–53.

40. Coll, *The Deal of the Century*.

41. Ibid., 256, 234.

42. Ibid., 188.

43. Ibid., 267.

44. Canada Minister of Communications, *House of Commons, Debates*, February 27, 1969, p. 6,016.

45. On these battles, see Schultz, "Partners in a Game without Masters," and Schultz and Alexandroff, *Economic Regulation and the Federal System*.

46. Lawrence Surtees, *Wire Wars: The Canadian Fight for Competition in Telecommunications* (Scarborough Canada: Prentice-Hall, 1994), p .58.

47. See Richard Schultz, "Winning and Losing: The Consumers' Association of Canada and the Telecommunications Regulatory System, 1973–1993," in G. Bruce Doern et al., eds., *Changing the Rules: Canadian Regulatory Regimes and Institutions* (Toronto: University of Toronto Press, 1999), pp. 174–200.

48. Surtees, *Wire Wars*.

49. Ibid., 93.

50. Ibid., 95.
51. For a summary of the American experience during this period which reflected these fears, see Hudson Janisch, "Winners and Losers: The Challenges Facing Telecommunications Regulators," in W. T. Stanbury, ed., *Telecommunications Policy and Regulation: The Impact of Competition and Technological Change* (Montreal: Institute for Research on Public Policy, 1986).
52. Personal communication.
53. Marcel Masse, "Looking at Telecommunications: The Need for Review" (notes for an address to the Electrical and Electronic Manufacturers' Association, Montabello, Quebec, 20 June 1985).
54. Richard Schultz, "Regulating Conservatively: The Mulroney Record," in Andrew Gollner and Daniel Saleé, eds., *Canada under Mulroney: An End of Term Report* (Montreal: Vehicule Press, 1988). On the deregulation of these industries in the U.S., see Martha Derthick and Paul J. Quirk, *The Politics of Deregulation* (Washington, D.C.: Brookings Institution Press, 1985).
55. CRTC, "Competition in the Provision of Public Long Distance Voice Service and Related Matters," Telecom Decision CRTC 92-12.
56. J. Stefan Dupré, "Reflections on the Workability of Executive Federalism," in Richard Simeon, ed., *Intergovernmental Relations* (Toronto: University of Toronto Press, 1985).
57. Personal communication.
58. This analysis draws on T. D. Hancock, "Regulated Competition: Resale and Sharing in Telecommunications," *Media and Communications Law Review* 2 (1991): 257–96, and on confidential interviews with participants conducted by Schultz as part of a larger project on the politics of communications in Canada.
59. CRTC, "Resale and Sharing of Private Line Services," Telecom Decision CRTC 90-3.
60. See Robert J. Buchan and Christopher C. Johnson, "Telecommunications Regulation and the Constitution: A Lawyer's Perspective," in Robert J. Buchan et al., eds., *Telecommunications Regulation and the Constitution* (Montreal: Institute for Research on Public Policy, 1982), p. 120.
61. Surtees, *Wire Wars*, 111.
62. *Alberta Government Telephones v. Canadian Radio-television and Telecommunications Commission*, 2 SCR 225 (1989).
63. Richard Schultz and Mark Brawley, "Telecommunications Policy," in G. Bruce Doern, Leslie A. Pal, and Brian W. Tomlin, eds., *Border Crossings: The Internationalization of Canadian Public Policy* (Toronto: Oxford University Press, 1996).
64. N. Luhmann, *The Differentiation of Society* (New York; Columbia University Press, 1982), cited in R. A. W. Rhodes, *Understanding Governance* (Buckingham, U.K.: Open University Press, 1997).
65. Here we borrow and extend a point made by N. Luhmann in *The Differentiation of Society* (New York: Columbia University Press, 1982), cited in R. A. W. Rhodes, *Understanding Governance* (Buckingham, UK: Open University Press, 1997).

5

TOBACCO CONTROL

DONLEY T. STUDLAR

IN ONE OF THE FEW DIRECT COMPARISONS OF TOBACCO CONTROL POLICY IN
Canada and the United States, Kagan and Vogel pose the question "Which is more
remarkable?":

> Twenty-five years after their hazards have been widely publicized,
> cigarettes—highly addictive, extremely dangerous, unnecessary
> products—continue to be sold and consumed in huge volumes.
>   Within the past decade or two, despite the objections of economically
> powerful tobacco industries and of millions of smokers (a sizable
> proportion of the electorate), virtually every democratic industrialized
> nation has enacted laws that curtail cigarette advertising, impose new
> taxes on cigarettes, and prevent smoking in public places where citizens
> have long been accustomed to light up at will.[1]

This amounts to asking, Is the glass half-full or half-empty?—or, in the context of
this chapter, is it more remarkable that governments have imposed so many losses
on tobacco interests or, perhaps, so few, as scientific information about the hazards
of tobacco use has proliferated over recent decades and public concern has grown?
    Tobacco control, both through the budget (taxes and subsidies) and through reg-
ulation, is a pertinent contemporary issue to which to apply the concept of loss
imposition. In both the United States and Canada, tobacco control has developed

into a major public policy controversy over (only) the past forty years, and at an accelerating pace over the past two decades. It involves the attempt of a long-established policy community to preserve as much of the status quo as possible in the face of a rising tide of information and public concern about tobacco use as a health hazard—especially in its most popular form, cigarette smoking. Groups have formed around the issue, at several levels of government and across industrialized societies, to challenge established policies of tobacco promotion with minimal regulation. Public health and citizen antitobacco groups have lobbied for governments to take action against tobacco usage and those who benefit from it. They refer to a tobacco "pandemic," a public health hazard that dwarfs others of recent vintage.

The history of public policy in regard to tobacco, however, is permeated with contradictions, U-turns, and difficult choices, perhaps even more than with respect to public policy on other issues. This is because of the economic, social, and cultural importance of tobacco, and because of the political interests that have formed around it.[2] The relatively short history of governmental policy on tobacco control vis-à-vis the entrenched interests defending a legal product economically beneficial to substantial sectors of the country make it a critical issue for the politics of loss imposition. This study examines how governments in Canada and the United States have attempted to impose losses on tobacco economic interests—which are both industrial and agricultural but also geographically concentrated—in favor of the more diffuse interests of public health and revenue enhancement, and with what success. What institutional factors, we ask, help explain what was done—and what was not done?

THEORY: LOSS IMPOSITION, INSTITUTIONS, AND POLICIES

R. Kent Weaver and others have argued that loss imposition is a key concept for the study of public policy.[3] Politicians are well aware that affected political interests are more sensitive to losses from public policy decisions than to potential gains from such decisions, thus they attempt to avoid and minimize loss imposition in a variety of ways. These methods of avoiding loss imposition may be as significant as alternative political goals, such as making good public policy or claiming credit.

Weaver[4] outlines eight blame-avoiding strategies for avoiding, delaying, deflecting, or diffusing responsibility for loss imposition: (1) agenda limitation (avoiding blame by keeping potentially costly choices from being considered); (2) redefining the issue (developing new policy options that diffuse or obfuscate losses); (3) throwing good money after bad (providing resources so as to prevent constituencies from suffering losses); (4) passing the buck (deflecting blame by forcing others to make politically costly choices); (5) finding a scapegoat (deflecting blame by blaming others); (6) jumping on the bandwagon (deflecting blame by supporting a politically popular alternative); (7) circling the wagons (diffusing blame by spreading it among as many policymakers as possible); and (8) "Stop me before I kill again" (keeping credit-claiming opportunities that conflict with policy preferences from being considered).

In addition to the adoption of strategies for blame avoidance in loss imposition, other factors may also be important. Institutionally, each political system generates its own opportunities for making decisions that impose losses on organized interests while, if possible, avoiding blame. The "deadlock of democracy"[5] produced in the United States by the separation of powers, checks and balances, and the lack of cohesive political parties is renowned for making new policy, especially against established interests, difficult to enact. (The last factor means that individual leaders and legislators lack the protective cover of unified party positions for blame avoidance on controversial issues.) More recent accounts, however, have argued that there is more evidence of policy change in the U.S. than earlier studies found. In particular, the variety of institutional venues for policy conflict, including state and local ones as well as those at the federal level, encourage affected interests to "venue-switch" in an attempt to secure decisions favorable to their interests.[6] If loss imposition is avoided in one venue, then perhaps another, in which blame avoidance is not so overriding a consideration—the judiciary, for instance, or a level of government in which the opposition is at a disadvantage—may be willing to do so, even if the target changes somewhat in the process.

Whereas, in theory, clearer policy choices, involving more loss imposition and less blame avoidance, might occur in parliamentary systems, empirically this has not always been found to be the case.[7] Parliamentary systems come in different varieties, of course, and it is a mistake to think only in terms of the prototypical British model. Coalition governments may be especially prone to avoid loss imposition for fear of potential repercussions, either immediately or at the next election.[8] But even the policy choices of single-party majority governments on the British model, including Canada's, may not be definitive and loss-imposing. Though party discipline does provide a cover for individual legislators, a party entirely responsible for the conduct of government may be reluctant to risk its reputation and even its political fate by imposing losses on powerful interests. Moreover, especially in a political system such as Canada's, where the lines of political accountability do not culminate as unambiguously in Parliament and cabinet as they once did, there are also opportunities for venue-switching. In Canada, the courts, especially the Supreme Court, have become an increasingly important actor since the patriation of the Canadian constitution, and especially the addition of a Charter of Rights and Freedoms, in 1982.[9] In a progressively decentralizing federal system, the provinces have become more significant policy actors as well.

In addition, the institutions that facilitate different policy outcomes, including loss imposition, may not be the primary ones, parliamentary or presidential/congressional, but rather secondary or even tertiary ones. In the Weaver–Rockman classification, "first-tier" institutions refer to the basic differences between parliamentary/cabinet and presidential/congressional central government systems, fusion of powers versus separation of powers. Second-tier institutions consist of variations within the basic presidential or parliamentary systems, based on a threefold division of dominant single-party rule, party government, or shared (coalition) governance and on different electoral rules, especially the distinction between single-member district plurality and proportional-representation electoral systems.

Third-tier institutions include judicial review, federalism, bureaucratic character-istics, and secondary features of legislatures, such as organizational rules and bicameralism. Other, noninstitutional influences are political conditions and poli-cymakers' goals, socioeconomic conditions, and policy legacies. Weaver and Rock-man[10] conclude that second-tier institutions, especially electoral systems, and such third-tier institutions as judicial review, federalism, and bicameralism, along with socioeconomic factors and policy legacies, may be more influential in determining policy outcomes than primary institutions. The question of which institutions facilitate loss imposition, then, is an empirical one.

Some types of *policy* may also be more amenable to loss imposition than others. While analysts of comparative politics have traditionally focused on the differential impact of political institutions, more recently some have adopted Lowi's[11] lead in ex-amining whether it is political institutions or policy types that make more of a dif-ference in how issues are processed across countries.[12] While a coherent theory of how policy types relate to loss imposition has not yet been developed, there is the possibility of such a theory emerging as more policies are examined across more countries. Studying loss imposition in automobile insurance reform within Cana-dian provinces and U.S. states, Lascher[13] finds support for Weaver and Rockman's claim that parliamentary institutions make it easier to impose losses.

Loss imposition in tobacco control involves a complex mix of interests: some diffuse, some geographically concentrated into regions. The major contenders, at least in recent years, are the tobacco industries, on the one hand, and antitobacco campaigners from citizen activist and public health organizations on the other. The former are regionally concentrated in terms of production facilities, even if diffuse in marketing; the latter are diffuse. Other interested parties include tobacco grow-ers (heavily concentrated) and tobacco retailers (diffuse). Smokers are, of course, diffuse, as is the nonsmoking public, although the incidence of smoking does vary somewhat by province and state. Because of their special legal status in both coun-tries, aboriginals are involved to a degree as a locally concentrated interest. Most of the concentrated interests operate through regional economic and political groupings in both countries. Industrial and agricultural interests, for instance, tend to overlap in the same areas.

THE CONTEXT OF TOBACCO CONTROL IN CANADA AND THE UNITED STATES

Canada and the United States provide a good test for the impact of institutions on tobacco control. Canada is a federal parliamentary system with a fusion of legisla-tive and executive power, but with an expanding scope for the judiciary in policy formation; the United States is a federal presidential system, with separation of powers and checks and balances. Both have centralized bureaucracies under po-litical direction, but the United States has, in addition, semi-independent regulatory commissions, not entirely under the jurisdiction of the elected political executive. The two countries share the single-member district plurality electoral system, but since the 1920s Canada has continuously had three to five parties represented in the federal House of Commons, often on a regional basis, while in the United States the two umbrella parties have withstood all putative challengers since the Civil War.

Canadian parties are cohesive whereas U.S. parties lack consistent internal discipline, even if the two parties have increasingly become ideologically polarized in recent years. In Canada the two traditional major parties, the Liberals and the Progressive Conservatives, have been considered "brokerage" parties lacking major ideological differences, and even the New Democratic Party (NDP) has moderated its socialism over the years. But the two new parties represented in the federal parliament reform in the 1990s, the Bloc Québécois from Quebec and Reform Alliance from the West, are more ideological as well as regionally based.

U.S. legislators use their individual constituency profile independent of party to help achieve a high re-election rate, irrespective of countrywide electoral trends.[14] On the other hand, Canadian federal legislators, bound by party identity, see their re-election prospects ebb and flow with partisan tides and have one of the lowest re-election rates among Western democracies.[15]

Despite discernible and persistent differences, especially in their people's willingness to trust government to act in the public interest, Canada and the United States share a large array of values and, if anything, are becoming even more convergent in recent times.[16] Each country is the other's most important trading partner, and there is also considerable population contact between the two countries through travel, media, and other forms of communication. Furthermore, their proximity and shared use of a dominant language means that events in one country are readily transmitted to the other, albeit there is more attention paid to the United States in Canada than vice versa ("the longest one-way mirror in the world"). It is also relatively easy for policy communities, both governmental and nongovernmental, to communicate with each other across the border.

Thus there is considerable "lesson-drawing," both positively and negatively, across this international boundary. Even if most of this is done by Canada, based on knowledge gained about developments in the United States,[17] there is also increasing evidence that lesson drawing occurs in reverse as well.[18] Presumably lessons about loss imposition are also transferable. Certainly this was attempted by United States tobacco companies in their media campaign against the Senate version of the National Settlement in 1998, when they employed former Canadian officials to testify about the problems associated with raising tobacco taxes, based on the smuggling crisis in Canada in 1993–94.

There are considerable similarities between the two countries, too, with respect to the social and economic context of tobacco control policy. Since 1971 Canada's health care system has been based on universal public insurance, while the United States relies on a mixture of financing but primarily on private insurance; nevertheless, health problems, spending, and outcomes are broadly similar.[19] In addition, over the past quarter-century both countries have reoriented public policy toward more preventive health measures, including tobacco regulation.[20] Many epidemiological studies based in the United States have Canadian components, as does at least one U.S. National Cancer Institute program designed to enable communities

TABLE 5-1
Tobacco and Smoking Data, U.S. and Canada

	Canada %	United States %
Smoking Prevalence		
Mid-1960s	50	42
Mid-1980s	38	30
1999	25	22
Lung Cancer, Age-Standardized Annual Death Rate per 100,000		
Males (early 1990s)	82.9	85.9
Female (early 1990s)	31.5	36.9
Total Deaths Attributed to Smoking (1995)		
1995	46,000	529,000
	(23% of total)	(24% of total)
Economics of Tobacco		
Arable land (hectares), 1985	39,893	278,430
1995	31,140	277,630
	(0.1% of total)	(0.1% of total)
World production share, 1990	1.1%	9.8%
Employment in		
tobacco manufacturing, 1990	5,000	49,000
	(0.4% of total)	(0.4% of total)
Annual cigarette production, 1994	49,000,000	725,600,000

Sources: National Population Health Survey, 1996, Statistics Canada; Office of Smoking and Health, Centers for Disease Control and Prevention, 1999; World Health Organization, 1997; Canada Tobacco Use Monitoring Survey, 1999.

to organize to combat tobacco use.[21] Although smoking spread earlier in the United States than in Canada, it also began to decline earlier there.[22] Even in the face of more stringent taxes and federal regulations on cigarettes since the mid-1980s, Canadian tobacco consumption is still somewhat higher than in the United States.[23]

Tobacco agriculture plays a similar role in the economies of the two countries as well. In Canada, 90 percent of tobacco agriculture is concentrated in the province of Ontario, with small amounts in Quebec, New Brunswick, and Nova Scotia (and formerly in Prince Edward Island). Ontario is the fourth largest tobacco producer among states and provinces in North America, after North Carolina, Kentucky, and Tennessee. Tobacco manufacturing is also similar in terms of its share of the respective economies—though, as with tobacco agriculture, it is on a far larger scale in absolute terms in the U.S., and the U.S. has a bigger share of the world tobacco market, including exports. (See table 5-1.) In each country, manufacture of tobacco products is dominated by a few producers. In Canada, tobacco manufacturing is more concentrated than in the U.S, with the headquarters of all three major companies in Quebec.

With tobacco production playing a significant role in the economies of the two most populous provinces, there is a regional dimension to the politics of tobacco in Canada, as there is in the United States, where tobacco production is concentrated in a few states in the Southeast. Fully 93 percent of tobacco agricultural production comes from six states (North Carolina, Kentucky, Tennessee, South Carolina, Virginia, and Georgia), and the top six tobacco manufacturing states (North Carolina, Virginia, Kentucky, Georgia, New York, and Tennessee) account for about 98 percent of the total.[24] Despite other similarities, in neither country has the population acquired a taste for the other's cigarettes; only a tiny portion of consumption is imported from the other country. In summary, once the relative scales of the two countries are taken into account, there are more similarities than differences in the sociology and economics of tobacco production and consumption in the U.S. and Canada.

TOBACCO TAXATION, REGULATION, AND LOSS IMPOSITION

The politics of tobacco control in the two countries have had periods of divergence and convergence. Table 5-2 presents a detailed comparison of federal action in the two countries on a range of tobacco control measures. This section will concentrate broadly on two policy areas of tobacco control: budgetary allocations, especially taxation of cigarettes and subsidies to tobacco agriculture, and regulatory policy with regard to tobacco sales and advertising. The United States took the lead in early regulation of tobacco through officially stated concern, health warnings, and broadcast bans while at the same time maintaining nominally static taxation rates. Canada soon followed in all of these respects, albeit with a "voluntary" industry code, until the early 1980s, when it began to raise federal taxes on cigarettes and other tobacco products; thereafter it established incentives for farmers to leave tobacco agriculture and attempted to regulate tobacco sales and advertising in the late 1980s in ways that went far beyond anything tried in the United States. Then, in the mid-1990s, the United States began to make similar attempts to regulate tobacco and to impose some modest tax increases on cigarettes.

How can loss imposition capacity help explain the roles of the two federal governments on tobacco control—embracing both regulatory policy and taxes—since the early 1960s? After the first decade of concentrated attention to tobacco regulation, Friedman[25] argues, the United States was the clear leader over Canada in governmental control of tobacco products (as indicated, e.g., by loss imposition) because semi-independent regulatory commissions, such as the Federal Trade Commission and the Federal Communications Commission, were willing to impose health warnings and to limit the impact of tobacco advertising, which, in turn, prompted Congress to act. In Canada the major outcome of policy deliberation was an informal agreement between the federal government and tobacco companies not to advertise on television and radio and a voluntary health warning on cigarette packages. By the mid-1990s, however, these relative positions had been reversed, with Canada the clear leader over the United States in tobacco control,[26] arguably without a major change having occurred in the political institutions in either country or in the

TABLE 5-2
De Facto Federal Laws and Regulations Concerning Tobacco, by Type, Country, and Year

	U.S.	Canada
Advertising		
Regulatory restrictions on specific practices	1938–71 (25+ times)	
Broadcasting banned	1970	1971 (voluntary)
Broadcasting counteradvertising allowed	1967	1967
Health warnings on advertisements	1972 (billboards, periodicals)	1975 (text,voluntary) 1984 (billboards, voluntary)
Advertising banned		1988(X)
Advertising restricted	1996 (X), 1998 (S)	1997
Sponsorship restricted	1998 (S)	1988
Sponsorship banned	1996 (X)	1997
Only preexisting company logos allowed	1996 (X)	
Trademarks on non-nicotine products banned	1996 (X)	1988 (X)
Trademarks on non-nicotine products restricted	1998 (S),	1997
Cartoon characters banned	1998 (S)	1997
Real or fictional persons and animals banned		1997
Lifestyle advertising banned		1997
Material misrepresentations banned	1998 (S)	1997
Paid film promotions banned	1998 (S)	1997
Black-and-white ads	1996 (X)	
Sales		
Sales to age 18 and above only	1996 (X)	1993
Vending machines restricted	1996 (X)	1993
Vending machines banned		1997
Kiddie packs banned	1996 (X), 1998 (S)	1993
Single-cigarette sales banned		1997
Free samples banned	1996 (X)	1988, 1997
Free samples restricted	1998 (S)	
Mail-order sales restricted		1997
Discounts and prizes banned		1971 (voluntary) 1988, 1997
Environmental Tobacco Smoke		
Airline no-smoking (domestic)	1987 (two-hour flights, partial) 1989 (comprehensive)	1987 (two-hour flights) 1988 (comprehensive)
Airline no-smoking (international)	1994 (partial)	1994 (partial)
Federal government facilities (comprehensive)	1997	1989
Residual Regulatory Authority, Contents Disclosure		
Broad executive authority over tobacco	1996 (X)	1997
Tar and nicotine levels on packages	1970 (voluntary)	1975 (voluntary)
Toxic contents on packages		1988, 1993, 2000
Tar and nicotine contents on ads	1970 (voluntary), 1984	1975 (voluntary)
Additives reported to government agency	1984	1988

TABLE 5-2

De Facto Federal Laws and Regulations Concerning Tobacco, by Type, Country, and Year *(continued)*

Taxation		
Taxation increased	1983, 1990, 1997	1981–89, 1991 1996, 1999, 2001
Taxation reduced due to smuggling		1952, 1953, 1994
Special levies on tobacco companies	1998(S)	1992, 1994, 1997, 2001
Taxation on purchases in duty-free shops		2001
Agricultural Alternatives		
Transitional funds for tobacco farmers	1998 (S)	1987
Litigation against Tobacco Companies		
Smuggling	1999	1999
Health care cost recovery	1998 (S), 1999	
Federally Funded Program for Community Action	1987, 1991, 1998	1994 (X), 2001
Health Warning Labels		
First warning labels	1965	1971 (voluntary), 1988
Attribution of warning	1964	1971 (voluntary), 1997
Warning labels' language strengthened	1970, 1985, 1996 (X)	1989, 1990, 1993, 1997, 2000
Rotating warning labels	1985	1989
Warning labels on front of packages		1989
Black-and-white warning labels only		1993
Graphic warnings on packages		2000
Federal preemption laws on warning labels	1965, 1970	
Package warnings; no liability protection		1988
Warning labels on noncigarette products	1986 (smokeless only) 2000 (cigars)	1988 (all)
Package Insert Warnings		1988 (authorized) 2000 (implemented)
Education	*several years*	*several years*
General Learning Tools		
First official expression of concern re: tobacco and health	1957	1963
First legislative committee investigation and hearings	1958	1969
Subsequent major legislative investigation and hearing	1994	2000
Chief medical officer reports	1964–2000 (26 times)	1964
Other major agency reports	1993	1983
Healthy public policy	1980	1974

Note: Except where noted, dates are based on passage of legislation, not on implementation dates, which vary. (X), overturned by court ruling or otherwise abandoned; (S), national policy resulting from state lawsuits.

economics of tobacco. In 1990 the Sixth World Conference on Smoking and Health in Perth, Australia, passed a resolution commending the Canadian government for "its leadership in improving the health of Canadians and for setting an outstanding example in comprehensive tobacco control policy."[27] By contrast, a 1994 report by the U.S. public health advocacy group Coalition on Smoking or Health contended that Congress and most federal agencies had done little to combat tobacco use.[28]

In a comparison of the two countries at the time, Kagan and Vogel[29] argue that it was a combination of political institutions and political culture, but especially the latter, that allowed Canada to leap ahead in tobacco regulation. Adopting the traditional perspective that Canada has a more collective political culture, which allows for a greater degree of governmental action once a problem is identified, they contend that Canadian leadership in the "second wave" of tobacco control policy in the 1980s and early 1990s was due to this cultural characteristic, supported by the capacity of Canadian political institutions to impose policy once the cabinet agrees. In contrast, in the United States the second wave of tobacco control policy relied more on initiatives taken by state and local governments than on federal government policy.

But the comparative policy situation only a few years later did not reveal such sharp differences. Canada has suffered some setbacks in tobacco control.[30] In early 1994 the federal Liberal government, in concert with five Eastern provinces, reacted to a tobacco smuggling crisis by lowering taxes on cigarettes by almost 50 percent, an episode discussed later. In 1995 the Supreme Court of Canada overturned the major piece of legislation regulating tobacco, the Tobacco Products Control Act (1988). After considerable delay, new federal legislation, the Tobacco Act of 1997, was enacted, but the tobacco companies immediately challenged that act in court. In addition, the federal government later delayed implementation of the stringent rules on tobacco company sponsorship of cultural and sporting events, a major source of revenue for those activities and a relatively more important outlet for tobacco company advertising in Canada than in the United States. In 2000, though, Canada again became a world leader in one dimension of tobacco control: introducing graphic package warnings on cigarettes. Moreover, there has been more frequent and wider-ranging tobacco control activity in the provinces in recent years as well.[31]

If Canada's previous international leadership role in tobacco control has been compromised, however, the position of the United States in tobacco control has risen. The Food and Drug Administration (FDA), supported by President Bill Clinton, declared in 1996 that it had regulatory power over tobacco as a drug, a position that it had previously been reluctant to assert. This strongest-ever federal executive commitment to tobacco control was challenged in the federal courts by the tobacco companies, however, and in 2000 the U.S. Supreme Court ruled 5–4 against current FDA authority over tobacco.

That comparatively unusual U.S. way of making public policy, through litigation, subsequently asserted itself again.[32] As a growing number of U.S. states sued tobacco companies to recover the costs of state public health care programs necessitated by the effects of smoking, many of them joined a "national settlement" with the industry to provide a resolution, one involving regulation as well as finance. Since it included a specific legitimization of the disputed FDA authority over tobacco as well as protection for the companies from further individual lawsuits, the settlement required approval by Congress for enactment. Once it reached the U.S. Senate, however, citizen activist and public health groups, encouraged by the White House, managed to get the required amount of the financial payment from tobacco companies raised from $369 billion to $517 billion. Declaring that the price was too high, the tobacco companies turned against the deal, and the agreement failed to pass for lack of a 60 percent majority to cut off debate. Nevertheless, in the wake of this collapse, four individual states—Mississippi, Florida, Texas, and Minnesota—made individual out-of-court settlements with the tobacco companies worth $41 billion, and in November 1998, a "master settlement agreement" included the remaining forty-six states and some municipalities for a total of $206 billion, along with agreed limitations on tobacco advertising and lobbying activities. Since these agreements did not include FDA authority or litigation limits, they did not require congressional approval.

In 1999 the U.S. Justice Department sued the tobacco companies for recovery of *federal* health care costs. There were also two modest federal tax increases in the 1990s. In summary, by the late 1990s the United States, led by the FDA and the states but with presidential support, had moved toward greater control over tobacco.

Federal Taxation: Canada and the United States

In examining long-term federal budgetary action on tobacco through taxation and subsidies, what is most apparent is that there is greater willingness to impose losses on the tobacco industry and on tobacco agriculture in Canada than in the United States. Despite the tax reductions in Canada in 1994 and the tax increases in the United States in 1989 and 1997, over an extended period Canada has been more willing to impose tax increases on tobacco products. Since the mid-1980s, taxation has been a major instrument of revenue enhancement as well as tobacco control—and one which, it has been argued, was quite successful in reducing smoking in Canada until 1994.[33] In fact, Cunningham[34] contends that Michael Wilson, finance minister in the Progressive Conservative government of Brian Mulroney (1984–93), did more to limit smoking than any other individual in Canada. Nevertheless, the relative impact of taxation versus regulation on tobacco consumption continues to be a subject of debate.[35]

Despite the steep increases in tobacco taxation in the 1981–93 period, when adjusted for inflation and disposable income, cigarettes in Canada were cheaper in 1993 than in 1949. Nevertheless, the tobacco companies were not pleased with a federal tax increase of 360 percent (from C$0.42 to C$1.93) from 1985 to 1993, and they expressed their discontent on several occasions.[36] The Mulroney government, however, was more concerned with deficit reduction—and, eventually, with reducing teenage smoking—than with placating the industry. By 1994 Canadian federal and provincial taxes accounted for an average of almost 70 percent of the cost of cigarettes.

The attempt to reduce cigarette consumption through taxation was compromised by a growing smuggling problem—stemming from the large difference in the price of cigarettes between Canadian provinces, especially the populous ones of

Ontario and Quebec, and nearby U.S. states—which reached its zenith in early 1994. By 1991 cigarette manufacturers and retailers were encouraging tobacco purchasers to send preprinted protests about taxation to their federal and provincial governments. Cigarette prices in Ontario, at an average of C$4.80 (U.S. $4.08) per pack, were nearly twice as high as in the bordering U.S. states of Minnesota, Michigan, and New York, where average prices ranged from C$2.19 to C$2.48 (U.S. $2.12, $1.86, and $2.09, respectively; at 1991 exchange rates), owing largely to lower state taxes on tobacco.[37] Even though Americans do not consume large quantities of Canadian-blend cigarettes, those can be legally exported to the United States without incurring Canadian taxes. As prices rose in Canada in the late 1980s and early 1990s, largely as a result of tax increases, exports of Canadian cigarettes to the United States rose from less than three billion in 1990 to seven billion in 1991, ten billion in 1992, and 18 billion in 1993, constituting fully one-third of the total Canadian output.[38] Many of these cigarettes found their way back to Canada, especially through the Mohawk St. Regis–Akwesasne reserve on the border between New York and the Canadian provinces of Quebec and Ontario. Although the legal price of cigarettes in Quebec was similar to that in Ontario, widespread smuggling led to estimates that some two-thirds of the sales in Quebec were of contraband cigarettes at less than half the legal price.

By February 1994 the problem had reached a crescendo, and the Liberal federal government of Premier Jean Chrétien—urged on by the Quebec Liberal government, which was expecting a tough provincial re-election fight against the separatist Parti Québécois later in the year—decided to combat the smuggling problem. The federal government rejected calls from several provincial health ministers, the public health community, and antitobacco activists to reimpose a severe but short-lived cigarette export tax that the previous Conservative government had employed in 1992 to combat smuggling. It was widely suspected that the federal Liberals did not want to enact a policy that might cost tobacco-related jobs in Quebec and subject their provincial counterparts to criticism from the separatists. Instead, the two governments formulated a complicated plan to lower tobacco taxes by two-thirds through matching cuts, which put additional pressure on other provinces in the region vulnerable to smuggling. Ontario and other provincial governments east of Quebec grudgingly agreed to lower taxes. (Newfoundland lowered taxes only in Labrador.) Although there were some offsetting taxes imposed on tobacco companies to placate health-conscious interests, effectively this was a 50 percent cut in the price of cigarettes in the participating provinces, including the two most populous ones, Ontario and Quebec. This policy reversal led to a plateau in smoking reduction—and, by some estimates, to an increase, especially in youth smoking.[39]

By 1997 the cost of cigarettes in Ontario was 62 percent of the January1994 price and, at C$2.99 per pack, was lower than in any bordering province or state, owing to increases in prices and taxes in the United States as well as to the Canadian tax reductions (even though 31 percent of the 1994 reduction had been restored) and the decline of the Canadian dollar against its U.S. counterpart. In the wake of the Master Settlement Agreement (MSA) leading to price increases on U.S. cigarettes, the price gap between the eastern provinces of Canada and their U.S. neighbors has widened. Despite further federal-provincial coordination of tax increases in 1999 and 2001, cigarette prices in Ontario and Quebec are still below that of any U.S. state after the MSA, which led to price increases of 33 percent in the first year. Meanwhile, in New York State several officials of RJR–MacDonald Inc. pleaded guilty to complicity in the earlier smuggling operations. In 1999 the Canadian federal government filed a civil lawsuit in the United States to recover the tax revenues from contraband cigarettes, which it alleged had been lost through the illegal conspiratorial activities of tobacco companies, principally RJR–MacDonald Inc. The judge ruled, however, that a foreign government could not file such a suit in the U.S.

Despite the U.S. federal deficit problems of the 1980s and 1990s and various proposals to increase cigarette taxes dramatically, in the United States federal taxation has lagged. Since 1951 there have been only three modest legislated federal tax increases on cigarettes, two of which involved delays in implementation: $0.08 in 1982 (implemented in 1983), $0.08 in 1989 (phased in at $0.04 each in 1991 and 1993), and $0.15 in 1997 (implemented in two phases, $0.10 in 2000 and $0.05 in 2002). Several states, however, have raised their cigarette taxes more steeply, with Massachusetts the highest at U.S. $1.51 per pack. Altogether, however, federal and state taxes in the U.S. accounted for only 30.5 percent of the price of cigarettes in 1997, down from 48.7 percent in 1955.[40] Even if one considers the cost of the MSA as a de facto tax increase, the U.S. still taxes cigarettes at a relatively low rate compared with other Western democracies. Only the very highest-taxation states, such as New York, even approach the taxation levels of the lowest Canadian provinces, such as Ontario. Proposals for substantial increases in federal cigarette taxes, notably the $0.75 per-pack increase proposed as part of President Clinton's National Health Security Plan in 1993 and an increase of $1.25 per pack in the National Settlement, have foundered with the collapse of those bills. In both instances, opponents portrayed these plans to a tax-resistant public as major tax increases.

Agricultural Subsidies: Canada and the United States

In Canada, tobacco farming, while subsidized in various ways (including research and marketing boards) by the government, does not receive direct price supports as in the U.S. As part of the government's comprehensive tobacco control policy and to assist passage of the Tobacco Products Control Act, the Tobacco Diversification Plan was announced in 1987, to provide financial compensation to farmers exiting tobacco production and to aid in developing alternatives to tobacco agriculture. These programs have had some success in reducing the number of farmers dependent on tobacco (whereas a comparable reduction has not occurred in the United States, see table 5-1).[41] Even in Ontario, tobacco is only the eighth leading cash crop in an agricultural economy that is itself less than 2 percent of the total provincial Gross Domestic Product. While there has been no concerted effort to drastically reduce tobacco agriculture in Canada, there is little indication of substantial public support for helping tobacco growers—in contrast to the United States, where their problems generate more sympathetic governmental policies at both federal and state levels.

U.S. federal agricultural subsidies for farmers to grow tobacco for a guaranteed price as long as they stick to their federal allotment have continued even in the wake of agricultural reforms.[42] In fact, one of the major concerns of tobacco-producing states and their representatives in Congress has been to get the industry to help tobacco farmers, both through an individual agreement between manufacturers and growers[43] and through use of the MSA money. Tobacco companies have agreed to extend some help to affected farmers, which helps maintain grassroots political support for the industry. Tobacco-producing states have also, in some instances, used their settlement money to assist tobacco farmers.[44]

Regulation: United States and Canada

After the introduction of health warnings and the ban on broadcasting of cigarette advertising in the United States between 1965 and 1970, federal government skirmishing with the tobacco industry resulted in little substantial regulation. During the 1980s, Surgeon General C. Everett Koop, the government's chief medical officer but one without an agency to direct, became the most prominent antismoking campaigner, declaring in 1982 that "cigarette smoking is clearly identified as the chief preventable cause of death in our society." Reports on the health effects of environmental tobacco smoke, especially the Surgeon General's Report of 1986, led to a series of measures restricting smoking in government buildings and on common carriers coming under federal law, culminating in an international airline treaty with Canada and Australia in 1994.[45] After a herculean struggle, in 1984, four stronger, more specific health warnings on cigarette packages were legislated, but they were neither as blunt nor as prominently displayed as the warnings in Canada that emerged from 1988 and 1992 enactments.[46]

U.S. federal government agencies have provided financial aid and incentives to the states for community-based programs to reduce tobacco use and prevent underage purchase of tobacco products.[47] In 1994, prominent investigative hearings on the tobacco industry were held by the House Subcommittee on Health and the Environment, chaired by Representative Henry Waxman of California. Although tobacco company executives denied that cigarettes were damaging to health and the Justice Department investigated possible antitrust violations in this episode, no legislation or prosecutions resulted. The 1994 "report card" on federal smoking prevention policies issued by the Coalition on Smoking or Health gave Congress, the White House, and most federal agencies grades of D or F.[48]

Until President Clinton announced in 1995 that the FDA would claim authority over tobacco as a drug and proclaim rules regulating its sale, there was no attempt at a comprehensive federal tobacco control policy. Nevertheless, long-proposed Department of Labor (DOL) regulations on environmental tobacco smoke in all workplaces, supported by Clinton's Secretary of Labor, languished. The otherwise antitobacco Clinton administration shrank from supporting the DOL initiative, partially because of lack of strong support from organized labor.[49] The National Settlement and the MSA were supported by the Clinton administration, although it did not take a principal role in any of the relevant negotiations. Subsequently, and despite congressional opposition mainly from Republicans, the Clinton Justice Department sued tobacco companies for Medicare costs. The Bush administration has indicated that it would attempt to settle this lawsuit out of court.

Since 1971, the Canadian federal government had relied on a voluntary agreement among tobacco companies not to broadcast advertisements and to provide a health warning on cigarette packages. In the early 1980s federal and provincial health ministers, who shared authority over health policy, began to discuss more restrictive regulatory action regarding tobacco products.[50] The issue rose to prominence on the federal political agenda in 1986 with the publication of New Democratic Party MP Lynn McDonald's private member's bill restricting smoking in public places and federally regulated workplaces and providing for regulation of tobacco under the Hazardous Products Act. The growing public health lobby threw its support behind McDonald's bill.

After negotiations with the tobacco industry over a voluntary agreement to deal with smoking prevention concerns collapsed, the Conservative government, led by Health Minister Jake Epp, introduced its own bill in 1987 providing for a comprehensive policy of tobacco regulation, which became the Tobacco Products Control Act (TPCA) (1988). This act prohibited advertising of tobacco products, banned special promotions for tobacco products (free distribution, discount coupons, gifts, or lotteries) and the use of tobacco trademarks on other products, and mandated prominent health warnings (originally four different ones, the largest in the world at the time) and lists of toxic constituents on packages, but did allow use of tobacco company corporate names (but not brand names) in the sponsorship of entertainment events. Despite some government reservations, McDonald's bill, the Nonsmokers' Health Act, became law as well.[51] This was followed in 1993 by the Tobacco Sales to Young Persons Act, which restricted sales to minors. After the Supreme Court of Canada struck down the TPCA in 1995 on narrow constitutional grounds, the Tobacco Act (1997) restored federal government regulation over tobacco but permitted advertising in "adult" venues and allowed for some other, limited exceptions; it also contained a provision enabling the government to enact further tobacco control measures under executive authority without having to go through the legislative process. This is similar to the authority claimed by the Food and Drug Administration in the United States.

Furthermore, Canadian federal regulations, unlike those in the United States, do not preempt potentially stronger provincial action in some areas.[52] Any provincial law regulating tobacco products is permissible as long as it does not weaken the requirements of Canadian federal laws. As in the United States, provincial laws regarding tobacco vary considerably.[53]

COMPARING LOSS IMPOSITION IN TOBACCO CONTROL

When it comes to actual loss imposition on tobacco companies and agriculture, the record of the Canadian federal government is generally superior to its counterpart in the United States. Despite the tax rollback in 1994, federal cigarette taxes have risen more in Canada over the past forty years than in the United States. Although government assistance has not been eliminated, Canada has instituted more active programs to reduce the size of tobacco agriculture. Tobacco regulation, through such policies as strong, prominently displayed health warnings on cigarette packages and permissive rather than preemptive federal policies vis-à-vis provincial legislation, have been consistent since the late 1980s, despite some legal setbacks.

Ironically, even though many observers have increasingly characterized Canadian federalism as highly decentralized—and as perhaps even deserving of the description "confederation"—it is the United States in which, despite federal preemption, the states have set the pace with respect to tobacco control. This is true in terms of both taxation and regulation and was most recently apparent in litigation, the MSA, and tax increases in 2002. Despite much public information and research money spent, the U.S. federal government, both legislative and executive, has done relatively little in a definitive way in terms of direct policy adoption with respect to tobacco control, whether one considers subsidies to tobacco farmers, aid to tobacco companies seeking markets abroad, taxation, or regulatory measures. What the U.S. federal government *has* been able to do is provide assistance to tobacco control efforts at other levels of government and in other venues, through public information, health promotion, and funding—as in the Surgeon General's reports, the Waxman Committee hearings, local capacity-building financial assistance through the Department of Health and Human Services, and presidential support for the FDA rule and the National Settlement (see table 5-2). These efforts have aided loss imposition; but, with the removal of FDA authority over tobacco, the United States still lacks a comprehensive tobacco control policy at the federal level. The de facto "comprehensive" policy is the MSA, but it has significant loopholes, especially as compared with its abortive predecessor, the National Settlement. Despite some compromises and setbacks, especially on federal taxation, Canada still has a comprehensive tobacco control policy, albeit a more modest one than envisioned in the early 1990s.

In terms of loss imposition on geographically concentrated versus diffuse constituencies, the two countries have exhibited both similarities and differences. Both have found it easier to impose losses on geographically diffuse rather than geographically concentrated constituencies. The principal geographically diffuse constituencies are smokers and tobacco retailers, and in both countries smokers have increasingly been curbed and taxed, with little effective response from them. This is due, in large part, to the fact that many smokers consider themselves victims rather than supporters of tobacco, as is shown by the booming industry in "quitting" techniques. Where feasible, of course, smokers and their survivors have also sued tobacco companies as responsible for their health problems. Smokers' rights organizations in both countries rely heavily on tobacco industry funding to support them and have been notably unsuccessful, especially on the federal level.

Similarly, retailers are a diffuse constituency, although tobacco often amounts to a substantial portion of total sales, especially for small vendors. Thus they are sometimes difficult to organize in opposition to federal and state or provincial regulations and taxation. Nevertheless, tobacco retailers in Quebec played a considerable role in the smuggling crisis of 1994 by selling cut-rate cigarettes in defiance of the law, and retailers have also sometimes organized effectively in other provinces and states. This case illustrates that tobacco retailers may be more effective in avoiding loss imposition if they can use geographical concentration as leverage for their economic concerns.

Geographically concentrated agricultural interests in tobacco have been more successful in opposing loss imposition in the United States than in Canada. In both countries, tobacco production has been declining. United States tobacco manufacturers, with their worldwide markets, have increasingly relied on supplies from growers abroad. But no Canadian province approaches the levels of the tobacco-producing U.S. states in terms of economic dependence on tobacco: Tobacco accounts for just 6 percent of agricultural receipts in Ontario, as compared to 24 percent in Kentucky, 15 percent in North Carolina, 13 percent in South Carolina, and 12 percent in Tennessee.[54] There has been less public sympathy for tobacco farmers in Canada and more attempt to move them into other crops than in the U.S. A substantial electoral constituency for tobacco agriculture simply does not exist at any level of government in Canada—in contrast to the United States, where such a constituency holds impressive sway in many municipal governments and a few states (as reflected in the low level of tobacco product taxation in major producing states)—and even in the U.S. Congress.

Since the share of the economy devoted to tobacco agriculture and manufacturing is similar in the two countries, this is one situation where political institutions make a difference. Canada has only ten provinces, whereas the United States has fifty states; in some of those states, tobacco is a major interest. Similarly, on the federal level, the institutions of the U.S. presidential system, acting especially through the Congress, have acted to protect tobacco interests from loss imposition. If one considers only the top six tobacco-producing states, they account for twelve U.S. senators, or 12 percent of the total, in a body that is fully coequal with the House of Representatives; if one takes the sixteen significant tobacco-producing states, there are thirty-two senators with ties to tobacco agriculture. Because of the threat of the filibuster (unlimited debate), increasingly it takes sixty senators to pass controversial legislation. Furthermore, traditionally many of the senators from tobacco states were able to accumulate vast amounts of seniority in a one-party Democratic South, thus enabling them to gain powerful Committee chairmanships—including Agriculture, in which they were in a position to kill proposed legislation endangering the interests of their powerful constituents. Without the necessity to vote in line with the party leadership's wishes—even those of the president, if he were of the same party—these powerful, entrenched senators could protect tobacco against attempts to tax and regulate it. Moreover, they had similarly powerful counterparts in the U.S. House of Representatives, even if that body is substantially larger (435 members). Even though some of these political characteristics, such as the one-party South and the allocation of committee chairs through seniority in the House of Representatives, have been altered, others, such as a lack of party cohesion mandated by party leaders and the importance of serving local constituency interests, have continued.

In Canada matters are very different. The Senate is a weak body, and party, not constituency, is the most powerful impetus. Furthermore, it takes only a bare majority of those voting to pass legislation, and committee chairs are not powerful, independent actors. In the Canadian House of Commons, majority party cohesion is based on what the prime minister and cabinet desire. Although there is more scope for voicing constituency interests than in the Senate, voting along party lines is paramount. Furthermore, committees have little power to stifle legislation, and, until 2002, the government chose committee chairs, rewarding its loyal supporters.

Thus, in the U.S. presidential system, there are more potential veto points than in the Canadian parliamentary one. The relative outcomes for tobacco agriculture have in part resulted from that difference, even as some of the political conditions have changed over the years. Tobacco agricultural interests have still been able to maintain influence, even as Republicans have increasingly been elected to political office in the relevant states. That influence is related to the system of campaign finance in the United States, which relies heavily on almost unlimited private funding, a fungible partisan resource. Some interests even contribute to both parties in a race to be sure of having access to whichever one is elected.

Within the federal government, the serious regulatory and tax initiatives on tobacco in the United States have all come from the executive branch, either the semi-independent regulatory agencies such as the Federal Trade Commission and the Federal Communications Commission, other offices such as that of the Surgeon General, the Food and Drug Administration, the Treasury Department (with respect to taxes), or even, in recent years, the president himself. Congress's role consistently has been to protect tobacco interests, agriculture and industry, from loss imposition by the executive branch and, more recently, from potential losses slated to be incurred under the National Settlement with the states, once the agreement became too costly for the tobacco companies to bear. Congress has preempted and limited agency authority, reduced tax demands, and, in general, compromised tobacco control when it has not killed it outright.

Of course, tobacco interests have considerable power in the U.S. executive branch as well. The secretary of agriculture, for one, has acted to protect tobacco farm subsidies, as occurred in the Carter administration when the secretary of health, education and welfare, Joseph Califano, suggested that they be phased out. When Califano embarked on a campaign to reduce smoking in 1978, he found that loss imposition on tobacco interests constituted a formidable challenge: "The anti-smoking campaign generated more political opposition than any other effort I undertook at HEW."[55] The Commerce Department and the cabinet-level Office of the U.S. Special Trade Representative have promoted markets for U.S. tobacco products abroad, especially in less economically developed countries, irrespective of the status of tobacco in other areas of the executive branch. Although this practice has been curbed somewhat in recent years by the Doggett Amendment, which limited such promotions except where there is discrimination among tobacco products of the same type, it has not been eliminated.[56]

In Canada, there is more of a sense of cabinet and party unity. If a federal or provincial executive decides to impose losses on tobacco, then the legislature is unlikely to be of much assistance to tobacco interests resisting those losses. This is especially true with respect to taxation losses imposed through the budget, since Parliament can reject an executive budget only at the cost of voting the government out of office, as occurred in 1980 with the minority Conservative government of Premier Joe Clark. Thus, battles on taxation in Canada are largely intraexecutive ones, and tobacco interests have only limited institutionalized lobbying power, primarily through the Ministry of Agriculture in the federal and Ontario governments. This power has often proved to be of little moment against the combined power of the Finance Ministry, searching for revenue, along with the Health Ministry. In order to persuade the cabinet, tobacco interests have typically needed to appeal to concerns beyond their immediate economic ones. The smuggling crisis of 1994 allowed tobacco companies to reverse a previous loss imposition through changing the focus of the issue. Cigarette taxes were no longer just a budgetary or smoking reduction issue, but one that had become complicated by aboriginal rights, the political situation in Quebec, and "law and order" concerns.[57] The issue became redefined in the minds of several political decision makers, and tobacco interests were able to reverse previous losses.

The government could have relied on an export tax on cigarettes, such as had been temporarily employed in 1992, or export stamps, invoked in 1992 but never properly implemented.[58] Instead of imposing losses solely on the tobacco companies and others who benefited from the smuggling, however, the government chose to capitulate to the pressure to lower taxes and cigarette prices, while providing some compensatory measures such as increased tobacco control funding for antitobacco forces.[59] Even though a reimposed export tax as well as a surtax on company profits were part of the policy package, this was more than offset by the federal and provincial tax reductions.[60]

Why was a policy more restrictive on tobacco companies not adopted? The 1992 export tax had excited vehement tobacco company opposition and was lifted after two months. The tobacco manufacturers had, among other things, threatened to move their operations to another country and had taken limited steps toward doing so. The combination of potential economic losses, the breakdown of law and order represented by smuggling, the possibility of armed confrontation with aboriginals, and the effect of all of these on the forthcoming Quebec provincial election were too much for the Liberal government to hold firm. In this case, it was the diffuse health care community suffered loss imposition.

Furthermore, even after passage of the Tobacco Act in 1997, the government delayed implementation and backtracked on sponsorship restrictions. Proud of its fiscal rectitude since taking office in 1993, the Liberal government has been reluctant to assume public financial support for arts and sporting events theretofore dependent on tobacco company support.

Canadian tobacco interests can alter, postpone, and, if an election is imminent, possibly even kill legislation by extending debate. They may also, as with the Tobacco Act, be able to win delays or amendments. For tobacco companies, time is literally money if regulations or taxes can be delayed. But in all of these instances, they have to get executive support rather than rely on the legislature to block or amend a government bill. In fact, in 1998 the Liberal government blocked a legislative initiative that would have imposed additional losses on the tobacco industry. Bill S-13, the Tobacco Company Responsibility Act, was proposed by Senator Colin Kenny in clear emulation of a similar policy linking tobacco taxes to antitobacco campaigns in California. An annual fee paid by Canadian tobacco manufacturers would have been devoted to tobacco reduction campaigns conducted by the federal government. Although professing sympathy for the bill's purpose, the government had it ruled out of order in the House of Commons on the basis that any revenue bill had to originate there rather than in the Senate. After Senator Kenny subsequently introduced similar bills, the government decided to preempt his initiative by providing more money for tobacco control in Canada through its newly announced Federal Tobacco Control Strategy. The concentrated power of the Canadian parliamentary system means that the key institution, as the source of policymaking and target for lobbying, is the executive. Tobacco companies have many powerful friends in high places in Canada, but once the battle in the executive is lost, they have had to rely on the judiciary—as a venue for *legal* action—not the legislature.

CONCLUSIONS: INSTITUTIONS AND LOSS IMPOSITION IN THEORETICAL PERSPECTIVE

How persuasive is the case for first-order political institutions—that is, parliamentary-presidential differences—as a major influence on loss imposition capacity in tobacco control in Canada and the United States? Following Lascher,[61] I shall provide a summary sketch of possible alternative explanations for policy differences. As he indicates, comparisons of the U.S. and Canada with respect to the same policy have the advantage of yielding sharp and consistent differences vis-à-vis the test variable (parliamentary versus presidential institutions) as well as similarities vis-à-vis many control variables.

First, there are several factors that qualify as third-tier similarities.

(1) Similar social and economic configurations for tobacco production and consumption.

(2) Similar cultural values and incentives for politicians. Recent evidence suggests that previous differences in the political cultures of the two countries are eroding and have largely disappeared. Thus, there is a mix of free enterprise/balanced budget/individual rights/public health values and concerns in both countries affecting tobacco control. Even though public opinion about taxes is very similar in the two countries, Canada's general tax levels are higher, and, given its more vulnerable position in international financial markets, Canadian elites have been more willing to raise taxes to cope with budget deficits.[62] U.S. elites have been more inclined to embrace the antitax sentiments of the electorate.

(3) Similar policy inheritances. Both countries took action against tobacco, albeit through differing institutional channels, in the late 1960s and early 1970s. The U.S. legacy was, if anything, stronger because of government mandates imposed on the tobacco industry, while Canada's was a "voluntary" agreement with the tobacco

industry designed to ward off government regulation. But negotiated agreements with affected private interests for regulatory purposes are a bureaucratic tradition inherited by Canada from its British forebears.

(4) Similar definitions of the public policy problem. The basic questions in both countries were the same: how much to tax tobacco for public health and revenue purposes and how much to regulate tobacco for public health purposes. How to prevent teenagers from smoking is a major concern in both countries but is more emphasized in the United States.

(5) Similar proposals for addressing the problem. Although the same proposals did not emerge in both countries at the same time, in each country the approaches have been familiar. What began as a novel approach in either country—legislation against tobacco advertising, steep tax increases on cigarettes, special taxes and fees on tobacco companies, or products to provide for health promotion, even litigation against tobacco companies—has spread across the border.[63]

(6) Similar interest group involvement. A familiar set of interests appears in both countries: tobacco companies, tobacco farmers, tobacco vendors, public health advocates, and anti-tobacco groups. In the U.S. attorneys for both sides are more prominent, because of the legalistic political culture. An assessment of the relative strength of interest groups in the two countries appears below.

Second-Tier Explanations

Second-order features are of some relevance to differences in loss imposition. The single-member district plurality electoral system in both countries puts a premium on geographical and regional representation. In the United States, a free-for-all campaign finance system enables groups such as tobacco companies with large amounts of resources to compound the lack of executive and legislative party cohesion in the first tier by throwing their support to candidates who espouse positions favorable to their interests.

The enormous financial clout of big tobacco has been invoked to support the individual campaigns of its allies, which buttresses the high return rate of incumbent Congressmen in the U.S., irrespective of party. In Canada, there is no such opportunity for the tobacco industry, since spending on behalf of individual candidates is limited, support of an agreed-upon party line is reinforced by the capacity of party leaders to intervene in parliamentary candidate selections, and election outcomes are heavily dependent on the relative popularity of parties, not that of individual parliamentary candidates. This results, as we have noted, in high levels of turnover, with incumbents poorly insulated from electoral waves against their party.

Ironically, what these institutional circumstances have led to, especially in recent years, is more partisan polarization on tobacco issues in the United States than in Canada. The decline of the Democratic party in the U.S. South has allowed the business-oriented interests and antiregulatory attitudes of the Republican party to coalesce with the regional economic interests of tobacco growers and manufacturers. Tobacco control even became a campaign issue in the U.S. presidential race in 1996 when Republican candidate Bob Dole denied the addictive nature of tobacco and promised to fire FDA commissioner David Kessler (also a Republican), while President Clinton and Vice President Gore were critical of the tobacco industry. Yet in the presidential election of 2000, even a televised debate in Winston-Salem, North Carolina, did not induce the candidates to discuss tobacco.

The Republican congressional leadership is also overwhelmingly from the South. When the Balanced Budget Amendment of 1997 (BBA) emerged from a House–Senate Conference Committee for final passage, it originally included a new provision allowing the tobacco companies a federal income tax deduction representing the cost of the federal cigarette excise tax increase of 15 cents, in the event of passage of the National Settlement.[64] Republican majority leaders in both chambers professed ignorance of how the provision—apparently a legislative "immaculate conception"—had become part of the bill, and it was subsequently removed after the bad publicity.[65] Though the loose party cohesion in the U.S. Congress also allows some Republicans, such as Senator John McCain (a leader in the fight for the National Settlement), C. Everett Koop, and David Kessler to be antitobacco icons, the patterns of congressional voting on tobacco-related bills, of legislative hearings on tobacco issues, and, most tellingly, of political contributions—in which the largest single contributors are the tobacco companies, with over 80 percent of their largesse going to Republicans—point to the underlying partisan interests.[66] As the BBA episode indicates, the Republican party does not always want its tobacco connections publicized because of their poor public image. Nevertheless, partisanship and political financial contributions continue to define major avenues for tobacco interests to protect themselves from loss imposition at the federal level, even though whether tobacco money "buys votes" or merely reinforces the ideological inclinations of conservative legislators remains debatable.[67]

In Canada, on the other hand, partisan and electoral factors have rarely been involved in tobacco policy. Operating under rules of party discipline and cohesion very different from those influencing legislators in the United States, even Canadian MPs from tobacco regions are insulated from constituency complaints. With respect to a party in government, once the prime minister and cabinet decide policy, then the legislative party is expected to follow, at least with their votes. Perhaps more interestingly, however, opposition parties in Canada have not made tobacco into a partisan issue—except, in a limited way, the Bloc Québécois, which has acted sporadically to defend the interests of the tobacco manufacturers, retailers, and "champion smokers" of its home province. But the BQ lacks the power to block legislation, and there is near-unanimity among the other parties about the broad principles underlying tobacco regulation. In contrast to its many policies similar to those of U.S. Republicans on tobacco control, Reform Alliance was critical of the Liberal government for not pursuing more aggressive regulatory measures. The pro-business Conservative government of Brian Mulroney was the first to enact federal tobacco regulatory policies along with steep increases in tobacco taxes.

There is no recent evidence of tobacco becoming an issue in Canadian federal elections. Canadian campaign finance rules[68] limit the impact of contributions from the tobacco industry, especially at the local level. Thus, whatever divisions exist between and within parties over tobacco have tended to be blurred in public, especially at election time, with the exception of the Liberals' espousal of tax reductions to combat the smuggling crisis in anticipation of the Quebec election of 1994. But if the Liberals have wavered in imposing loss imposition on the tobacco companies because of their now-strong electoral base in Ontario (and on account of a leadership cadre largely drawn from Quebec), it is not an issue that they want to display in their election campaigns. In summary, there has been less evident partisanship on the tobacco control issue in Canada than in the United States in recent years, which is at least partially attributable to the opportunities for interest groups in the U.S., especially business groups, to wield financial power in political campaigns.

The electoral cycle does not appear to have been an important determinant of loss imposition in tobacco control in Canada except in one instance, that of the provincial election in Quebec in 1994. Otherwise, federal tobacco control measures in Canada have been introduced at various times: annually in budgets and, in fact, closer to the next election than the previous one in the case of regulatory legislation (Tobacco Products Control Act, Tobacco Sales to Young Persons Act, and Tobacco Act). Public opinion generally has constituted what analysts call a "permissive consensus" in favor of tobacco control; and with deficit reduction a paramount concern for both Progressive Conservative and Liberal governments over the past two decades, tobacco interests have not been able to focus on antitax sentiments. Their most effective lobbying against federal policy, outside the courts, was in connection with the recission of the export tax in 1992 and the federal tax reduction of 1994.

In the United States, the electoral cycle is significant for loss imposition insofar as it relates to partisanship, campaign contributions, and re-election prospects for officials. President Clinton's endorsement of the FDA regulations in 1995–96 allowed him to appeal to suburban voters, especially women, with public health concerns, while his opponent became identified with the tobacco industry. The National Settlement would probably have had a better chance of passage if it had not been considered by the Senate in an election year, when tobacco interests could portray it as a "tax grab." But in the United States, with congressional elections every two years, almost every year is an election year.

Third-Tier Explanations

Some third-order differences also have an effect on tobacco control policy. In particular, the availability of a judiciary able to make politically significant decisions has influenced the course of policy in both countries. In the U.S., judiciaries on the state level have allowed individual smokers and states in the U.S. to force the industry into costly settlements, which raise the price of cigarettes. Although the judiciary has acted as a limiting force in loss imposition on the federal level in both countries, in Canada the decision overturning the Tobacco Products Control Act was so narrowly drawn that a new Tobacco Act replaced it within two years. If that act eventually were to be overturned by the Supreme Court of Canada, former Liberal Health Minister David Dingwall has recommended that the Canadian government use the seldom-invoked "Notwithstanding Clause" of ultimate parliamentary supremacy over the judiciary to keep it in force.[69] In the United States, the Supreme Court decision against FDA authority over tobacco was more critical, because Congress is unlikely to grant such authority in the foreseeable future except on severely restricted terms. Thus the possibilities of tobacco companies' avoiding loss imposition by utilizing the judiciary are contingent upon their influence in the legislative branch. The separation of powers in the presidential system gives the industry greater opportunities to avoid loss imposition through legal action, in contrast to what happened in Canada once the TPCA was overturned.

In both countries, federalism provides additional venues for loss imposition. So far this has been more important in the United States, but there are indications that the provinces in Canada are becoming more active.[70] Through the National Settlement and the MSA as well as other activities, concerted action by the U.S. states has imposed more substantial losses on the tobacco industry than has the federal government, even though the first-order institutional configuration of the two levels is similar. While tobacco-growing states were reluctant to sue the industry and join the settlement negotiations, unlike in the U.S. Congress they had no power either to veto the process or to logroll in an attempt to obtain favors from other states. Furthermore, since the process was a judicial one rather than one of executive-legislative decision making, separately elected attorneys general could, in some instances, act independently of the wishes of their governors. (Mississippi, the first state to sue the tobacco companies, was the most prominent instance.) Thus the pro-tobacco states became part of the Master Settlement Agreement against their inclinations, being unable to compromise or to veto the process, as happened when the National Settlement was presented to Congress.

Strong bicameralism, a feature of a presidential system not shared with most parliamentary systems,[71] is of some relevance, because it allows greater opportunities for affected tobacco interests to avoid loss imposition. The U.S. Senate has consistently acted to protect tobacco. On the other hand, weak bicameralism in Canada protected the tobacco industry from Senator Colin Kenny's bill.[72]

Tobacco control policy outcomes, especially in Canada, have often been portrayed as a result of relative interest group strength.[73] But are there really substantial differences in the power of industry and public health groups in the two countries? In both countries, antitobacco and public health groups have improved in organizational capacity, financial undergirding, and diffuse public support over the past two decades. What is remarkable about the Canadian antitobacco lobby is that it has been aggressive in a political culture that normally does not encourage publicly assertive behavior from interest groups.[74] Thus it stands apart more from other Canadian interest groups than from U.S. ones, although in the early 1990s even U.S. antitobacco interests found the Canadians remarkably assertive. This aggressiveness, however, has not prevented the Canadian antitobacco lobby from suffering losses on some issues, especially the smuggling/taxation controversy and the question of cultural and sports sponsorship. In both countries, the tobacco industry has not been reluctant to voice its own interests, though preferring to use executive and judicial channels rather than conduct public campaigns.

First-Tier Explanations

The clearest difference in terms of the impact of the two first-order institutional systems, parliamentary versus presidential, lies in the role of the executive, especially the chief executive, in each system. In Canada's parliamentary system, before a bill is sent to parliament, the cabinet as a whole, including the ministers responsible for health, agriculture, commerce, and the budget, must agree to back the bill. This may lead to extensive delays and consultations before a bill is presented, as happened in the case of some tobacco control measures, but once the legislation is presented, party cohesion behind a majority government (assuming there is one) assures that it will pass into law, with whatever loss imposition ensues for affected interests.

In the United States, by contrast, even the executive is fragmented, as Secretary Califano discovered when he tried to enlist support from President Carter and the secretary of agriculture for his tobacco use reduction initiative in 1978. In Canada, though the health minister may lead the government's effort to get a regulatory bill passed while the finance minister leads on budgetary matters, including taxation, the prime minister is ultimately responsible for these as well as other matters on the government's legislative agenda. If the prime minister decides to impose losses on any group—be it tobacco companies, tobacco farmers, or even the public health community, as in the 1994 smuggling crisis—there is little to stop him as long as he has cabinet backing.

On the other hand, in the United States the president has been less able to impose losses on affected groups, especially economically and politically powerful ones. Presidents from Johnson to Carter shrank from a confrontation with tobacco interests;[75] others were simply uninterested, or unsympathetic to antitobacco concerns. President Clinton was the first U.S. chief executive to endorse a tobacco control agenda incorporating both increased taxation and greater regulation, some thirty years after the first Surgeon General's Report warning of the dangers of tobacco use. Even then, aside from encouraging and endorsing the FDA's assertion of authority over tobacco products, he was able to act as little more than a consultant and cheerleader for the National Settlement. He was not a direct negotiating participant and did not have the power to command party support in Congress for its adoption. U.S. states, both individually and jointly, have had more power to impose losses because they have been able to act in a highly unified manner potentially legally and financially perilous for tobacco companies. In short, the capacity of the president to impose losses on tobacco control is extremely limited, even more so in the wake of the Supreme Court decision against FDA authority over tobacco.

Given the growing convergence of political cultures in the United States and Canada, it would appear that political institutions are perhaps more important in terms of loss imposition in tobacco control than Kagan and Vogel[76] realized. As has been argued with respect to other issues,[77] parliamentary institutions, dominated by the executive, make loss imposition easier for governments to achieve, even given the greater accountability of such systems. Blame avoidance is also more difficult, although hardly impossible, for the executive in such systems. Friedman[78] is correct in that Canada's parliamentary institutions had greater potential for imposing losses on tobacco interests but, through the mid-1970s, had not exercised that potential. Once the long-term health hazards associated with tobacco, both direct and environmental, became clearer and as the diffuse support for tobacco control became greater (as measured, for example, by the massive reduction in the percentage of the population smoking since the 1950s, when over half the population of both countries did so), the Canadian federal government was able to subordinate the concentrated economic interests of tobacco production to the larger collective interests of deficit reduction and public health to a considerable degree. In the United States, the same evidence of health hazards, much of it first discovered in U.S. research, has proven more difficult to incorporate into public policy, especially on the federal level. Entrenched interests, even narrow ones with a declining basis of public support, have more opportunities for institutional blockage of loss imposition in a presidential/congressional system with multiple veto points.

The specific imposition of losses in tobacco control, as with any other policy, depends on the contingencies of particular pieces of proposed policy. Loss imposition on politically powerful interests is never easy. Some institutions, however, allow more opportunities for such a policy. In general, extended consideration of the course of tobacco control in Canada and the United States since the mid-1960s indicates that first-order differences between parliamentary and presidential institutions allow more opportunities for loss imposition in a parliamentary system.

Nevertheless, overall outcomes with respect to tobacco control policy in the United States and Canada have increasingly converged, even if through different processes. On the federal level, Canada has been better able to impose losses on business through regulation, incentives to leave tobacco growing, and, with some qualifications, taxes. But in the United States, state and local jurisdictions have in some instances compensated for a weaker federal tobacco control policy with respect to regulation, taxes, and even agriculture by using such unusual mechanisms as referendums and litigation for policy purposes as well as by taking advantage of federal grants for community action. Emulation across levels of government has also been a factor in yielding similar outcomes despite often dissimilar processes of policymaking.

NOTES

1. Robert A. Kagan and David Vogel, "The Politics of Smoking Regulation: Canada, France, the United States," in Robert L. Rabin and Stephen D. Sugarman, eds., *Smoking Policy: Law, Politics, and Culture* (New York: Oxford University Press, 1993), p. 22.
2. Lee Fritschler and James M. Hoefler, *Smoking and Politics: Policy Making and the Federal Bureaucracy*, 5th ed. (Upper Saddle River, N.J.: Prentice Hall, 1996); Frank R. Baumgartner and Bryan D. Jones, *Agendas and Instability in American Politics* (University of Chicago Press, 1993); Rob Cunningham, *Smoke and Mirrors: The Canadian Tobacco War* (Ottawa: International Development Research Centre, 1996).
3. R. Kent Weaver, "The Politics of Blame Avoidance," *Journal of Public Policy* 6 (1986): 371–98; Paul D. Pierson and R. Kent Weaver, "Imposing Losses in Pension Policy," in

R. Kent Weaver and Bert A. Rockman, eds., *Do Institutions Matter? Government Capabilities in the United States and Abroad* (Washington, D.C.: Brookings Institution Press, 1993); see also Edward Lascher, Jr., "Loss Imposition and Institutional Characteristics: Learning from Automobile Insurance Reform in North America," *Canadian Journal of Political Science* 30 (1998): 143–64.

4. Weaver, "The Politics of Blame Avoidance," 384–90.

5. James MacGregor Burns, *The Deadlock of Democracy: Four-Party Politics in America* (Englewood Cliffs, N.J.: Prentice Hall, 1963).

6. Baumgartner and Jones, *Agendas and Instability in American Politics*, 31–35.

7. R. Kent Weaver and Bert A. Rockman, eds., *Do Institutions Matter? Government Capabilities in the United States and Abroad* (Washington, D.C.: Brookings Institution Press, 1993).

8. Weaver, "The Politics of Blame Avoidance," 371–98.

9. Christopher Manfredi, "The Use of United States Decisions by the Supreme Court of Canada under the Charter of Rights and Freedoms," *Canadian Journal of Political Science* 23 (1990): 499–18.

10. Weaver and Rockman, *Do Institutions Matter?*, 445–61.

11. Theodore H. Lowi, "American Business, Public Policy, Case Studies and Political Theory," *World Politics* 16 (1964): 677–15.

12. T. Alexander Smith, *The Comparative Policy Process* (Santa Barbara, Calif.: ABC-Clio, 1975); Gary P. Freeman, "National Style and Policy Sectors: Explaining Structured Variation," *Journal of Public Policy* 5 (1986): 467–95.

13. Lascher, "Loss Imposition and Institutional Characteristics," 158–59.

14. David K. Mayhew, *Congress: The Electoral Connection* (New Haven, Conn.: Yale University Press, 1974).

15. Richard E. Matland and Donley T. Studlar, "Determinants of Legislative Turnover: A Cross-National Analysis" (paper presented at the European Consortium of Political Research, Bordeaux, France, April 1995).

16. Seymour M. Lipset, *Continental Divide: The Values and Institutions of the United States and Canada* (New York: Routledge, 1990); Ronald Inglehart, Neil Nevitte, and Miguel Basanez, *The North American Trajectory: Cultural, Economic, and Political Ties among the United States, Canada, and Mexico* (Hawthorne, N.Y.: Aldine De Gruyter, 1996); George Perlin, "The Constraints of Public Opinion: Diverging or Converging Paths?" in Keith Banting, George Hoberg, and Richard Simeon, eds., *Degrees of Freedom: Canada and the United States in a Changing World* (Buffalo: McGill-Queen's University Press, 1997).

17. Colin J. Bennett, "The Formation of a Canadian Privacy Policy: The Art and Craft of Lesson Drawing," *Canadian Public Administration* 33 (1990): 551–70; George Hoberg, "Sleeping with an Elephant: The American Influence on Canadian Environmental Policy," *Journal of Public Policy* 11 (1991): 107–32; Donley T. Studlar, *Tobacco Control: Comparative Politics in the United States and Canada* (Orchard Park, N.Y.: Broadview Press, 2002), chap. 6.

18. Barry G. Rabe, *Beyond NIMBY: Hazardous Waste Siting in the United States and Canada* (Washington, D.C.: Brookings Institution Press, 1999); Studlar, *Tobacco Control*, 203–55.

19. Jonathon Lemco, ed., *National Health Care* (Ann Arbor: University of Michigan Press, 1994).

20. Howard M. Leichter, *Free to Be Foolish: Politics and Health Promotion in the United States and Great Britain* (New York: Cambridge University Press, 1991).

21. Ontario Tobacco Research Unit, *Monitoring Ontario's Tobacco Strategy: Progress toward Our Goals* (October 1995).

22. Roberta G. Ferrence, *Deadly Fashion: The Rise and Fall of Cigarette Smoking in North America* (New York: Garland Publishing, 1989).

23. Cynthia Callard, "The Canadian Set-Back: Tobacco Use in Canada, 1986–1997," (paper presented at Tenth World Conference on Smoking or Health, Beijing, China, 1997).

24. Centers for Disease Control and Prevention, *State Tobacco Control Highlights—1996* (Atlanta, Ga.: Centers for Disease Control and Prevention, National Center for Chronic Disease Prevention and Health Promotion, Office on Smoking and Health, 1996).

25. Kenneth M. Friedman, *Public Policy and the Smoking-Health Controversy* (Lexington, Mass.: Lexington Books, 1975).

26. Studlar, *Tobacco Control*, 125.

27. Cunningham, *Smoke and Mirrors*, 297.

28. Warren E. Leary, "A 30-Year Report Card on Smoking Prevention," *New York Times*, January 12, 1994.

29. Kagan and Vogel, "The Politics of Smoking Regulation," 40–45.

30. Cunningham, *Smoke and Mirrors*; Callard, "The Canadian Set-Back."

31. Studlar, *Tobacco Control*, chap. 4.

32. Peter Pringle, *Cornered: Big Tobacco at the Bar of Justice* (New York: Henry Holt, 1998); Carrick Mollenkamp et al., *The People vs. Big Tobacco: How the States Took on the Cigarette Giants* (Princeton, N.J.: Bloomberg Press, 1998); Peter Jacobson and Kenneth E. Warner, "Litigation and Public Health Policy Making: The Case of Tobacco Control," *Journal of Health Politics, Policy and Law* 24 (1999): 769–804.

33. Murray Kaiserman and Byron Rogers, "Tobacco Consumption Declining Faster in Canada Than in the U.S.," *American Journal of Public Health* 81 (1991): 902–4.

34. Cunningham, *Smoke and Mirrors*, 122.

35. Michael Licari and Kenneth Meier, "Regulatory Policy When Behavior Is Addictive: Smoking, Cigarette Taxes, and Bootlegging," *Political Research Quarterly* 50 (1997): 5–24.

36. Cunningham, *Smoke and Mirrors*, 123–25.

37. *The Tax Burden on Tobacco*, 32 (Washington, D.C.: The Tobacco Institute, 1997): 117.

38. Cunningham, *Smoke and Mirrors*, 126.

39. Cunningham, *Smoke and Mirrors*, 16; Callard, "The Canadian Set-Back," 10–13.

40. *The Tax Burden on Tobacco*, 32: 259.

41. Cunningham, *Smoke and Mirrors*, 186–88.

42. Richard Lugar, "A Good Time to End Tobacco Quotas," *New York Times*, April 7, 1998.

43. "Tobacco Fund for Farmers," *New York Times*, January 22, 1999.

44. Richard Wolf and Martin Kasindorf, "Big Plans for Big Tobacco's Big Payoff," *USA Today*, November 22, 1999; Ed Gibson, "Smoke and Mirrors: Contrasting Policies for the Tobacco Settlement Allocation in Two Southern States" (paper presented at the Southern Political Science Association, Atlanta, Georgia, November 9–11, 2000).

45. Ken Kyle and Fran Du Melle, "International Smoke-Free Flights: Buckle Up for Take-Off," *Tobacco Control* 3 (1994): 3–4.

46. Michael Pertschuk, *Giant Killers* (New York: W. W. Norton and Co., 1986); Cunningham, *Smoke and Mirrors*, 116–28.

47. Marc Manley et al., "The American Stop Smoking Intervention Study for Cancer Prevention: An Overview," *Tobacco Control* 6 (1997): S5–S11.

48. Leary, "A 30-Year Report Card on Smoking Prevention," *New York Times*, January 12, 1994, 28.

49. Don Delducci, "OSHA Should Rewrite Its Workplace Smoking Plan." *Pittsburgh Post-Gazette*, October 6, 1996.

50. Cunningham, *Smoke and Mirrors*, 68.

51. Kagan and Vogel, "The Politics of Smoking Regulation"; A. Paul Pross and Iain S. Stewart, "Breaking the Habit: Attentive Publics and Tobacco Regulation," in Susan Phillips, ed., *How Ottawa Spends, 1994–95* (Ottawa: Carleton University Press, 1994).

52. Fritschler and Hoefler, *Smoking and Politics*, 90, 112–13.

53. National Clearinghouse on Tobacco and Health, *Canadian Law and Tobacco* (www.cctc.ca/ncth/docs/legislation, 1999); and Dana Shelton et al., "State Laws on Tobacco Control—United States, 1995," *Morbidity and Morality Weekly Report, CDC Surveillance Summary*, vol. 44 (Atlanta: Centers for Disease Control and Prevention, 1995), pp. 1–28.

54. Centers for Disease Control and Prevention, *State Tobacco Control Highlights—1996*.

55. Joseph A. Califano, *Governing America: An Insider's Report from the White House and the Cabinet* (New York: Simon and Schuster, 1981), 184.

56. Morton Mintz, "Tobacco Roads: Delivering Death to the Third World," *The Progressive*, 55 (1991): 24–29; Glenn Frankel, "The Tobacco Pushers: How the U.S. Government Helped Recruit New Cigarette Smokers Overseas," *Washington Post* (weekly edition), November 25–December 1, 1996; John Bloom, "International Interests in U.S. Tobacco Legislation," *Policy Analysis No. 3* (Advocacy Institute, Health Science Analysis Project, 1998) Washington D.C.

57. The Canadian experience with smuggling in the early 1990s has been portrayed in the United States as an argument against higher federal taxation of cigarettes. See Jacob Sullum, *For Your Own Good: The Anti-Smoking Crusade and the Tyranny of Public Health* (New York: The Free Press, 1998). More generally, antitobacco lobbyists have been accused of essentially advocating the prohibition of smoking, thus inviting the problematic consequences attending the earlier federal prohibition of alcohol products in the United States.

58. Cunningham, *Smoke and Mirrors*, 127–29.

59. Cunningham, *Smoke and Mirrors*, 132.

60. Colin Kenny, "Smoking Out Smugglers," *Montreal Gazette*, February 10, 1999.

61. Lascher, "Loss Imposition and Institutional Characteristics," 159–63.

62. Perlin, "The Constraints of Public Opinion"; George Hoberg, Keith Banting, and Richard Simeon, "North American Integration and the Scope for Domestic Choice: Canada and Policy Sovereignty in a Globalized World" (paper presented at the Association for Canadian Studies in the United States, Pittsburgh, November 18–21, 1999).

63. Studlar, *Tobacco Control*, chap. 6.

64. Jacobson and Warner, "Litigation and Public Health Policy Making," 790.

65. Charles Lewis and the Center for Public Integrity, *The Buying of the Congress* (New York: Avon Books, 1998).

66. Jill Abramson, "Tobacco Industry Gave Big to Parties in States Where It Faced Attack," *New York Times*, June 8, 1998.

67. Stephen Moore et al., "Epidemiology of Failed Tobacco Control Legislation," *Journal of the American Medical Association* 272 (1994): 1171–75; John Wright, "Tobacco Industry PACs and the Nation's Health: A Second Opinion," in Paul S. Herrnson, Ronald G. Shaiko, and Clyde Wilcox, eds., *The Interest Group Connection: Electioneering, Lobbying, and Policymaking in Washington* (Chatham, N.J.: Chatham House, 1998).

68. Dianne L. Alexander et al., "Tobacco Industry Campaign Contributions in Ontario, 1990–95," *Canadian Journal of Public Health* 88 (1990–95): 230–31.

69. The Notwithstanding Clause in the Canadian Constitution of 1982 provides that Parliament remains the supreme authority by virtue of invoking the clause for a period of five years, sequentially if necessary, to maintain a law declared invalid by the Supreme Court. It has only rarely been used to overturn court decisions, however, and never on the federal level. Thus the effective power of the Supreme Court of Canada has grown since 1982.

70. Studlar, *Tobacco Control*, chap. 4.

71. Arend Lijphart, *Democracies: Patterns of Majoritarian and Consensus Government in Twenty-one Countries* (New Haven, Conn.: Yale University Press, 1984).

72. "Your Move, Mr. Rock," *Montreal Gazette*, December 5, 1998.

73. Morton Mintz, "No Ifs, Ands, or Butts," *Washington Monthly* 22 (1990): 30–37; Pross and Stewart, "Breaking the Habit," 155–57.
74. Paul Pross, *Group Politics and Public Policy*, 2d ed. (Toronto: Oxford University Press, 1992).
75. Califano, *Governing America*, 182–97.
76. Kagan and Vogel, "The Politics of Smoking Regulation," 40–45.
77. Weaver and Rockman, *Do Institutions Matter?* 445–61; Lascher, "Loss Imposition and Institutional Characteristics," 159–63.
78. Friedman, *Public Policy and the Smoking-Health Controversy*, 155.

6

CLOSING MILITARY BASES

LILLY J. GOREN AND P. WHITNEY LACKENBAUER

Domestic military base closures never seem to constitute easy decisions for democratic governments either to make or to implement. Both the United States and Canada have faced a number of expected difficulties in their respective efforts to consolidate and modernize their domestic basing situations. Over the past quarter of a century, both countries have run into significant roadblocks every time the military requested that elected representatives consent to the closure of military bases.

Although the number of bases in the United States (historically and currently) dwarfs the relatively tiny number in Canada (at approximately a 20:1 ratio), and would thus make the issue seem almost incomparable on grounds of magnitude, several salient factors make this case study relevant. In both countries, extraneous infrastructure costs were seen as representing a significant portion of military expenditures. Furthermore, in both Canada and the U.S. there is the complication of the distribution of military bases across the country. Both Canada and the U.S. faced a situation where any particular area or region might find their "defense dollar" losses apparently greater than another region's or area's losses. Both countries' basing structures had grown up and evolved in a haphazard manner, mostly rooted in responding to various threats over extended periods of time. Certain U.S. bases, for example, were first built to protect against the British invasion in the War of 1812, or to get B-47s with atomic bombs as close to the Soviet Union as possible before the age of intercontinental missiles and jet planes. In Canada, the Second

World War necessitated the development of a huge number of bases for infantry and air training across the country, and strategic considerations during the cold war led to the creation of installations for early warning radar lines across the Arctic and mid-North.

There are, of course, political reasons behind some basing decisions as well. In the United States, during the military buildup under the Reagan administration in the 1980s there was a conscious effort to "spread the wealth" and make sure that there were bases in as many districts and states as possible, thus ensuring ongoing support from Congress for these expenditures. All these efforts helped to distribute military bases throughout the United States. Similarly, repeated Canadian governments throughout the 1970s and 1980s stressed the socioeconomic benefits of military bases for their host communities and the role of a broad, regionally balanced basing structure in national development.[1]

The closing of any single base will affect the particular community or area where that base has been established; thus it is clear that the "pain" from base closings tends to be highly concentrated geographically. The losses from gun control among gun owners and enthusiasts and from pension cuts among old-age pensioners are also concentrated in an identifiable group, but these groups are quite geographically dispersed (though there is the rural-urban and East-West split among gun enthusiasts). Military bases, however, can be viewed as huge funnels of material benefits that can be specified spatially. The concentric ring of benefits emanates out from a dense core of the town or city closest to the base, to the region, and finally to the state or province. For the most part, loss imposition through closure of a base is consequently highly visible and has a clear and delimited range of impacts. The benefits of such closures, however, are as widely dispersed as those that accrue from gun control and pension retrenchment. Moreover, unlike some cases of geographically concentrated losses, such as the establishment of a repository for high-level nuclear wastes where imposition of costs on one community is likely to lead to all other areas being spared those costs, closing some bases *may* lead to other bases being spared or even expanded, but it may also have the opposite effect: Proponents of retrenchment, emboldened by success in one round of retrenchment, may try, and have tried, to secure more closings.

Base closures contrast with and complement some of the other topics covered by this study. They are not, generally, as symbolically driven an issue as gun control. The losses imposed by closing military bases are primarily material in nature: the loss of jobs, both civilian and military; the withdrawal of the economic stimulus to a city and region that comes from a base; and the extra tax revenue generated for state and provincial economies. Naturally, "ways of life" are sometimes invoked to resist a closure (in the form, for example, of the idea of some historical or organizational link between a base and its surrounding region or area), but for the most part, the arguments are nakedly material. The closure of major (and even minor) military installations in a region can have highly visible impacts on areas already suffering from weak economies and with bleak economic prospects for the future.[2]

All of these considerations would lead us to expect that base closings would be very difficult for governments to impose, and relatively easy for potential losers to resist. In institutional terms, there is an additional reason for this difficulty (on the part of governments) and this advantage (on the part of potential victims). Since bases are located in a specific area, their loss can be clearly identified with a political representative. Both congressional and Westminster-style parliamentary systems organize political representation among geographical lines, so any type of loss imposition that has a clearly geographical delineation will be quite tricky. Reinforcing this is the problem of regional rivalries. Virtually every country is divided along regional lines in some fashion, and politics everywhere involves treating different regions with some measure of fairness—that is, not consistently and deliberately advantaging or disadvantaging one region over another. And any closure runs the risk of being framed as an attack on a particular region.

We will observe these dynamics in both the U.S. and Canadian cases. But we will also see that the challenge of military base closures has generated some creative politics of loss imposition that allowed much more of such loss imposition than might have been expected.

THE UNITED STATES PROCESS: THE BASE REALIGNMENT AND CLOSING COMMISSION (BRAC)

The politics of military base closures should be particularly difficult in a political system like that of the United States, where, as former House Speaker Thomas P. (Tip) O'Neill put it, "All politics is local:" where congressional committees with jurisdiction over military bases tend to overrepresent districts containing bases, and where gridlock and inaction are institutionally privileged over decisive change. Given the potential dislocation that can result from a base closure, "the conventional wisdom holds that base closures end congressional careers, and few legislators are willing to sacrifice themselves."[3] Legislators could attempt to distance themselves from political blame by delegating authority for closures to the executive branch, and for quite some time this century this is how base closure decisions were made—by the executive branch in some capacity. But legislators have a not entirely unreasonable notion that Defense Department closure initiatives are likely to be either heavily biased in favor of the president's party,[4] or targeted at those members who didn't or don't support the president's defense policies.[5] Since the end of World War II, domestic base closures have always tread a fine line between parochial and partisan politics, on the one hand, and national security needs on the other.

These theoretical presuppositions suggest that closing military bases in the United States would almost be a political impossibility once Congress got involved in the process—and an examination of the record of the history of closing bases from the mid- to late 1970s through the late 1980s would be consistent with those presuppositions. The military base structure was notoriously full of obsolete facilities, including a moat-encircled fort (later an army training center) in Virginia, originally built to defend against the British in the War of 1812, and another fort in Utah built to protect Pony Express riders from hostile Indians.[6] But the political obstacles to closing bases were so high that "the Department of Defense gave up even trying to close any major bases between 1979 and 1985."[7] No major domestic military bases were closed between 1977 and 1988, while thirteen new ones were opened, making a total of 312.[8] Although Secretary of Defense Robert McNamara came up against little concerted opposition from Congress in regard to his selections for base closures in the early 1960s, by the late 1980s Secretary of Defense Frank Carlucci suggested that "the Pentagon was tied up in knots forever by endless procedures and litigation and political pressure to the point where the Defense Department finally throws up its hands and says, 'We just cannot do this. We cannot devote the time and resources to it.'"[9]

Most secretaries of defense who followed Robert McNamara were not as lucky as he was in selecting domestic military bases for closure and succeeding in closing them down. The Kennedy and early Johnson administrations went about closing military installations with little regard for political considerations or sensitivity to congressional reactions. Secretary of Defense McNamara, at Kennedy's request, compiled extensive lists of closures and made these decisions in the context of a strong policy consensus within the United States that Communism and Communist countries needed to be contained, and that the military had to be prepared for that mission. This policy consensus helped to solidify the role of the Pentagon and the Executive as *the* locus for military policy decisions and choices. During this period, the case was made that the decisions of the secretary of defense and the sitting president should not be frivolously disputed by elected representatives because that might lead to the appearance of weakness and divisiveness, which could easily be exploited by the Soviet Union and its allies.[10]

Congress Becomes More Involved

The changes that enabled substantial congressional involvement in the decision-making process started to come in the 1970s, after the initial military consolidation following the United States departure from Southeast Asia. In 1976, when 147 bases were proposed for closure or realignment, Congress fought back in a more concerted way than it had in the past. Numerous pieces of legislation were passed by Congress; when these were taken all together, they effectively tied up the entire base-closing process "in knots," as former Secretary of Defense Carlucci put it. The first piece of legislation "required a one-year notice prior to closure of a base employing 500 or more civilians or 'reduction in the level of civilian personnel at any military installation by more than 50 percent.'"[11] The secretary of defense was also required to tender to the Committee on Armed Services "detailed justification of the proposed closure or reduction together with the estimated fiscal, economic, environmental, and operational effects of the proposed closure or reduction."[12] At the same time as this legislation was being fought over by the White House and the Congress, legislation requiring that the Defense Department comply with National Environmental Policy Act (NEPA) regulations was put into effect. By reorienting the decision-making process in this way, Congress was more or less "setting up shop" in an area that had long been the realm of the Department of Defense, with some minor influence from the White House (mostly via the National Security Council) and maybe a word or two from senior senators or members of Congress with special expertise in defense matters. Thus, in the late 1970s, Congress engaged in a form of "covert politics" with regard to base closure decision-making policy. Legislators were not outwardly blocking or thwarting policy decisions or the decision-making process through the available overt or openly visible means of doing so, such as resorting to a filibuster, amending a bill to death, or tying up the legislation in committee. Rather, the obstructive behavior was covert, typically extending over a long period of time, and leading to so much frustration on the part of those trying to accomplish certain goals that they finally gave up.

The Stealth Commission: The BRAC Is Created

By the late 1980s, it was clear that the process for closing military bases in the United States was riddled with problems, more so than ever before. Those problems included excessive delays, vigorous congressional objections, expensive litigation, and repetitious environmental impact statements. As one scholarly observer put it: "The new institutional mechanisms [put in place by Congress in the late 1970s] so lowered the marginal cost of resisting major base closures and realignments that it became politically untenable for an individual member of Congress not to block closures and realignments."[13]

All that changed, however, with the creation of a new process for closing military bases in 1988. The new process (altered in some significant ways in 1990) works like this: The military services indicate to the secretary of defense those bases that they would like to close; the secretary makes additions or deletions from this list and sends it to a temporary, independent commission, which then prepares its own list after a review that includes analysis of available data and public hearings. The commission makes up a final list and sends it to the president, who can either accept it and submit it to Congress or reject it—but he cannot make additions to or deletions from the list. Once it is approved by the president, base closings will proceed unless both houses of Congress pass a joint declaration disapproving the list within forty-five working days—but, once again, they cannot make changes to the list by adding to or subtracting from it or substituting individual bases or groups of bases.[14] And even if both houses pass such a declaration, it is subject to a presidential veto, meaning that a two-thirds majority in each chamber would have to pass it again for it to take effect.

In theory, at least, this mechanism offers several advantages insofar as imposing regionally concentrated losses. It places detailed decision making in the hands of a body that is not concerned about reelection; indeed, it goes out of business after it has made its recommendations. It places pressure on the president and the Congress to approve the work of a body that they have themselves created.[15] And instead of there being multiple congressional hoops to jump through in order to secure base closures, it is opponents of base closures who must, now, quickly build support—in both houses of Congress. Legislators do not have to put their fingerprints on a base closure, so to speak, by voting for it directly. So long as the number of affected districts—and, in the Senate, affected states—is kept below a majority (or even two-thirds) in at least one chamber, the short-term incentive for most members is to vote not to overturn the commission's recommendations.[16] (The calculus of legislators may be different if they think that acceptance of a round of base closings sets a precedent making it more likely that there will be later rounds affecting their own constituents.) And if one chamber fails in its bid to overturn the commission's recommendations, members of the other chamber are off the hook entirely from even having to vote: There is little incentive for legislators to force an embarrassing roll call vote on their colleagues, since a single chamber's opposition would not overturn the commission's recommendations anyway. Moreover, the second through fourth rounds of base closures were all authorized by a single piece of legislation in 1990, further lowering the probability that a legislator might be punished by his or her constituents for voting to put the process in place.[17]

WHY THE BRAC?

Why would legislators in the United States adopt such a procedure? Public choice theory suggests that legislators are unlikely to adopt new procedures that produce outcomes harmful to a majority of those approving the procedures unless they are unable to accurately predict the outcomes of those new procedures. While it is certainly true that legislators could not predict precisely which bases would be recommended for closure, the general outlines of the scope of closure and the types of bases likely to be closed were known with reasonable accuracy before the initial base closure procedure was put into effect.[18] A more plausible interpretation of legislators' behavior is that they were amenable to a procedure that (1) allowed them to express a personal preference for governmental economy and efficiency and (2) enabled them to cast a politically popular vote in favor of that preference, for which they could claim credit from constituents while simultaneously (3) protecting them from the wrath of an intense minority of their constituents when base-closing decisions were made and (4) allowing them to protest loudly against individual base closures affecting their constituents, while ensuring that their protests would not be effective. In short, it is less important that the base-closing procedure provides a Rawlsian "veil of ignorance" for *legislators* with respect to which bases are likely to be closed than that it does so for *constituents*. Legislators may actually agree that bases should be closed, but fear the political consequences; in shielding constituents from this knowledge, legislators are protected from blame.

It is also helpful to recognize that not all legislators are likely to have the same preference for preserving congressional discretion over military base closings. That motivation is likely to be especially strong among the congressional committees with jurisdiction over military issues, for whom delegation of authority cuts into their jurisdiction and removes a potential legislative currency.

It should thus come as no surprise that the idea for a military base closing commission came not from committee leaders but from a member of the then-minority party, Representative Dick Armey of Texas (subsequently House majority leader), who favored giving Congress no opportunity at all to overturn an independent commission's recommendations. Four separate committees in the House of Representatives all claimed jurisdiction to evaluate and mark up the BRAC legislation.[19]

While committee leaders initially proposed weaker alternatives to Armey's bill,[20] Congress eventually agreed to a stronger version incorporating the fast-track joint resolution as a congressional check on the commission's actions. By outlining such circumscribed provisions for disapproving of the base closing and realignment list, the law goes far to ensure that individual members' political interests are protected, since each member can lobby, protest, and make a case while the commission is deliberating but would find it nearly impossible to prevent the process from proceeding once the decisions were made.

The BRAC (Base Realignment and Closing Commission) legislation refers a resolution of disapproval to only one committee in each house—the Committee on Armed Services—and the respective committees must discharge the resolution within a twenty-day period, or "at the end of such period, [such committee shall be] discharged from further consideration of such resolution, and such resolution shall be placed on the appropriate calendar of the House involved."[21] Also, there is a prohibition on committee or floor amendments to BRAC recommendations. Congress may not tinker with the package that is presented to it; either it is rejected or it goes into effect, whereupon the secretary of defense commences closure of the recommended bases.

The initial commission's recommendations, for closure or partial closure of ninety-one bases and "realignment" of fifty-four others, were made public at the end of December 1988.[22] And in April 1989 the House rejected a joint resolution of disapproval by an overwhelming 381–43 vote.[23] While powerful legislators tried to win exemptions for bases in their states, alleging factual errors in the commission's decision-making process, the Bush administration refused to go along, with then–Defense Secretary Dick Cheney arguing that "It was a package, and if we get into the business of pulling out individual bases, I'm fearful the entire package will come apart and I'll end up without any bases closed."[24]

While there was some speculation among those in the press that the first round of base closures led to a much longer list of closures than had been anticipated in Congress,[25] members and staff who worked with the 1988 commission suggested that, in fact, the list could have been much longer, but the commissioners tried instead to strike a balance of some kind between too much and too little. The suggestion, from one of the senior staff members on the 1988 commission, was that while there was a "list of other bases that [the commission] was looking at, . . . and perhaps would have liked to have closed . . . but there was a kind of a sense, not that we could quantify it, that maybe this would go too far and we didn't want to over-tax the system."[26] But nothing succeeds like the success of a depoliticized decision-making process when the issue is loss imposition, or so it seemed. In 1990, when Defense Secretary Dick Cheney announced, as part of President George H. W. Bush's annual budget request, a package that included a few dozen base closures, there was quite a rumble through Congress, especially from Democratic members who said that their districts had been specifically targeted: Twenty-nine of the thirty-five major domestic base closures proposed by the defense secretary for consideration were in Democratic districts.[27] Congress blocked Cheney's plan, and Armed Services Committee chair Les Aspin immediately offered legislation establishing another base closure commission, along much the same lines as the 1988 commission. This new independent commission would go into effect three different times, for three separate rounds of closure decisions: in 1991, 1993, and 1995. By moving to establish a new BRAC, the Democratic members would, they hoped, avoid the charge that they were spendthrift while weakening the power of the administration over outcomes. They would also look less like they were "speaking out of both sides of their mouths," since they had been calling for defense budget cuts in the face of the end of the Cold War at the same time that they were then complaining about the cuts that came in their districts or states.

The Second BRAC: Fine-Tuning Dedistributive Policymaking

The subsequent BRAC looked and acted a little bit differently than the 1988 version. These alterations were mostly due to some of the complaints that had been filed against the first commission. Since there had been some questions about the independence of the initial BRAC, there was a new requirement that the General Accounting Office, Congress's autonomous investigation and auditing arm, provide the commission with its own analysis of the money-saving potential of the Defense Department's recommendations to the commission.[28] After holding public hearings (which were mandated by the new legislation but had not been required of the first commission), the commission deliberated in public on a final list; its deliberations were even televised live on C-SPAN.[29] The 1991 commission largely followed Cheney's recommendations, advising the closure of twenty-five bases with a loss of 100,000 civilian and military jobs; the House rejected a Joint Resolution to overturn the recommendation by a vote of 364-60.[30] Another round of base closure proposals in 1993 was highly controversial because its effects were concentrated in California, but it ended up producing the most ambitious round of closings to date, embracing thirty-five major and ninety-five smaller bases.[31] While legislators and local officials tried a variety of maneuvers to keep their bases from being closed, the process, and the overall result, remained largely insulated from their efforts.

Several years earlier, after a first-round list had been submitted by the BRAC, many elected representatives had tried to hold up the appropriations necessary to close the designated bases and had also demanded that the procedures used for selecting bases be investigated for possible inconsistencies, but they did not interfere with the actual workings of the 1988 BRAC. But in 1991 there was a bit of a shift, with input from elected representatives coming *before* the BRAC had started its evaluations.

This shift in responses is a direct result of the change in the BRAC legislation and the way the decision-making procedures were to operate, since the Defense Department now had to draw up a list of bases for closure and realignment and then present that list to the BRAC for analysis. This returned the procedure, in many ways, to the way base closures had been done in the past, when the secretary of defense would begin by submitting a list of bases to Congress. But the difference here—both from the 1988 BRAC and from the way base closings had been accomplished in the past—was that the process was protected and insulated from partisan or parochial politics.

Along with the reworking of the BRAC procedure, there was a newly opened avenue to try to influence the commission's decisions and evaluations; this is what prompted the outspoken and immediate responses from elected officials. They were hoping to redirect the commission's attention during its four-month period of scrutinizing and analyzing the secretary's recommendations. The task for members of Congress and/or agitated members of a community was to focus the commission's attention on a particular installation and suggest that the Department of Defense had somehow been remiss in its analysis of that particular installation and had inappropriately included it on the list for closure or realignment. The commission was fully within its authority to "add, delete, or modify the secretary's list"[32]; the job of the commission was specifically to "ensure that the proposals submitted by [DOD] did not deviate substantially from the force-structure plan and the eight [congressionally approved] selection criteria."[33] The newly open procedure, along with this mandate to make sure that the Defense Department had been true to the evaluation criteria for selecting bases, meant that elected officials started to reorient their behavior with regard to the base closure decision-making process. They now worried that if they did not publicly take *some* action, their constituents would blame them if bases were closed in their districts and states. Faced with public hearings, public announcements of the bases to be closed, and a somewhat established, longer-term system, politicians could not reasonably be expected to refrain from trying to influence the base closure process. And try they did.

During the 1970s and 1980s, those who had lobbied members of Congress to keep their bases open had been grassroots organizations, generally without that much sophistication. What had to be done in those days consisted mostly of bringing the issue to the attention of the appropriate congressional delegation. After that, the affected members would do the rest of the lobbying, urging their colleagues to vote with them and so on. This was not to be the case with the newly implemented BRAC process. Those who hoped to keep their base open would have to find some means of convincing the commission that the Defense Department had made a miscalculation by putting the base on its list in the first place. This took a little more sophistication and creativity and possibly more professional lobbying methods. Thus, with the three BRAC rounds that came out of the 1990 legislation there was an opening up of opportunities for professional consultants, public presentations, new arguments for keeping bases open, and manipulation of the system—for real hopes and attempts to influence and change the outcomes of the process. The city of Charleston, South Carolina, for example, spent about $1 million to make its case to the BRAC, hiring consultants, putting together facts and figures and reports, and presenting information to the BRAC when it came to investigate the Charleston case. Members of Congress and various communities also hired former staff members from the BRAC to advise them during subsequent rounds when their bases were under consideration.

Elected representatives also pursued the usual routes of trying to get what they wanted by holding up appointments to the commission and attempting to frustrate the appropriations process where and when possible. With these political maneuvers in the House and the Senate came some political maneuvering by the White House, which selected more overtly political and partisan appointees for the commission and offered up less controversial lists from the Defense Department of bases to be closed. In addition, fewer bases were selected for closure in the period prior to the 1996 election year, and there was an attempt to avoid base closures in states that had some political weight with respect to the forthcoming primary season or presidential election. Indeed, there have been no BRAC rounds since 1995 in large part because of partisan concerns, many of which stem from the way the Clinton administration acted during and after the 1995 round of closures. This observation is directed specifically at the Clinton administration's response to the BRAC's selection of Kelly Air Force Base in Texas and McClellan Air Force Base in California for closure, and its subsequent move to "privatize in place" the tasks that were performed at these two bases, thereby mitigating the political repercussions of those "closures."[34] This action by the Clinton administration incensed some House Republicans, particularly Rep. Dick Armey, and prompted a stonewalling of any more discussion of base closures or BRAC rounds until after the Clinton administration was out of office. Since the military spends two years preparing for the BRAC decision-making process, this "stonewalling" kept base closures off the table until, at the earliest, the inauguration of President Bush in January 2001. In fact, the Bush Administration pushed off any base closures until 2005—again, commencing the BRAC round after the general election of 2004.

At the same time, affected communities and their elected representatives used multiple strategies in attempting to slow the process, reverse the process, and lessen the pain involved in the process—and, particularly, to influence those making the decisions. With each round of closures, the commission felt pressure from these various actors. Bases were still selected for closure, but the final BRAC round selected fewer of them, and the openings for those who hoped to change outcomes became more discernible.

There was also an attempt to pit the institutions of government against one another—what Pal and Weaver call venue-shifting—in order to hold up the decision-making process. Opponents of closure of the Philadelphia Naval Shipyard (ordered in the 1991 round) mounted both a court challenge to the commission process and a legislative effort to subject the commission process to judicial review.[35] The Yard employed a significant number of people, both directly and indirectly, and its closure would certainly have been keenly felt in the immediate area—particularly during a recession, as was the case in the early 1990s. The case went all the way to the U.S. Supreme Court, where Senator Arlen Specter (R-PA) asked the Court to "declare that the Government's selection of military bases for closing or downgrading is subject to challenge in Federal court."[36] In the end, the Supreme Court unanimously rejected Specter's argument, explaining that it was not in the Court's purview to decide such questions.

The BRAC essentially remains a "creature" of the Congress, unlike other independent regulatory agencies or commissions. It remains such a creature because it does not operate entirely independently. While the process of congressional approval of BRAC decisions is extremely streamlined, those decisions can nonetheless not go into effect without getting that approval, which is not the case with the decisions made by independent regulatory commissions and agencies.

NOTHING SUCCEEDS LIKE SUCCESS

Between 1988 and 1995, the various incarnations of the Base Realignment and Closing Commission selected a total of approximately 534 domestic military bases for closure and/or realignment.[37] While the bulk of this figure is made up of smaller closures and realignments, each round of selections and recommendations did strike at major installations, with nearly 100 major bases being slated for closure or significant downsizing through this process.

Each round of closures also saw a greater reduction in the domestic base structure itself, with a total reduction over seven years of nearly 20 percent of the entire domestic base structure. The estimate of actual dollars saved by the closures can be calculated only over a period of time, since each round of closures also demands an initial one-time expenditure to pay for the expenses of closing down the selected bases.[38] In total, according to estimates, it was not until 1998 that the "cumulative savings of the four [BRAC] rounds completely offset the cumulative costs to date."[39] Through the year 2001, base closure savings are to reach a total of $14 billion, with annual savings of $5.6 billion in the year 2002 and in each subsequent year thereafter.[40] Given these significant cuts in the domestic base structure, the BRAC was seen by most elected representatives as having successfully executed a tough, loss-imposing decision-making process. And it did so in a manner that spared most members of Congress (and the president) from being blamed for the hardship visited upon their constituents as a result of those cuts. Essentially, the BRAC did what it was intended to do: make decisions that imposed losses while sparing elected representatives from being blamed for those decisions.

There were some differences in terms of the particular solutions that characterized the various BRACs; in particular, some key aspects of the first BRAC were not retained in the subsequent legislation because of the criticisms they engendered. Once the process was established, members were able to further refine its character and components, tweaking it so that the entire decision-making process was streamlined at the same time that it was made more legitimate. Professionalism and oversight, of various kinds, were increasingly incorporated into the BRAC decision-making process. These, combined with the mandate for open hearings and visits to communities, established a process that was generally accepted as legitimate and respectable. These alterations in the way that the commission went about its business also changed the BRAC from a secretive and stealthy organization to a more open and accessible one, allowing for public involvement and for professional evaluation of its decisions. All this helped the BRAC to do its job more effectively and efficiently. At the same time, because its operations were becoming more and more accepted (and even praised by those who had had any contact with the process), the newly implemented tools also helped to close down many avenues that might have been used to undermine the work of the commission.

The BRAC has had a long-term effect on the entire base closure decision-making process, changing the way these decisions are made. It is doubtful that domestic military bases will ever again be closed without a commission guiding the process, making the decisions, and cushioning the political shocks. This conclusion was recently confirmed by the passage of legislation creating a new BRAC round in 2005. In the face of new demands and spending increases following the events of September 11, 2001, Congress discussed the need for military efficiency and effectiveness, which meant the closing of additional outdated bases. And that would only happen if a commission made the decisions.

THE CANADIAN CASE

In Canada, the post–World War II period was marked by the construction of military bases, training centers, and depots across the country. There were occasional rationalizations with resources, but Canadian military base closures did not arrive on the policy agenda until the mid-1960s, with the advent of initial rumors of systematic closures in 1969.[41] The new government led by Pierre Trudeau had launched a review of foreign policy that had inevitable consequences for rethinking the nature of the country's defense posture, and consequently its defense facilities. The new government was also trying out the first of many systems to control its expenditures and had set a target for national defense that could be met only through rationalization of bases. Indeed, serious discussions of base closings in Canada have all been driven by this dual dynamic of changes in defense policy (a result of changes in the global strategic balance) accompanied by a fresh round of efforts to get the government's fiscal house in order.

In 1969 a special National Defence Task Force was established to study every base and station in Canada. By August of that year, the task force had come up with two lists of bases compiled on the basis of four criteria: military role, capital investment, involvement with the local community, and civilian jobs. As one senior defense official explained, the first list consisted of bases that would be "least painful to close. . . . They are the ones where we think there is the best chance of finding alternative uses for the base and alternative employment for the civilian staffs involved."[42] This list consisted of four bases that were eventually closed: Canadian Forces Military Complex Ville La Salle in Quebec and three facilities in Ontario.[43] These certainly fit the criterion of the "easy list": All of them, with the exception of the radar base in Clinton, Ontario, were depots with relatively few military or civilian personnel who might lose their jobs, and they lent themselves to easy disposal or sale to the private sector.

The potential impact of the second list of bases—presumably with deeper community roots and wider economic spin-offs—made implementation more challenging. An interdepartmental committee (concerned with everything from regional and economic issues to manpower) explored the broad implications of potential closures beyond the purely defense concerns, and even consulted with provincial authorities.[44] Assurances were sought from the prime minister even before the cabinet made its decision, and the issue was clearly linked to the question of regional economic stimulation.[45] The government, fully realizing some of the liabilities associated with loss imposition, floated several tactics to diminish the possibility of grassroots political retaliation. It offered compensation through either "adjustment" grants or some countervailing regional investment, and it tried to spread the pain over time by staggering the base closings.[46]

The federal cabinet itself had difficulty coming to a decision with respect to the second list of proposed closures.[47] A decision was supposed to have been made by October 1969, but federal decision makers faced a fierce lobbying campaign by officials from Prince Edward Island who feared the closure of the base at Summerside. In December 1969, the only official announcement on closures came not from the Defence Department but from Allan MacEachen, responsible for immigration but also the regional minister for Atlantic Canada: Summerside would stay open at least until 1973. In August 1970, defence minister Leo Cadieux announced the closure of air training bases at Rivers (affecting 843 military personnel and 204 civilians) and at Gimli (813 military and 206 civilians), both in Manitoba. Predictably, local opinion was aroused and delegations immediately traveled to Ottawa to try to reverse the decision.[48]

In the early 1970s, a budget freeze, coupled with inflationary pressures, left the Department of National Defence in a dismal financial state. Defence Minister James Richardson looked for ways to increase the portion of the defense budget available for capital expenditures (it had plunged to an all-time low in 1973) through in-house economies and base consolidations, and he commissioned studies to identify the Canadian Forces' future infrastructure needs.[49] The next round of potential base closings thus coincided with the Liberal government's austerity program of 1975–76. The Ministry of Defence again faced major budgetary cuts, and the Chief of Defence Staff, General J. A. Dextraze, spoke publicly about the need to consolidate facilities in order to permit better personnel decisions, in the face of new demands such as peacekeeping and the kinds of terrorist scenarios suggested by the 1976 Olympics.[50]

Rumors circulated about closures, most notably over the potential that Canadian Forces Base (CFB) Chatham in New Brunswick and some other Maritime bases would be shut down. MPs from the region grilled the defence minister, extracting a promise that no bases had been selected for closure "yet."[51] By March 1976, newspapers in the region were printing panic stories about the devastating impact of potential base closings.[52] As soon as the rumors surfaced, unions, businesses, and local politicians organized "massive protest rallies" at several Maritime centers. This tactic was a predictable response on the part of those resisting loss imposition: By broadening the circle of potential losers and implying that all bases in the region were potentially threatened, more people rallied to the cause. The regional dynamic also came into play because of a rumor that the air patrol functions performed by the now obsolete CF-101 escort jet designed to carry fuel and weapons over long ranges located at Maritime bases would be moved to Quebec, along with a fleet of new fighter aircraft; the perceived favoritism to Quebec incensed Maritime spokespeople.[53] The protests proved effective: Chatham was not closed until 1994, although Prime Minister Pierre Trudeau tried again in 1982 (and backed down in the face of loud protests).[54]

In April 1976 the issue of base closures was turned over to a cabinet committee. After a month of deliberation, however, the defence minister admitted that the committee was stalled. Protests from affected areas, along with public and private appeals by members of Parliament to the minister, stressed the economic effects that potential closures would have on communities.[55] By July, in the face of these reactions, the government simply gave up. Countrywide pressures, coupled with disagreement within the governing caucus, meant that the Liberal government "indefinitely postponed potentially contentious decisions on closing or partly closing military bases."[56] A revised, reduced list of closures was drafted over the summer and submitted to the cabinet in October 1976, but once again this generated a storm of protest across the country.[57] In the end, only one base was closed (in Toronto, Ontario) and another transferred (from Edmonton, Alberta, to Petawawa, Ontario), together affecting only 150 civilian jobs. No bases in eastern Canada were touched—not even Summerside, P.E.I., which had been on the chopping block for years and was avowedly maintained for regional development rather than defense purposes.[58]

Although the Department of National Defence had determined a "blueprint" for military infrastructure by 1976, a lack of political will hindered any significant action to close surplus bases during the 1970s and 80s. As the auditor general's office later surmised, "government concern about the impact of base closures on local economies and the potential political fallout led to indecision." There was no established governmental framework to deal with local economic impacts (although there was overlapping jurisdictional interest between several federal departments and agencies). As a result, "National Defence . . . continued to bear the cost of keeping bases open even as budgetary pressures increased."[59] In the battle between local economic interests (which translated into political support) and Defence Department economies and effectiveness, the latter was consistently losing out.

Conservative Government Attempts at Base Closures

The next round of Canadian closures began in the late 1980s, again under the joint pressure of a defense policy review and fiscal constraints. Brian Mulroney's Tory government, elected in 1984, had promised—at that point, without much success—to do something serious about the federal budget deficit. As the Cold War came to a close, Canada's broad strategic outlook and domestic expenditures clearly needed reevaluation.

The military had long supported reductions in facilities, since this would free up money for badly needed new equipment. It now awaited a decision by the Mulroney government (now early in its second term in office) to facilitate a reallocation of resources. The perceived success of base conversions in the United States and Canada, coupled with the need to reduce infrastructure as "an inevitable consequence of changing military requirements," justified immediate rationalization, according to a Department of National Defence release. Although past governments had resisted base closures because of the financial impact on communities, the situation had now "come to a head: in two decades the size of the Canadian Forces has dropped by one third, without a corresponding reduction in support infrastructure." The choice was now "between cutting operational effectiveness—thus national security—or cutting an inefficient infrastructure."[60]

The 1989 federal budget announced a total of fourteen closures and reductions,[61] most prominently in P.E.I., Ontario, Manitoba, and New Brunswick, all of which had received repeated reprieves in the past. At the time, Manitoba and New Brunswick were withholding support for the Meech Lake constitutional accord, which the Mulroney government strongly supported. These provincial choices, therefore, coupled with the consideration that Quebec was least affected by the defense cuts,[62] suggested that decisions might have been targeted to punish recalcitrant provinces while placating Quebec for political reasons.[63]

Protests were predictably loud. Moreover, the scale of the loss imposition generated precisely the type of coalition building one might expect in this situation: The affected communities banded together to resist the cuts.[64] Rallies were held in virtually every affected community; delegations were sent to Ottawa; and premiers visited the national capital to lobby on behalf of their provinces. P.E.I. residents even tried to enlist God on their side: Prayers were said in virtually every church on the island.[65] This was entirely understandable, since CFB Summerside was P.E.I.'s largest industry after agriculture. The island's lobbying campaign—honed through years of practice—included Premier Joe Ghiz, all the members of the provincial Legislative Assembly (regardless of party stripe), chambers of commerce and unions, the Public Service Alliance of Canada, the largest protest march in provincial history (with about 6,000 participants), and protests on Parliament Hill in Ottawa. Remarkably, given the history of Canadian base closures, Prime Minister Brian Mulroney held firm, although he promised some form of federal compensation.[66] In the end, the base was closed; but Summerside received the Goods and Services Tax Processing Centre to mitigate the impact.[67]

In September 1991, Marcel Masse, the minister of defense, issued a statement on defense policy that clearly pointed to further base closings and reductions. He announced that Canada's two overseas bases in Germany would be closed. Domestic infrastructure would be the subject of another committee study, called the September Review, stipulating that if Canada wished "to ensure that a satisfactory level of funding is available for the procurement of equipment, redundant or unnecessary infrastructure should be eliminated *immediately* in order to recover the savings thus realized."[68] The acrimony and maneuvering generated by the 1989 closures doubtless encouraged the minister to copy an American strategy for depoliticizing the proposed closure of bases.[69] Masse appointed an Advisory Group on Defence Infrastructure (MAGDI) to develop a decision-making framework (in part based on "the experience of foreign governments in dealing with identical problems of rationalization") and to report within six months. Part of the advisory group's mandate was to consider the socioeconomic impact of "adjustments," taking into account governmental programs, regional equity, and Canada's French-English duality. It was not charged with identifying specific facilities for closure.[70]

The advisory group reported in June 1992, urging the establishment of a Review Panel on Defence Infrastructure to ensure that decisions to close bases were based on security reasons rather than regional development. After making inquiries and holding hearings, the review panel would be free to modify the proposals it received from the minister of national defence before sending them to the minister and the government. If these recommendations were accepted without amendment, the report would be forwarded to a Parliamentary Committee (including opposition party members) that would, after up to thirty days of hearings, be able to vote for or against the report as a package before the final decision was made. In a departure from past processes, Dr. Katy Bindon, an expert on military history and strategy, argued that the proposed process imposed a greater degree of accountability and transparency, as well as a "timeframe . . . in which there is a multifaceted assessment of the basis of [each] recommendation and the arguments in support of it." The process could not be "entirely painless," she argued, but could certainly be more "felicitous than it has been."[71] Nevertheless, the minister of national defence delayed action.

The appeal of the proposed procedure, designed to be as nonpartisan as possible while placing significant constraints on governmental decision-making power, lay in the notion that the government itself would not be held accountable for the "pain'" inflicted on communities. Coming as it did late in the Conservative administration, however, some observers accused the government of simply using this advisory committee process as a politically motivated delay tactic to avoid announcing any base closures before the next election. They pointed to the American BRAC process as an indication that the decision-making process could be expedited if the government so desired.[72] As events unfolded, all of these procedural changes were rendered moot when an election was called and the Liberals were swept into power with a majority government.

The Liberals Come to Power

The Liberal *Red Book*, the Liberal Party's Agenda and Platform, committed the party to $1.3 billion in federal cuts in 1994–95, of which nearly half would come from the cancellation of the EH-101 helicopter program and other defense programs.[73] As promised, the new government initiated a review of defense priorities, but it undertook serious reforms before the final report was issued. The February 1994 budget announced the single largest program of base reductions and closures in Canadian history: Four large bases and two military colleges would be closed in the next three years, and sixteen smaller installations would be shut down or have their operations scaled back. Perhaps even more surprisingly, the minister of national defence warned that the government's fiscal position would permit only modest compensation, in special cases, for these closures; there would be "no more Summersides," because the government "just [did not] have the millions of dollars to replace the economic activity." The government estimated that these actions would save $850 million over five years, and by 1997–98 would produce annual savings of $350 million.[74] The 1995 federal budget announced the closure of nine more facilities.

The Department of National Defence's rationale for the reductions and closures was remarkably blunt and dismissive of the extensive consultation procedures recommended by the advisory group.[75] The constraints of prolonged public discussion and committee oversight were cast aside in the name of expediency and efficiency. While the lack of input elicited criticism from opposition MPs and from the media in affected areas, the Liberals achieved results, and they could turn to their *Red Book* promises of immediate and drastic reductions for justification. Defence Minister David Collenette, defending his government's actions, shifted blame to the previous administration: "For 10 years the Conservatives sat here in the biggest postwar economic boom and did not deal with the tough questions of surplus military infrastructures. They just sat on them and saddled Parliament with the consequences of their action. . . . They should be ashamed of themselves. . . . The Conservatives should have taken these tough decisions and not left them to us."[76] The collapse of the Conservative Party in the 1993 election meant that there was no force to counter this delegation of responsibility.

It took more than twenty-five years to close CFB Chatham after the intention was first announced in 1970. Department of National Defence officials publicly admitted in their budget documents that the department had been planning facility closures for years. Why, after decades of paralysis, was the Liberal government able to move so quickly and so drastically to impose these difficult losses on communities across the country? There were several key factors. First, by 1994 the government was able to convincingly claim that the federal budget deficit was at a point of crisis. With virtual unanimity in the country that "something had to be done," there was a rare opportunity to impose losses not just in the defense budget but across the board. As a result, the Liberals were prepared to act promptly and confidently, early in their administration. Second, the 1994 reductions were spread out across the country, and the defense budget was careful to document precisely how evenhanded the cuts were.[77] Third, while the budget had sternly warned that compensation would be minimal, it was still offered in some cases. Saint-Jean-sur-Richelieu, Quebec, the site of a military college, received $25 million and a refitting of the facilities for new academic uses. Cornwallis, Nova Scotia, received $7.5 million and would be home to a Canadian International Peacekeeping Centre, and Chatham received $17 million (including an armored vehicle renewal contract for which the region had no existing infrastructure).[78] Fourth, the Liberals faced a unique configuration of opposition parties, all of whom supported deficit reduction (albeit the Bloc Québécois [BQ] and New Democrats did so somewhat less fervently than the others). Although opposition members attacked the government over specific closure decisions, they did not challenge the notion that a widespread reduction in infrastructure was badly needed. Moreover, both the BQ and Reform parties had their power bases in specific regions of the country; as such, their opposition to Liberal decisions focused on areas they represented, allowing the government to dismiss their criticisms as narrow and self-centered.

Protests against Proposed Closures

Protests over the 1994–95 closures were different from those voiced in 1989. The debate in the House of Commons was predictably and thoroughly partisan. The Bloc Québécois focused its energies on protesting the closure of the College Militaire Royal (CMR) in Saint-Jean, the only French-language military school in Canada. With another referendum on Quebec sovereignty pending, the highly publicized, vociferous debate largely dissipated when Saint-Jean was slated to became a "megaplex" training facility in 1995.[79] Reform Party members attacked the absence of a parliamentary review process with respect to the closure decisions.[80] Moose Jaw MP Allan Kerpan advocated that an ad hoc committee of MPs with bases in their ridings (electoral districts) be established so that communities and parliamentarians could contribute information to the decision-making process. Such accusations and suggestions did not influence the process at all; the Liberal response was that the Reform Party's own deficit reduction agenda confirmed the need for the expedited process,[81] and decision-making power remained centralized in the cabinet.

The Liberal government justified the 1994 cuts on the basis that a regional balance had been struck, and that the majority of closures had come in Liberal constituencies,[82] thus the need to maintain a regional balance to the cuts was no longer aa key a criterion in 1995. Whereas the Liberals could plead a wide dispersion of loss in 1994, Reform-voting constituencies in Alberta and British Columbia took the brunt of the 1995 cuts. As a result, the most enduring criticisms came from the Western provinces.

Calgary, Alberta, was the hardest hit of any city in the country. Senior defense officials, fed up with years of uncertainty and tenuous negotiations over a training area on aboriginal lands, supported the closure of Harvey Barracks and the return of the Sarcee Training Area to the Tsuu T'ina First Nation in 1994. This sealed the fate of the rest of CFB Calgary. Although the cabinet decided to close the entire base in 1994, it did not publicly announce the decision until the following year's budget, catching many Calgarians by surprise. The large and prosperous city could certainly absorb the economic shock of the loss, but local spokespeople questioned the motives for the closure and its dubious financial justification. Edmonton, which had elected two Liberal members to Ottawa, stood to benefit from the transfer of soldiers and concomitant spending, including a large appropriation for new construction originally planned for Calgary. Rumors linked the closure of CFB Calgary with the need to console Edmontonians who had lost a squadron of Hercules aircraft that had been moved to Winnipeg, the riding of the minister of foreign affairs and international trade. In the latter case, critics noted that the Winnipeg airport would have been no longer viable without this transfer, and that the minister's riding needed to be compensated for the loss of a regular force regiment moved to CFB Shilo.[83] In addition, the dubious nature of the financial figures cited by the military when justifying the relocation to Edmonton became a source of significant controversy as the expected costs of the move rose exponentially. In the end, even a petition signed by more than ten thousand Calgarians protesting the closure posed little concern to the government in Ottawa.[84] The city was the heart of Reform country and would remain so whether the base was closed or maintained.

The closure of CFB Chilliwack—also located in a riding held by a Reform MP—was similarly controversial, though for different reasons. The Army appeared to have vigorously opposed the closure in internal departmental memoranda, on the basis that it needed a base to support domestic operations in British Columbia (such as emergency response), and that the excellent condition of the infrastructure, the low maintenance costs at Chilliwack, and the high capital costs of moving elsewhere would offset the proposed benefits.[85] More important, the closure of the base would result in no operational field force presence west of the Rockies and would hurt lower mainland British Columbia reserve units. These concerns, expressed within the Department of National Defence and in Parliament, did not prevent the closure. While some parts of Chilliwack eventually remained open, the Canadian Forces Officer Candidate School moved from Chilliwack to the megaplex in Saint-Jean. The minister of national defence dismissed opposition concerns as reflecting selected reading of internal documentation that failed to take into account the full range of advice provided to the deputy minister and the chief of defence staff, coupled with a "not in my backyard" mentality.

The Office of the Auditor General of Canada joined opposition MPs in criticizing the process employed by the federal government, stressing that base closure decisions needed to be based upon defense requirements and not political criteria. It applauded the BRAC legislation in the United States for "streamlining the political process and virtually [eliminating] political bartering" while facilitating community input and long-term planning by all stakeholders, and recommended that Canada adopt an independent, open process akin to the American model (and that proposed by the MAGDI in 1992) should further base closures or reductions be necessary. The clear force structure requirements, careful business planning, and transparent, independent review process characteristic of the American model were preferred, in the auditor general's report, to the secrecy and surprise that were hallmarks of Canadian rationalizations in 1994 and 1995.[86] The report highlighted the "cost and social advantages" of the American approach; but the political and institutional imperatives to adopt such a procedure do not exist in Canada.

The power to close and reduce bases in Canada was clearly concentrated in the governing party. By 1994, early in their first mandate, the majority Liberal government was willing to use this power and to bear the political costs of imposing base closures and reductions. Whatever the sentiments of citizens in constituencies (especially those represented by opposition MPs) that were affected by the closures, there was little recourse to influence the process except through efforts to embarrass the government through the media or through their local representative in the House of Commons. Although the Liberals were ultimately accountable for their decisions, blame was averted by casting the closures and realignments in terms of deficit reduction, the military's self-professed need to divest itself of surplus infrastructure and consolidate, and the opposition parties' partisan interest in specific ridings. There was no broad threat to the notion that base closures were needed and on a sweeping scale. In short, the Liberals accomplished their political objectives through enforced consensus, without delegating authority to an autonomous, consultative body or dispensing large amounts of compensation to affected communities.[87] Therefore, with the scars of the 1970s and 1980s now removed from the federal political psyche, there is no reason to expect that further military base and infrastructure reduction in Canada will not resemble the base reductions of the mid-1990s.

REFLECTIONS ON THE TWO CASES

The U.S. and Canadian experiences with military base closures show strong similarities. Both countries went through prolonged periods of minimal base closures, and both countries moved much more strongly in the late 1980s to impose closures, impelled in large part by a combination of high budget deficits, high expectations for a big defense "peace dividend" with the end of the Cold War, and a realization that continuing defense obligations (made more real for the United States by the Gulf War and for Canada by new peacekeeping commitments) could be sustained in the new fiscal environment only by streamlining defense infrastructure.

The methods used by the two countries to impose closures differed in some respects and in magnitude. The United States implemented a new procedure of independent commissions that combined a highly visible evaluative process, some public consultation, and a heavy dose of insulation of elected politicians from political blame. The Canadian Advisory Group was modeled on this experiment, but when the Liberal Government came into power, the advisory group was scrapped and the government reverted to an ad hoc, budget-driven process, imposing facility closures in 1994 and 1995. Both countries used insulation mechanisms to avoid blame, but the Liberals were able to implement base closures at the beginning of their governing mandate in part because they could shift the blame to the Conservatives—who, they argued, had not been able to close any bases at all during their ten years in power. In the end, both countries successfully closed down and realigned enough bases to have an impact on their respective defense budgets. The U.S. cut about one-fifth of its total domestic base structure; the Canadians cut nearly half of theirs.[88]

Two intertwined differences, one in the respective political environments and the other in the two countries' political institutions, seem central in explaining the different paths taken by the two governments. The first difference is the greater salience of regional cleavages in Canada than in the United States. While regional divisions are by no means absent in the United States, the sense that any defense cutbacks in a region represent an affront to an already aggrieved and mistreated region (a self-perception shared by almost all regions in Canada) has mostly weak parallels in the United States. Legislators from several regions did lambaste the insensitivity of Washington-based bureaucrats in drawing up lists considered for closures, and charged that their regions were being singled out unfairly.[89] California officials, for example, charged in 1994 that their state had suffered 70 percent of the job losses entailed by the first three rounds of base closures despite the fact that only 15 percent of military personnel were based there.[90] State and regional congressional delegations often worked together to block specific base closures in many cases. But the sense of grievance was, on the whole, much more localized, and thus less politically explosive, in the United States.

Paralleling and reinforcing this difference was the role of the cabinet in Canadian base closures, a role that has no parallel on the U.S. side. Canadian cabinets are composed of elected politicians, and they are constructed to be both regionally representative and regionally sensitive.[91] While the cabinet often delegates decision-making authority to specialized bodies like regulatory commissions, it almost always retains ultimate authority to overturn politically sensitive decisions made by those bodies. In the Canadian context, with decision-making power vested in the governing party, there was no *need* to establish "nonpartisan" commissions to determine what bases should be closed or realigned. While this concentration of authority and accountability alarmed the Conservative Party during its tenure in government, the Liberals have used the direct, government-centered decision-making powers at their disposal to great effect over the last decade. Furthermore, for the Canadian cabinet to bind itself to the decisions of an independent body in a meaningful way would be a much bigger leap than for legislators in the U.S., where such delegations of authority are common and where the courts (notably in the *Chadha* decision on the legislative veto) have limited legislative efforts at more limited delegations of authority.[92] Members of Congress did try to make use of the courts to avoid implementation of base closure decisions, but with no success; in this decision-making arena, the courts proved to be of little salience or use as a means of venue-shifting.

The use of an independent commission to decide on military base closures in the United States provides an interesting contrast with the case of pension cuts, as outlined in chapter 2. Although several prominent commissions have been appointed to propose Social Security reforms, politicians in the United States have never been willing to give the proposals made by those commissions the same procedural protections that were accorded the base-closing commission, because (1) the policy preferences of many legislators were much more strongly against cutting Social Security, (2) the scope of the delegation of authority with respect to Social Security would be much higher and its political salience much greater, and (3) the risk is much higher that future political opponents would later be able to generate blame against incumbent decision makers, and their constituents would punish them for voting for delegation of authority in the event that the commission did recommend cuts. The general lesson here is that politicians in the United States are likely to approve highly binding delegations of authority only when the political stakes are perceived to be relatively small, or when there is a broad agreement or consensus on outcomes but a need to provide political cover from a minority of constituents, or when both are true.[93]

In the base closure case study, institutions did matter, at least to a degree. The presidential–congressional system in the United States, characterized by divided government during the period under consideration, could not employ the kind of blame-shifting techniques that aided the new Liberal government in Canada in making and implementing significant base closures during the same period of time. The Liberals' electoral mandate, along with the fiscal crisis of the early 1990s, allowed the Westminster system in Canada to impose loss without the concomitant fear of blame that members of the U.S. Congress were working hard to avoid while making and implementing the same decisions in their system. The unitary government in Canada, in this context, eased the process, whereas the diffuse quality of the electoral system in the United States made the creation and use of the BRAC absolutely necessary, particularly in the face of divided government and the need to generate some kind of consensus on this issue.

NOTES

1. See Brigadier General G. G. Bell, "The Armed Forces and the Civil Authority: Two Aiding National Development," *Behind the Headlines* (December 1972): 7–14.
2. See, for example, "Shutdown of forces base will knock N.B. town flat," *Calgary Herald*, November 10, 1981, and the Canadian Department of National Defence (DND) budget impact statements for 1994 and 1995, which detail anticipated socioeconomic impacts on communities.
3. Kenneth R. Mayer, "Closing Military Bases (Finally): Solving Collective Dilemmas through Delegation," *Legislative Studies Quarterly* 20, no. 3 (August 1995): 396. See also Bob Benenson, "Members Hustle to Protect Defense Jobs Back Home," *Congressional Quarterly Weekly Report* 48, no 2 (January 13, 1990): 87–90.
4. Mayer, "Closing Military Bases," 398–99.
5. Representative Dick Armey (R-TX) explains some of the instances where this fear of political retribution via base closures has come into play. See Richard Armey, "Base Maneuvers: The Games Congress Plays with the Military Pork Barrel," *Policy Review* (winter 1988):, 73. See also L. Goren and P. W. Lackenbauer, *The Comparative Politics of Military Base Closures: A United States–Canadian Case Study of De-Distributive Decisions and Domestic Military Bases.* (Oreno, Maine: University of Maine Press, Canadian American Public Policy Occasional papers series, vol. 23, Sept. 2000).
6. Mike Mills, "Members Go on the Offensive to Defend Bases," *Congressional Quarterly Weekly Report*, 46 (July 2, 1988): 1815–17.
7. Mayer, "Closing Military Bases," 394. See also Charlotte Twight, "Department of Defense Attempts to Close Military Bases: The Political Economy of Congressional Resistance," in Robert Higgs, ed., *Arms, Politics, and the Economy: Historical and Contemporary Perspectives* (New York: Holmes & Meier). The key provision impeding military base closures was a requirement that detailed environmental impact studies be conducted with respect to any base closure proposal. See Mike Mills, "1976 Law Poses Key Hurdle to Closing Bases," *Congressional Quarterly Weekly Report* 48 (July 2, 1990): 1817.
8. Phil Kuntz, "House Panels Differ over Base-Closing Bill," *Congressional Quarterly Weekly Report*, 46 (June 11, 1988): 1619.
9. *H.R. 1583 to Establish the Bipartisan Commission on the Consolidation of Military Bases,* Hearing before the Subcommittee on Military Installations and Facilities, 100th Cong., 1st sess., March 17, May 18–19, and June 8, 1988, 120.
10. Casimir David Hadwiger, "*Military Base Closures: How Congress Balances Geographic and General Interests*" (Ph.D. diss., University of California, Berkeley, 1993): 57.

11. Ibid., 77.

12. Ibid.

13. Twight, "Department of Defense Attempts to Close Military Bases," 262.

14. Defense Base Closure and Realignment Act of 1988, section 208 [Public Law 100-526], Defense Base Closure and Realignment Act of 1990, section 2903 (e), section 2904 (a) [Public Law 101-510]. See also Christopher Deering, "Congress, The President, and Automatic Government: The Case of Military Base Closures," in James A. Thurber, ed., *Rivals for Power: Presidential-Congressional Relations* (Washington, D.C.: Congressional Quarterly Books), pp. 153–69.

15. Each Base Realignment and Closing Commission is to be composed of members who are appointed by the president and approved by the Senate. The appointments are to be made in consultation with the majority and minority parties in both houses so as to make sure that the commission has a partisan balance.

16. The first round of base closings under the independent commission process contained one potential roadblock that could (and almost did) kill the process: a requirement that normal procedures be used to appropriate funds needed to implement base closures. In the subsequent legislation that set up the later rounds of base closures, funds were both authorized and appropriated in advance. See Mayer, "Closing Military Bases," 401.

17. Mayer, "Closing Military Bases," 406.

18. Representative Richard Armey (R-TX), the author of the BRAC legislation, was unabashedly clear that he was modeling the BRAC on the more useful and successful characteristics of the Social Security reform effort of 1982–83. See Paul Light's *Artful Work: The Politics of Social Security Reform* (New York: Random House, 1985) for more details on the Social Security Commission of 1982–1983, which created and put through the Social Security reforms in 1983.

19. The four committees were Armed Services, Merchant Marines and Fisheries, Government Operations, and the Rules Committee.

20. See Phil Kuntz, "House Panels Differ over Base-Closing Bill, *Congressional Quarterly Weekly Report* (June 11, 1988): 1619–20, and Mike Mills, "Members Go on the Offensive," 1815.

21. Defense Base Closure and Realignment Act of 1990, section 2908 (c) [Public Law 101-510], 104 Stat. 1817 (1990), 10 USC 2687 note.

22. Defense Secretary Frank Carlucci had already appointed a commission before the 1988 legislation was passed, but the legislation defined the procedures by which its recommendations could be rejected by Congress.

23. "House Clears the Way for Base Closings," *Congressional Quarterly Weekly Report*, 47 (April 22, 1989): 918.

24. Cheney is quoted in Pat Towell, "On Base Closings, No Hill Reprieve," *Congressional Quarterly Weekly Report*, 49 (September 30, 1989): 2576. See also Mike Mills, "Challenge to Base Closings Fizzles on House Floor," *Congressional Quarterly Weekly Report*, 47 (August 5, 1989): 2062–64. Secretary of Defense Cheney's comments offered the same argument that the Supreme Court later made when it was confronted with a complaint about the BRAC process and the desire by some elected representatives to have certain bases taken off the list after the fact.

25. Press speculation at the time suggested that about two dozen bases were likely to be closed. See Associated Press, "Panel Expected to Favor Closing Two Dozen Military Bases," *Washington Post*, December 14, 1988, A4; "Bye-Bye Bases," *National Journal*, October 15, 1988: 2624.

26. Interview with Jay Winik, Washington, D.C., 5 May 1998.

27. See Mike Mills, "Cheney's Plan for Shutdowns a New Salvo in Long Fight," *Congressional Quarterly Weekly Report* 48 (February 3, 1990): 340–42.

28. See Elizabeth A. Palmer and Pat Towell, "Cheney Reveals New Hit List; Members Feel the Pain," *Congressional Quarterly Weekly Report*, 49 (April 13, 1991): 931–32.

29. Barton Gellman, "Base-Closing List Likely to Stick Despite Flack," *Washington Post*, July 2, 1991, A4.

30. Elizabeth A. Palmer, "Commission Spares Just a Few from Cheney's Hit List," *Congressional Quarterly Weekly Report*, 49 (July 6, 1991): 1845–48; Elizabeth A. Palmer, "Bush Approves Panel's List, Dashing Members' Hopes," *Congressional Quarterly Weekly Report*, 49 (July 13, 1991): 1915; Elizabeth A. Palmer, "Opponents Lose Final Bid to Save Installations," *Congressional Quarterly Weekly Report*, 49 (August 3, 1991): 2190.

31. See Elizabeth A. Palmer, "Megaports to Keep Navy Afloat As Other Facilities Close," *Congressional Quarterly Weekly Report*, 51 (July 3, 1993): 1755–58.

32. Defense Base Closure and Realignment Commission, *1995 Report to the President*, Previous Base Closure Rounds (Washington, D.C.: GPO, 1995): 5, subsection chap. 4.

33. Defense Base Closure and Realignment Commission, *1991 Report to the President*, Executive Summary (Washington, D.C.: GPO, 1991): v.

34. Texas and California, *but particularly California*, were considered keys to Bill Clinton's re-election strategy and subsequent success in 1996. California, in 1995 and 1996, was still working its way out of the recession of the early 1990s, and more closures of large bases in California would, potentially, have worked against Mr. Clinton in his bid for California votes. Thus the "privatization in place" mechanism kept the base (and the jobs) more or less as it was before it was selected for closure by the BRAC.

35. *Dalton v Specter*, 511 U.S. 462 (114 S. Ct. 1719, 1994).

36. "High Court Hears a Senator," *New York Times*, March 3, 1994, section A–16.

37. See Defense Base Closure and Realignment Commission, *1995 Report to the President*, Previous Base Closure Rounds, subsection chap. 4, for precise details.

38. The BRAC had been instructed to take this calculation into effect when making its decisions, since the selected bases are to reach a point of net savings rather than expenditures within a five- or six-year period.

39. Defense Base Closure and Realignment Commission, *1995 Report to the President*, Executive Summary, v.

40. Ibid.

41. Following the unification of the Canadian Forces, there were several closures and reductions in 1966, related to an attempt to rationalize the over 100 training centers that the military maintained across the country. See "Ottawa May Close Centralia Air Base," *Globe and Mail* (Toronto), May 9, 1966; "Churchill to Lose Navy," *Winnipeg Free Press*, September 14, 1966.

42. Clive Baxter, "Bad News on Base Closings Comes Soon," *Financial Post*, August 9, 1969.

43. Clive Baxter, "Want to Buy a Base? Ottawa Selling Some," *Financial Post*, November 29, 1969.

44. Dr. J. C. Arneil, Assistant Deputy Minister (Finance), Department of National Defence [hereinafter DND], SCEAND, (March 26, 1971): pp. 20: 15–16; Mr. D. H. W. Kirkwood, ADM (Policy), DND, SCEAND, (March 28, 1974): pp. 7: 16–17.

45. Scott Young, "No Firm Commitment, but PM Sympathetic on Base-Closing Issue," *Globe and Mail* (Toronto), July 25, 1969.

46. "Defence Closedowns to Take Some Years," *Montreal Star*, July 29, 1969.

47. "Defence Base Closings, Cuts, to Be Staggered," *Ottawa Journal*, July 29, 1969.

48. "To Fight Air Base Closure," *Winnipeg Free Press*, August 28, 1970; Paul Pihichyn, "Government May Delay Closures," *Winnipeg Free Press*, November 19, 1970. For a list of closures from 1965 to 1972, including the number of displaced personnel by site, see Lieutenant-Colonel J. Gardam, Directorate of Base Planning, DND, SCEAND (March 16, 1972): p. 5: 18.

49. Gerald Porter, *In Retreat: The Canadian Forces in the Trudeau Years* (Ottawa: Deneau and Greenberg, 1978), 8–11.

50. "Forces Thin, Gov't Studies Cutting Bases," *Ottawa Journal*, November 26, 1975. On the need for closures, see also Hon. James Richardson, Minister of National Defence,

Statement on Defence Expenditures for 1976–77, Appendix Q, SCEAND, (April 13, 1976): p. 35: 29.

51. "No Decision Made on Base Closures," *Ottawa Citizen*, January 27, 1976; SCEAND, (May 6, 1976): 39:19–20, 23; (May 13, 1976): p. 35: 19.

52. Greg Coolen, "Economic Nightmare," *Chronicle-Herald* (Halifax), March 23, 1976.

53. John Porteous, "Maritime Bases 'On Alert' over Rumours of Closings," *Financial Post*, April 3, 1976.

54. "Shutdown of Forces Base Will Knock N.B. Town Flat," *Calgary Herald*, November 10, 1981; "N.B. Businessmen Fear CFB Chatham to Close," *Globe and Mail* (Toronto), February 5, 1984; DND, news release, May 22, 1984.

55. Victor Mackie, "Plan to Close Bases Stalled in Committee," *Ottawa Journal*, May 27, 1976.

56. "Ottawa Postpones Plans to Trim Military Bases," *Globe and Mail* (Toronto), July 26, 1976.

57. National Defence Headquarters Study Directive S61, "Infrastructure Rationalization" (Directorate of History and Heritage 78/154), November 30, 1976; Victor Mackie, "Military Base Cuts Reduced," *Ottawa Journal*, October 6, 1976; "Pressures Force Ottawa to Reduce Base Closures," *Albertan*, October 6, 1976.

58. John McHugh, "CFB London to Remain Open," *London Free Press*, November 30, 1976; Hon. B. J. Danson, Minister of National Defence, SCEAND, (November 29, 1976): pp. 2: 14–15; (December 1, 1976): pp. 3: 24–5; (March 8, 1977): pp. 6: 37–40; General Dextraze, SCEAND, (March 10, 1977): pp. 7: 14–32. On the rationale for maintaining CFB Summerside, see Third Report to the House, SCEAND, (June 29, 1972): p. 19: 9; SCEAND, (May 6, 1975): p. 20: 36.

59. Report of the Auditor General of Canada, 1994, chap. 26: Infrastructure Reductions, www.oag-bvg.ca/domino/reports.nsf/html/9426ce.html.

60. DND, "Base Reconstruction" (backgrounder), May 1989.

61. Canada, Department of Finance, *The Budget Speech*, (April 27, 1989): 6.

62. The loss of the Mont Apica radar site was offset by a mobile radar establishment at Bagotville.

63. Michel Rossignol, *Military Base Closures* (Ottawa: Library of Parliament, 1993); *Canada's Defence News Bulletin* 3/18 (May 3, 1989). The resounding Conservative majority in the House of Commons (168 seats, compared with 83 for the Liberals and 43 for the NDP, as of January 1989) led to a politically predictable result, with most of the basic closures and cuts hitting ridings with Liberal representatives.

64. Carey French, "Communities Join Forces against Base Closings," *Globe and Mail* (Toronto), May 2, 1989. See also SCEAND, (June 26, 1989): pp. 4:14–17.

65. John Lyons, "Prairie Effort Trails Island Lobby," *Winnipeg Free Press*, June 30, 1989.

66. Roy Wood, "PM Stands Firm on Base Closing despite Ghiz's Plea," *Montreal Gazette*, July 11, 1989; Julian Beltrame, "6,000 Islanders Protest Base Closing," *Calgary Herald*, May 15, 1989.

67. Peter C. Newman, "Time to Gut Our Biggest Landlord," *Maclean's*, March 7, 1994, p. 44.

68. Quoted in "Comments: A Non-Interview with Marcel Masse," *Esprit de Corps* (April 1992): p. 13.

69. "How to Streamline our Defence System," *Maclean's*, August 19, 1991.

70. Statement by the Honourable Marcel Masse, September 17, 1991.

71. SCEAND, (June 16, 1992): p. 26: 14.

72. See, for example, SCEAND, (October 21, 1991): p. 7: 15.

73. Liberal Party of Canada, *Creating Opportunity: The Liberal Plan for Canada* (Ottawa: Liberal Party of Canada, 1993): 111.

74. Hugh Winsor, "Collenette warns of Base Closings," *Globe and Mail* (Toronto), February 18, 1994; Jeff Sallot, "Four Military Bases Wiped off Map," *Globe and Mail* (Toronto), February 23, 1994.

75. DND, *1994 Budget*, 19.

76. Canada, House of Commons, *Debates* [hereinafter *Hansard*], (February 23, 1994): 1744.

77. The high per capita military cuts in Atlantic Canada, the minister argued, reflected the disproportionate number of bases built in the region during the Second World War that had never been closed. See Sallot, "Four Military Bases Wiped off Map."

78. "$1 Million Is Enough, Ottawa Says," *Montreal Gazette*, June 13, 1996; Jean-Marc Jacob (Charlesbourg, BQ), *Hansard* (November 21, 1995): 16584; DND, "Cornwallis: A Canadian International Peacekeeping Training Centre" (backgrounder), February 1994. There were also criticisms of so-called "closures" of bases that were in some cases not closed completely but reduced to "detachment status." See, for example, Robert Sheppard, "The Way to 'Close' a Military Base," *Globe and Mail* (Toronto), November 22, 1994.

79. David Johnston, "Defence Fallout," *Montreal Gazette*, February 26, 1994; Anne McIlroy, "Quebec Signs Deal for Military College," *Calgary Herald*, July 20, 1994; Rheal Seguin and Susan Delacourt, "PQ Wants Military College Left Open," *Globe and Mail* (Toronto), October 19, 1994.

80. *Hansard* (February 24, 1994), 1819.

81. *Hansard* (February 17, 1994): 1517; see also (February 3, 1994): 885.

82. See Hon. David Michael Collenette, *Hansard* (February 23, 1994): 1744. The 1993 election saw the Liberals win a majority government with a power base in the Maritimes, Ontario, and Manitoba. The Bloc Québécois won 54 of 75 seats in Quebec, and the Reform Party won 50 of 72 seats in Saskatchewan, Alberta, and British Columbia.

83. See Letter, General A. J. G. D. de Chastelain, Chief of the Defence Staff, August 5, 1994; CFB Calgary Closure—Master Implementation Plan; Annex D to (A) 94/0156 (VCDS), July 1994 (acquired under Access to Information); Stephen Harper (Calgary West, Reform), *Hansard*, (March 23, 1995): 10885; *Hansard* (online version), September 19, 1994, www.parl.gc.ca/english/hansard/previous/092_94-09-19/092SM1E.html.

84. Stephen Harper, *Hansard* (October 5, 1995): 15253; (June 3, 1996): 3325.

85. The Land Forces Command (LFC) also opposed the closures of Detachments Moncton and Toronto and stated that the potential savings at Montreal, Toronto, and London were likely inflated. Col. J. R. P. Daigle, G3, "Executive Summary of Program Review" (secret memorandum) (October 14, 1994): pp. 1–2, Annex D (acquired under Access to Information).

86. Report of the Auditor General of Canada, 1994, Report of the Standing Committee on Public Accounts to the House of Commons, 12 June 1995 www.oagbvg.gc.ca/domino/reports.nsf/.

87. Of the fifty-two bases, stations, and detachments maintained by the military in 1994, only twenty-four remained by the end of 1999. Minister Compendium of Changes in the Canadian Forces and the Department of National Defence, www.dnd.ca/eng/min/reports/Compendium/Change2.htm.

88. Closing a base is often a rather expensive undertaking, because there may be significant environmental cleanup costs before the area can be opened for civilian uses. The two countries' defense budgets have only recently begun to see the full results of the base closings of the early 1990s.

89. See, for example, Elizabeth A. Palmer, "Commission May Help Ease Members' Unsavory Task," *Congressional Quarterly Weekly Report*, 49 (March 2, 1991): 555.

90. William Claiborne, "California Seeks to Fend Off Further Closings of Military Bases," *Washington Post*, (December 10, 1994): A3.

91. See Herman Bakvis, *Regional Ministers: Power and Influence in the Canadian Cabinet* (Toronto: University of Toronto Press, 1991).

92. Immigration and Naturalization Serv. v. Chadha, 462 U.S.919 (1983). The Supreme Court struck down what had become known as the "legislative veto." This was action

by Congress to stop the executive branch from going forward in certain and various activities. For a much more detailed analysis of this topic, see Jessica Korn, *Power of Separation: American Constitutionalism and the Myth of the Legislative Veto*, (Princeton, N.J.: Princeton University Press, 1996).

93. R. Kent Weaver, "Is the Congress Abdicating Power to Commission?" *Roll Call*, (February 12, 1989): 5; Mayer, "Closing Military Bases," 408–10.

7

SITING NUCLEAR WASTE

BARRY G. RABE

Nuclear reactors have generated significant quantities of electricity and related varieties of waste products in both Canada and the United States for nearly a half-century. During much of that period, these facilities and their wastes were hardly seen as forms of loss imposition. To the contrary, the construction and commissioning of new nuclear power facilities were distributional goods, energetically pursued and enthusiastically welcomed by many of the Canadian and American communities fortunate enough to be selected to host them. In many respects, site selection for nuclear power plants resembled the distributional politics of hospital expansion or highway construction, with any sense of "loss" felt primarily in those communities that were unsuccessful in securing one.

These facilities were highly attractive to communities, offering immediate access to state-of-the-art electrical generating capacity that was widely expected to be "too cheap to meter." More important, they promised a significant economic development boost, with large numbers of high-paying jobs that appeared secure for decades to come. The opening of nuclear power plants in various states and provinces regularly provided an opportunity for credit-claiming by elected officials who could brag of their involvement in the siting process; ribbon-cutting ceremonies were often crowded with officials from all levels of governments eager to get into the photograph. Many communities with substantial nuclear power plants or related research centers became known as "Ph.D. capitals" and boasted unusually high rates of per pupil expenditures for public school students, owing to the high property tax revenues generated by these facilities. "This was at a time when the *Weekly Reader*, which we all had as children, proclaimed the wonders of the atom," recalled former Nevada Governor and Senator Richard Bryan. "Nevada was very much enthralled by being on the cutting edge. Hey, I was excited about it."[1]

Such enthusiasm was neither confined to Nevada nor to the earliest years of nuclear energy in the late 1950s and early 1960s. As recently as 1975, President Gerald Ford endorsed a doubling in the number of nuclear power plants over the next decade. At nearly the same time, George Gathercoal, the chairman of Ontario Hydro, the public utility for Canada's most populous province, called for an increase in the number of nuclear plants within the province from 20 to 160 by the year 2000.

Amid this early enthusiasm, there was very little discussion of the variety of waste products generated by nuclear reactors. Nuclear waste was simply not an agenda item in either Canada or the United States, reflecting a confidence that sophisticated technical solutions would safely resolve this issue over time. Intensive research programs sponsored by both federal governments, examining options that ranged from chemical neutralization of waste to nonreturning launches into outer space, were expected to deliver politically painless answers to this inconvenient aspect of nuclear reactor operation. Meanwhile, early attempts to store certain quantities of waste away from the site of nuclear reactors were not controversial, as reflected in six American communities that raised no opposition to hosting facilities to store so-called "low-level" nuclear wastes during the 1960s and early 1970s.

The politics of nuclear power and nuclear waste has been transformed in more recent decades. Canada has not opened a new nuclear power plant since 1980, and the newest American facility was opened in 1982. Once seen as marvels of technological skill and operational efficiency, the 124 nuclear power plants located in the two nations are increasingly regarded as millstones in a deregulatory environment for electricity generation and distribution. It is difficult to foresee any circumstances under which a new nuclear plant, even one featuring superior technology, would be sited in any state or province in the coming decades. Any possibility of future plant siting was even further diminished in the aftermath of the September 2001 terrorist attacks, which focused new attention on nuclear plants and waste sites as possible targets for future attack.

A series of factors have contributed to this sea change in political fortunes with respect to nuclear power, including the transformation of nuclear waste from a nonissue into an extreme form of geographical loss imposition. The once-anticipated technological fix for waste disposal has yet to materialize, leaving some form of burial deep within geological formations as the preferred option of the present. However, at the same time that the siting of new nuclear plants has ground to a halt, efforts to site high-level nuclear waste repositories have triggered outraged opposition in all Canadian and American communities considered to date as possible site candidates. Consequently, every nuclear reactor in Canada and the United States has become an inadvertent storage site for nuclear waste, awaiting the resolution of politically charged controversies in each country regarding the location of permanent host sites. For now, storage occurs either in water-filled cooling pools indoors or in nearby canisters composed of concrete and steel.

This chapter will focus on the form of waste that tends to trigger the most intensive public concern: high-level nuclear waste. This type of waste consists primarily of spent fuel residuals from nuclear reactors. Referred to as "rods" in the United States and "bundles" in Canada, these wastes resemble hefty fireplace logs and include tubular zirconium alloy sheaths that contain ceramic uranium oxide pellets. In one respect these wastes appear less burdensome than virtually any other form of waste, in that their sheer volume is quite minimal compared with the amounts of low-level nuclear waste as well as so-called hazardous (or toxic) wastes. Collectively, American and Canadian nuclear power plants have generated approximately the same volumes of high-level nuclear waste per capita in each nation. Given the high concentration of this tonnage, however, the actual space consumed by the wastes is far less than the vast amounts of materials deposited in familiar solid waste landfills. The average amount of high-level nuclear waste produced each year by a nuclear plant would, if compacted, fit into a phone booth; in fact, one commonly noted assessment concludes that all of Canada's current high-level nuclear waste would fill three regulation-sized hockey rinks up to the top of the boards.[2] Any seeming advantage for waste management posed by the relatively compact nature of the waste, however, is countered by the intense and enduring nature of the public health threat posed by exposure to these materials. Unlike other forms of nuclear waste with fairly rapid processes of decay and consequent decline in radioactivity, these wastes have been irradiated with by-products that must be isolated from human contact for a minimum of 10,000 years, and possibly for as long as 100,000 years. This fact gives rise to the popular description that such waste requires at least "one hundred centuries of solitude."[3]

These qualities contribute to making high-level nuclear waste disposal a unique case among loss-imposing policies. The severity of the potential risks imposed by permanent disposal techniques may be so great, vis-à-vis both the threat to human health and the length of the time commitment necessary for implementation, that it may trump various institutional explanations that would anticipate some variation in national outcomes in the two countries. Actually, in some respects, there are important similarities in these cases between the two countries. Both faced very similar policy inheritances from nuclear waste disposal in recent decades. In both, this unexpectedly serious problem represented a notable departure from the pattern of relative calm, involving heavily subsidized nuclear industries and low-profile nuclear subgovernments, established during the first quarter-century of policy. Moreover, both nations gave their respective *federal* governments unusually early and extensive authority over most key policy issues concerning nuclear power and waste, contrary to the more varied patterns of responsibility characteristic of other areas of environmental federalism.

Aside from these similarities, substantial political and institutional differences have not led to any final outcome differences to date, although the United States is clearly closer to a possible long-term strategy. Any anticipated Canadian advantage with respect to moving legislation forward, given its comparatively concentrated authority and reduced number of veto points, has not translated into specific policy outputs. In fact, Canada's original nuclear energy legislation, enacted in 1946, was never amended or supplemented until 1997. This new legislation, the Nuclear Safety and Control Act, does not address many of the most controversial issues surrounding future waste disposal; rather, it essentially codifies safety and health regulations developed by national ministries during recent decades. In contrast, the presumably hamstrung U.S. Congress has taken more legislative steps, particularly between 1982 and 1992, and again in 2002, but none of these actions has led to any final loss imposition decisions regarding waste disposal. Other significant institutional factors, such as the impact of varying election cycles, seem largely irrelevant in this case.

Consequently, high-level nuclear waste disposal siting may be characterized by so intensive a loss-imposing potential as to defy conventional institutional explanations. As one senior Natural Resources Canada official noted, "I would hate to be bound today by some irrevocable decision my Victorian forefathers made for me centuries ago."[4] Yet any decision involving irretrievable burial, the prevailing disposal concept in Canada and the United States in recent decades, has precisely such binding features. Other wastes, including less intensive radioactive ones, involve far less of a risk to human health and are a threat for far shorter periods of time. Most other forms of loss imposition can be reversed, whether by reopening a closed military base or restoring a pension cut. But the proposals for so-called "permanent disposal" of high-level nuclear waste are in essence as permanent as public policy can become. Institutional differences may matter little when governments face such a challenge, resulting in a common preference for more "temporary" approaches, such as on-site storage, while public deliberation and research over various technical options continue, perhaps for decades to come.

TYPE OF LOSS IMPOSITION

Given the uncertain life span of nations, much less the environmental regulatory policies of individual governments, this long-term horizon for waste decomposition poses considerable risk to any community assigned to manage these wastes. Federal authorities in both Canada and the United States have endorsed the idea of establishing a single repository in each nation to assume perpetual responsibility for all high-level nuclear waste that has been generated to date or will be created once current facilities are decommissioned. Both have also supported reliance on deep burial within a geological formation, such as a mountain range. If established, all high-level nuclear waste generated in both nations would be shipped to the designated site in the host province or state. It would, under most recent plans, be buried in such a way that it could never be extracted and would be constructed with such elaborate protective features as to be able to withstand a direct nuclear bombing or any conceivable terrorist act.

Such a policy area thus constitutes an extreme version of geographically concentrated loss imposition. Any governing community or jurisdiction within which the repository area was sited would live with the consequences of this imposed loss for, at minimum, a time span more than forty times longer than the history of the American republic. "Clearly here we enter the realm of what can only be called 'political science fiction,'" explained policy analyst Robert Paehlke during 1996 Canadian government hearings. "We cannot even assume that there will be a Canada in 1998, let alone in 11998."[5] Extensive research on the perception of various types of risk consistently concludes that the public deems a high-level nuclear waste management facility to pose far greater risks than other facilities, such as nuclear power plants, nuclear weapons production facilities, chemical manufacturing plants, and prisons.[6] According to one synthesis of these findings, such wastes "are perceived as representing very high risks, which the public characterizes as immense, dreaded, catastrophic, unknown, uncontrollable, and inequitable."[7] Historian Spencer Weart concludes that, unlike other significant forms of risk, nuclear wastes create "feelings of awe and terror, little different from what we might feel if confronted with a mad scientist's monster or a divine apocalypse."[8]

High-level nuclear waste management, therefore, goes far beyond most other likely forms of geographical loss imposition, such as military base closure. In fact, the intensity of public sentiment on the issue, along with the strategy of concentrating the entire nuclear waste (i.e., the entire loss) of a nation at a single site, may give this case unique features from the standpoint of loss imposition. But, as in other cases, there are clearly identifiable winners and losers in the event that the single-site strategy is implemented in either Canada or the United States.

Potential Winners

Successful siting of a single repository would offer an opportunity for massive reallocation of responsibility for high-level nuclear waste. For all of the states, provinces, communities, and facilities that currently host nuclear power reactors and are required to store high-level waste on site, concentrated loss imposition on the host community would create a redistributive opportunity to export their wastes. At present, the de facto practice of storage involves the sites of 103 American nuclear power reactors in thirty-one states and six Canadian sites with twenty-one nuclear power plants, located in three provinces. Nineteen of the Canadian plants are in Ontario, which tends to cluster multiple plants in neighboring settings, thereby leading to shared storage arrangements.

This export possibility may explain the broad support for repository siting among most elected officials representing jurisdictions that would gain an export destination. In the United States, many members of Congress and governors from both parties in states with nuclear power plants have strongly endorsed the export option—as long as their jurisdiction is not the ultimate host. For example, Senator Ernest F. Hollings (D–SC) agreed to support 1997 legislation designed to increase the likelihood that Nevada would become the national high-level waste host once he secured a provision that South Carolina would be eliminated from any consideration as a temporary storage site. This was particularly important in his state, given its long-term operation of one of the few remaining low-level nuclear waste sites (opened in the 1960s) and its possible candidacy for a role in expanded storage. Upon securing this provision, Hollings exulted: "We have slammed the door shut on anyone who thinks they can use South Carolina as a national dumping ground for the country's high-level radioactive waste."[9] This type of support has consistently crossed partisan lines and has been strongest from representatives of jurisdictions with the greatest existing waste burden. Siting of a repository would clearly provide elected representatives of these jurisdictions with an opportunity to claim credit for transferring a nasty problem to another geographical area while avoiding blame for any problems that might stem from such on-site storage. Similar political support from potential nuclear waste-exporting jurisdictions has also been evident in Canada.[10]

Perhaps the greatest beneficiaries from the creation of a repository, however, would be the nuclear power industry and electric utility officials. The inability to ship high-level waste to a permanent site only compounds the uncertainty surrounding the future of nuclear power generators in Canada and the United States. This is a particularly serious problem for those facilities with limited available space for on-site storage, for which the absence of external waste management may preclude long-term plant operation.

Repository creation would not necessarily give nuclear power a new lease on life in Canada or the United States, but it would clearly remove a major impediment to the continued operation of existing plants and to any serious discussion of new facility construction. It would also provide a boost for much-maligned federal agencies, such as the U.S. Department of Energy and Atomic Energy of Canada Limited (AECL), and increase the future viability of their nuclear energy activities. Elimination of the biggest environmental barrier to nuclear power would also serve to bolster the strongest pro-environment argument for nuclear power. Approximately one-third of greenhouse gases generated in Canada and the United States come from electricity generation, primarily through the burning of coal and other fossil fuels for power. Given the growing concern over the contribution of these gases to global warming, the fact that nuclear power plants release no greenhouse gases is a significant attraction in terms of their continued operation.[11] Neither Canada nor the United States has taken the sort of serious loss imposition steps inherent in any greenhouse gas reduction strategy, but the recent growth in these emissions would expand markedly if current nuclear power generating capacity was replaced with fossil fuel–burning capacity.

It is also conceivable that a jurisdiction could perceive itself as a winner in the event that it agreed to accept a waste repository. There has been some industry-led exploration in both Canada and the United States of communities that might be sufficiently desperate for economic development that they would consider site hosting to be a worthwhile trade-off. Some of this discussion has centered on Canadian aboriginal or Native American populations in remote locations with enormous economic problems. This approach is consistent with siting strategies for other wastes that have emphasized economic "compensation" packages as a mechanism to secure support, although substantial research suggests that compensation alone is insufficient to gain public support for controversial facilities. The limitation of this strategy would seem especially applicable to the case of high-level nuclear waste, given the extreme risks and the attendant level of public anxiety and concern. Nevertheless, it is not impossible that site acceptance might hinge on the host community's depiction of itself as an economic winner in such a political transaction.

Potential Losers

Successful resolution of the search for a single site in either Canada or the United States would impose an extraordinary loss upon the host jurisdiction. The area surrounding the facility would be uninhabitable for generations. Public health risks could be severe for anyone living as far as 100 miles away from the facility in the event that a natural disaster such as an earthquake or a human disaster stemming from facility mismanagement or sabotage were to occur. There would also be a significant possibility of long-term economic repercussions for the surrounding region, given the likely undesirability of pursuing investment or taking up residence within any area perceived as threatened by its relation to the facility.

Most communities that have received the slightest indication that they might be a candidate for host status have tended to respond with anger and vigorous political opposition, indicating a perceived fear of catastrophic loss if siting were to proceed. In recent years, as Nevada emerged as a possible high-level nuclear waste site, political survival in the state has hinged at least in part on articulating unequivocal opposition to the possibility of siting and taking all conceivable steps to delay or thwart the siting process. For example, Nevada Representative John Ensign used a series of procedural maneuvers to help derail a 1997 legislative proposal that would have increased the likelihood of his state becoming the primary high-level waste recipient for the nation. He also expressed outrage at his fellow Republican colleagues, all from other states and eager to impose a significant loss on Nevada: "I told [Texas Representative Dick] Armey that he and [then-Speaker] Newt [Gingrich] screwed us. They told me I have to be reasonable. I said, 'Don't come to me telling me I have to be reasonable when you have just broken into my house and are threatening my children.' That's the way I feel about this bill."[12]

Individuals who would be directly affected by proximity to a repository constitute a unique category among those who would suffer imposed losses in this case. They are not, however, alone among potential losers. The transfer of high-level nuclear waste from multiple storage facilities near existing reactors to a single location would neither be automatic nor risk-free. In the event that a Nevada site became a high-level repository for the United States, it would receive more than 100,000 waste shipments over a thirty-year period following its opening. Those shipments would pass through more than forty states via either rail or highway, and at least fifty million Americans would live or work within a half-mile of at least one of those shipment routes.

Little is known about the reliability of current transport methods for high-level nuclear waste, in large part because these wastes have remained stationary. Survey analysis reveals that more than 80 percent of Americans "would not be willing to live near a transportation route," and recent experience in Europe suggests the likelihood of strong public opposition to any proposed shipments of high-level nuclear waste to various storage facilities.[13] Critics of a repository siting effort have labeled this the "Mobile Chernobyl" effect and have visited likely transit points in a national waste shipment process, such as Chicago, Denver, and St. Louis, attempting to build opposition to any use of local transportation routes to move high-level nuclear waste. These concerns, which revolve around a potential diffusion of the loss imposed through facility siting, are somewhat less salient in Canada, since the vast majority of nuclear facilities are located in a single province. The physical expanse of Ontario, however, and the broad distribution of its nuclear plants around the province suggest that the issue of more geographically diffuse loss imposition could surface in Canada as well once waste transport routes to a single repository were determined.

Potential Winners and Losers under an On-Site Storage Strategy

Neither Canada nor the United States seems likely to break ground any time soon with respect to a single repository for high-level nuclear waste. This suggests that, at least in the near term, loss imposition will continue to be distributed more broadly among all of the current plant sites storing these wastes. In fact, many analysts suggest that such a strategy for waste management might be desirable in future decades, considering current political and technical doubts concerning a single repository. Given the likely opposition in either nation to any proposed siting, this could remain both countries' de facto high-level nuclear waste strategy for many decades to come.

Extended storage of high-level nuclear waste at its various points of generation creates a different set of potential winners and losers than does a single-repository approach. The most obvious winners would be jurisdictions that would be relieved, at least temporarily, of the possibility of assuming responsibility for all of their respective nation's waste. Virtually every elected official in Nevada, the primary target of the American siting process, would exult in the event of a formal commitment to on-site storage. These officials would have considerable opportunity to claim credit for this policy shift, attributing the change to their vehement opposition to single-repository siting. Such an extension of the process for making permanent waste management decisions would also create winners among those communities that would cease to be threatened by the shipment of wastes to a central site via nearby transportation routes.

Any community that currently hosts a nuclear power plant would emerge as a potential loser under this arrangement. Moreover, many of these plants are located in fairly populous urban or suburban areas, placing large numbers of citizens within relatively close range of the stored wastes. As plants have increasingly moved toward some form of dry container storage system as cooling pools have reached capacity, there have been a few incidents involving equipment breakdowns. Concerns have been greatest among those plants where storage takes place close to major water bodies, including a number of plants in both Canada and the United States that are adjacent to one of the Great Lakes. These incidents have not resulted in any major releases of radioactivity, but they suggest that no current system for management of these wastes is foolproof.

Still, the growing trend toward on-site storage has triggered relatively little public attention or outcry in either Canada or the United States. This may reflect the gradual, ongoing process of on-site storage that has been taking place for many years with minimal visibility at most nuclear power plants, along with a higher level of comfort with respect to storing only wastes generated locally rather than those from across the nation. This perception, of course, could change rapidly in the event that a major incident occurred involving on-site storage that attracted significant public attention and triggered public concern.

CROSS-NATIONAL COMPARABILITY

There are strong similarities to many key aspects of the development of nuclear power and the formation of relevant policies in Canada and the United States in past decades, suggesting considerable comparability in the contexts in which high-level nuclear waste policy has been developed. These similarities originate in the very launching of the domestic nuclear experiment in the post–World War II era. Federal governments in both Canada and the United States embraced nuclear power in the late 1940s and 1950s as a key component in postwar industrial policy. Both governments heavily subsidized research and development of nuclear power, whereas alternative energy sources received considerably less support. As political scientist Thomas Birkland has noted in the American case, "The nuclear industry was created, financed, promoted, and underwritten by the federal government and a vast scientific, technical, academic, and military infrastructure. Nuclear power was not to be an ordinary industry."[14] Canada's nuclear industry received a comparable range of assistance and followed the American pattern of rapid construction of nuclear power plants in the late 1960s and early 1970s.[15]

This pattern of federal government involvement also extended to the regulatory process that would be developed to authorize plant construction, monitor facility operation, and oversee waste management. Well before either federal government explored the possibility of significant command-and-control environmental programs, both enacted legislation and created specialized agencies to oversee most aspects of the nuclear power process. These policies provided minimal opportunity for citizen participation or for the involvement of local, state, or provincial governments. States and provinces did retain authority to develop either public corporations to manage nuclear plants or public utility commissions to oversee the practices of one or more nuclear plants operated by privately owned utilities. But these activities were guided by a complex system of federal rules and standards and were heavily dependent upon federal subsidies. Even as the United States—and, to a lesser extent, Canada—began to expand the federal government's regulatory role in environmental policy in the 1970s and 1980s, nuclear power retained an unusually high degree of federal involvement. This dominant federal role in high-level nuclear waste remained evident in the last decade, despite the devolution during this period of a number of environmental regulatory functions to states and provinces.[16]

These federal policies have been implemented by institutions created in large part to support the expanded development of nuclear power. The organizations with primary oversight of most federal environmental programs, such as Environment Canada or the U.S. Environmental Protection Agency, have had limited involvement in any aspect of nuclear power or nuclear waste policy. Instead, entities such as the Nuclear Regulatory Commission and the Department of Energy in the United States and Natural Resources Canada and Atomic Energy of Canada Limited have retained dominant roles. Given their dual responsibilities for promoting nuclear power expansion and overseeing regulatory compliance, they have tended to function as relatively insulated subgovernments. These institutions have become accustomed to working very closely with the parties they regulate and have proven reluctant to open their decision-making processes to include subnational governments, the general citizenry, or critics of the nuclear industry.

These similar institutional structures in the U.S. and Canada have produced a strikingly similar degree of reliance on nuclear power. Canadians and Americans consume nearly identical amounts of electricity per capita, and both received approximately one-fourth of that electricity from nuclear sources during the 1980s. That level of reliance has dropped somewhat in more recent years, with nuclear plants providing approximately 22 percent of American electricity and 18 percent of Canadian electricity in 2000. This places the two nations close to the worldwide average of 17 percent reliance on nuclear power sources among developed nations, between such extreme cases as the Netherlands at 4 percent and France at 76 percent. Both Canada and the United States also have jurisdictions that are either heavily reliant on nuclear power or totally dependent upon nonnuclear sources. Ontario and Illinois, for example, rely on nuclear plants for nearly 60 percent of their electricity, while seven provinces and nineteen states have never had a single nuclear power plant within their boundaries.

Both nations also anticipate a gradual decline in their reliance on nuclear power as an energy source in coming decades, as existing facilities begin to reach the end of their operational lives and new nuclear plants appear unlikely to be sited. The United States has cancelled 112 proposed nuclear plants since 1979, and nuclear-dependent Ontario may have signaled the demise of prospects for new plants in Canada with the cancellation of twelve proposed new plants in 1992. Widely publicized episodes, most notably the 1979 Three Mile Island incident in Pennsylvania and the 1986 Chernobyl explosion in the former Soviet Union, provided "focusing events" that contributed to public resistance to the construction of additional plants, which was already growing in both nations.[17] Other incidents in both nations had already triggered some public attention about nuclear plant safety, beginning with a 1952 explosion in a nuclear research reactor in Ontario that led to the disintegration of several fuel rods and the release of gaseous fission products to the atmosphere.[18] During the 1990s, a continual series of smaller mishaps and extended plant closures in a number of settings in both nations served to further undermine public confidence. When uneasiness over these incidents was coupled with other concerns over nuclear power, including growing uncertainty over cost overruns and waste management, nuclear subgovernments in both Canada and the United States began to lose their unquestioned footing over nuclear power development by the late 1970s and early 1980s.

Interregional Equity

These significant similarities, however, should not overshadow important contextual differences in the cross-national comparability of the Canadian and American cases. Perhaps most importantly, there are fundamental differences in the extent to which, despite federal government dominance of policy in both countries, high-level nuclear waste management is seen as either a national or more regionally based problem. In the Canadian case, it is almost universally assumed that any waste management solution—whether a single repository, on-site storage, or some other alternative—will be resolved within the boundaries of Ontario. The province operates nineteen of Canada's twenty-one nuclear power plants, with the two additional ones located in Quebec and New Brunswick. A limited amount of nuclear research continues in Manitoba and uranium is mined in Saskatchewan, but neither of these activities generates high-level nuclear waste. Other western provinces, such as British Columbia, have imposed a formal moratorium on any future construction of nuclear power plants, and Alberta is sufficiently rich in oil and natural gas resources to have never seriously considered the siting of a nuclear power plant.

Consequently, the problem of high-level waste in Canada is concentrated in the eastern half of the country. Moreover, any serious discussions of waste management options involving repository siting in recent decades have consistently assumed that some area or areas of Ontario would be the ultimate resting place. Intraprovincial distributional issues could complicate siting process implementation, as has already occurred in efforts to site low-level nuclear waste facilities in the province,[19] but interprovincial or interregional equity in assuming responsibility for high-level nuclear waste management has not been an issue in Canada.

That degree of geographical and jurisdictional certainty is in vivid contrast to the American case, where interstate and interregional tensions have dogged deliberations over high-level nuclear waste management for decades. Nuclear power plants continue to operate in thirty-one states and virtually every state has received some consideration as a possible repository host at some time in past decades, whether or not it hosts one of these plants. No state has been at all receptive to becoming the national host for waste generated in so many states. Early 1980s plans to promote regional equity by opening two permanent sites, one on each side of the Mississippi River, collapsed into a concerted congressional effort to impose a single site in Nevada, with burial proposed within a mountain range approximately 100 miles northwest of Las Vegas. Nevada does not have a single nuclear power plant, though it may at times receive some of its electricity from nuclear sources transmitted through its regional electricity grid.

In addition to all the other factors mitigating against siting in the United States, this interstate and interregional equity issue has long been pervasive. In the United

States, unlike in Canada, there is simply no single state so dominant in nuclear waste generation that it emerges as an obvious siting host. Even Illinois, the state with the highest level of reliance on nuclear power for its electricity, generates less than 10 percent of the United States's high-level nuclear waste, whereas Ontario generates more than 90 percent of Canada's output.

Exports and Imports

Canada is not, however, independent of cross-boundary considerations in developing its policy for high-level nuclear waste. Although some destination or destinations in Ontario are universally regarded as the final resting place for Canadian waste, Canada remains very active in exploring the possibility of exporting its standardized nuclear reactor technology to other nations. Advocates of this export strategy contend that rapid resolution of the siting issue is crucial to future export, both to demonstrate to potential investors that a site can be opened and to hold out the possibility that a Canadian disposal site might be available to accept high-level nuclear waste generated abroad.

The export of Canada's nuclear expertise has long been a central component in the national policy toward nuclear power and a rationale for enormous public subsidies to such crown corporations as Atomic Energy of Canada Limited and Ontario Hydro. Whereas the United States encouraged a number of alternative reactor designs to be developed by competing private firms, backed by federal research grants and other subsidies, Canada took a more uniform approach. "Unlike the British and the Americans, the Canadians brought out a single line of reactors and concentrated on them," according to historian Robert Bothwell, "ensuring that Canada's limited resources in science, engineering, and money would not be squandered by being spread too thin."[20] The export potential of the so-called Candu reactors has been thought far greater than that of reactors manufactured by American firms, owing both to their standardized design features and to the fact that they are powered directly by natural uranium that is mined from the ground. Most American and European reactors, by contrast, utilize enriched uranium, requiring a much more complex technology. For developing nations eager to create nuclear power capacity, the Canadian technology was thought particularly attractive. By the late 1990s, eighteen Canadian reactors were either in operation or under construction in such diverse nations as Argentina, India, Pakistan, Romania, and South Korea.[21]

Canadian repository siting advocates repeatedly point to these export possibilities as a mechanism to revive the moribund domestic fortunes of nuclear power. But these considerations also contribute to a common concern that any Canadian site for high-level nuclear waste could become a magnet for wastes from other nations. This concern has become a central consideration in Canadian deliberations. It surfaced repeatedly during extended federal governmental hearings on the feasibility of a geological repository during the 1990s, with fears being expressed concerning the possibility of waste imports both from American plants and from those nations operating Canadian reactors. Siting opponents noted previous statements from federal officials that a permanent site would "provide the ability, in the future, to integrate power plant sales with waste management services, giving the Canadian industry a unique advantage in the export market."[22] In response, a representative of an environmental group noted during the hearings that "I think Canada might be a little bit of a naïve boy scout in its willingness to take other people's nuclear waste."[23]

Concern about becoming a magnet for the high-level nuclear waste of other nations has not surfaced as a serious issue in deliberations over siting in the United States. The American federal government has not followed the Canadian approach in actively promoting nuclear plant exportation, nor has it given any indication of receptivity to importing wastes in the event a repository were opened. Occasional concerns about Canadian waste in select states have almost exclusively been confined to solid and hazardous wastes. Consequently, America's cross boundary concerns over high-level nuclear waste remain focused on interstate rather than international shipments.

THE MULTIPLE DIMENSIONS OF NUCLEAR WASTE

High-level nuclear waste may occupy a unique position among various types of waste that call for long-term management and facility siting. Many of these other waste types may present less severe and enduring public health threats and thereby create more political opportunity for cooperative approaches to waste management. Even among nuclear wastes, there are two categories of domestic waste with very different qualities from high-level wastes, as well as a range of waste categories associated with military weapons construction, storage, and dismantling. Each of these varies so greatly in volume, location, and intensity of radioactive properties as to present potentially different management challenges and opportunities than high-level wastes. Low-level nuclear waste from domestic sources, for example, comprises materials that have been contaminated with limited amounts of radioactive substances through either electricity generation or research involving nuclear materials. Unlike the concentrated rods and logs of high-level waste, low-level materials include a wide range of contaminated clothing, packaging, animal carcasses, medical fluids, and power reactor liquids. In contrast to the 10,000- to 100,000-year time span within which high-level nuclear wastes must be isolated from human exposure, low-level nuclear wastes cease to pose a public health threat after much shorter periods of time. So-called "mixed wastes" also contain nuclear material but constitute even less of a long-term exposure risk, involving small amounts of materials with low levels of radioactivity that have been integrated with solid or hazardous wastes.

Different wastes may pose very different challenges for management and siting. High-level nuclear wastes pose enormous human health risks over very extended periods of time in the event of exposure but are limited in volume; it is technically feasible to conceive of a single facility managing decades of these wastes generated across the entire nation. Solid waste stands at the other end of the risk continuum. It poses very limited threats to human health given most standard management methods; but nations such as Canada and the United States generate massive volumes of such wastes, making the idea of a single waste repository inconceivable in either nation. Other types of waste, including the range of nuclear materials, hazardous wastes, and biomedical wastes, pose differing kinds of risk and volume challenges.

In turn, each type of nuclear waste poses somewhat different disposal issues than high-level wastes. With respect to low-level nuclear waste, for example, neither Canada nor the United States has opened a new waste disposal facility in the past two decades; the United States has been successful in keeping a pair of aging facilities operational. In Canada, a process that borrowed from earlier hazardous waste siting successes by emphasizing a voluntary approach to siting and substantial public participation did result in a volunteer host community in northern Ontario; this potential agreement was derailed over local and federal inability to reach accord on a compensation package. Three Toronto-area communities that have substantial deposits of low-level nuclear waste from very early decades of nuclear activity have responded to this breakdown with a plan to share responsibility for the waste through burial mounds constructed in each community.

THE EVOLUTION OF AMERICAN AND CANADIAN POLICY FOR HIGH-LEVEL NUCLEAR WASTE: 1970–2000

The considerable overlap in the development of nuclear power in the United States and Canada also coincides with the challenges the two countries have faced in attempting to manage high-level nuclear waste. Both began to explore waste facility siting possibilities in a serious manner in the late 1960s and early 1970s. The hostile reaction of prospective host communities in both nations was an early indication that facility siting would not be easily implemented. Subsequently, the two nations have taken somewhat different paths, involving different federal institutions and strategies in pursuit of a common goal: designation of a single geological repository to handle each nation's wastes for centuries to come. Neither of these approaches has yet resulted in facility construction, however, leaving the common outcome of on-site storage as increasingly distinctive siting processes are implemented.

The American Case

The American odyssey of high-level nuclear waste siting began in a quiet fashion in the late 1960s. Federally sponsored research examined a wide range of possible disposal options and initially focused upon waste burial in underground salt mines. This research was almost exclusively technical in nature, dominated by the physical sciences. At this point, officials of the federal government and the nuclear power industry gave little if any thought to the political or social ramifications of siting, assuming that the central issue was finding and rapidly utilizing the most efficient technology rather than developing a politically acceptable siting process. Any public concerns over potential risk from proximity to such a site, it was assumed, could be mitigated by generous economic development packages and demonstrations of technical competence.

The first hint that this optimism over siting was misplaced came in the early 1970s. The Atomic Energy Commission (the predecessor to the current Nuclear Regulatory Commission and the dominant regulatory force in the early decades of domestic nuclear policy) concentrated its siting plans on an abandoned salt mine near Lyons, Kansas. The Lyons site was selected from among a series of candidates where preliminary research on salt mine disposal was being conducted. The site selection followed a classic top-down process common in other waste management contexts during the 1970s and 1980s: It emphasized technical siting criteria and was averse to virtually all forms of involvement by state and local officials or the general public. In fact, less than three months before Lyons was officially selected even the governor of Kansas had not yet been informed by the Atomic Energy Commission (AEC) that it was a site candidate.[24]

State and local officials registered strong opposition to the proposed facility and the state's congressional delegation successfully amended the AEC authorization bill, blocking further work on the Lyons site. Continued site analysis indicated a series of potential problems that brought into question its technical suitability. Consequently, the AEC withdrew its siting plan, and its successor siting bodies, the Energy Research and Development Administration (ERDA) and later the Department of Energy, renewed the search process. ERDA began to review prospects for a high-level repository in the mid-1970s and conducted analyses at sites in thirty-six states. As in the Kansas case, many states responded angrily to the discovery that they had become unwilling site candidates. In 1976, Michigan Governor William Milliken implored ERDA to halt its exploration of a possible site near Alpena, in the northeast corner of the state's lower peninsula. The Michigan legislature, in turn, passed legislation banning nuclear waste disposal within its boundaries. Michigan was soon joined by other states, all eager to make formal declarations of their opposition to the possibility of becoming a national high-level nuclear waste repository. By the end of the decade, nineteen states had imposed legislative bans on repository siting within their boundaries and six had banned construction of any new nuclear reactors until a disposal method for high-level waste had been established.[25] Additional states passed comparable legislation in subsequent years, with repository siting bans in effect in two-thirds of the states, including Nevada, by the early 1980s. It was very doubtful that these state bans could sustain court challenges, however, given consistent U.S. Supreme Court treatment of waste as governed by the interstate commerce provisions of the Constitution and thus falling under federal purview.

The once quiet field of nuclear waste repository siting, then, like the issue of nuclear power generally, was enmeshed in controversy by the 1980s. In response, the nuclear industry began to pressure Congress and the Reagan administration for legislative direction to guide the future of high-level nuclear waste management. The early 1980s were not a time conducive to enactment of legislation in most areas of environmental policy, given the enormous tensions between legislative and executive branches. Nonetheless, a broad coalition emerged in 1982 that crossed partisan and regional lines and produced the Nuclear Waste Policy

Act (NWPA), the first detailed American legislative pronouncement on the management of high-level nuclear waste. Despite the complex and increasingly contentious nature of this issue, the legislation passed the House by a 256–32 vote and the Senate by a voice vote under a unanimous consent agreement. The bill was quickly signed by President Ronald Reagan and widely heralded as an important step toward resolving this issue.

Several important features of this legislation contributed to its broad base of support. First, it endorsed balanced regional assumption of responsibility for waste management, calling for two high-level repositories, one to be located on each side of the Mississippi River. This served to build support from western-states legislators, who had become increasingly fearful that their vast expanses of territory, much of which was under the ownership of the federal government, made their states likely hosts for a single, national repository.

Second, the legislation created a Nuclear Waste Fund to cover all of the costs of facility siting and ultimate operation. This fund established a fee of $0.001—a tenth of a cent—per kilowatt hour on all purchases of electricity from the nation's nuclear power plants. This user fee approach had considerable appeal to legislators from both parties as it promised to create adequate funding for waste management without appearing as a new tax or an addition to the federal deficit. In turn, the fee was set sufficiently low as to be unlikely to trigger any awareness or opposition from ratepayers.

Third, the act was designed to foster cooperation between federal siting agencies and potential host states through a series of measures. These included requirements that the Department of Energy reach "written, binding agreements on screening and characterization studies with those states designated by the president as potential sites,"[26] along with federal grants that participating states could use to hire consultants and conduct their own site evaluations. In addition, the legislation allowed any potential host state to veto its designation, although such a veto could be overridden by a vote of both houses of Congress.

Fourth, the NWPA began a process of shifting the legal and economic liabilities of the waste from the nuclear industry to the federal government. The nuclear industry enthusiastically welcomed this provision, as did many legislators who saw this as a significant step toward establishment of a reliable national system for waste management. Finally, many supporters of the legislation saw it as a step to boost the long-term fortunes of nuclear power in the United States amid enduring concern over the continued availability of other energy sources, particularly imported oil.

The Department of Energy quietly issued new siting guidelines and began collecting fees, but the siting process became controversial as soon as specific candidate sites began to be mentioned. In February 1985, the DOE designated three sites for extensive evaluation as the potential western site: Deaf Smith, Texas; Hanford, Washington; and Yucca Mountain, Nevada. Each of these areas had some prior experience with nuclear technology: A nuclear weapons testing site had operated near Yucca Mountain for many decades, for example. In January 1986, twelve eastern candidate sites from seven states (Georgia, Maine, Minnesota, Mississippi, New Hampshire, Virginia, and Wisconsin) were selected for similar consideration as the potential eastern site. Local reaction to these announcements was extremely negative, particularly near sites located east of the Mississippi. Under enormous political pressure, Energy Secretary John Herrington announced in May 1986 that his department would suspend its search for an eastern repository and instead concentrate siting efforts on a single facility in the West.

Congress quickly moved to ratify this decision and enacted the Nuclear Waste Policy Amendments Act in 1987. This legislation represented a significant departure from its 1982 predecessor, as it terminated any possibility of a deliberative review of multiple site candidates. Instead, it embraced Herrington's decision to cease consideration of sites east of the Mississippi and went one major step beyond the secretary in designating Yucca Mountain as the lone national candidate for further site characterization analysis. There was remarkably little congressional deliberation over this proposed change.

Opposition was concentrated in the small Nevada congressional delegation, which condemned the legislation as the "Screw Nevada Bill." Some sympathy was also evident from representatives of other western states and from fervent opponents of the nuclear industry. These sentiments were overwhelmed, however, by the political opportunity that representatives from other states gained to shift all waste management responsibility to Nevada and thereby avoid any blame for possible consideration of sites in their state or region. As James Flynn and colleagues have noted, this policy shift "was widely viewed as a thinly-veiled attempt to enhance the reelection prospects of several senators from the eastern half of the country and to defuse political opposition to the repository from the more populous states."[27] Among the three potential western candidates, Nevada clearly lacked the congressional clout of either Texas or Washington. Texas had a much larger delegation in the House and such congressional leaders as Speaker of the House Jim Wright and Senate Finance Committee chair Lloyd Bentsen. Washington also had a large representational base, which included House Majority Leader Thomas Foley. In contrast, Nevada had a relatively inexperienced delegation of two senators and one member of the House. Its most influential legislator, former Senate Commerce Committee chair Howard Cannon, had been defeated in 1982 in an attempt to win a fifth consecutive term.

There was little of the credit-claiming among legislators that accompanied the 1982 Nuclear Waste Policy Act, which generated self-congratulatory claims of innovativeness and fairness. Instead, Congress worked across partisan and regional lines to craft a modified approach that, if implemented, would get 98 of 100 senators and 434 of 435 House of Representatives members permanently off the hook with respect to high-level nuclear waste management. Advocates of this approach such as Luther Carter, a journalist whose writings have had considerable influence on the past two decades of federal policy for high-level waste, lauded the Yucca siting decision as a way to avoid "elegant but impractical national site screening strategies" and "procedural marathons." He urged the Department of Energy to move rapidly to cut a deal with Nevada officials, emphasizing generous economic compensation packages and input on such issues as shipment routes as ways to build support for the single repository.[28]

Congress continued to operate in the spirit of the 1987 legislation five years later by attempting to clear away one potential hurdle to development of the Yucca Mountain facility. Although the Department of Energy had retained primary authority for most aspects of site assessment process and development, the Environmental Protection Agency used its authority to propose "cumulative exposure standards" for Yucca or any other federal facility. Given the extended periods of risk posed by exposure to high-level wastes, however, any facility might have considerable difficulty meeting such a standard. In response, Congress attached an amendment to the 1992 Energy Policy Act that eliminated those proposed standards, although only in the case of Yucca Mountain. Instead, Congress required that EPA utilize "individual-dose" standards, which measure one-time exposure rates. Rather than attempt to demonstrate that Yucca Mountain would meet cumulative exposure standards over a period of at least 10,000 years, this legislatively revised standard instead requires the Department of Energy to make the easier case that "a single large dose of radiation is unlikely to be released."[29] As in the case of the 1987 amendments, this 1992 legislative tinkering received broad support in both the Senate and the House.

When combined, the 1987 and 1992 legislation was widely expected to eliminate hurdles to opening a high-level nuclear waste repository in Nevada. After a series of conflicts and delays during the Clinton presidency, the Bush administration and Congress gave strong support in February 2002 to accelerate the siting process. Nonetheless, a series of strong barriers, both physical and legal in nature, remain, adding to the uncertainty of whether the Yucca Mountain facility will ever be constructed.

SCIENTIFIC RESERVATIONS

One of the initial attractions of Yucca Mountain as a potential repository site was its imposing geological expanse. Located in a relatively isolated area within a deep range of mountains, Yucca gives every outward appearance of being a massive, stable place for entombing America's high-level nuclear waste. The mountain and its surrounding area receive only six inches of rain each year, most of which is drawn out of the soil rapidly by evaporation and vegetation, making it unlikely that surface water would reach deeply buried wastes. Since Yucca's designation by the Department of Energy as the preferred national site, however, a series of seismic incidents and research findings have contributed to growing uncertainty about the technical suitability of the site.

Earthquakes have been an ongoing problem in Nevada and in the area surrounding the proposed site. Nevada has experienced more earthquakes than all states other than Alaska and California in recent decades. Fault lines run parallel to the east and west sides of Yucca Mountain, and a third fault cuts across the mountain. Many of the recent earthquakes near Yucca Mountain have been relatively minor, registering a magnitude of less than 3 Richter scale points. But several of them have been more serious and may suggest an intensifying period of seismic activity. For example, a 5.6-magnitude earthquake struck Yucca Mountain in June 1992, knocking out windows, cracking walls, and bringing down ceiling panels at the Yucca Mountain Project field operations center, located only twelve miles from the proposed repository site. Additional earthquakes hit the area during the late 1990s, including a series of six during January 1999. One of these had a 4.7 magnitude and caused damage at a proposed waste storage site adjacent to the proposed repository site.[30]

Recent studies have confirmed that earthquake, as well as volcanic, activity may be considerably more likely and frequent in the Yucca Mountain area than initially thought. A 1998 study sponsored by the National Science Foundation and the Nuclear Regulatory Commission concluded that the Yucca site may be at least ten times more susceptible to earthquakes and lava flows than previous studies acknowledged. It also concluded that the earth's crust at Yucca is stretching at least ten times faster than was assessed in previous studies, making future seismic episodes potentially more dangerous than anticipated. At least two volcanoes are known to have erupted in the vicinity of Yucca Mountain within the last 5,000 years, approximately one-half of the minimum time period for which a repository would have to provide secure storage.

Even groundwater has emerged as a nagging scientific uncertainty. The Yucca Mountain aquifer is used by regional residents and farmers and falls under U.S. EPA standards. As was the case with cumulative exposure, the agency has proposed a much more rigorous standard than that favored by the Department of Energy and facility advocates. EPA supports a millirem standard identical to that enforced in tap water and at Superfund cleanup sites under federal safe drinking water legislation. Department of Energy officials and other analysts contend that imposing such a standard on Yucca-area water might be impossible to attain and might thereby thwart future licensure approval.

POLITICAL OPPOSITION

Each scientific challenge to the safety of the proposed Yucca site has been widely touted by opponents as evidence that the plan is fundamentally flawed. Nevada elected officials, at both state and federal levels, have proven masterful at taking each new study or episode and securing significant national media exposure. In turn, the state has used virtually every conceivable tactic to delay—and ultimately to prevent—the Yucca site from ever being developed. The siting issue has become so central to Nevada politics that election campaigns are increasingly concentrated on the issue of which candidate is most firmly opposed to siting and will take the most effective steps to block the facility. Some have begun to characterize any positive reference to any aspect of the Yucca Mountain proposal as the "third rail" of Nevada politics, as 1998 Democratic gubernatorial candidate Jim Neal discovered when he expressed some willingness to enter into negotiations with federal authorities over Yucca Mountain if elected and was widely denounced for the statement.

Nevada members of Congress have sought to build coalitions to increase doubt over the desirability of Yucca Mountain through a variety of mechanisms. During 1998, Senators Harry Reid and Richard Bryan launched a national tour of sites likely to become major nuclear waste shipment points in the event the Yucca Mountain facility is opened. They declared this to be their "Mobile Chernobyl" campaign and emphasized that a single repository would not eliminate potential exposure for the rest of the nation. Reid has been extremely effective in sustaining this effort, even maintaining on his Senate website (reid.senate.gov) detailed projections of likely transit routes for each individual state.

State officials from Nevada have matched the ferocity of opposition demonstrated by their federal-level colleagues. State agencies continue to explore every conceivable method to delay or deter the construction of a Yucca site, such as blockage of water permits or restricted use of transportation routes. Nevada has also sustained the Nevada Agency for Nuclear Projects (NANP) to conduct an aggressive anti-Yucca lobbying campaign in the state and around the nation. The agency was initially created by the Nevada legislature in 1985 and focused on research, much of which was subsidized by the federal government. "But as soon as we realized that Congress was not interested in our research and was only interested in making Yucca the only site in the nation, the gloves were off," explained NANP Executive Director Robert Loux. "We still do research, only with state money, but also play a political role, facilitating environmental and other groups, working with reporters, and advising our elected officials."[31] Other organizations have joined this effort, with resolutions of opposition to Yucca Mountain siting approved by such diverse organizations as the Nevada State Medical Association, the Nevada Resort Association, the Nevada State Firemen's Association, and the Nevada Parent Teachers Association Board of Directors, as well as numerous municipalities and counties.

All of these state-based political resources were put to use during the second Clinton administration in successfully opposing various initiatives to bring high-level nuclear waste to Nevada. Under proposed Nuclear Waste Policy Act amendments, the Department of Energy would have created a "temporary" national storage facility at the Nevada Test Site, a former nuclear weapons testing facility that adjoins the proposed Yucca Mountain site, by 2003. Such a facility could operate without all of the testing and safeguards required of a permanent repository and would use a system of monitored retrievable storage (MRS). The proposed amendments would have represented a formal reversal of the 1987 legislation, which prohibited the construction of such a facility in Nevada, or anywhere in the nation, under any circumstances before a construction license was issued to the permanent repository. As in 1987 and 1992, many representatives of waste-generating states responded favorably, eager to find some way to maximize the likelihood of waste export to Nevada. The proposed amendments quickly gathered more than 100 cosponsors in the House and seemed headed for rapid passage by both chambers. "We need to get started with a safe, centralized facility," commented Alaska Republican Senator Frank Murkowski in endorsing the proposed legislation. "The time is now. Nevada is the place."[32]

Various forms of the proposed amendments were consistently thwarted through the very end of the Clinton presidency. The Nevada congressional delegation played a significant role in this reversal, stoking concerns over nuclear waste transportation and with respect to the future prospects for nuclear power. "I ask you not to make my home state the nuclear toilet for the country," said Nevada Representative Shelley Berkley in testimony before the Senate Energy Committee, chaired by Murkowski.[33] Senator Reid proved particularly effective in sustaining enough of an opposition coalition to block Senate debate in 1998 and 1999. In turn, the Clinton administration and its respective energy secretaries (Hazel O'Leary, Federico Pena, and Bill Richardson) consistently expressed the president's commitment to veto any MRS proposal. Instead, the president and his cabinet members endorsed continued exploration of the Yucca Mountain process, thereby delaying any decision until after Clinton left office. Even once the legislation cleared the Senate and significant differences with the House had been resolved, it was clear that the Senate lacked the votes to override Clinton's 2000 veto. This strategy offered multiple political benefits for the Clinton administration, allowing it to avoid alienating antinuclear groups, by blocking any siting for at least the near term; to avoid alienating pronuclear groups by keeping alive the long-term option of Yucca; and to simultaneously offer a significant political boost to Reid's ultimately successful 1998 re-election campaign.

The second Bush administration signaled a more positive outlook on Yucca, linked to its larger energy proposals, which endorsed an expanded role for nuclear power. An all-star lineup of lobbyists, including former New Hampshire Governor John Sununu, former Democratic vice presidential candidate Geraldine Ferraro, and former Nevada Governor Robert List, led a formidable coalition headed by the U.S. Chamber of Commerce and the Nuclear Energy Institute. Energy Secretary Spencer Abraham endorsed their views in a January 11, 2002, recommendation to President Bush to move forward with Yucca siting. Abraham argued that Yucca had been proven viable and offered protection to the environment and to the viability of nuclear power plants. He also linked approval to the nation's new concerns over homeland security, noting that "we should consolidate the nuclear wastes to enhance protection against terrorist attacks by moving them to one underground location that is far from population centers."[34]

President Bush endorsed Abraham's recommendation one month later, setting the stage for the next set of battles. Nevada and its governer, Kenny Guinn, used its powers under the NWPA to register formal opposition to Bush's decision, but solid majorities in both the Senate and the House overrode the opposition in mid-2002. While many media accounts implied that the siting issue was now resolved, however, this is not necessarily the case. The latest congressional action is only a prelude to formal license review by the Nuclear Regulatory Commission. The U.S. General Accounting Office, reflecting the views of the project contractor, has already raised 293 technical concerns that it contends must be addressed before license application can begin. Nevada-based opponents are also collecting resources for a Nevada Protection Fund to sustain an all-out legal assault against the proposal; and finally, Reid and allies, such as Las Vegas Mayor Oscar Goodman, are relaunching the "Mobile Chernobyl" campaign with new intensity, attempting to build on recent ordinances by Denver and St. Louis to ban movement of any high-level nuclear waste through their cities. As Reid noted the day after Bush's announcement: "Coming soon to a highway near you . . . the deadliest substance known to humankind! It sounds like a

Hollywood thriller, but this is not just a plot for a scary movie. This is President Bush's plan, one that could feed plots for terrorists hell-bent on destroying America."

The Canadian Case

Canada began to explore options for high-level nuclear waste at about the same time and in much the same way as the United States. New nuclear plants were built with water-filled storage bays to cool high-level wastes and prepare them for eventual shipment to a central disposal facility. Serious research began in the early 1970s on the best technology and siting criteria for such a facility. Much of Canada's nuclear power infrastructure was already operational before these reviews had made much progress, but it was commonly assumed that this was simply a technical problem that could be easily resolved, given Canada's growing prowess in all aspects of nuclear technology.

Formal work on waste management began in 1972 through a joint committee directed by representatives of Atomic Energy of Canada Limited, Ontario Hydro, and Hydro Quebec. This committee quickly concluded that some form of geological disposal at a single site was the best method for Canada to address the high-level nuclear waste issue. In response, AECL and the Ministry of Energy, Mines and Resources (MEMR) agreed in 1974 to support research directed primarily at examining disposal options involving burial deep in geological formations within the Ontario portion of the Canadian Shield. This research began with little public deliberation in several communities with a prior history of involvement in nuclear research, including those in Chalk River, Ontario, and Pinawa, Manitoba. But the first indication of the potential political complexity of the high-level waste issue occurred in Madoc, Ontario, in 1977, once local citizens discovered that such research would also be conducted in their community. At a public meeting in March 1977, AECL representatives attempted to explain their plans to a "hostile, placard-waving audience of about 1,100, which included many of the antinuclear leaders from across the country."[35] Public concern was concentrated not on the issue of hosting a research facility but on the growing belief in the community that AECL had already selected nearby Mount Maria as the permanent repository site. Public opposition in Madoc continued after this meeting, and local representatives in the national and provincial legislatures convinced MEMR to ban both the AECL and the Geological Survey of Canada from doing any further work related to nuclear waste management in the area.

This experience had a chilling effect on the early optimism that waste management would be a quiet, technocratic exercise. But whereas the United States reacted to such initial expressions of opposition with an aggressive set of legislative and bureaucratic steps designed to create a central facility, Canada responded with a more deliberative process that continued throughout the 1990s. "The Madoc incident prompted a complete rethinking of the approach to site selection and the field research program," recalled historian Donald Hurst. "It was decided that it was both impractical and unfair to ask communities to consider hosting a waste disposal facility before they could be assured beyond a reasonable doubt that it was safe."[36]

The Madoc experience was sobering, but it did not halt consideration of siting options. In fact, a 1977 report commissioned by MEMR concluded that deep burial constituted the best long-term approach, dismissing other options such as reprocessing, surface storage, or disposal in ice sheets, outer space, or beneath the floor of the sea. This document, widely known as the Hare Report after its chair, Kenneth Hare, endorsed deep disposal in rocky geological formations but also supported further research on such alternatives as salt mines and shale deposits.[37] The Hare Report did not rule out the possibility of establishing more than one facility over several decades but emphasized that the first facility should be sited in Ontario, owing to its expected dominance among Canadian provinces in waste generation. Attentive to the Madoc incident, the report also emphasized the need for extensive public discussion and assurances of broad public support before any siting strategy was implemented.

The federal minister of energy, mines and resources and his Ontario counterpart responded to the Hare Report with a 1978 joint statement that directed AECL to refine the concept of deep geological disposal. This assignment reflected an intergovernmental division of labor that concentrated research and planning for long-term management of high-level nuclear waste in federal hands. In turn, Ontario would assume responsibility for developing strategies for temporary storage and for transportation of wastes to a central site. The joint statement endorsed an extensive AECL program of research and development designed to verify "that permanent disposal in a deep underground repository in intrusive igneous rock is a safe, secure and desirable method of disposing of radioactive waste."[38] A subsequent joint statement in 1981 emphasized that site selection would not occur until after a full federal public hearing and approval of the concept by federal and provincial governments.

During a ten-year period in which the Congress enacted three major pieces of nuclear waste legislation and the Department of Energy moved forward to narrow site selection, AECL conducted an elaborate technical evaluation of waste disposal options. Nearly a decade after its initial federal-provincial charge, AECL presented a detailed blueprint that both reiterated support for deep geological disposal and established a process to guide site selection for a single repository. The AECL report anticipated a twenty-five-year period for siting and construction, beginning with a broad review of the technical suitability of potential host sites. It endorsed finding a site somewhere within the Canadian Shield in Ontario, which embraced more than 75 percent of the province's 412,581 square miles. Detailed siting criteria would be used to eliminate inappropriate sites, such as those located in zones with possible seismic activity or risk of groundwater contamination. Construction would entail a system for implantation of the wastes in specially designed hardrock mines located 500 to 1,000 meters beneath the pre-Cambrian shield. Additional protection would be provided by engineered barriers built around the wastes. AECL expressed considerable confidence that there would be a large number of technically suitable sites available and announced at a 1989 public briefing that at least 1,300 Ontario sites appeared upon initial analysis to be "technically acceptable."[39]

AECL was less detailed in explaining its plan for final site selection and public participation. It did suggest that after a detailed review of alternative sites revealed technically viable candidates, volunteer host communities would be sought. Further comparison of site characteristics would be conducted, leading to a final selection of the best site from among those with communities supportive of the proposed project. In this sense, AECL did respond to the public participation portion of its charge from the federal and provincial governments. It also employed some of the participatory language increasingly being employed by Canadian provinces in this period, which were exploring voluntary programs for hazardous waste facility siting that involved extensive public awareness and input into facility design and sought formal expression of community support before hosting a facility.[40] This aspect of its proposal, however, remained far less developed than the technical endorsement of deep geological storage.

AECL continued its research efforts and attempted to build public support for its proposal after release of its plan. In turn, the Canadian nuclear industry spent $4 million dollars between 1987 and 1991 to build support for nuclear power and increase public confidence in the federal government's capacity to manage high-level nuclear waste safely. But neither the federal government nor AECL had the authority to move forward on implementation without completion of further review. Under Canadian law, the AECL proposal had to be reviewed under the federal Environmental Assessment and Review Process. Such an assignment was somewhat unique for this review process, which usually examines the environmental ramifications of a specific site proposal. In this case, the review was to examine all aspects of the proposed concept, in that no specific sites had yet been designated.

After a year of consultation with provincial governments and other stakeholders in the three provinces that generate high-level nuclear waste, the federal minister of the environment appointed a Nuclear Fuel Waste Management and Disposal Concept Environmental Assessment Panel (the Seaborn Panel) in October 1989. Chaired by Blair Seaborn, a retired senior civil servant who had formerly served as deputy minister of Environment Canada and chair of the Canadian delegation to the International Joint Commission, the panel comprised eight members and was supported by a four-person secretariat and a Scientific Review Group.

AECL and proponents of an accelerated siting process hoped for a rapid completion of the review and a strong endorsement of their proposal. They were disappointed on both counts. The Seaborn Panel evolved into a three-phase marathon encompassing dozens of hearings that involved a total of 531 speakers and 536 written submissions. The panel and its advisors sought input from virtually every conceivable academic discipline and category of Canadian stakeholder, including representatives of Canadian aboriginal groups, environmental advocacy groups, and communities with some prior involvement in nuclear power and waste generation. Its final report was delayed repeatedly and was not ultimately released until February 1998, nearly a decade after its charge was issued. Critics contend that the panel lost focus after its initial years of operation and thereby extended an assessment process that should have taken two or three years into an exercise that lasted nearly a decade. Supporters of the Seaborn Panel respond that such an exhaustive and extensive process was essential. "We had to take a very broad scope and involve a broad range of people," recalled Guy Riverin, who served as a senior staff advisor to the panel. "The issues were very complex and there was no specific site to focus the review. When you get into the ethical and social issues, as we did, that takes time. We've seen some Royal commissions that have taken a lot longer than the Seaborn Panel."[41]

Beyond the delays, the contents of the report cast fundamental doubts about key elements of the AECL proposal. The report did affirm that "from a technical perspective, safety of the AECL concept has been on balance adequately demonstrated for a conceptual stage of development." It also did not rule out the possibility of long-term reliance on a single geological repository for Canadian high-level nuclear waste. The report did, however, find the AECL proposal suspect from a "social perspective." In fact, it concluded: "As it stands, the AECL concept for deep geological disposal has not been demonstrated to have broad public support. The concept in its current form does not have the required level of acceptability to be adopted as Canada's approach for managing nuclear fuel wastes."[42]

As an alternative, the Seaborn Report established a multiphase plan that would radically alter the previous direction of federal policy if implemented. Initially, the federal government was urged to outline a new plan for waste management and create a new federal entity, a Canadian Nuclear Fuel Waste Management Agency (NFWMA), "to manage and co-ordinate the full range of activities related to all nuclear fuel wastes produced in Canada." Creation of such an agency would not eliminate existing bodies, such as AECL, but would become dominant in this policy area. "If there is to be any confidence in a system for the long-term management of nuclear fuel wastes," asserted the report, "a fresh start must be made in the form of a new agency." NFWMA would also oversee development of a new fund to cover all costs related to high-level nuclear waste management. This fund would be generated by owners of facilities producing high-level nuclear waste, comparable to the American Nuclear Waste Fund, whereas Canadian government funding for all of its activity related to nuclear power and waste has historically come from general revenues rather than user fees.

This first phase was intended to create a new institutional footing for future policy and, as well, to begin to foster an atmosphere of trust. Subsequently, the NFWMA would launch an extensive process of informing and communicating with the public and of exploring all options for waste management. These options would include the AECL approach of deep geological disposal but would also include alternatives such as above- or below-ground storage at a centralized location or expanded reliance on storage at nuclear plant sites. The new agency would also be expected to develop methods to "measure the broad public support needed" to proceed toward a siting process. This would involve development of a series of mechanisms to measure general public sentiment, such as polls, and tools that could be used to gauge the consent of potential host communities, such as referenda .[43]

Active development and implementation of a siting process could begin only after these consultations; siting would occur only among communities that had formally volunteered after extended processes of public deliberation. The process would consider all essential safety and technical considerations, in concert with efforts to most fairly define surrounding communities that should have direct input into siting decisions. The report also endorsed creation of "community liaison groups" for any possible host community that would "involve citizens substantively in all stages of decision-making." [44]

Only after completion of these steps and the emergence of one or more self-declared volunteer communities would facility development and operation become possible, said the report, which set no timetable for completion of the siting process and suggested that development of a single repository might prove undesirable and unnecessary. The report supported continued reliance upon on-site storage as a "possible long-term approach to managing wastes" that was "already widely considered to be safe, economical, and acceptable."[45] Among Ontario reactors, it contended, existing storage space was sufficient to accommodate all high-level wastes that were expected to be generated through 2035, which would mark the end of all of the reactors' life cycles. The report notes that storage eliminates transportation risks and also retains the option of retrievability in the event superior management methods are discovered in future decades or generations.

The response to the Seaborn Report has been decidedly mixed. Environmental groups in particular have supported its key tenets of expanded public involvement, a voluntary siting process, and serious consideration of on-site storage as the dominant long-term strategy. But organizations more closely associated with nuclear power in Canada have responded negatively. The *Bulletin of the Canadian Nuclear Society* has criticized the "social perspective" concerns of the report as "an absurd notion."[46] The official Canadian government response to the report, released by Natural Resources Canada in December 1998, endorses some of its broad goals but dismisses several key recommendations; it sidesteps the on-site storage issue and reiterates support for an active facility siting initiative. The government's response also rejects the proposed creation of the NFWMA, suggesting that the federal government expects provincial utilities from Ontario, New Brunswick, and Quebec to "establish a waste management organization, incorporated as a separate legal entity, with a mandate to manage and coordinate the full range of activities relating to the long-term management, including disposal, of nuclear fuel waste."[47]

The official federal response also suggested that many of the provisions of the Seaborn Panel had already been put into effect through a Canadian Nuclear Waste Policy Framework that was quietly established by Natural Resources Canada in July 1996. The framework addresses all forms of Canadian nuclear waste by means of very general points, presented in a five-sentence document. It reiterates federal responsibility for assuring "safe, environmentally sound, comprehensive, cost-effective" waste disposal and calls upon the waste generators to assume responsibility for funding and managing waste disposal. The framework was the product of 1995–96 deliberations between Natural Resources Canada and approximately eighty stakeholders, primarily involving representatives of organizations that generate some form of nuclear waste and of the provinces in which they are lo-cated. Environmental groups and the sorts of diverse stakeholders so central to the Seaborn Panel review were not included in this process. This document has pro-vided Natural Resources Canada with a tool with which it could rebut those provi-sions of the Seaborn Report that it finds objectionable and declare that it was al-ready pursuing those aspects of the report that it supported. But it is sufficiently vague as to give little concrete direction to future policy, and it has never been invoked as a basis for legislation.

The only area in which Parliament has made a formal decision on nuclear waste policy involved passage of the 1997 Nuclear Safety and Control Act (NSCA). This act represented Parliament's first major pronouncement on high-level nuclear waste since the 1946 Atomic Energy Control Act, which it replaced. The legislation renames some existing institutions (the Atomic Energy Control Board, for exam-ple, became the Canadian Nuclear Safety Commission as of May 2000), but its most important step involved updating health and safety standards. "This was simply a case of the Government getting its house in order," explained Peter Brown, direc-tor of the Uranium and Radioactive Waste Division of Natural Resources Canada. "The legislation had not been updated in over half a century, and this basically cod-ified what was already being done in practice in terms of health and safety stan-dards."[48] The new legislation also included a provision calling upon the owners of nuclear power plants to set aside funds to cover the costs of eventual plant closure and waste management disposal. There are no specific revenue-generating mecha-nisms included in the legislation, however, and no trust fund to cover disposal costs has been created. The legislation takes no steps toward the creation of a new, over-arching regulatory agency, and it did not address issues of waste facility siting. It breezed through Parliament with little discussion and minimal opposition from industry or environmental groups.

The NSCA may have represented a federal effort to deflect the then-anticipated findings of the Seaborn Report as well as respond to changing market conditions with respect to electrical power generation. As the Seaborn Panel's deliberations dragged on and assumed more and more of an antinuclear tone, the Seaborn Report was increasingly expected in the years leading up to its 1998 release to be critical of earlier approaches to siting. The NSCA legislation gave Parliament an opportunity to make some alterations, including cosmetic name changes, so as to appear to be taking significant action in advance of the report. At the same time, provincial utili-ties holding nuclear reactors in their portfolio, most notably Ontario Hydro, have in-creasingly looked for ways to minimize their nuclear liabilities and attempt to sur-vive potential privatization initiatives. The possible establishment of funds to cover plant closure and waste management may well make Ontario Hydro and other Cana-dian nuclear plants more attractive to potential investors. The legislation clears the way for such transactions, and the Natural Resources Canada reaction to the Seaborn Report suggests that deference to these provincial utilities is an increasing federal priority. If authority is decentralized and privatized in this way, the federal government might relieve itself of a substantial future burden and also avoid blame for any future problems emanating from nuclear power. None of this, however, moves Canada closer to any long-term decisions on how it will manage high-level nuclear waste.

CONCLUSIONS

Processes

Both the United States and Canada launched their loss imposition efforts with respect to high-level nuclear waste at about the same time, in accordance with very similar processes. These relied upon federal government agencies to develop technical criteria to select a single site as a geological repository for all of the waste generated in each nation. They presumed sufficient agency competence both to make key technical decisions and to resolve any siting-related issue with the host community or region. For most of the 1970s, this was a low-saliency issue, seen as essentially technical in nature.

By decade's end, these processes began to appear suspect—which was most evident in the public outcries in Lyons, Kansas, and Madoc, Ontario, against the possibility of these towns being selected as siting hosts. At this point, however, the two nations chose markedly different approaches as they attempted to continue their loss imposition processes. Although parliamentary systems are generally thought more capable of decisive action in loss imposition owing to their fewer veto points, the United States Congress proved far more decisive than the Canadian Parliament: Congress established a coalition that cut across party lines to pass three major pieces of high-level nuclear waste legislation between 1982 and 1992. The 1982 Nuclear Waste Policy Act set forth detailed guidelines for siting. Subsequent pieces of legislation enacted in 1987 and 1992 attempted to streamline the siting process and concentrate loss imposition on a single area: Yucca Mountain, Nevada. Senate and House representatives from states other than Nevada held an overwhelming voting advantage over the Nevada delegation, and the ability to impose the sizable loss represented by a geological repository on such a politically weak state proved consistently appealing. These detailed congressional directives gave the federal Department of Energy license to move rapidly toward site selection and construction, and it has vigorously pursued Yucca Mountain siting in subsequent years.

The Canadian process has not deviated from its initial pattern of delegation to federal agencies. Parliament ended a half-century of relative silence on high-level nuclear waste with enactment of the 1997 Nuclear Safety and Control Act. This belated gesture, however, makes only limited changes in the governance arrangements for waste management, does not address facility siting, and followed decades of delay in devising a federal process for loss imposition in nuclear waste disposal. Respective federal ministries, boards, and commissions have all contributed to an extended period of proposal generation and review. Two of the most significant initiatives (such as the 1987 AECL proposal and the 1998 Seaborn Report) have each consumed virtually a decade of preparation time. Nearly fifty years after construction of Canada's first nuclear reactor for research, Canada still has no detailed blueprint, legislative or bureaucratic, to guide site selection with any precision. There are no specific sites currently under consideration, enormous uncertainties about the future direction of such initiatives, and no consensus among the various agencies and commissions that have had a central role in this policy area in the past decade. The lone point of agreement, evident throughout this extremely deliberative process, is that any waste management strategies will ultimately be implemented within the boundaries of Ontario, given its dominance in Canadian nuclear power and waste generation. This eliminates the cross-jurisdictional controversies so central to the American process but has not facilitated consensus building in Canada.

Outcomes

Despite these notably different processes and the more aggressive American approach to siting, the outcomes of attempted loss imposition remain, to this point, identical in the two nations. Neither the United States nor Canada has opened any facilities to manage high-level nuclear wastes. Both continue to rely exclusively upon storage in cooling pools and sophisticated containers at the site of every nuclear power plant in the two nations. In both nations, the reality of high-level nuclear waste management involves storage at dozens of places—and this form of loss imposition has received relatively little public attention, even in communities neighboring these de facto waste management sites. This relative calm regarding storage has contributed to its emergence as an alternative to siting a central repository—one that distributes responsibility for waste management geographically rather than imposing it on a single locale in each nation.

Nonetheless, the United States could be heading into the final stages of a process that could result in development of a massive national facility, the long-debated Yucca Mountain site. The Bush administration has accelerated a process for siting that has advanced in fits and starts for over two decades, and it could result in significant facility development by the end of the current decade. Of course, if the Yucca proposal collapses for any reason, there is literally no alternative site or siting process, reflecting the steadfast focus on Yucca. In contrast, Canada adheres to on-site storage as it lumbers through another decade of trying to define a siting process.

Process vs. Outcomes

The case of nuclear waste disposal illustrates the potential for very different policymaking processes to produce outcomes that may ultimately be either very different or very similar in the long term. To the present, the different loss imposition processes resorted to by the United States and Canada in this case have resulted in identical outcomes in terms of the management of high-level nuclear waste. In the event of successful siting of Yucca Mountain, however, outcome differences would become substantial, with the United States having a single repository for disposal of all of its high-level nuclear wastes. The inability of either process, after decades of debate and analysis as well as the expenditure of billions of dollars in both nations, to impose loss through facility siting suggests that high-level nuclear waste may possess unique features that make any form of loss imposition other than on-site storage extremely difficult.

Explanatory Factors

The greater likelihood of a loss imposition outcome involving selection of a single site in the United States reflects the relative strength of its federal government in the area of environmental policy. Despite the numerous ways in which institutional arrangements can restrict the ability of the American federal government to impose losses, it does have an established track record of nearly four decades in enacting loss-imposing environmental legislation. Medium-specific federal legislation that follows a command-and-control process is well established in the American system, supplemented by a series of exacting programs related to hazardous and nuclear wastes, endangered species protection, and pesticides management. Indeed, during the decade-long period in which Congress enacted three major bills governing high-level nuclear waste, it also enacted extraordinarily detailed legislative reauthorizations of federal air pollution control and hazardous waste cleanup programs that were packed with loss-imposing decisions.

Moreover, the intergovernmental dynamics of high-level nuclear waste disposal provided a substantial opportunity to lower institutional barriers to the establishment of new policy. Unlike regulatory programs that pit multistate regions against one another with respect to controls on massive quantities of pollution generated by numerous sources (such as air pollution), high-level nuclear waste disposal involves a relatively small amount of an exceedingly undesirable waste product. Since it is produced in so many states, all of which have an incentive to ship the wastes to another location for perpetuity, federal legislation offers an attractive means of ganging up politically on a single jurisdiction and designating it as the host. Having a state such as Nevada, with limited numbers of elected representatives, a politically weak congressional delegation, and an abundance of sparsely populated territory, makes the task all that easier.

Canadian institutional arrangements may seemingly offer a more streamlined opportunity for loss imposition, but this has clearly not been the outcome with respect to nuclear waste and many other areas of environmental policy. Canadian federal jurisdiction over most areas of environmental and natural resource protection is very limited constitutionally, and has followed a trend toward even greater decentralization in recent years. Parliament has never passed any federal legislation in such areas as cleanup of abandoned hazardous waste dumps or endangered species protection, and its medium-specific programs in such areas as air and water pollution are vague declarations of concern that delegate most decision making to provinces and other stakeholders. Even Canada's eagerness to play the role of "moral superpower" in building coalitions to reach international environmental agreements is increasingly undermined by the inability of its federal government to impose the losses needed to implement its part of international bargains.

Canada's federal government has retained jurisdiction over most aspects of nuclear waste, but its elected officials have treated that subject with as much caution as they have most other areas of environmental policy. This has left enormous latitude to federal agencies and commissions, facilitating a prolonged style of deliberation that does not lend itself to imposing specific losses. Moreover, the Ontario-centered nature of the nuclear waste problem eliminates the incentive for provincial representatives in Ottawa to use federal legislation to geographically shift the burden of waste management.

Nonetheless, the continued inability of either the United States or Canada to reach closure on a loss-imposition strategy—and the possibility of continued stand-off over an indefinite period in both nations—suggests that traditional explanatory factors for outcome differences may be insufficient in this case. High-level nuclear waste may occupy a unique category in terms of its ability to defy prospective loss-imposing strategies. The volume of this waste is exceedingly small—yet its potential health risks are so severe and long-standing that it may prove beyond the capacity of most governments to convince potential losers to accept the necessary loss. Instead, the common reaction around the world to a wide range of proposed siting processes calling for a single repository has been the intense, aggressive opposition that North America has seen in Kansas, Ontario, and particularly Nevada. For virtually every other type of waste material, one can highlight some pattern of successful waste imposition strategies in both Canada and the United States. But the basic qualities of high-level nuclear waste may generate such public fear and political opposition that any combination of deliberation, analysis, and compensation may prove insufficient to allow loss imposition in the form of single-facility siting to take place. In both nations, on-site storage remains the prevailing method of disposal, owing both to their common inability to impose concentrated loss through a single site and to a much higher apparent public tolerance for this method. This appears consistent with a growing trend among many other western governments, including the United Kingdom and Germany, to abandon earlier plans for a single repository in favor of various types of "temporary" or "interim" storage methods.[49]

Techniques and Strategies

Blame avoidance opportunities abound in the case of high-level nuclear waste, and different institutional actors in the United States and Canada have utilized various strategies in attempting to facilitate—or avoid—loss imposition. Initially, both the United States and Canada turned to technical experts lodged in federal agencies to guide loss imposition. Both assumed that technical criteria would guide site selection and that economic compensation packages and safety assurances would override any conceivable opposition. Thereby, it was assumed, politicians would not have to take responsibility for loss imposition and could instead characterize the process as a technical exercise, conducted by agency officials with advanced degrees in the physical sciences.

Such blame avoidance was proven likely to fail by the end of the 1970s, leading to different strategies in the two nations during more recent decades. In the United

States, blame avoidance took multiple forms for representatives of different institutions, all promising some potential cover from this issue. For at least 98 percent of the members serving every Congress during the past two decades, the most obvious method of blame avoidance has been steadfast support for siting a single geological repository in Nevada. For waste-generating states, such a siting strategy would allow their officials to avoid blame for any possible problems stemming from on-site management or from possible consideration of them as a siting host. For nonwaste-generating states, such a strategy removes them from possible siting candidacy and from the blame likely to be affixed to elected officials if that candidacy proceeded. For former President Clinton and Vice President Gore, the Yucca designation process provided a convenient mechanism to avoid any final decision on repository siting during their terms in office. The Clinton administration neither endorsed nor opposed Yucca during its eight years, instead insisting that extensive technical review must be completed before any decision was possible and that this could not be finished until after it left office. Its opposition to the late 1990s proposal to create a "temporary" national storage facility at the Nevada Test Site was a further resort to blame avoidance, since congressional enactment of such legislation would have required the president to make a decision on this alternative approach and, in effect, on Yucca Mountain as the permanent site.

For the Department of Energy, the three pieces of federal nuclear waste legislation passed between 1982 and 1992 gave it a fairly clear blueprint for how to proceed with siting and the capacity to deflect blame by simply following specific legislative orders. And for Nevada elected officials, blame avoidance has entailed efforts to thwart rather than facilitate loss imposition. Vocal disassociation with any aspect of the Yucca Mountain proposal has become a staple strategy for electoral success in Nevada, with accompanying efforts to find any conceivable political or technical method to delay or block the strategy likely not only to provide opportunities for blame avoidance but to facilitate credit-claiming as well.

The entering Bush administration was widely expected to replace the timidity of the Clinton administration with intensified support for Yucca siting as part of an overall effort to sustain—and possibly expand—the role of nuclear power as an American energy source. Energy Secretary Abraham and President Bush did move rapidly in 2002 to try to remove remaining obstacles to Yucca siting. In so doing, they built on post September 11 concerns about the potential vulnerability of dozens of storage sites to future terrorist acts. However, potential obstacles to Yucca siting remain, especially as opponents attempt to shift the focus to the risks posed by nuclear waste transport to a single facility.

Blame avoidance has taken a somewhat different turn in Canada, reflecting the different institutional processes governing loss imposition by the federal government in environmental policy. For members of Parliament over several decades, nonaction and deference to federal agencies and commissions have provided cover from any blame associated with high-level nuclear waste management. Parliament remained silent on the issue between 1946 and 1997, allowing an extraordinarily deliberative process of study and review to proceed. Since no prospective sites have ever been announced, by Parliament or by any federal agency, no riding has been gripped by concern over loss imposition involving site hosting. Delay as a blame avoidance tactic has also been evident in federally designated review bodies, most notably the Seaborn Panel. This commission took nearly a decade to review virtually every conceivable dimension of high-level nuclear waste management in Canada and concluded that a long-term process of building trust was necessary before any serious consideration of siting could take place. It provided only a very general outline of the future course of Canadian policy, essentially advising the Canadian government to start from scratch, with new institutions and an extended process designed to build public trust.

These respective strategies have contributed directly to the current outcomes in the two national settings. Congressional determination to impose a repository on Yucca Mountain has not faltered, but Nevada opposition and other factors have delayed the implementation of its goals. Canada has retained a deliberative posture that appears to leave it no closer to loss imposition through repository siting than it was thirty years ago. Despite these differences in blame avoidance strategies, the current outcomes with respect to high-level nuclear waste management remain identical, at least at present. In both nations, continued resort to on-site storage capacity retains support from virtually all forces with some reason to want to avoid blame for siting any geological repository. On-site storage may, in fact, become the primary blame avoidance recourse for siting critics who lack any waste management alternative to creation of a single facility.

OVERALL EVALUATION AND GENERALIZABILITY

Local capacity to block proposed geographical losses has grown dramatically in both the United States and Canada in recent decades. The term NIMBY (for Not in My Backyard) is used increasingly to describe reactions to a range of controversial geographical loss imposition proposals—ranging from the sorts of waste management facilities discussed above to other unwanted facilities, including prisons, drug and alcohol treatment facilities, hospices, homeless shelters, recycling centers, cellular phone towers, shopping centers, large churches, and public housing, among others. But if one were to create a continuum ranking the intensity of political opposition and fear in reaction to various proposed types of facilities, those intended to manage high-level nuclear waste would occupy the extreme high-fear end. The health risks imposed by exposure to high-level nuclear waste, unlike those associated with other kinds of waste, are well established and severe. Moreover, the centuries of secure isolation required for successful management are politically and technically staggering.

For other types of concentrated geographical losses, an array of techniques may prove effective in making loss imposition more palatable or even desirable. In such cases, institutional and other political differences may have a far greater impact than in a case such as high-level nuclear waste, where the severity of potential loss imposition may override any institutional factors. Even in the case of waste management, there appears to be enormous variation in the prospects for cooperative resolution according to waste category and the type of risk it is perceived to impose.

In the case of those types of waste that appear to pose very limited risks to human health or property values, there may be considerable opportunity to establish new waste management facilities with public support. In the area of solid waste (more commonly known as garbage), numerous landfills and other waste management facilities have been opened in both Canada and the United States in recent years. Earlier concerns about a looming crisis in solid waste management capacity have largely disappeared, at least for many regions in both nations. In this case, solid waste is familiar to all citizens and poses a far smaller set of human health risks than high-level nuclear waste. A combination of more open siting negotiation processes, multifaceted compensation packages to host communities, and increasingly sophisticated waste management methods have helped defuse tensions in this area. In turn, unexpected growth in solid waste recycling rates in many states and provinces has dramatically reduced the anticipated volumes of waste requiring management.[50] Siting conflicts still emerge, perhaps most notably in Ontario, and some jurisdictions and waste management firms have poor track records with respect to siting. Nonetheless, the solid waste case reinforces the notion that geographically concentrated loss imposition through facility siting can be resolved cooperatively, at least in waste areas other than high-level nuclear waste.

The case of hazardous waste stands somewhere between the extremes of solid waste and high-level nuclear waste. These wastes pose more significant human health risks than solid waste but are generally accepted to be less threatening than high-level nuclear waste, in terms of both the intensity of the health risk posed and the time period for which isolation from human contact is required. In these cases, siting efforts have generally proven more conflictual than in the case of solid waste but have achieved more agreements (or near-agreements) than with respect to high-level nuclear waste. In the case of hazardous waste, the combination of an open deliberation process with formal agreements for sharing the responsibilities of waste management among multiple communities has actually resulted in multiple volunteers offering to host major hazardous waste management facilities in certain jurisdictions.[51] This type of approach to siting is reflected in the broad model outlined in the Seaborn Report. In turn, low-level and mixed nuclear waste siting efforts have been less successful overall than those for hazardous waste, but there have been occasional signs of success, most recently in Ontario and in keeping existing American facilities operational.

Ironically, the areas of hazardous waste, low-level nuclear waste, and mixed nuclear waste management appear somewhat more promising with respect to siting cooperation but also bear one striking similarity to the case of high-level nuclear waste. Despite all of the attention concentrated on the development of sophisticated waste management facilities, these other waste types have also tended to follow the high-level nuclear waste pattern of increasing reliance upon on-site management. Most low-level nuclear waste in both nations is managed through storage near nuclear power plants, or near those medical and research facilities that generate such waste. In the case of hazardous waste, some method of on-site disposal, treatment, or storage is used for most of the waste generated in both countries. As in the case of high-level nuclear waste, this development does not reflect any formal plan or official federal, state, or provincial policy. In fact, the far greater quantities and sources of these wastes, as opposed to those associated with high-level nuclear waste, raise serious questions about governmental capacity to monitor waste management and assure regulatory compliance.

The on-site approach may possess a number of political advantages over single-facility siting in both nations, regardless of larger political and institutional factors. Familiarity with a particular risk is commonly thought by risk analysis experts to reduce public concern over potential dangers.[52] Even if the risk is posed by nearby high-level nuclear waste, years of proximity to its storage at a nuclear power plant may serve to mitigate apprehension over that potential risk. And the familiarity factor may be enhanced by the significant number of jobs commonly supported by continued nuclear plant operation, as well as the sizable contributions the facility makes to local tax coffers. Contrary to conventional depictions of waste management as concentrated in low-income, predominantly minority areas, many nuclear power plants—and their waste storage facilities—are located in relatively affluent areas, and their operation contributes to local financial well-being.

The presence of exclusively local wastes at on-site storage facilities may further contribute to citizens' relative comfort with this management technique; local reluctance to assume responsibility for waste generated in other jurisdictions is a significant contributor to many NIMBY-type cases of siting opposition.[53]

At the same time, support for on-site storage may reflect lack of public awareness rather than familiarity. On-site storage generally occurs quietly, accompanied by few if any formal public hearings or permit review processes. Environmental groups and the media, as well as scholarly analysts, pay relatively little attention to this phenomenon. Governments tend not to establish commissions or environmental assessment processes that might open on-site storage to significant public scrutiny and generally tend to avoid drawing attention to this practice. In fact, whereas most Canadian and American citizens might be expected to vehemently oppose the creation of a high-level nuclear waste facility in their area, many of the citizens living near a de facto waste storage site may simply be unaware of its existence.

Whatever the reason, on-site management has been perceived with respect to a range of hazardous and nuclear wastes—not solely high-level nuclear waste—as posing far less risk and producing far less political acrimony than is created by facilities that accept wastes from multiple points of generation. Given this pattern, high-level nuclear waste may share at least some common loss imposition characteristics with other, less lethal, types of waste. From a technical, economic, and human health standpoint, one can continue to debate the desirability of this method of waste management. But for policymakers in both Canada and the United States, keeping waste close to its generating source has been the easiest way to impose loss without triggering the sort of uproar so common if the imposition is concentrated in a single geographical locale. Perhaps in no area has this strategy proven more desirable than for the waste that poses the harshest and longest threat to human health: high-level nuclear waste. This pattern may endure in both nations, although the

Bush administration push to open Yucca Mountain, along with the post–September 11, 2001, recognition that all sites holding such wastes could constitute a dangerous target for terrorism, may serve to fundamentally alter this reality in coming years.

NOTES

The author is grateful for the very helpful comments of Leslie Pal, Kent Weaver, George Hoberg, and anonymous reviewers on earlier versions of this chapter, and for the assistance of Carole Shadley, Kate Irvine, and Alex Belinky.

1. Scott Sommer, "Bryan: Nevada's Nuclear Attitude Has Undergone Transformation," *Las Vegas Review-Journal*, March 5, 1999, 10B.

2. Canadian Nuclear Fuel Waste Disposal Concept Environmental Assessment Panel, *Report of the Nuclear Fuel Waste Management and Disposal Concept Environmental Assessment Panel* (February 1998): 12.

3. James Flynn et al., *One Hundred Centuries of Solitude: Redirecting America's High-Level Nuclear Waste Policy* (Boulder: Westview, 1995), p. 20.

4. Interview with Peter A. Brown, Natural Resources Canada (Ottawa, August 31, 1999).

5. Robert Paehlke, "Practical Notes Related to High-Level Nuclear Waste Management" (paper presented to Canadian Nuclear Fuel Waste Disposal Concept Environmental Assessment Panel, March 22, 1996).

6. Michael E. Kraft and Bruce B. Clary, "Public Testimony in Nuclear Waste Repository Hearings: A Content Analysis," in Riley E. Dunlap, Michael E. Kraft, and Eugene A. Rosa, eds., *Public Reactions to Nuclear Waste: Citizens' Views of Repository Siting* (Durham, N.C.: Duke University Press, 1993), pp. 89–114; Doug Easterling and Howard Kunreuther, *The Dilemma of Siting a High-Level Nuclear Waste Repository* (Boston: Kluwer, 1995); Richard G. Kuhn, "Social and Political Issues in Siting a Nuclear-Fuel Waste Disposal Facility in Ontario, Canada," *The Canadian Geographer* 42, no. 1 (1998): 14–28.

7. Flynn et al., *One Hundred Centuries of Solitude*, 72.

8. Spencer Weart, "The Heyday of Myth and Cliché," in Len Ackland and Steven McGuire, eds., *Assessing the Nuclear Age* (Chicago: University of Chicago Press, 1986).

9. Margaret Kriz, "A Political Controversy over Nuclear Waste," *National Journal*, (May 10, 1997): S34.

10. William C. Gunderson and Barry G. Rabe, "Voluntarism and Its Limits: Canada's Search for Low-Level Radioactive Waste Facility Sites," *Canadian Public Administration* 42, no. 2 (summer 1999): 193–214.

11. Walter A. Rosenbaum, "The Good Lessons of Bad Experience: Rethinking the Future of Commercial Nuclear Power," in Pauline Vaillancourt Rosenau, ed., *Public-Private Policy Partnerships* (Cambridge, MA: MIT Press, 2000), pp. 59–76.

12. Tony Batt, "Ensign Takes on GOP over Nuclear Waste," *Las Vegas Review-Journal* (October 29, 1997): 1A.

13. Kate O'Neill, "Yucca Mountain and Mobile Chernobyl," *Environment* 41, no. 9 (May 1999): 34–35.

14. Thomas Birkland, *After Disaster: Agenda Setting, Public Policy, and Focusing Events* (Washington, D.C.: Georgetown University Press, 1997), p. 106.

15. Donald G. Hurst, ed., *Canada Enters the Nuclear Age: A Technical History of Atomic Energy of Canada Limited* (Montreal: McGill–Queen's University Press, 1997); Ronald J. Daniels, ed., *Ontario Hydro at the Millenium: Has Monopoly's Moment Passed?* (Montreal: McGill-Queen's University Press, 1997); Robert Bothwell, *Eldorado: Canada's National Uranium Company* (Toronto: University of Toronto Press, 1988).

16. Barry G. Rabe, "Power to the States: The Promise and Pitfalls of Decentralization," in Norman J. Vig and Michael E. Kraft, eds., *Enviromental Policy: New Directions for the Twenty-first Century*, 5th ed. (Washington, D.C.: Congressional Quarterly Press, 2003), pp. 33–56; Patrick C. Fafard and Kathryn Harrison, eds., *Managing the Environmental Union: Intergovernmental Relations and Environmental Policy in Canada* (Kingston: Queen's University School of Policy Studies, 2000).

17. Birkland, *After Disaster*; 106–30. Frank Baumgartner and Bryan Jones, *Agendas and Instability in American Politics* (Chicago: University of Chicago Press, 1993).

18. Hurst, *Canada Enters the Nuclear Age*, 14.

19. Gunderson and Rabe, "Voluntarism and Its Limits," 193–214.

20. Robert Bothwell, *Nucleus: The History of Atomic Energy of Canada Limited* (Toronto: University of Toronto Press, 1988), pp. 445–46.

21. Daniels, *Ontario Hydro at the Millenium*, 325.

22. Dave Plummer, "Nuclear Waste: Coming Soon to a Hole Near You?" *Canadian Dimension* 30, no. 5 (September 19, 1996).

23. Mark Nichols, "Nuclear Mausoleums: Two Scientists Fear That Buried Radioactive Fuel Might Explode," *Maclean's*, March 20, 1995.

24. Easterling and Kunreuther, *The Dilemma of Siting a High-Level Nuclear Waste Repository*, 30.

25. Robert J. Duffy, *Nuclear Politics in America: A History and Theory of Government Regulation* (Lawrence: University Press of Kansas, 1997), chap. 7.

26. Ibid., p. 186.

27. Flynn et al., *One Hundred Centuries of Solitude*, 40.

28. Luther J. Carter, *Nuclear Imperatives and Public Trust: Dealing with Radioactive Waste* (Washington, D.C.: Resources for the Future, 1987), pp. 425–27.

29. Flynn et al., *One Hundred Centuries of Solitude*, 42.

30. Keith Rogers, "Two Temblors Rock Plateau at Test Site," *Las Vegas Review-Journal*, January 26, 1999, 1A; "Another Quake Hits Test Site," *Las Vegas Review-Journal*, January 28, 1999, 1B.

31. Interview with Robert Loux, (Carson City, Nevada, August 24, 1999).

32. Margaret Kriz, "Outvoted, Nevada Still Says No!" *National Journal* (March 30, 1996).

33. Dow Jones News Service, "U.S. Senators from Nevada Sponsor Nuclear Waste Bill," March 24, 1999.

34. Matthew L. Wald, "Nevada Site Urged for Nuclear Drop," *New York Times*, January 11, 2002.

35. Hurst, *Canada Enters the Nuclear Age*, 380.

36. Ibid., p. 384.

37. A. M. Aikin, J. M. Harrison, and F. K. Hare, *The Management of Canada's Nuclear Fuel Wastes: Report of a Study Prepared under Contract for the Ministry of Energy, Mines and Resources* (Ottawa: Ministry of Supply and Services, 1977).

38. Minister of Energy, Mines and Resources Center, and Ontario Energy Minister, *Joint Statement on the Canada/Ontario Radioactive Waste Management Program* (June 5, 1978), pp. 1–2.

39. "1,300 Ontario Sites 'Acceptable' for Nuclear Waste," *Ottawa Citizen*, October 20, 1989, A4.

40. Barry G. Rabe, *Beyond NIMBY: Hazardous Waste Siting in Canada and the United States* (Washington, D.C.: Brookings Institution Press, 1994).

41. Interview with Guy Riverin, Health Canada (Ottawa, August 30, 1999).

42. Canadian Nuclear Fuel Waste Disposal Concept Environmental Assessment Panel, *Report*, 41.

43. Ibid., 74.

44. Ibid., 78.

45. Ibid., 71, 135.

46. Robert Lewis, "The Nuclear Waste Muddle," *Maclean's*, May 4, 1998.
47. Natural Resources Canada, *Government of Canada Response to Recommendations of the Nuclear Fuel Waste Management and Disposal Concept Environmental Assessment Panel* (Ottawa: Natural Resources Canada, 1998), p. 7.
48. Interview with Peter A. Brown, Natural Resources Canada (Ottawa, August 31, 1999).
49. Flynn et al., *One Hundred Centuries of Solitude*, pp. 14–16; Steven D. Chandler, *Radioactive Waste Control and Controversy: The History of Radioactive Waste Regulation in the UK* (Amsterdam: Gordon and Breach, 1997).
50. David H. Folz, "Municipal Recycling Performance: A Public Sector Environmental Success Story," *Public Administration Review* 59, no. 4 (July/August 1999): 336–45.
51. Rabe, *Beyond NIMBY*.
52. Howard Margolis, *Dealing with Risk: Why the Public and the Experts Disagree on Environmental Issues* (Chicago: University of Chicago Press, 1996), chap. 5.
53. Rabe, *Beyond NIMBY*.

8

GUN CONTROL

LESLIE A. PAL

On the surface, Canadian and American gun control policies appear to fit the usual stereotypes. The U.S. has relatively permissive laws, particularly with respect to handguns, while Canada is currently implementing one of the most comprehensive legislative regimes of universal firearms registration in the world. Rates of gun ownership and of gun-related violence in the U.S. easily eclipse Canadian rates. The U.S. is by no means uniformly marked by strong public support for loose gun laws, and public opinion in recent years has swung gradually toward a pro-control stance as their pro-control counterparts. This coincides closely with efforts since 1990 to tighten Canadian gun laws. Likewise, the anti-gun control interest groups take similar positions and articulate similar arguments with the same fervor as on both sides of the border.[1] Indeed, the National Rifle Association (NRA) in the U.S. has offered tactical advice to its counterpart in Canada, the National Firearms Association.

These similarities do not mean that circumstances are identical in the two countries, but they do suggest that gun control generates roughly the same types of political forces in Canada and the U.S. A key difference in outcomes—Canadian federal governments have been markedly more successful in passing gun control legislation in the 1990s than U.S. federal governments—may result from institutional differences between the two countries and how they channel similar political forces. If gun control is viewed as an instance of loss imposition on gun enthusiasts, it may be that the U.S. congressional system permits opponents of

233

control to pressure their government more effectively. The looser party system in the U.S. means that coalitions can be built within and across parties in a way that is not possible in Canada's parliamentary system. The concentration of power in the Canadian executive also means that once a legislative decision has been taken, it dominates the agenda and has a high likelihood of successful implementation.

Generally speaking, this indeed seems to capture what has happened in the two countries. Even after the horrors of Littleton, Colorado (on April 20, 1999) and subsequent killings, the NRA and its allies have managed to stall efforts to introduce tighter gun control. In Canada, on the other hand, Bill C-68 was successfully passed in the teeth of substantial party, interest group, and provincial opposition. However, as we will note below, the Canadian government still faces problems in implementing its new legislation. As well, the Canadian success obscures the fact that the government was forced to respond to criticisms of the bill. The executive power can be checked to some small degree in the party caucus and, in typically Canadian fashion, by provincial opposition.

ANALYTICAL AND METHODOLOGICAL ISSUES

Theorizing Loss Imposition

Political institutions establish the rules of the game that define who has power and influence, which alternatives are compared and selected, access to veto points, and, in any given case, the objectives and strategies of policymakers and interest groups. For politicians, what this boils down to is the institutional capacity that they have to strategically manage the imposition of loss (e.g., spread it out over time, groups, or space; make side deals; compensate losers in some fashion) and protect themselves from blame: "Politicians must, therefore, be at least as interested in *avoiding blame* for (perceived or real) losses that they either imposed or acquiesced in as they are in 'claiming credit' for benefits they granted."[2] For opponents of any given loss, the institutional variable amounts to how much access to and influence over decision makers they can realistically have.

Considering only institutions for the moment, the success that politicians have in imposing loss and the success that losers have in resisting it would seem to depend on several generic features. As discussed in the introduction to this volume, those can include concentration of authority, the number and capacity of potential vetoers, and the ability of voters to punish loss-imposing politicians. In comparing the U.S. system with Canada's, these variables suggest, on balance, a greater capacity to impose loss under parliamentary institutions. The Westminster system concentrates authority in the prime minister and the cabinet—indeed, in the Canadian case, to an extent that seems to exceed Britain's and other similar systems, like Australia's and New Zealand's.[3] Party discipline means, at least when the government has a majority of seats (and governments in Canada have ruled with majorities in all but nine years since 1945), an almost complete control over the legislative agenda. Governments can also be more easily blamed, of course, but given national rather than local electoral campaigns, and control over the timing of elections within the required five-year limit, governments can usually counteract any punishment that might be exacted in the ballot box.

These broad, first-order effects are complicated by second-order variations, such as divided government in the American case and majority or minority government status in the Canadian case. Therefore, while we might expect loss imposition to occur more frequently and efficiently in Canada than in the U.S., specific outcomes are likely to depend on the nature of the issue and the degree to which it amplifies first-order or second-order effects.

The type of loss being imposed can pose different types of challenges for political decision makers. The key categories would appear to be (1) losses that are geographically concentrated, affecting one community or a region; (2) losses that are geographically dispersed but inflicted on an identifiable group, such as pensioners; (3) losses that affect business; and (4) losses that are primarily symbolic or value-based rather than material.[4]

Gun control falls in the last category, though there are material consequences for the firearms industry[5] and for those who depend on firearms for their livelihood (e.g., hunters, hunting guides, farmers, and outfitters).[6] In fact, virtually every political issue has a symbolic or value component,[7] but issues that are primarily symbolic or value-based have three key characteristics: (1) Issues of this type (e.g., abortion or homosexuality) tap into fundamental debates about differing "ways of life" and are not primarily about material impacts; (2) in turn, these debates about "ways of life" are often deeply connected to debates about fundamental political liberties; and (3) losers in symbolic politics sense that their "social worth" is being demeaned and diminished. The gun control issue resonates across all three dimensions. In both the U.S. and Canada, gun use is higher among rural than among urban residents, and higher among Southern states and Western and Northern provinces and regions than in the East.[8] Guns have also been portrayed as a "freedom" versus "governmental control issue" (more, as we note below, in the U.S. than in Canada), thus pitting individualist values against more collectivist ones. Finally, the debate between opponents and proponents of gun control is often marked by negative imagery designed to devalue the other side: Gun owners are depicted as "rednecks," for example, whereas control opponents are freedom-hating authoritarians. This combined emphasis on way of life, core political values, and status gives symbolic issues their charge. Imposing losses in this context is particularly challenging and dangerous—and, unsurprisingly, politicians are normally reluctant to upset any stable status quo.

What does all this mean in terms of loss imposition in the guise of gun controls? First, because it is a symbolic issue, we would expect that attempts to impose losses that would go unremarked in other policy areas (as in the case of registration of motor vehicles, for example) will be vigorously resisted as threats to ways of life. Second, given the different roots of the gun control issue in the U.S. (discussed below), we would expect that resistance to be more widespread in the United States. Third, as this is a symbolic issue, once the lines are drawn, it will be more difficult for politicians to avoid blame through such means as compensation or grandfathering. They may use these techniques, but they are likely to be relatively ineffective in satisfying potential losers. Finally, we would expect gun control to be more easily blocked in the U.S. system than in Canada's. With fewer access points for pro-gun interest groups, and more concentrated authority in a government willing to go ahead with controls, we would expect loss imposition through gun control to be more successful in Canada than the United States.

Comparing the Countries

Before discussing the different policy trajectories on this issue in the two countries, it is important to highlight some key contextual differences. We will return to these in the conclusion in an attempt to gauge the impact of institutions and issue type.

Perhaps the most important, if amorphous, contextual difference between the countries on this issue is the existence of what Richard Hofstadter and others have called a "gun culture" in the United States.[9] There is a sort of romanticism about firearms in the U.S. that has no counterpart in Canada. Their different cultures are reflected in patterns of firearm use. Table 8-1 shows that with a population about nine times as large as Canada's, the United States has thirty times as many firearms. Whereas in Canada handguns make up about 16 percent of all firearms, they account for about 34 percent of all firearms in the U.S. Table 8-1 also shows that death rates involving firearms (per 100,000 of the population) are much higher in the U.S. than in Canada, as are rates for murders with firearms and robberies with handguns. The total percentage of homicides with firearms in the U.S. is more than double Canada's.

The existence of a "gun culture" and the prevalence of the use of firearms in the U.S. do not mean that Americans are uniformly pro-gun. Public opinion polls over the past two decades have consistently shown strong majority support for gun controls, and when driven by singularly horrific events (massacres or attempted assassinations) or worries about crime, this support has spiked even higher.[10] There are local, state, and federal regulations and statutes governing the import, purchase, use, and transport of firearms: There are over 20,000 regulations at the local and state levels alone, and large municipalities have also passed legislation. The resulting patchwork of federal and state legal regimes leaves various loopholes. For example, federal law prohibits anyone under the age of 21 from purchasing a handgun from a federally licensed dealer, but it is legal for such persons to possess handguns and to purchase them from private collectors. Many provisions, such as background checks, are not well implemented.

Counterbalancing this is the American constitutional reference to the bearing of arms, the Second Amendment,[11] and the existence (as of 2002) of "right-to-carry" legislation in thirty-three states. Many Americans assume that these provisions mean that they have a constitutionally protected right to bear arms.[12]

The legal context for firearms legislation in Canada is very different. There is not even the possibility of suggesting a specific constitutional support for the right to bear arms, though opponents of gun control do highlight the impacts on personal freedoms and privacy. The 1999 appeal to the Canadian Supreme Court argued

TABLE 8-1
Canada–U.S. Comparison, 1998

	Canada (million)	United States (million)
Population	30.2	270
No. of all firearms	7.4	222
No. of handguns	1.2	76
Total firearms deaths*	4.2	11.4
Murders with firearms*	0.5	4.4
Murders with handguns*	0.23	3.3
Robberies with handguns*	18	63
% of homicides with firearms	27.3%	66%

*Rate per 100,000
Source: Coalition for Gun Control, www.guncontrol.ca/Content/Cda-US.htm

primarily that the Firearms Act contravened provincial jurisdiction over property and civil rights, but this is an argument of jurisdiction, not of personal freedoms per se. In the U.S., federal legal authority over firearms has been based primarily on the commerce power (article 1, sec. 8) of the Constitution (Congress has the power to "regulate Commerce with foreign Nations, and among several States, and with Indian Tribes"). The first case to define the clause (*Gibbons v. Ogden*, 1824) established a distinction between intrastate and interstate commerce, and concluded that Congress's power extended only to the latter. However, in cases involving the 1887 Interstate Commerce Act and the 1890 Sherman Antitrust Act, the Supreme Court reasoned that where interstate and intrastate commerce were so mingled that regulation of interstate commerce required incidental regulation intrastate commerce, such regulation could be allowed. This line of jurisprudence was substantially extended through the Depression until, for example, in the case of the Fair Labor Standards Act, the Supreme Court held that Congress had the power to regulate intrastate commerce if such commerce had an effect on interstate commerce or if that regulation could be viewed as a means of achieving a legitimate congressional end (e.g., *United States v. Darby*, 1941). The commerce power thus became the basis for the regulation of interstate sale of firearms, but also for various gun-related activities. The link with commerce could be tenuous. For example, the 1990 Gun Free School Zones Act prohibited the possession of a firearm in or near a school on the basis of its effects on commerce. In what may signal the beginning of a shift in the Supreme Court's view of the commerce power, in 1995 the act was struck down as extending beyond the constitutional authority of Congress.[13]

Canadian firearms law has been a matter of federal jurisdiction because, until the 1995 Firearms Act, it had been included as part of the criminal law through the criminal code of Canada.[14] Provinces implement federal regulations, but there is no doubt that Ottawa has broad capacity, based on its exclusive jurisdiction over criminal law, to regulate firearms.[15] This is both an advantage and a disadvantage from the point of view of Canadian authorities. It means, on the one hand, that Ottawa has a legislative and regulatory capacity that in principle eclipses anything Washington has. Since implementation depends on the provinces, however, Ottawa has relatively little leverage should provinces refuse to enforce the criminal code.

A final consideration is the nature of gun control legislation and regulation itself. Typically, there are three main dimensions of control: the gun owner or user, the gun itself and associated equipment (e.g., ammunition), and its use. Gun control regulations can be notoriously complex and difficult to fathom or compare because they can vary independently along all three dimensions. Typical provisions pertaining to the person using a gun, for example, include age restrictions, required training in the use of firearms, mental competence, the existence of a criminal record, and social and psychological stability. As for the gun itself, certain guns can be completely restricted, as can certain enhancements (rapid fire, for example, or silencers), and some or all guns can be required to be registered in some fashion (and again, there can be variations in the way in which such records are kept and accessed).

As for use, everything from storage to transportation of firearms can potentially be regulated. Table 8-2 provides some examples of different types of regulations along each dimension, along with descriptions of the typical parameters defining weak and strong gun control regimes. It is important to note that policymakers can tweak any given requirement independently of others: Higher age restrictions on gun purchases, for example, can vary independently of provisions for background checks or regulations on storage and transport.

There is no country in the world that does not have some rules about gun users, guns themselves, and the use of firearms. Weak regimes tend toward minimalist requirements on the user or owner (relating to age or police record, for example), on the gun itself (banning only military-type weapons, for example, or enhancements clearly designed to facilitate crime or murder), and on use (such as those relating to transport across jurisdictions). The U.S. regime at the national level is generally considered weak because it is light on all three dimensions. The new Canadian regime is considered strong because it has multiple requirements for the user, numerous restrictions and bans on various types of firearms as well as universal registration, and detailed regulations on storage and transportation.

IN THE UNITED STATES

For many, the key to understanding the trajectory of gun control legislation in the U.S. is the strength of the gun lobby, and in particular the NRA. The NRA was formed in 1871 as an association to promote military marksmanship after the sometimes dismal performance of Union soldiers in the Civil War.[16] By the 1960s it had become one of the best organized lobbies in the world.[17] It has, however, suffered setbacks in recent years, most notably on account of the Oklahoma City bombing. (Timothy McVeigh was an NRA member, and there had been meetings between NRA officials and the Michigan militia.[18])

The first federal gun control legislation in the U.S. was enacted in 1927; it prohibited sales of handguns through the mail, though the act was toothless without enabling regulations. This was followed by the generally uncontroversial

TABLE 8-2
Dimensions of Gun Control

Dimension	Objects of Regulation	Weak-Control Regime	Strong-Control Regime
Gun User	• age • criminal and police records • psychological state • type of owner (collector, hunter, shooting club member) • civil status (citizen of state, aboriginal) • training in use • requirement of references • requirement for license	• lower age thresholds (e.g., 16) • focus on criminal record only • no references required • background check done quickly, without waiting period or "cooling-off" period before actual possession • no requirement for license	• higher age threshold (e.g., 21) • social as well as criminal considerations, with references from third parties required • lengthy background check • cooling-off period • specific training required • user must have a license or permit
Gun and Equipment	• import and export restrictions • permits/licenses • prohibitions of certain types (assault weapons) • ammunition • safety devices • barrel types • silencers	• loose restrictions on import and export • no requirement for individual permit or registration of firearm • prohibited list is short; all other firearms permitted • narrow restrictions on types of ammunition, safety devices, etc.	• lengthy prohibited list includes some powerful hunting rifles as well as handguns • import and export are tightly controlled • universal registration of each firearm • safety devices are enforced
Use	• transport • storage • display (e.g., for businesses, clubs) • concealment • proximity to certain types of establishments (e.g., schools)	• storage restrictions mostly to protect minors • transportation restrictions pertain only when crossing jurisdictions • concealment is permitted	• transportation from site to site is regulated • storage requirements are detailed • concealment is not permitted

National Firearms Act of 1934, which focused on weapons used by gangsters (short-barreled shotguns, rifles, and machine guns). This was followed in 1938 by the Federal Firearms Act, which gave the Treasury Department the power to develop a national licensing system for dealers, manufacturers, and importers. No major gun control initiatives were launched again until the mid-1960s.

Spitzer observes, with respect to these early efforts, that they were all compromised by the ability of the gun lobby (essentially the NRA) to weaken or narrow provisions in committee, without (as would happen later) the issue ever coming out for a fight on the floor of the House or Senate.[19] Virtually all subsequent national U.S. gun control legislation has faced the same challenge. In 1963 the Senate Judiciary

Committee began hearings on a bill to ban mail-order handguns; the bill "never left committee, owing to pressure applied by the NRA and its allies."[20] President Johnson continued to propose stronger control measures each year but was only successful in 1968. Title IV of the Omnibus Crime Control and Safe Streets Act of 1968 (which restricted transport of pistols and revolvers across state lines and prohibited the purchase of handguns by nonresidents in a state) couched gun control in the context of crime control, thereby clearly identifying the benefit group as law-abiding citizens, and was passed one day after Senator Robert Kennedy's assassination and two months after Martin Luther King, Jr., was killed.

President Johnson was unhappy with the gun control provisions in the act—which addressed only sawed-off shotguns, machine guns, mufflers, and silencers; destructive devices such as grenades and missiles; and handguns—and backed the introduction of new gun control legislation that proposed, remarkably for the time and well ahead of any contemporaneous Canadian proposals, universal firearms registration and owner licensing for hunting rifles and shotguns. The House version of this bill was held up in the Rules Committee by committee chair and gun control critic William Colmer (D–Miss.), and was released only after he had extracted a promise to soften the licensing and registration provisions. Even so, the bill encountered four days of debate in the House of Representatives, forty-five attempts to amend, and five roll call votes. In the Senate the "bill was delayed and weakened by gun control opponents."[21] The bill passed both the House and the Senate, went to conference committee, and was signed by President Johnson on October 22, 1968. The Gun Control Act prohibited the interstate transportation of firearms, banned sales to felons and incompetents, and strengthened some regulatory oversight of weapons such as machine guns, silencers, mines ,and missiles.[22] President Johnson, noting how weak the legislation was, commented that stronger measures had been blocked by "a powerful gun lobby."[23] One year later, key provisions of the act requiring registration by purchasers of shotgun and rifle ammunition were repealed through an amendment to a tax bill.[24]

The anti–gun control lobby returned in 1986 with the successful passage of the Firearms Owners Protection Act, which weakened certain provisions of the 1968 act by relaxing the prohibition on the interstate sale of rifles and shotguns and reducing access by legal authorities to records of sales kept by gun dealers. (The original act said that those records would be available to the secretary of the treasury at all times; now those records were otherwise protected unless the secretary had a warrant in connection with the investigation of a specific offense.) The bill was first introduced in the Republican-controlled Senate in 1982 and then again in 1984; it was finally debated and passed (79–15) in 1985. It faced strong opposition in the Democratic-controlled House of Representatives, and a broad coalition of pro–gun control interest groups was organized, including many law enforcement associations. Initially it looked as though the bill would be killed in the Judiciary Committee, whose chair (Peter Rodino, D–N.J.) was firmly against it. A successful discharge motion forced the committee to report a compromise bill out to the floor of the House in the hopes of forestalling the original version, but this failed, as did a series of amendments offered by William J. Hughes (D–N.J.). A version of the bill with some gun control measures was eventually passed. The acrimony of the debate in the House led to some further unusual maneuvers (such as the subsequent passage of a clarifying bill), but the event as a whole demonstrated the capacity of groups to access political institutions, first through sympathetic Republican senators, and then (crossing party lines) via a sympathetic Democratic congressman. By the same token, however, it took two years to get the bill onto the floor of the Senate, and the House version should have died in committee; it was because of some extraordinary parliamentary maneuvers that the bill was finally passed at all. According to Spitzer, presidential influence in the process was negligible.[25]

The social and political context changed in favor of gun control in the early 1990s. The Brady bill, for example, which sought to impose a mandatory waiting period to allow a background check and provide a cooling-off period for some purchasers, was first introduced in Congress in early 1987. President Reagan did not himself support the provisions of the bill until the very end of his presidency, and neither did his successor, President Bush. While Bill Clinton did not explicitly campaign in favor of gun control, his platform contained a range of measures to fight crime. Once elected, Clinton introduced an omnibus crime bill in 1993 that contained both conservative elements (like stronger death penalty provisions) and liberal ones (such as a waiting period for handgun purchases) and that set the stage for the eventual passage of the Brady bill. The change in social context was equally important: Public opinion, in part owing to concerns about rising gun-related crime and to the 1993 siege in Waco, Texas, was more supportive of gun control.[26]

It was against this backdrop that the omnibus crime bill encountered difficulty in the House when it was introduced in the fall of 1993. Brady bill supporters pushed for a freestanding bill, which they thought would have a greater chance to pass, but Judiciary Committee chair Jack Brooks (D–Texas), a gun control opponent, initially disagreed. He finally agreed to a freestanding bill, but voted against approval both in committee and later on the floor.[27]

At this stage, it seemed clear that there would not be enough votes to carry the bill, and so opponents had to stage a rearguard action to limit their losses. An interesting technique was a successful amendment that introduced a five-year phaseout of the waiting period. From the point of view of loss imposition theory, this is a counterpart to "grandfathering"—except that rather than imposing losses in the future, it exacts them now, with a guarantee that they will be phased out (unless reenacted).[28] The bill passed the House by a vote of 238–189 largely along party lines, but 54 Republicans voted for it and 69 Democrats against. The bill faced a Republican filibuster in the Senate, so one amendment was passed to further weaken the five-day waiting period; somewhat surprisingly, the steam went out of the filibuster, and the bill passed the Senate on November 20, 63–36. President Clinton signed it on November 30.[29] Most observers at the time agreed that the shift in public opinion, and its subsequent reflection in a bill that directly confronted the NRA and its lobby, was the big story behind the legislation.

An assault weapons ban was the other big issue in the last decade; it stemmed from the 1989 Stockton killing of five children and wounding of twenty-nine others by a man with an AK-47 assault rifle. There were immediate calls for bans on automatic and semiautomatic weapons (ones that can fire large numbers of bullets with a single pull of the trigger). President Bush, an NRA member and formerly an opponent of restrictions on such weapons, changed his view and imposed a temporary import ban by executive order in March 1989; the ban was expanded by President Clinton.

The proposal for a *legislated* ban came from Senator Dianne Feinstein (D–Calif.) in the form of an amendment to the omnibus crime bill being debated in the fall of 1993. Her amendment proposed to specifically outlaw the sale and possession of nineteen categories of assault weapons, but it also provided a list of 650 manual and semiautomatic guns used for sport and hunting that would be exempted. There was also a ten-year sunset provision.[30] The amendment was very astutely designed from a loss imposition perspective: It was limited in time and scope; and, more importantly, it neutralized the "thin edge of the wedge" argument that the difficulty of distinguishing types of weapons would lead effectively to a wider ban than intended. The amendment passed narrowly, but it looked like it was headed for defeat in the House; at this point President Clinton lent strong support to the provision, but Jack Brooks once again worked hard to have the amendment defeated in the Judiciary Committee. In a surprise reversal, Henry Hyde (R–Ill.) decided to vote for the amendment in committee, and it passed on April 26.[31] Whereas a similar provision had been defeated by some seventy votes two years earlier, this time, in a dramatic seesaw battle on the floor, the ban won by two votes (216–214) on May 5, 1994. Gun control opponents had assumed that the amendment would not survive a House vote and so had to scramble that summer; Jack Brooks chaired the conference committee and worked hard to weaken the provisions of the ban.[32] Negotiations were protracted, and eventually the assault weapons ban was accepted on the condition of weakening the Brady bill provisions (by exempting pawn shops from having to conduct background checks). But then the crime bill lost a procedural vote when it came back to the floor of the House.

The bill was also coming under attack in the Senate. In a series of dramatic procedural votes in both the House and Senate, the bill finally passed. The hurdles had, notably, come from a more unified Republican party voting more closely along party lines; the victory was in part due to the special efforts made by President Clinton. The November 1994 congressional elections gave the Republicans control of both the House and the Senate, however, for the first time in forty years, and they were determined to revise the crime control bill that had passed just months before. The issue simmered for over a year, occasionally coming to the fore in connection with a longer debate on counterterrorism measures, and on March 22, 1996, the House voted to repeal the assault weapons ban by 239–173. The GOP leadership in the Senate (especially Bob Dole) showed no interest in taking up the bill.

The momentum on gun control in 1997–98 shifted to the state and local levels, as well as to the courts. In 1997, the Supreme Court struck down the background checks provisions of the Brady law as a violation of the Tenth Amendment's provisions on separate state sovereignty.[33] And borrowing from the successful litigation settlement of $206 billion between forty-six states and the tobacco industry in November 1998, individuals and local governments launched lawsuits against gun manufacturers to recover damages incurred in their communities. The

NRA and its allies responded by trying to ban such suits. In February 1999, Georgia (under Gov. Roy Barnes (D), who had been endorsed by the NRA in his 1998 election bid) passed legislation that prevents cities from suing gun manufacturers. The likelihood of legal success in such suits is not great, but even by late 1999 they had resulted in the beginnings of negotiations among gun companies and some cities to explore ways of enhancing the design and safety of firearms. The Clinton administration supported suits by public housing projects against the firearms industry as well,[34] and in March 2000 reached a deal with Smith & Wesson on safety measures in return for protection from litigation.

President Clinton's January 19, 1999, State of the Union address called for renewed attention to gun control, both in the sense of specific provisions—such as restoring the five-day waiting period for buying a handgun and extending the Brady bill to prevent juveniles who commit violent crimes from buying a gun—and in terms of a broader plan to ensure school and community safety.[35] The April 20, 1999, Littleton, Colorado, tragedy refocused public attention on gun violence,[36] and President Clinton lost little time in calling for an array of gun control measures, including a three-day cooling-off period prior to all handgun sales, an increase in the legal age for handgun possession from 18 to 21, and fines and jail terms for parents who let guns fall into their childrens' hands.[37]

The president had asked House Judiciary Committee chairman Henry Hyde to introduce his proposed new package, but the action started in the Senate, with votes on background checks at gun shows and a juvenile justice bill that had been languishing for eighteen months, after a delicate standoff between those who feared it was too hard on teens and those who worried about its crime provisions leading to more gun control. The Senate majority Republicans introduced half-hearted gun control measures under the pressure of public opinion, hoping to stave off stronger Democratic proposals; a weak gun show bill was defeated in mid-May by a vote of 51–47. Then a slightly stronger version was introduced through an amendment by Democrats Frank R. Lautenberg (N.J.) and Bob Kerrey (Neb.), requiring criminal background checks for all sales at gun shows and for persons seeking to purchase their own guns at pawnshops; this passed by a 51–50 vote, with Vice President Gore casting the deciding vote. (In the U.S. system, the vice president breaks ties in the Senate.)

The juvenile crime bill, containing new gun control provisions (a ban on the importation of high-capacity ammunition clips, and a requirement for the sale of lockboxes with each gun purchase) passed by a strong majority of 73–25. These were stunning outcomes and were widely considered to constitute a major defeat for the NRA,[38] a sign that the Republicans (especially Majority Leader Trent Lott) had lost control of the issue in the Senate, and an indication that the terms of debate had shifted: Being anti–gun control now appeared to conflict with the Republican position on taking strong measures to deal with crime.[39]

Separate votes were arranged in the House on juvenile justice and gun control. Under the pressure of public opinion, Speaker Dennis Hastert (R-Ill.) and Judiciary Committee chairman Henry Hyde (R-Ill.) had already offered to support control measures that would address public safety. On June 18, 1999, the Republican majority in the House watered the gun control bill down with an amendment that would give small vendors twenty-four hours to conduct background checks on potential purchasers but allow them to sell the firearm anyway if the check was not completed in time. Democrats thought this was worse than no bill and so joined the anti–gun control group—the vote was 280–147—to defeat the measure. (The NRA was reputed to have spent $1.5 million in lobbying against the bill.[40]) This left, however, a version of a juvenile crime bill—without gun control measures—which passed in the House on June 17 (by 287–139), and the Senate version, *with* gun control measures. Since Republicans controlled both chambers, it gave them a renewed ability, after their Senate debacle, to name the members of the conference committee that was to reconcile the bills and report in September 1999.

The conference committee opened hearings on August 6. However, the Democrats also threatened to use appropriations bills that would be coming up in the fall (particularly for the Treasury and the Post Office) as another possible route to keep gun control measures on the legislative agenda. Despite suggestions of compromise from high-ranking Republicans, the conference committee stalled almost immediately, meeting only once;[41] the bill died at the end of the congressional session in 2000. While there were other skirmishes regarding gun control throughout the year (for example, around the Elementary and Secondary Education Act, observances of the one-year anniversary of the Columbine High School massacre, and the May 14 "Million Mom March"), nothing of substance emerged from Congress.

On January 18, 2000, President Clinton announced plans to increase funding for the enforcement of existing gun control measures by 25 percent, or $280 million. The NRA and congressional critics had consistently argued that the real failing of gun control was not weak laws but weak enforcement, and this presidential announcement was designed to outflank gun control opponents and garner more political and financial support for the Bureau of Alcohol, Tobacco and Firearms.[42] Clinton's proposal was eventually whittled down by Congress in the appropriations process;[43] by March 2000 the administration had changed tactics and struck a deal with Smith & Wesson (a major U.S. firearms manufacturer) to offer safety locks with all handguns and work on "smart gun" technology, in exchange for being dropped from the lawsuits launched by cities.[44]

By the time that George W. Bush assumed the presidency, gun control was nowhere on the national domestic agenda as a defining issue. The Bush agenda, instead, focused on missile defense, tax cuts, abortion (reproductive technologies), and education. In March, in partial response to yet another gun-related massacre (school shootings on March 5 that killed two students and wounded thirteen others), House Republicans announced their intention of proposing a $1.5 billion program of grants to states and localities to deal with juvenile justice issues—but this program would not involve controversial gun control measures.[45] As of September 11, 2001, the bill had not reached the floor of the House, after which the administration's and Congress's agenda changed dramatically as a result of the attack on the World Trade Center towers. The agenda was now to be dominated by homeland security issues, defense, and pursuit of the war against terrorism.

Gun control at the federal level *has* occurred in the U.S., and losses *have* been imposed, but largely by virtue of (1) association with assassination (Robert

Kennedy, Martin Luther King, Jr.), attempted assassination (President Reagan and his press secretary, James Brady), or senseless massacre (the 1989 Stockton killings, Columbine), (2) a strong presidential push (President Clinton), or (3) executive order. All other attempts at gun control at the federal level have been blocked in the legislative process because of several factors. The first is the ability, in a congressional system with loose party discipline, of the legislative allies of the NRA to block or impede legislation they do not like. The second is the fluidity of coalitions in a congressional system: Several versions of bills can be on the table at any one time, and with only loose and broad lines of division among pro–and anti–gun control legislators, the kaleidoscope of potential allies and opponents is constantly shifting. The third is the ability of the NRA to exact punishment on members of Congress if they support gun control. Spitzer argues that this power is more apparent than real, but concedes that the "perception of NRA strength and its 'hassle factor' can be inhibiting forces."[46]

Nonetheless, the shift in public opinion in the summer of 1999, reflected as it was in part in the convergence around the juvenile justice bill in both the House and the Senate, caused the NRA to adopt a more cautious approach in its fall lobbying: It was prepared, for example, to allow some new controls on juvenile possession of firearms in order to defeat the proposed waiting period for purchases at gun shows. Hardline NRA supporters openly criticized the organization for backing down.[47] The NRA also supported a get-tough-on-gun-crime program called Project Exile, pioneered in Virginia,[48] which was the basis for then–Texas Governor Bush's initiative on guns in the wake of the Fort Worth shootings.[49]

IN CANADA

Canada's first formal legislation on gun control was enacted in 1892 as part of the first Canadian criminal code and required a "certificate of exemption" to carry a pistol (unless the owner had cause to fear assault or injury). The law continued to evolve, but restrictions were primarily aimed at handguns, with a more relaxed regime in effect for rifles and shotguns. In 1951 the registry system for handguns (automatic firearms were included as well) was centralized with the Royal Canadian Mounted Police.

By the 1960s, the legal provisions with respect to various types of firearms were intricate and confusing, and criminal code amendments in 1968 attempted to develop a more coherent firearms control regime. Since then, Canada has extended and developed that regime on three occasions: in 1977, in 1991, and most extensively, in 1995. The 1968 law[50] defined three categories of weapons, and the legislative changes of 1977 and 1991 for the most part simply extended their scope, along with the penalties for violation. As we shall see, the technical nature of the changes made in the 1977 and 1991 revisions was relatively uncontroversial (though of course there were critics) as compared with the storm of protest that blew up around the sharper loss imposition contained in Bill C-68, which eventually became the Firearms Act.

The 1968 amendments were originally introduced in 1967 by then Justice Minister Pierre Trudeau as part of the omnibus criminal code Bill C-195. The bill died when the 1968 election was called and was then reintroduced by the new justice minister, John Turner, as Bill C-150. The bill *was* controversial—but less because of the provisions on gun control than because of its liberalization of the laws on abortion, homosexuality, and lotteries. Most public criticism and debate focused on the first two of these components, and Turner's second-reading introduction of the bill and the opposition's reply barely mentioned the firearms clauses.[51] The sheer size of the bill also attracted procedural debate, since the opposition would have preferred to slice up its 126 pages (with 120 clauses) into separate bills. The government refused, and to make sure the message was clear, Turner pointed out that "the government fully endorses this bill. It is a government bill, bears the government stamp and will be supported by the government. We feel bound to the bill as the principal item of social reform in this session of parliament. It is identified with our prime minister and party."[52]

The three categories defined in 1968 were prohibited weapons, restricted weapons, and unrestricted weapons. The original 1968 definition of "prohibited weapons" included muzzle silencers, switchblades, and any other weapon the federal cabinet should choose to define as prohibited. Possession of a prohibited weapon (aside from by police and military personnel in pursuit of official duties) carried a sentence of up to five years in prison. Restricted weapons included handguns, short-barrel semiautomatic weapons, telescoping firearms, and, again, any other weapon the cabinet should choose to so define. Canadians could possess restricted firearms, but only with a registration certificate for the weapon issued by a local registrar of firearms. The certificates specified the proper use and transport as well as production of these weapons. Unrestricted weapons were the residual category, and from 1968 to 1977 included most rifles and shotguns used for recreational shooting or hunting. No registration certificate was required for unrestricted weapons, though users still had to have a permit for firearms use.

The next effort at tightening controls was Bill C-83 in 1976, but it died when that session of Parliament was ended (in Canada, all bills are termintated when a parliamentary session or sitting ends and must be re-introduced in the new session).[53] The government then introduced a new package of criminal code amendments in 1977 (Bill C-51) that tied tighter gun control to greater police powers to fight crime. (Wiretaps, for example, were made easier.) The bill passed the Commons, 95–40, but 150 MPs did not vote.

The 1977 amendments[54] to the criminal code accomplished several things. First, the definition of prohibited weapons was expanded to include automatic weapons and sawed-off rifles. Second, the restricted category was expanded to include semiautomatics with short barrels. Third, and most controversially, a new certification process for gun owners and users was introduced in the form of a "firearms acquisition certificate" (FAC). FACs were good for five years and were required in connection with all transfers of firearms (either as sales or gifts) after the legislation came into effect in 1978. FACs were designed as *acquisition* and not *possession* permits: Someone who had legally acquired a nonrestricted firearm with a FAC would not have to renew that FAC for simple possession of the same firearm. Persons already in possession of a firearm before the legislation came into effect likewise did not require a certificate (though if they were to purchase or receive one afterwards, a FAC would be required). Furthermore, a single FAC was sufficient for a number of acquisitions of nonrestricted firearms. FACs were issued by a "firearms officer" (so designated by the RCMP or the attorney general of a province, usually a member of the local police force).

The new regime combined new, more expansive controls—ones that went beyond the previous "permit" approach—on *who* could possess a firearm, as well as on firearms themselves. Police powers under the legislation were quite broad. For example, if a peace officer believed on reasonable grounds that an offense had been committed, he or she could search a person, vehicle, or premises (other than a dwelling) without a warrant.

This remained Canada's gun control regime until 1989, when a new round of legislative amendments were introduced and eventually passed in 1991 as Bill C-17. The stimulus for change came from two events that year. The first was the Stockton massacre. As in the U.S., this tragedy opened up the debate on semiautomatic weapons, which in Canada were "restricted" but available for sale under certain conditions. The second event was the December 6 killing of fourteen female engineering students by Marc Lépine at the École Polytechnique at the Université de Montréal. In this case, the crime was specifically targeted against women: Lépine's suicide note made it clear that he intended to kill women, and his rampage was marked by shouts that "You're all a bunch of feminists!"[55] The Tory government had already introduced legislation in May 1989 in response to the Stockton shootings that would have prohibited fully automatic weapons or automatic weapons that that had been converted to semiautomatic ones;[56] after the Montreal massacre, there were renewed calls for more extensive gun control.[57] The government had won 44 of its 169 seats in Western Canada (25 in Alberta) and, unsurprisingly, initially rebuffed these demands under Doug Lewis, minister of justice at the time. The Tories faced strong cross-pressures in this period: The Montreal killings played well politically for the Bloc Québécois (which was formed in 1990 after the collapse of the Meech Lake Accord; Lucien Bouchard resigned from the Tory caucus and took five Quebec members with him, along with one Liberal), in that they could press for strong gun control measures with the backing of Quebec public opinion. However, the Reform Party was making gains in support in the West, where gun control was not popular. The Tory coalition was a Mulroney creation that had patched together Quebec and the West; gun control and the Lépine killings threatened to become a wedge issue that would drive the coalition apart. Alberta Tory MPs had also been weathering the impact of the immensely unpopular Goods and Services Tax.[58]

When Kim Campbell became minister of justice in early 1990, it was increasingly difficult to resist the pressure to do something, especially as the government had already signaled an earlier willingness to address some aspects of gun control through restrictions on automatic weapons. Campbell introduced Bill C-80 in June. She formed a special committee (rather than using the Standing Committee on Justice and the solicitor general) and tried to have it rush its approval of the bill without public hearings. The MPs reacted to pressure from pro–gun control advocates who hoped to tighten the legislation and heard witnesses over the summer.[59] In September Campbell began to meet with backbenchers to line up support, but faced resistance for the reasons cited earlier. She also established the Canadian Advisory Council on Firearms, with fifteen members representing various stakeholders: the legal and medical professions, urban safety experts, competitive shooters, hunters, law enforcement agencies, aboriginal peoples, and experts on firearms.[60] By November, Campbell had decided on the basis of these consultations and the report of the Special Committee (which contained thirty-two recommendations for amendments) that she would have to drastically change the bill, requiring another review in the cabinet and new legislation.

Bill C-17 was introduced on May 30, 1991, and was effectively the government's response to the committee report, incorporating many of its recommendations for stronger controls. The bill moved all converted semiautomatics into the prohibited weapons category, though as in the 1977 legislation, current owners had their guns grandfathered as long as they were gun collectors and applied for registration before 1992. The Canadian Advisory Council on Firearms developed a point system to determine which weapons should be restricted or prohibited; as a result of this list, over thirty firearms were added to the prohibited list in 1992 (though these could also be grandfathered). A controversial new regulation prohibited most "large-capacity" magazines, setting limits of ten rounds for all semiautomatic handguns and five rounds for center-fire semiautomatic rifles and shotguns.

Bill C-17 also introduced a clearer and more stringent definition of a "gun collector," tightened up the FAC process, implemented a requirement of mandatory safety training (in cooperation with the provinces), and extended storage and display regulations to all firearms. The government explicitly rejected the option of universal registration of firearms as being too expensive, too time-consuming for law enforcement officers, and ineffective.[61] It also sought to defuse the issue of unaccountable regulatory power (regulations pertaining to gun control were made by cabinet) by introducing a unique procedure whereby proposed regulations would first be tabled in the House for consideration.[62]

Though there was opposition to these changes, it was relatively muted, for several reasons. First, the Montreal massacre significantly altered the "atmospherics" of the gun control debate in Canada, by linking gun control directly to the issue of violence against women. Second, there was no Canadian interest group lobby that could even approach the resources and sophistication of the NRA. The Canadian Wildlife Association actually supported some aspects of the bill, such as mandatory training for first-time gun owners and storage regulations;[63] the prime opponents were the Shooting Federation of Canada and the National Firearms Association. They were facing off (as they would later, with Bill C-68) against the Coalition for Gun Control (headed by Wendy Cukier), the Victimes de Polytechnique (represented by Suzanne Laplante-Edwards, who lost her 21-year-old daughter, Anne-Marie, at the Polytechnique), and women's groups galvanized by the sexist dimension of both the Lépine killings and gun violence in Canada generally. Third, the changes were largely technical, and although they represented some important departures, for the most part they built on the existing regime and simply broadened and deepened it. Moreover, the government's use of grandfathering (which had also been used in the 1977 legislation) effectively neutralized the key "losers" and shifted losses to the future. Finally, the Tories faced an opposition that largely welcomed the bill and indeed would have supported even stronger controls.

The bill was passed in the Commons on November 7, 1991, by a vote of 189–14. It then passed unanimously in the Senate on December 5, one day before the anniversary of the deaths at the Polytechnique. The process was not over, however, since the Minister of Justice still had to table regulations that would be reviewed by a parliamentary committee. The committee reported in June 1992, with thirty-seven recommendations. The implementation of the new regulations was kicked off with a one-month amnesty on November 1 that enabled owners of illegal or unregistered firearms to turn them in without penalty.

The Tories were routed in the 1993 election, and the Liberal Party had promised to introduce gun control legislation as part of its 1993 "Red Book" platform on crime.[64] The bill it eventually introduced completely changed Canada's gun control regime, making it one of the toughest in the world. The rhetoric and legislative maneuvering around the bill was reminiscent of the American dynamics around the gun control issue: extreme statements by opponents that this was communistic or fascistic legislation, demonization of the conflicting sides, and extraordinary interest group mobilization. Dozens of new anti–gun control groups were formed across the country, and several pro–gun control groups achieved high profiles despite having a relatively weak membership base. Unlike in the U.S., however, the government was able to impose its will—though it did have to amend the legislation in various ways and deal with a backbench revolt in the Commons and a rearguard action in the Senate.

After several months of cross-Canada consultations in 1994, the new minister of justice, Allan Rock, announced in late November that a new firearms control program would be legislated in the coming year. Bill C-68 was introduced in the House of Commons on February 14, 1995, and eventually passed by the House, with a number of amendments, on June 13, 1995. The legislation had several key features. First, it would take most of the regulatory provisions regarding firearms out of the criminal code and place them in a new Firearms Act. Second, it reorganized and redefined the categories of restricted and prohibited firearms. Third, once it was fully implemented (and this might take until the year 2003), *everyone* (with the exception of police and the military) in possession of a firearm would have to have a license. Licenses would have to be periodically renewed, and the conditions of renewal were similar to, but expanded upon, the old FAC requirements. Fourth, every firearm in a person's possession would have to be separately registered; again, this would be phased in over time. Both licenses and registration certificates would have fees attached in order to cover the costs of implementation. Fifth, the bill introduced mandatory minimum sentences of four years in prison for certain offences involving the use of firearms (e.g., robbery, sexual assault with a weapon, extortion). Sixth, it made failure to comply with licensing and registration procedures a criminal offense. And finally, it gave police and inspectors broader powers of investigation, allowing for search and seizure of guns and waiving the requirement for judge-approved warrants.

The legislation initially looked like a winner. Polls in Canada regularly showed levels of support for stricter gun control of 70 percent and above. But, as *Maclean's* reported in June 1995, Rock had "clearly underestimated the potential strength of the opposition to his legislation."[65] In terms of our model of loss imposition, strong opposition was precisely what might have been anticipated. Bill C-68 was not cosmetic or incremental; it introduced a whole new regime. The licensing and registration provisions affected every gun owner in the country (amounting to about three million people), sharply defining the losing group. By imposing hefty registration and licensing fees, it also imposed material losses. Finally, the introduction of criminal penalties for failure to comply with licensing and registration requirements gave the appearance of directly attacking gun owners' "way of life" and devaluing it. While these dynamics of loss imposition were understandable and even predictable, however, the success of the resistance will depend to a large degree on the permeability of political institutions to that opposition. In the U.S. case, as we saw, gun control opponents have access to congressional representatives who in turn can tie up the legislative process. In the Canadian case, it was not so easy.

Initial opposition came in the form of rallies held across the country by gun owners groups (and the formation of dozens of new organizations at the local level). In late January 1995, Rock weathered a Liberal Party caucus meeting at which many MPs, especially those representing rural ridings, criticized the scope of the legislation as well as its feasibility.[66] On the eve of introducing the bill, Rock appeared defiant and gave no sign that he was prepared to consider amendments. In part this was tactical, but it may also have reflected the fact that the prime minister strongly supported the bill and that opponents tended to come from regions in the country (e.g., Alberta) where Liberals were weak anyway. Interestingly, the NDP (with the exception of Svend Robinson) did not support the bill, reflecting provincial opposition from Saskatchewan's NDP government. So, in an odd marriage, the NDP and the Reform parties formed the nucleus of opposition in the House of Commons—supported, however, by as many as two dozen Liberals who spoke publicly against the legislation.[67]

The government succeeded in having the bill pass second reading and referred it to committee on April 5, 1995, with the help of the Bloc Québécois (173–53). However, amidst complaining that the Reform Party had launched a filibuster and had taken up too much time on the bill, a motion was passed to limit debate.[68] Three Liberal backbenchers voted with the opposition[69] they were immediately removed from their committee assignments.[70] However, forty-nine Liberal MPs either stayed away for the vote or tried to abstain,[71] responding no doubt to the prime minister's announcement of the seriousness of voting against the party in this instance.[72] By the end of April, in short, the government knew that more than fifty of its own MPs were unhappy with the legislation.

Just as significant, however, were critical positions on the bill taken by the Canadian Medical Association (which did not believe that registration would affect crime or suicides),[73] the Canadian Bar Association,[74] the Canadian Civil Liberties Association,[75] and the Canadian Criminal Justice Association—all of which objected to the search and seizure provisions. These prominent groups were joined by the governments of Alberta, Saskatchewan, Manitoba, Yukon, and the Northwest Territories, in addition to some aboriginal organizations.[76] The provincial governments objected to many of the same features (e.g., broad search and seizure provisions, criminalization of the failure to register firearms), but their principal criticism related to the efficacy and eventual cost of implementing the licensing and registration provisions. The governments of the Yukon and Saskatchewan even suggested exemptions for themselves, along with introduction of the bill on a pilot basis in other jurisdictions.[77] Even the Bloc Québécois changed its position on the bill, which initially had been very supportive, and on May 17 demanded fourteen amendments.[78]

Bowing to these pressures (and particularly to the objections of the Canadian Bar Association), Allan Rock appeared before the Commons Justice Committee on May 19, 1995, and proposed a series of changes to soften Bill C-68. Principal among them were the partial decriminalization of failure to first-time register[79] and a new provision that would require police to have a search warrant to investigate the home of anyone with fewer than ten firearms.[80] This maneuver served to shore up support from the legal community, and the Bar Association announced its strong support for the bill as amended.[81] Several days later the prime minister reiterated that Ottawa would pay for the national registry, though provinces would still be responsible for enforcing the bill.[82] Cost estimates varied widely, with Ottawa insisting that the registry would cost only $85 million (to be recovered from fees charged to gun owners), whereas Quebec was complaining that the bill would cost $300 million in that province alone. (By November 2000, Treasury Board officials informed a Senate committee that the total cost of administering the new program over its first seven years would be $689 million; by January 2002 the government had decided to privatize most of the registration and licensing functions.[83])

Rock's moves were buttressed by yet another prime ministerial statement to the effect that he would not brook any rebellion by his backbenchers.[84] This was important, since MPs opposing the legislation could take some comfort from sagging public support for the bill. Polls showed that while a national majority still supported gun control, the bill was strongly opposed in some parts of the country (e.g., the prairies).[85]

The result was that the bill easily passed third reading in the Commons on June 13, 1995, by a vote of 192–63. However, nine Liberals broke ranks and voted against the bill, as did eight of the nine NDP MPs, all but three Reform MPs, and both Tory MPs. The Bloc Québécois voted with the government. But Bill C-68 then had to go to the Senate, and the anti–gun control lobby began to target the Conservative-dominated upper chamber in its last-ditch efforts to stop the legislation.[86]

The Senate Committee on Constitutional and Legal Affairs held hearings in late September and early October 1995 and in November introduced eight major amendments to the bill, which Allan Rock immediately said were unacceptable. In a surprise move, however, seven Tory members of the committee broke ranks and voted against the amendments, killing the committee report. Despite an acrimonious debate in the Senate, the bill passed unamended on November 22, 1995, 64 votes to

28, with eleven senators abstaining.[87] The new Firearms Act (S.C. 1995, c. 39) was given Royal Assent on December 5, 1995, and came into force on January 1, 1996, except for key provisions (e.g., registration) requiring enabling regulations, which would come into force on October 1, 1998. In order to develop those regulations, Rock appointed a Users Group on Firearms. The registration system would be implemented in two phases, the first requiring that all firearms owners would have to acquire a license by 2001, the second requiring universal registration by 2003. The User Group had representatives of hunters, gunsmiths, gun clubs, firearms retailers, the police, competitive shooters, aboriginals, outfitters, firearms safety trainers, and collectors.[88] It then took almost two years for the government to table and revise regulations before Parliament.

This long process of regulatory enactment gave the government time to defuse criticisms, to shift the debate to more technical terrain, and to try to accommodate opponents. However, it also gave those opponents additional time and opportunity to attack the legislation. In early 1997, for example, the Assembly of First Nations threatened to take the government to court if aboriginals were not exempted from the registration and storage regulations (though it had no objection to the handgun provisions).[89] The National Firearms Association saw an opportunity as the June 2 federal election approached and urged its members to vote strategically for anyone (including the Bloc) who might defeat a Liberal.[90] Gun control did not become a national issue, however, gaining prominence only in occasional remarks by party leaders and in specific rural and Western ridings.[91] Reform won twenty-four of twenty-six ridings in Alberta, out of a total of sixty seats (but none in Ontario, where it had hoped for a breakthrough), and its pro-gun platform probably did it no harm, though it likely did not generate any new support, either.

As part of his new government, the prime minister appointed Anne McLellan from Edmonton as justice minister, and she promised full support for the provisions of the act.[92] She almost immediately began to feel the continued turbulence underlying the gun issue, however. Three weeks after the election, the government of Alberta asked the Alberta Court of Appeal to rule on the constitutionality of the Firearms Act. The government argued that it was unconstitutional because, rather than being based in criminal law, it relied on licensing and registration provisions relating to legal activities and was thus a violation of provincial jurisdiction over property and civil rights. (Alberta was joined by the governments of Saskatchewan, Manitoba, Ontario, the Yukon, and the Northwest Territories, along with the Shooting Federation of Canada and the Alberta Fish and Game Association as interveners.[93]) The three prairie provinces and the Northwest territories had already opted out of a cost-sharing agreement for administering the former gun law, in the fear that the new law would be too complex, cumbersome, and expensive.

Yet another setback was a report by the government's own User Group that the gun law would create a black market for weapons; Justice Minister McLellan maintained that the law would go ahead and be implemented (in terms of licensing and registration requirements) nonetheless.[94] As well, information was released that implementation costs would be higher than estimated. Original cost estimates of registration had been $85 million, but in September 1998 the Justice Department indicated that they would be higher, though it did not specify by how much.[95] This was a critical admission, since opponents had long held that the real costs of universal registration would be significantly higher than forecast.[96]

Gun owners planned a last-ditch protest on September 22, 1998, and organized a rally on Parliament Hill that reportedly drew 10,000 people.[97] The day before, McLellan had announced a delay in the implementation of the act until December 1, 1998, on the grounds that more time was required for the training of law enforcement officers, but this continued to feed the controversy over costs.[98] The government's fortunes improved on September 29, 1998, however, when the Alberta Court of Appeal ruled in a 3–2 decision that the Firearms Act was constitutional.[99] Despite an eventual appeal to the Supreme Court (which, in June 2000, unanimously found that the Firearms Act was a valid exercise of the federal government's criminal law jurisdiction[100]), the Alberta defeat paved the way for the rollout of the regulations, as scheduled, on December 1, 1998. Two months before the act was to finally be in force, however, McLellan announced a series of softening amendments to the regulations. These changes resulted from consultations with the Users Group on Firearms, the same group of stakeholders that had criticized the department's implementation plans earlier that summer, and relaxed some provisions on handguns, through grandfathering and an amnesty.

The dynamics of loss imposition in this case were clearly more advantageous to the federal government, because political institutions gave it the ability to insulate itself to some degree from the political pressure of a well-organized constituency. The legislation was amended only slightly; and because of its majority, the government controlled the legislative process in the House completely. The threat of a backbench revolt did stimulate some amendments after second reading, as did the partial reversal by the Bloc, but the prime minister made it clear that Bill C-68 was a party vote. The only sources of serious and effective opposition were the provinces and the Senate. The Western provinces disagreed in principle with the bill, and later, other provinces (e.g., Ontario and Newfoundland) expressed concerns about the costs of implementation. In the Senate, ironically, the ability of Tory senators to break party ranks without any serious penalty permitted them to defeat committee amendments to the legislation. This factor has worked the other way in the U.S., but principally because congressmen have to face election. It is interesting to speculate what might have happened, ceteris paribus, had the anti–gun control lobby been exercising pressure on members of an elected upper chamber.

CONCLUSIONS

Processes

An ironic difference in the processes surrounding gun control is that the U.S., which has been much less successful in imposing controls at the national level, has also consistently generated more bills with proposed controls than Canada has. These bills are, of course, sponsored by individual representatives as well as by the executive from time to time, whereas in Canada, the legislative agenda is tightly controlled by the government, starting with the prime minister. So Canadian legislative initiatives have been fewer, but almost all of them have resulted in successful passage and only modest amendment. Whereas, in the U.S. case, presidents (with the exception of Johnson and Clinton) have had relatively little impact on the issue and on the processes leading to legislation.

Several other important differences characterized processes in the two countries. First, while there were similar parliamentary maneuvers by opponents to block control measures in both countries, these were much more successful in the U.S. than in Canada. In particular, gun control bills in the U.S. get buried in committee and soon die and disappear; congressional committees are much more congenial arenas for lobbyists than the floors of the House or Senate. In the Canadian case, the government had greater capacity for agenda control throughout the process and could stare down opponents, both in the House and within its caucus. Second, elections seem to have played no role in the Canadian case; gun control legislation was driven by the same types of crisis events as in the U.S., with the exception of Bill C-68, which was linked to an election promise in the Liberal Party Red Book. In the U.S. case, the de facto two-year electoral cycle is what gives lobbying groups, and the NRA in particular, their leverage over politicians. Third, regulations play a much greater role in Canada and give the federal government considerable scope in making secondary law that does not need to go continually before a legislature. The federal government has the authority, grounded in its jurisdiction over criminal law, to make regulations (which, however, must be reviewed by the House of Commons) pertaining to guns, their ownership, and their use. This removes at least part of the issues under debate from the public forum into a more bureaucratic venue.

A final note concerns the *rhythms* of reform. It is interesting that major legislative initiatives to tighten controls in both countries were undertaken in the late 1960s, the late 1980s, and the mid-1990s. The drivers were often different, but Canadian debates have been affected by U.S. events, such as assassinations and killing sprees. It is an interesting example of emulation, though in this case in response to the horror of such events and the ensuing public outrage. The Canadian twist is that the emulation of this outrage usually results, unlike in the U.S., in legislation. A good example is the impetus that the Stockton shootings gave to the Conservatives in 1989, which was then hugely amplified by the Lépine massacre. If there has been a roughly similar rhythm in the past, however, it is unlikely to continue. Canada's Firearms Act represents a substantial and comprehensive gun control regime, so that events south of the border are no longer likely to generate demands for legislative change the way that they can be expected to in the U.S. Canadian policy in this area (barring reversals by the courts) is likely, therefore, to become more regulatory in nature. In Canada the losses have already been imposed—whereas in the U.S., the dynamics of loss imposition are likely to resume in the event of future sensational gun-related events.

Outcomes

In terms of the descriptions outlined in table 8-2, Canadian legislative efforts have led to a strong gun control regime, whereas the U.S. has a weak one. Especially after implementation of the Firearms Act, Canada will have strong controls with respect to all three dimensions: gun owners, guns themselves, and gun use. Put simply, all owners will have to be approved for a license, all guns will be registered; there are significant prohibitions and restrictions with respect to the types of firearms that may be legally used, and there are detailed provisions regarding every conceivable aspect of use, from storage to display to transportation. At the state and municipal level, the U.S. also has examples of regimes that approximate the Canadian one (e.g., New York City), though without universal registration; only handguns require registration. At the national level, however, the U.S. regime is weak in its review of gun owners, is relatively relaxed with respect to the types of firearms that can legally be owned, and has few restrictions on use. In part this reflects the constitutional capacities of the two national governments. In Canada, full jurisdiction over the criminal law allowed Ottawa to legislate and regulate along all three dimensions; whereas the American federal government bases its authority on the commerce clause, and so has had to concentrate on aspects of gun control that can plausibly be connected to trade, exchange, or commerce. There has been a strong focus on imports and exports, on crossing state lines, and on sales, but very little on use.

Accordingly, the outcomes of the loss imposition strategies pursued in the two countries were quite different. Though this is clearly a matter of (our) judgment, the difference in outcomes seems greater than the difference in processes. As mentioned above, the players, the alignments, and the discourses were similar. Certainly the evidence from some U.S. states shows that the country as a whole is far from the stereotype of a uniform gun-loving culture. Many Americans want stronger gun control, and there have been numerous and repeated attempts to strengthen existing controls at the national level, though most have failed. What explains these divergent patterns of outcomes?

Explanations

Earlier, we mentioned the role of the NRA and election contributions as crucial to the American case. We also noted some cultural and social differences between the two countries that might help explain different outcomes. It is now time to look more closely at those explanations. If cultural, social, and historical differences were *that* important, then there should be less broad public support in the U.S. for gun control than there currently is, and states and municipalities should not have as many laws as they do. By the same token, Canada also has its equivalent to the NRA, along with a broad and vocal opposition to gun control.

The key difference would seem to be in the way that the social and political forces coalescing around the gun control issue are channeled through institutions. The evidence would seem to support the view that loss imposition is more difficult in the U.S. than in Canada on symbolic issues. Most gun control initiatives never got out of congressional committees, and when they did, they faced huge hurdles in both the House and the Senate. The capacity of individual legislators in the U.S. system to block bills or amend them has no parallel in Canada. The number of veto players is much larger in the U.S. case, as is the scope for legislative action to block or stall bills. It is important to remember that loss imposition in the case of gun control involves introducing legislation to change an existing situation; all that potential losers have to do is defeat the initiative and protect the status quo. And while the NRA is powerful, it also has a "target-rich environment" of committees and legislators who are engaged in an almost constant electoral campaign.

In the Canadian case, some Liberal backbenchers and the conservative opposition expressed the same views as the "gun lobby" does in the U.S., but their impact on the progress of legislation was nil—it could not be blocked. They did effect some amendments, but in comparison with what is possible in the U.S., these were minor. In characteristic Canadian fashion, the only institutionally effective opposition came from the (western) provinces and the territories; their court actions and their refusal to administer the regulations under old agreements seem to have been a key factor in slowing the government down in the implementation of the 1995 act. It should be noted, however, that in the cases of both Bill C-17 and Bill C-68, the government faced significant opposition from within its own caucus. While the conventional wisdom that a majority government in a Westminster system can virtually ignore the opposition seems well supported in this case, the role of the governing party's caucus was surprisingly important. In the case of both those bills, the government felt enough pressure that it made small amendments and constantly battled with its own backbenchers. As well, in the Bill C-68 case, the role of professional organizations such as the Canadian Medical Association and the Canadian Bar Association proved unexpectedly strong.

In short, the U.S. has not lacked for gun control advocates or legislation. Presidents and powerful congressional representatives alike have supported gun control. But whereas in Canada this political support could be translated by an executive into legislation, steered through the House and Senate, and passed over objections and opposition, in the U.S. it could be blocked over and over again because of the characteristics of the institutional playing field. Does this mean that the U.S. is incapable of legislating stronger controls? Obviously not, since controls have been instituted nationally over the last thirty years. But institutional impediments in the U.S. demand that there be some galvanizing event, something that propels the issue onto the public stage long enough to forge consensus. It must be remembered that the U.S. is an immensely complicated and diverse country, and that there is a certain wisdom in the way its institutions demand substantial consensus in order for national policy to get made.

Reflections on the Issue

There are also some conclusions that can be drawn regarding the nature of the gun control issue. First, while guns are clearly a symbolic issue, recent developments in the U.S. show that there is a strong material aspect to it as well. The firearms industry, from manufacturers to collectors, is not negligible as a material support for anti–gun control movements in both the U.S. and Canada. Second, as a symbolic issue, it is worth noting that gun control (unlike abortion) seems to be a telltale for attitudes toward government itself. To be anti–gun control is to generally support more libertarian positions; the militia mentality represents the extreme version. Those ideologically committed *to* gun control fall on the other side of the political spectrum. Some of the potency of the gun issue, therefore, may come less from its "way of life" character than from the baggage it carries regarding attitudes toward the role of the state.

Third, whereas it is often argued that symbolic issues do not lend themselves to trade-offs or compromise, the gun issue does to the degree that it can be packaged as part of a crime control strategy. President Clinton used this tactic well in simultaneously proposing more gun control and tougher provisions concerning the death penalty. Both of these are symbolic issues, but they can be "traded" in the sense that someone wanting one might be prepared to swallow the other. The Canadian case reflects several interesting strategies. "Grandfathering" was made extensive use of in both the Firearms Act and its predecessors. The reliance on regulations rather than legislation helped defuse the issue and keep it in the realm of the technical. It can also stretch out the implementation process so gradually (consider, for example, the reliance on repeated amnesties) that this can help defuse opposition. The appointment of various types of advisory groups also brings those groups into the process, defuses the emotional dimension of the issue, and once again deflects it onto technical terrain. Issues like gay rights and abortion do not appear to have the same broad potential to be defused by gradual implementation, exemptions for certain subgroups, or technical discourse.[101]

What does the gun control issue tell us about comparative U.S./Canada institutions? It tells us that those institutions matter a great deal, especially if elections, federalism, and the courts are brought into the mix. A broadly similar issue with broadly similar forces surrounding it took a very different course and met with different results, primarily because of differences in political institutions. Institutions are not destiny; wild cards occasionally pop up in the deck. At the time of writing, however, the two countries appear to be on very different trajectories, leading to continued and substantial divergence in this policy field.

NOTES

1. The Littleton, Colorado, killings in particular may have shifted public opinion, especially among women. See Dan Carney, "Lawmakers Rethinking Assumptions about Politics of Gun Control," *Congressional Quarterly Weekly Report* (September 4, 1999): 2051–53. See also Michael Janofsky, "Concerns about Guns Put New Pressure on State Legislators," *New York Times*, January 4, 2000.
2. R. Kent Weaver, "The Politics of Blame Avoidance," *Journal of Public Policy* 6 (1986): 372.

3. Donald J. Savoie, *Governing from the Centre: The Concentration of Power in Canadian Politics* (Toronto: University of Toronto Press, 1999), chap. 4; Jeffrey Simpson, *The Friendly Dictatorship* (Toronto: McCelland and Stewart, 2001).

4. Spitzer, following Tatalovitch and Daynes, classifies gun control as a "social regulatory policy," but also emphasizes the symbolic or value dimension. However, he argues that policies of this type are characterized by single-issue groups, weak presidential leadership, party polarization, and the salience of federalism, among other things. See Robert J. Spitzer, *The Politics of Gun Control*, 2d ed. (New York: Chatham House Publishers, 1998), pp. 5, 15–16; Raymond Tatalovitch and Byron W. Daynes, eds., *Moral Controversies in American Politics: Cases in Social Regulatory Policy* (Armonk, N.Y.: M. E. Sharpe, 1998).

5. Tom Diaz, *Making a Killing: The Business of Guns in America* (New York: The New Press, 1999), p. 7, conservatively estimates the wholesale value in 1995 of all firearms and ammunition manufactured in the United States to be $1.7 billion, with roughly a third made up of handguns, other firearms, and ammunition. If one includes the value of accessories and gun-related services, the total figure for the firearms and firearms-related industries could be significantly higher.

6. Part of the gun control debate is about the efficacy of legislation in controlling the criminal use of firearms. To the extent that legislation is effective in reducing the rewards of crime, this is potentially a major material impact, but it will not be considered here.

7. See Murray J. Edelman, *The Symoblic Uses of Politics* (Urbana: University of Illinois Press, 1964), and *Politics as Symbolic Action* (Chicago: Markham Publishing Co., 1971).

8. Richard Block, *Firearms in Canada and Eight Other Western Countries: Selected Findings of the 1996 International Crime (Victim) Survey* (Ottawa: Department of Justice, Canadian Firearms Centre, 1997). Nonetheless, because of the geographical concentration of the Canadian population, Statistics Canada estimates that 50.7 percent of all firearms in the country are owned by residents of Ontario and Quebec (28 percent and 22.7 percent, respectively). See Canadian Firearms Centre, *Estimated Number of Firearms and Households with Firearms in Canada, 1998* (Ottawa: June 1998). For U.S. data, see U.S. Department of Justice, Bureau of Justice Statistics, *Sourcebook of Criminal Justice Statistics 2000*, table 2.69. In the eastern U.S., only 28 percent reported owning a gun, whereas the figures for the Midwest and the South were 45 and 52 percent, respectively.

9. See William R. Tonso, ed., *The Gun Culture and Its Enemies* (Bellevue, Wash: Second Amendment Foundation, 1990).

10. Spitzer, *The Politics of Gun Control*, 118.

11. "A well regulated Militia, being necessary to the security of a free State, the right of the people to keep and bear Arms, shall not be infringed."

12. A useful pair of readings that illuminates the contrary positions is Warren Freedman, *The Privilege to Keep and Bear Arms: The Second Amendment and Its Interpretation* (New York: Quorum Books, 1989), and Stephen P. Halbrook, *That Every Man Be Armed: The Evolution of a Constitutional Right* (Albuquerque: University of New Mexico Press, 1984). The mainstream consensus in American legal opinion has been that the Second Amendment does not confer an *individual* right to bear arms, but recent thinking—even in liberal circles—has been changing. See Laurence H. Tribe, *American Constitutional Law*, 3d ed. (New York: Foundation Press, 2000).

13. *United States v Lopez*, 115 S. Ct. 1624 (1995).

14. In the United States, criminal law is primarily a matter of state jurisdiction. Activities related to the matters specifically entrusted to the central government can be prohibited by Congress and made criminal, but Congress has no power to define crime generally for the nation as a whole.

15. Donna Lea Hawley, *Canadian Firearms Law* (Toronto: Butterworths, 1988), pp. 1–3.

16. Edward F. Leddy, *Magnum Force Lobby: The National Rifle Association Fights Gun Control* (New York: University Press of America, 1987), chap. 5.

17. Osha Gray Davidson, *Under Fire: The NRA and the Battle for Gun Control* (Iowa City: University of Iowa Press, 1998), p. 35.

18. This setback in public opinion was balanced, however, by a surge in contributions. See "The Gun Lobby," *U.S. News & World Report*, May 22, 1995. The shootings at Columbine High School posed another recent public relations challenge, as the NRA carried through with its annual meeting in Denver, Colorado.

19. Spitzer, *The Politics of Gun Control*, 105.

20. Ibid.

21. Ibid., 108.

22. These were not legally available in most countries, and the act simply introduced some review over their purchase, import, and transfer. It did not prohibit, for example, the purchase of a machine gun or assault rifle. The federal licensing requirements imposed on anyone engaged in interstate traffic in firearms as an importer, manufacturer, or dealer, while light (one had to pay $1,000, be twenty-one years of age, and have no convictions or mental illness), did include all firearms. Another key point is that this legislation was intended to support state laws on gun control, and it required sellers to honor those laws. The overall intent was to control interstate commerce, but it was still possible for someone to go into a state and buy a gun, as long as he or she met the relevant state requirements. The would-be purchaser's compliance with those requirements was gauged by a questionnaire administered by the firearms seller, but there was no capacity to check the veracity of the answers.

23. Quoted in Wilbur Edel, *Gun Control: Threat to Liberty or Defense against Anarchy?* (Westport, Conn.: Praeger, 1995), p. 103.

24. Robert J. Spitzer, "Gun Control: Constitutional Mandate or Myth?" in *Moral Controversies in American Politics: Cases in Social Regulatory Policy*, ed. Raymond Tatalovich, Byron W. Daynes (Armonk, N.Y.: M. E. Sharpe, 1998), p. 179.

25. Ibid., p. 181.

26. Holly Idelson, "Gun Rights and Restrictions: The Territory Reconfigured," *Congressional Quarterly Weekly Report* (April 24, 1993): 1021–26.

27. Holly Idelson, "Brooks Puts Six Easier Pieces on Anti-Crime Program," *Congressional Quarterly Weekly Report* (October 30, 1993): 2978–80.

28. I owe this idea to Richard Lévesque.

29. The Supreme Court in *Printz v. United States* (1997) struck down the background check provisions of the Brady bill.

30. Holly Idelson, "Congress Responds to Violence; Tackles Guns, Criminals," *Congressional Quarterly Weekly Report* (November 13, 1993): 3127–30.

31. Holly Idelson, "House Nearing Showdown on Assault Weapons Ban," *Congressional Quarterly Weekly Report* (April 30, 1994): 1069.

32. Holly Idelson, "Democrats' Disagreements Delay, Imperil Crime Bill," *Congressional Quarterly Weekly Report* (July 23, 1994): 2048–49.

33. Dan Carney, "High Court Shows Inclination to Rein in Congress," *Congressional Quarterly Weekly Report* (January 25, 1997): 241–44. The case involved the issue of whether, as in the Brady case, "the federal authority can require local police to carry out federal statutes at their own expense, and potentially in violation of a state law."

34. David Stout and Richard Perez-Pena, "U.S. Laying Groundwork in Bid for Safeguards on Weapons," *New York Times*, December 8, 1999.

35. Transcript of the president's speech, *Congressional Quarterly Weekly Report* (January 23, 1999): 205–7.

36. The Pew Research Center noted that the Colorado school shootings were the third-ranked news story of the 1990s (out of over 600 national and international stories catalogued since 1990). See www.people-press.org/shooting.htm.

37. "Once Again, a Quick-Draw Debate in the Gun Wars," *Online U.S. News*, May 5, 1999, www.usnews.com/usnews/issue.

38. Helen Dewar and Juliet Eilperin, "Senate Backs New Gun Control, 51-50," *Washington Post*, May 21, 1999, A1.

39. Dan Carney, "Gun Control Backers Get Upper Hand as Senate Passes New Restrictions," *Congressional Quarterly Weekly Report* (May 22, 1999): 1204–5.

40. Jan Cienski, "Eight Weeks after Massacre, House Kills Gun-Control Bill," *National Post*, June 19, 1999, A1.

41. For example, House Judiciary Committee Chairman Henry Hyde (R-Ill.) was reported to have suggested background checks of twenty-four hours—extended to three days if they were not completed—for purchases at gun shows. *CNN/Allpolitics*, "Hyde Offers Gun-Control Compromise," September 22, 1999, http://cnn.com/ALLPOLITICS/stories/1999/09/22/gun.control.

42. Edward Walsh, "Clinton Plans Gun Initiative," *Washington Post*, January 18, 2000.

43. *Congressional Quarterly Almanac 2000: 106th Cong., 2nd sess.* (Washington, D.C., 2000), pp. 2–25.

44. Ibid.

45. "Juvenile Justice Program Bill Likely to Avoid Gun Debate," *Congresional Quarterly Weekly Report* (March 10, 2001): 545.

46. Spitzer, *The Politics of Gun Control*, 91.

47. Jim VandeHei, "GOP Takes Aim at NRA," *Roll Call*, August 12, 1999, pp. 1, 14.

48. NRA, "Bush Implements 'Texas Exile,'" www.nraila.org.

49. *CNN/Allpolitics*, "Bush Announces Gun Crimes Initiative in Texas," September 21, 1999, http://cnn.com/ALLPOLITICS/stories/1999/09/21/president.2000/bush.guns. The gun issue was threatening throughout the summer of 1999 to become the "wedge issue" some Democrats hoped it would be—with a spree of killings, culminating in Governor George Bush's own state of Texas. It was an issue in the presidential campaign, with Bush being attacked for signing a right-to-carry law in 1996 and for the summer 1999 shootings. His "Texas Exile" program was designed to be seen as a zero-tolerance approach to gun violations.

50. Sections 84 to 117, R.S.C. 1985, c. C-42, Part III.

51. See Canada, Parliament, *Debates of the House of Commons*, 28th Parliament, 1st sess. (January 23, 1968), pp. 4717–51.

52. Ibid., p. 4719.

53. The issue had been debated the year before, however, because of two gruesome killings that captured national attention. On May 28, 1975, a sixteen-year-old boy named Michael Slobodian killed a teacher and another student and wounded thirteen others at his high school in Brampton before killing himself. This led Solicitor General Warren Allmand to launch a departmental review of possible new gun control legislation. Then, on October 27, 1975, an eighteen-year-old Ottawa student named Robert Poulin shot and wounded six students at St. Pius X Catholic High School before killing himself. He had also handcuffed a girl to a bed in his basement, who then died in the fire he set.

54. S.C. 1976–77, c. 53.

55. "Man Kills Fourteen Women in Montreal," *Globe and Mail* (Toronto), December 7, 1989.

56. "Massacre Prompts Gun Control Debate," *Ottawa Letter*, December 11, 1989, p. 396. The concern with converted semiautomatics is that they can be converted back.

57. Kim Campbell, *Time and Chance: The Political Memoirs of Canada's First Woman Prime Minister* (Toronto: Doubleday, 1996), p. 141: "the Lépine killings had raised the profile and sensitivity of the issue dramatically."

58. Ibid., p. 147.

59. Geoffrey York, "Tories Shelve Plan to Rush Gun-Control Debate," *Globe and Mail* (Toronto), June 18, 1991, A8.

60. Campbell, *Time and Chance*, 153.

61. See Canada, Parliament, *Debates of the House of Commons*, 34th Parliament, 3d sess. (June 6, 1991), p. 1253.

62. The Standing Joint Committee for the Scrutiny of Regulations is mandated to review all regulations *after* they have been issued. This procedure gave Parliament the power to review regulations *before* they were implemented.

63. "Gun Controls Attacked by Shooting Federation," *Globe and Mail* (Toronto), September 1991, A7.

64. "In order to combat crime a Liberal government will work in a broad range of areas. To strengthen gun control, a Liberal government will, among other measures, counter the illegal importation of banned and restricted firearms into Canada and prohibit anyone convicted of an indictable drug-related offence, a stalking offence, or any violent offence from owning or possessing a gun." Liberal Party of Canada, *Creating Opportunity: The Liberal Plan for Canada* (Ottawa: 1993), p. 84.

65. *Maclean's*, June 5, 1995, 14.

66. "Gun Debate to Heat up as Rock Tables Bill," *Globe and Mail* (Toronto), February 14, 1995. Political observers noted that the divisions among opposition parties meant that the real debate over gun control was taking place within the Liberal caucus. Jeffrey Simpson, "The Only Real Debates Are Found Within the Caucus of the Liberal Party," *Globe and Mail* (Toronto), February 16, 1995, A22.

67. "MPs Debate New Gun Law with Passion," *Globe and Mail* (Toronto), March 29, 1995.

68. In fact, the government side claimed that this motion would actually take the Reform Party off the hook by forcing an end to its opposition to a widely supported piece of legislation. See Canada, Parliament, *Debates of the House of Commons*, 35th Parliament, 1st sess. (April 5, 1995), p. 11541, www.parl.gc.ca/englsh/hansard/previous/184_95-04-05/184G0E.htm.

69. They were Rex Crawford (Kent), Benoit Serre (Timisskaming–French River), and Paul Steckle (Huron-Bruce).

70. "Commons Passes Gun Controls," *Canadian News Facts*, June 1–15, 1995, pp. 5134–35.

71. There is no formal mechanism for the House to record abstentions (one can only stand with the "nays" or "yeas"), though MPs sometimes seek to have their abstention recorded in Hansard on a point of order. Several MPs had approached the Speaker to see if this might be possible in this case; he refused.

72. "Rock's Gun-Control Bill Approved in Principle," *The Gazette* (Montreal), April 6, 1995.

73. David Vienneau, "MDs Reject Registration in Gun Bill," *Toronto Star*, May 12, 1995.

74. David Vienneau, "Under Siege, Rock Likely to Amend Gun Control Bill," *Toronto Star*, May 13, 1995.

75. Tracey Tyler, "Gun Control Bill Attacked: Makes Police Too Powerful," *Toronto Star*, May 13, 1995.

76. "Rock Hints at Yielding More Ground on Guns," *Globe and Mail* (Toronto), May 16, 1995. Aboriginal criticisms focused on claims that the bill did not accommodate treaty rights and constitutional provisions with respect to their inherent right of self-government. See, for example, the submission by the Inuit Tapirisat of Canada, Standing Committee on Justice and Legal Affairs, 35th Parliament, 1st sess., no. 110 (May 19, 1995), pp. 110A:1–15.

77. "More Opposition to Gun Bill," *Canadian News Facts*, May 1–15, 1995, pp. 5117–18. See also Submission of the All Party Delegation of the Legislative Assembly of Saskatchewan, Standing Committee on Justice and Legal Affairs, 35th Parliament, 1st sess., no. 109 (May 19, 1995), pp. 109A:18–49.

78. "Bloc Flip-flops over Gun Bill," *Toronto Star*, May 18, 1995.

79. Failure to register a firearm would invite a fine of $2,000 and/or a six-month jail term. Persons so convicted would still have a criminal record, but would not be fingerprinted or photographed by the police.

80. "Measures to Soften Gun Bill Proposed," *Toronto Star*, May 20, 1995.

81. David Vienneau, "Firearms Bill Wins Backing from Lawyers," *Toronto Star*, June 6, 1995, A10.

82. Doug Fischer, "Ottawa Will Foot Bill for Gun Registry, PM Says," *The Gazette* (Montreal), May 25, 1995, A10.

83. Tim Naumetz, "Private Sector to Handle Gun Registry," *National Post*, January 26, 2002.

84. "Chrétien Threatens Gun Bill Rebels," *Toronto Star*, May 22, 1995.

85. Doug Fischer, "Majority Still Backs Gun Control," *The Calgary Herald*, June 2, 1995, A1.

86. "Gun Owners Target Senate Support," *Edmonton Journal*, July 1, 1995; "Group Fighting Gun Control Asks Senate to Kill Bill," *The Chronicle Herald* (Halifax), September 20, 1995.

87. "Bitter Gun Debate Silenced as Senate Passes Bill," *Globe and Mail* (Toronto), November 23, 1995. There were four petitions against the bill introduced by Senators, all signed by citizens of British Columbia, Alberta, Saskatchewan, and Manitoba. Three separate votes were held on third reading on November 22; eighteen Tories voted for the bill, and four abstained. Had they joined their colleagues in voting against the bill, it would have been defeated.

88. Canada, Department of Justice, "Biographies—User Group on Firearms" (press release, December 1995). The regional breakdown was: Ontario, 5; Quebec, BC, and NS, 2 each; Alberta, Manitoba, Yukon, and the NWT, 1 each.

89. Jim Morris, "Leave Us Out of the Gun Law, Aboriginals Tell Rock," *The Gazette* (Montreal), February 4, 1997, A6.

90. David Vienneau, "Gun Lovers Set Sights on Liberals," *Toronto Star*, May 3, 1997, E4.

91. Murray Campbell, "Gun Control Triggers Emotions," *Globe and Mail* (Toronto), May 23, 1997, A6.

92. Sheldon Alberts, "McLellan Sticks to Guns," *Calgary Herald*, June 12, 1997, A3.

93. Brian Laghi, "Alberta Court to Hear Gun-Law Challenge," *Globe and Mail* (Toronto), September 8, 1997, A4.

94. Chris Cobb, "Minister Fires Back," *The Gazette* (Montreal), May 5, 1998.

95. Jim Morris, "Gun Registry Costs to Increase," *Calgary Herald*, September 27, 1997, A1.

96. The Registry continued to be an issue. In November 1999 the Reform Party acquired a confidential and highly critical report on the implementation of the Registry conducted for the government by PricewaterhouseCoopers. See Norm Ovendon, "Consultants Find Gun Registry 'Inflexible and Inefficient,'" *Edmonton Journal*, November 24, 1999.

97. Chris Cobb, "10,000 Rally against Gun Law: Friends of Victims Defend Toughened Canadian Standards," *Ottawa Citizen*, September 23, 1998, A3. The same number was cited in Erin Anderssen, "Gun Owners Rally against Registry," *Globe and Mail* (Toronto), September 23, 1998, A3.

98. Department of Justice Canada/Canadian Firearms Centre, "Firearms Act to Be Implemented on December 1, 1998" (press release, September 21, 1998).

99. The victory was an ambiguous one, however, since four questions had been posed (two on licensing and two on registration). The two dissenting judges answered no to all four questions, making it a strong dissent and a sharply divided legal opinion.

100. *Reference re Firearms Act (Canada)*, 1 S.C.R. 2000.

101. The weight of most regulatory regimes that deal with the safety of objects (e.g., cribs, flotation devices, cigarettes, cars) is on the producer or manufacturer of those objects. End users and end use can then be regulated relatively lightly. The regulatory challenge with respect to firearms is that, of course, they are deliberately intended to be "unsafe." It is as though cigarettes were deemed to have a highly lethal potential to both their owners and third parties simply by virtue of possession, and that governments had a responsibility to pass regulations about individual handling and possession of cigarettes, as well as their use in public spaces. Imagine the challenge of regulating individual smoking and handling of cigarettes in this sense.

9

ABORTION

RAYMOND TATALOVICH

Abortion is the purest example of "symbolic" politics, involving the imposition of what Kent Weaver and Leslie Pal call "value-focused" pain. Today the scope of conflict over abortion rages over the entire U.S. political system, touching every branch of the state and national governments and extending to acts of violence by political extremists. In the United States abortion has been an ongoing controversy for more than a quarter-century, whereas in Canada a serious political debate over abortion started in 1988 but pretty much ended after 1990. Why and how the Canadian political regime was able to neutralize an issue that exploded onto the American political scene with such intensity is the fundamental question to be addressed in this chapter.

While all "moral" conflicts involve symbolic pain, they may involve other kinds of loss imposition as well. There is an element of self-interest going beyond symbolism when the National Rifle Association opposes gun laws, because there are hundreds of millions of guns in the United States, and gun owners constitute a sizable number of Americans. In the case of abortion, however, in no year have more than 1.5 million American women gotten abortions—and given that the rallying cry of pro-choice does not directly affect men and that pro-life women presumably have no desire to abort their pregnancies, abortion does not involve the personal self-interest of most Americans, or even of most women. Indeed, abortion engages *altruistic* motivations, not self-interested ones, because both sides of the abortion divide are fighting for the well-being of others: the women who might need or want an abortion or the unborn, who have no legal voice in the matter.

Moreover, even minor gun regulations or marginal restrictions on abortions seemingly impose tremendous "symbolic" pain on gun fanatics or pro-choice zealots, whose reactions, by the standards of most ordinary citizens, are well out of proportion to the amount of "pain" being imposed by government. This perception gap belies the importance of value-focused conflict, however, and explains why public opinion is more moderate than the views on either side of either dispute. The politician's problem is not that most voters oppose a middle position upholding a legal right to abortion with some restrictions, for most voters indeed favor this position.[1] Rather, the political problem is that well-organized, deeply committed, and highly vocal minorities on both extremes find any compromise of their beliefs to be unacceptable and are prepared to punish politicians who do not support them fully. For these voters, abortion is a "clash of absolutes"[2] that strikes at the heart of their deepest moral beliefs about the sanctity of life or a woman's right to control her own body. Perhaps even more than gun control, abortion is an issue wherein it is impossible for politicians to find a blame-avoiding middle ground that will satisfy all voters. Whether you advocate stronger or weaker regulations on abortion, ultimately abortion still involves the termination of potential "life" and thus encroaches on a fundamental value—whereas stronger or weaker regulations on guns need not infringe upon gun ownership as such.

Moral issues are different organizationally from economic issues, because grassroots mobilization and countermobilization usually take the form of single-issue groups.[3] Of course effective organization is no guarantee that both sides will be equally endowed with other political resources, although there is, in fact, a closer match of organizational strength between pro-life and pro-choice forces in the United States and Canada than there is vis-à-vis gun control. Pro-gun activists are far better organized than their opponents in the United States, whereas anti-gun forces are better positioned in Canada.

Adversaries engaged in "value-focused" conflict and symbolic combat do not agree to disagree. They talk past each other, because their values reflect fundamentally unlike premises. In talking to the public, each side will try to "define the agenda" in such a way as to cultivate a supportive public opinion. Surely nobody can claim to be "pro-abortion," given the negatives associated with that term—feminist Germaine Greer once said that being "pro-abortion" was like being "pro-amputation"—so those proponents reframe their objectives in libertarian language that will endear them, they hope, to classic liberals: that of protecting individuals from government coercion. Groups defending women's access to abortion thus label themselves "pro-choice": It is not abortion itself they are defending, they say, but a woman's right to choose and to control her own body. Contrariwise, groups that oppose abortion portray themselves as "pro-life" advocates who view the "unborn" as living beings, not simply worthless cell matter, and most Americans would agree with them. The pro-life cause persists because, notwithstanding the fact that the unborn have no legal rights or constitutional protections, ordinary Americans think that the fetus has "moral" claims to survive absent compelling reasons to the contrary.

TABLE 9-1
Differences between the U.S. and Canada on Abortion

Variable	U.S.	Canada
1995 population (in millions)	263	29.5
Percent Catholic[a]	20	33
Percent Evangelical	24	10
Total abortions	1,365,730 (1996)[b]	106,658 (1995)[c]
In hospitals (%)	92,890 (7)	70,549 (66)
In clinics (%)	1,234,580 (91)	35,650 (33)
In offices (%)	38,260 (3)	—
In the U.S.	—	459
1995 abortion ratio/rate[d]	26.0	28.2

[a]These are percentages of "committed" Catholics, as determined by survey screening questions. See Angus Reid Corporation, "Survey of 3,000 Americans and 3,000 Canadians Conducted September 19–October 10, 1996."

[b]Stanley K. Henshaw, "Abortion Incidence and Services in the United States, 1995–1996," *Family Planning Perspectives* 30 (November/December, 1998): 263–70, 287.

[c]Data from Canadian Institute for Health Information.

[d]The U.S. abortion ratio is the number of abortions per 100 pregnancies ending in abortion or live birth; the Canadian abortion rate is the number of abortions per 100 live births.

Yet there are several factors that might lead to a cross-national divergence between Canada and the United States with respect to abortion policy processes and outcomes (see table 9-1).

The most obvious potential source of divergence concerns matters of national beliefs. If one country has stronger pro-life views than the other, for example, we would expect these differences to be reflected in policy outcomes, and such differences might also influence the pain-imposing ability of subnational governments—states or provinces and municipalities. There are probably more similarities than differences in how Canadians and Americans view abortion—both publics are centrist—though, at the margins, it is likely that Canadians are more liberal than Americans.[4] Yet there are important regional variations: "Southerners are less supportive of access to legal abortion than are nonsoutherners in the United States," whereas "residents of Quebec are more supportive of abortion rights than are respondents residing in the English-speaking provinces."[5]

The acute sensitivity of the abortion issue also suggests several hypotheses about the role played by political institutions in explaining cross-national similarities and differences in policymaking and in policy outcomes. First, at the outset, most politicians will try to avoid contentious issues that pose a "zero-sum" conflict, because they risk deeply offending either side with a firm stand or alienating both adversaries with a wishy-washy voice of moderation. Faced with this political dilemma, they may prefer to "pass the buck" to institutions that are more insulated from blame, like nonelected judges, or allow "direct" democracy, wherein the people settle a policy question by referendum or plebiscite.

But sometimes—and both abortion and gun control are examples—political institutions are forced, *by* the nonelected judiciary, to address those issues. In the United States, pro-choice groups developed a litigation strategy precisely because the legislative strategy of gaining statutory reforms among the fifty states was so slow and indecisive. In Canada, although it was not until 1988 that the Supreme Court invalidated the 1969 criminal code on abortion, there were previous cases (notably in Quebec) when Dr. Henry Morgentaler violated the law by openly performing abortions, thereby forcing the provincial and national authorities to take a public stand in the ensuing legal proceedings.

Second, when faced with an adverse judicial pronouncement, groups opposed to the resulting policy are likely to lobby the elected branches when they feel that they have sufficient political leverage, and that approach would generally be more effective in the United States than in Canada, because the separation-of-powers system is more porous than the parliamentary one. Third, the obvious role of the judiciary in micromanaging abortion policy, especially in the United States, would, we expect, lead to a politicization of the judicial nomination process, since opponents of pro- or anti-choice judicial nominees have some prospects of defeating them during the Senate confirmation process. The more closed nature of the judicial appointment process in Canada inhibits these developments and makes them less visible if they do occur.

Fourth, while the relatively open processes of party candidate selection for elections to the Canadian House of Commons and the U.S. Congress offer an additional political venue to influence abortion policy, this is especially true in the United States, given its widespread use of primary elections and the weakened state of partisanship within the American electorate. American presidential elections are regularly touched by the abortion debate, unlike recent campaigns for the prime ministership in Canada.[6] Finally, if the conflict over abortion does become polarized along party lines—which has happened in the United States—the consequence may be policy instability caused by party turnover, or policy deadlock during periods of "divided government."

Potentially there are numerous "techniques of control" by which government authorities can regulate abortions, but many of these are minor inconveniences, while other, more significant hurdles have been disallowed by the U.S. and/or Canadian Supreme Courts (see table 9-2). Because the policy debate over abortion has been framed around three fundamental issues—(1) the legal *right* to abortion, (2) government *funding* of abortion, and (3) the *availability* of abortion services—case studies of those specific policies are provided to enable us to draw comparisons between the Canadian and American legal regimes regarding abortion.

ORIGINS OF THE ABORTION DEBATE IN THE UNITED STATES AND CANADA

The history of the abortion controversy shows remarkable similarities between the United States and Canada. By relating these historical developments in tandem, we

TABLE 9-2
Techniques of Control: Regulating Abortion Access

Technique	Permissive Policy	Restrictive Policy
Patient		
Legal requirement	elective	threat to life only
Informed consent	none	yes (written)
Spousal consent	no	yes
Spousal notification	no	yes
Parental consent (minors)	none	yes
Parental notification (minors)	none/with judicial bypass	yes
Waiting period	none	yes (24 hours)
Counseling on risks	no	yes
Counseling on alternatives	no	yes
Fetus		
Gestational period	1–9 months	1–3 months
Fetal viability testing	none	yes
Procedures		
Private facilities	offices/clinics/hospitals	hospitals only
Use of public employees	yes	no
Use of public facilities	yes	no
Public funding	any abortion	therapeutic only
Early abortion procedure	none	yes (saline method)
Late abortion procedure	none	yes (to enhance fetal survival)
Post-viability abortion	one physician	second physician required
Record-keeping	none	yes (to state authorities)
Public reporting	none	yes (with public access)
Pathology report	none	yes
Humane disposal of remains	none	yes

can more fully understand when and how regime differences affected the capacity of the respective governments to impose symbolic pain, and why the abortion controversy rages more intensely today in the U.S. than in Canada.

In the United States

Abortion was not prohibited or regulated in the United States until 1821, when Connecticut banned abortions after quickening. In 1829, New York State stipulated the first therapeutic exception, legalizing abortions "necessary to preserve the life of such mother . . . [when] advised by two physicians to be necessary for such purpose."[7] The New York law became a model for legislation adopted by virtually every other state, and these "original" antiabortion laws, prohibiting termination of pregnancy unless the life of the woman was endangered, remained in force until the 1960s.

Between 1966 and 1972, fourteen states "reformed" their criminal codes on abortion, adding more therapeutic exceptions, and four states—Alaska, Hawaii, New York, and Washington—actually repealed their original antiabortion laws, making it an elective procedure. Reformers rallied behind the American Law Institute (ALI) Model Penal Code, which urged the states to amend their abortion laws to take into account the physical or mental health of the mother, any physical or mental defect in the fetus, and pregnancy resulting from rape, incest, or felonious intercourse. Various ad hoc physician groups spearheaded this cause, which was endorsed by some religious denominations and professional associations (in the face of state legislative reforms, the AMA liberalized its abortion policy in 1967), and opinion polls indicated widespread popular support for abortion reform. In a relatively short period of time, then, a new policy consensus was emerging around abortion reform, not abortion on demand.[8] But activists soon abandoned reform in favor of outright repeal of all abortion laws, and they turned to the judiciary for a more decisive victory. (While antiabortion sentiments were expressed by the Roman Catholic Church at that time, there was no countervailing orchestrated campaign, from an antichoice perspective, *against* state abortion reforms.)

My own assessment is that "the Catholic church's moral position against abortion did not allow much room for compromise, and for this reason its position may not have seemed convincing within the context of the 1960s. Even the Catholic press admitted as much. As abortion politics entered the 1970s [however], the credibility of the church's position was strengthened because the debate now centered on elective abortion as a right. Furthermore, the Catholic church's articulation and sponsorship of the pro-life position created an atmosphere in which the debate over abortion became especially intense, ideological, and combative."[9] The 1970s political backlash resulted because the Supreme Court, by embracing elective abortion, imposed tremendous symbolic pain on the Roman Catholic Church and its allies, who were morally opposed to abortions. Beyond that, *Roe v. Wade* was judged to be a complete victory for legalized abortion, not the compromise that Justice Blackmun envisioned, because all but a few abortions are performed during the first trimester.

In Canada

Canadian abortion law followed English legal precedents. Abortion after quickening was a common-law offense in England until Lord Ellenborough's Act of 1803 codified postquickening abortion as a crime punishable by death. In 1837 the pre/post-quickening distinction was dropped, as was the death penalty, although later Section 58 of the 1861 Offences against the Person Act mandated that a woman who procured her own abortion was also guilty of a crime. Though Section 58 remained in force in Britain until 1967, it was challenged by the medical and legal professions because the 1861 law allowed no therapeutic exceptions for the life or health of the mother. What dramatized the disconnect between law and medical practice in England was the famous case of Dr. Aleck Bourne, who in 1938 aborted a fourteen-year-old who had been gang-raped by four soldiers. He invited the Crown to prosecute him, which it did, but the jury acquitted him after forty minutes of deliberation. Thus the Bourne defense ("defense of necessity") became standard in English common law.

The first Canadian criminal law on abortion was enacted in 1869, providing for life imprisonment for any person who procured a miscarriage. Before abortion reforms were enacted in 1969, the criminal code of Canada had three sections on abortion. Section 237 made abortion an offense for persons who procured it or performed it. Section 209 made the killing of an unborn child a crime, but allowed an exception for any person who, in good faith, considered it necessary to "preserve the life of the mother." Section 45 stipulated that anyone who performed a surgical operation to benefit a person, given her state of health and other circumstances of the case, was protected from criminal liability if the operation was done with reasonable care and skill—which essentially codified in Canada the English common-law "defense of necessity" standard. However the Bourne defense was not extended to eugenic reasons for abortion, like birth defects, nor were socio-economic conditions considered a justification for abortion. The thalidomide scare of the 1960s—the drug was linked to thousands of deformed fetuses in Western Europe, though far fewer in North America—was one reason for the abortion reform movements in England, Canada, and the United States.

According to Morton, "[t]wo professional groups, the Canadian Medical Association and the Canadian Bar Association, spearheaded the [reform] effort. They received moral support from the United Church, the largest Protestant denomination in Canada, which began to support wider access to abortion in 1960. Surprisingly, women's groups played only a marginal role at this stage of the reform movement."[10] Late in 1967 the Liberal government and its justice minister, Pierre Trudeau, introduced an Omnibus Criminal Code Reform Bill, which proposed over 100 changes to the criminal code, including the legalization of abortion when carrying a child to term would "endanger the life and health of the mother."

Including the abortion law changes in a large package prevented the measure from being singled out for criticism and possible blame-generating activity by its opponents. It was not until after the national elections of 1968, which returned the Liberals to power and catapulted Trudeau into the prime ministership, that conditions were ripe for passage of this landmark legislation. Originally the Omnibus Bill was treated like a "vote of confidence" in the government, insofar as Trudeau would not explicitly allow Liberal backbenchers a "free vote" so they could follow their own consciences, but ultimately pressure from Quebec Liberals forced the prime minister to grant a "conscience vote" on Clause 18 (the abortion provision) only. "In a classic display of political cowardice, sixty of the 155 Liberal members of Parliament somehow managed to be absent from Parliament when the vote was taken."[11] Overall, there were more abstentions than yeas or nays on the amendment to strike Clause 18, after which the whole legislative package was enacted.

As in the United States, the Roman Catholic Church was slow to countermobilize even as Parliament began deliberations, because of "social and doctrinal upheaval associated with the Vatican Council and the papacy of John XXIII. While Catholics themselves were debating doctrinal and social questions, their interventions in the public and Parliamentary discussions tended to reflect a certain hesitancy to promote traditional positions with complete enthusiasm."[12]

The 1969 criminal code amendment allowed an abortion to be performed by a qualified medical practitioner in an accredited or approved hospital if the therapeutic abortion committee of the hospital had issued a certificate stating that, in its opinion, the continuation of the pregnancy would or would be likely to endanger the woman's life or health. The law restricted the practice of abortions to hospitals accredited by the Canadian Council on Hospital Accreditation or the province; it excluded medical clinics and doctors' offices. There was no provision in the law compelling a hospital to set up a committee, and many hospitals did not do so.[13] Moreover, proponents of broader legalization argued that the requirement for hospital committee certification caused lengthy delays that placed women in unnecessary danger.

The amendment tried to strike a balance between pro-life and pro-choice interests, but it pleased neither side. For many years the debate centered on the requirements that abortions be approved by a hospital abortion committee and be performed in a hospital. When Dr. Henry Morgentaler began to fight the system by operating an abortion clinic in Montreal, he began a series of legal battles that served as the symbol and flashpoint for the entire abortion controversy in Canada over the next two decades.[14]

The first round of proceedings against Morgentaler ended with the rise to power of the Parti Québécois in 1976. The PQ Government not only dropped all legal proceedings against Morgentaler but also agreed to fund freestanding abortion clinics in the province. Since then, the PQ government has refused to enforce the criminal code on abortion, effectively allowing perhaps 30 percent of Canadian women open access to abortions. Although it seemed that the abortion controversy had been resolved, at least in Catholic Quebec, the issue was simply dormant, because women across Canada still had uneven access to abortion services. Nevertheless, the Trudeau government successfully avoided directly reopening the abortion issue. In 1978, Prime Minister Trudeau shrugged off an opposition request to tighten up the abortion law, saying: "It's not up to the Government to give the gift of life. This is up to God and to the parents."[15] Morgentaler vowed to make liberalization of the abortion law an election issue, but his efforts were unsuccessful.

In late 1982, however, Morgentaler began to actively campaign for the establishment of abortion clinics in major cities across Canada. Focusing on Winnipeg and Toronto, he tried to bypass what he still viewed as a "cumbersome, discriminatory and dangerous procedure for legal abortions."[16] The province of Ontario chose to prosecute Morgentaler for violating the federal abortion law, initiating a legal episode that lasted five years, finally ending with a Supreme Court ruling on January 28, 1988. It was this decision that set off Canada's latest abortion crisis.

ABORTION POLICIES IN THE UNITED STATES AND CANADA

Abortion Rights in the United States

The watershed in U.S. abortion policy was the Supreme Court's 1973 decision in *Roe v. Wade*, which extended the constitutional right of privacy to a woman's decision to terminate her pregnancy. *Roe* escalated rather than ended the abortion controversy, however, by encouraging countermobilization by antiabortion groups, led by the Roman Catholic Church. My own view is that the United States might well have avoided these traumatic politics had the Supreme Court followed its ruling in *United States v. Vuitch* (1971), which involved a challenge to the District of Columbia's antiabortion law. That lawsuit argued that the word "health" as it defined a therapeutic exception—"unless . . . done as necessary for the preservation of the mother's life or health"—was unconstitutionally vague, and a federal district court judge agreed.

But the majority opinion in *Vuitch*, by Justice Black for the Supreme Court, cited "common usage, [that] properly defines health as the 'state of being . . . sound in body [or] mind' [and] . . . in this light, the term 'health' presents no problem of vagueness. Indeed, whether a particular operation is necessary for a patient's physical or mental health is a judgment that physicians are obviously called upon to make routinely whenever surgery is considered." My assessment is that "[t]he *Vuitch* case may arguably be viewed, in retrospect, as a lost opportunity for the judiciary to join the emerging consensus favoring therapeutic abortions and thus settle the abortion dispute before it broke out as political war."[17]

The majority opinion in *Roe v. Wade* was authored by Justice Blackmun, who used a trimester framework to balance privacy rights and state interests. Because abortions during the first three months are safer than childbirth, he argued that "the attending physician, in consultation with his patient, is free to determine, without regulation by the State, that, in his medical judgment, the patient's pregnancy should be terminated. If that decision is reached, the judgment may be effectuated by an abortion free of interference by the State." During the second trimester, government may regulate abortions so as to preserve the mother's health, thus furthering a legitimate state interest, and during the third trimester the state can prohibit abortions unless they are deemed necessary to protect the mother's life or health. By its ruling, the high court held the challenged Texas statute to be unconstitutional, along with the laws of forty-five other states.

The legal niceties of *Roe v. Wade* were not appreciated by pro-life forces, who viewed the decision as an unmitigated defeat. Pro-life sympathizer John T. Noonan,

Jr., wrote that "*Roe v. Wade* and *Doe v. Bolton* [its companion case] may stand as the most radical decision ever issued by the Supreme Court."[18] The Vatican called it "morally monstrous," and the National Conference of Catholic Bishops argued that "Catholics must oppose abortion as an immoral act" and that "under Church law, those who undergo or perform an abortion place themselves in a state of excommunication."[19] A most virulent expression of outrage came from the *St. Louis Review*: "The appalling 7 to 2 U.S. Supreme Court decisions on abortion may well unleash an era of carnage and slaughter which could quickly eclipse the bloody record of Hitler's Germany. The Supreme Court's bizarre interpretation of the right to life of the unborn in our society has overnight transformed the United States into the Savage Stage."[20]

Almost immediately pro-life groups began to lobby Congress to reverse *Roe* by constitutional amendment, but without success. Beginning with the 1976 electoral cycle, they began to identify and target pro-abortion congressional candidates for defeat, with mixed results.[21] Members of Congress responded by trying to avoid the issue. Under the legislative rules of Congress, bills usually must be considered by a standing committee before they can be debated on the floor of the House of Representatives or the Senate, and a majority vote in the appropriate standing committee is needed for a bill to be "reported" to either floor. It is difficult if not impossible to overcome this procedural requirement, especially in the House of Representatives. Because Catholic Democrats faced cross-pressures from their party leadership (to favor the right to an abortion) and their own constituents and church (to oppose it), any abortion bill that reached the floor could be enacted by a coalition of Catholic Democrats and Republicans. To protect their Catholic colleagues while following the dictates of their party leadership, the Democrats who chaired the House and Senate judiciary committees, which had jurisdiction over abortion, typically refused to report out antiabortion legislation to the floor.

During the period 1973–85, 275 of the 498 antiabortion bills introduced into Congress were proposed constitutional amendments.[22] But none was reported out by a standing committee for a floor vote until June 28, 1983, when the Senate defeated, on a 49–50 vote, the Hatch–Eagleton amendment, which read: "A right to abortion is not secured by this Constitution." This unprecedented event occurred because the Republicans won a majority of Senate seats in the 1980 elections, which gave the GOP control over that chamber and its Judiciary Committee until 1987. Because constitutional amendments require passage by two-thirds of the House of Representatives and the Senate, plus ratification by three-fourths of the states, the odds of Hatch–Eagleton or any pro-life amendment being adopted are virtually nil.

The failure of pro-life groups to secure their objectives through legislation caused them to shift their attention to the judicial nomination and appointment process.[23] The election to the presidency of Ronald Reagan—a strong proponent of pro-life views who had relied heavily on Christian Right support during his campaign—gave antiabortion groups a strong opportunity to make their voices heard. Reagan's first opportunity to choose a Supreme Court justice came early in his administration: In 1981 Reagan nominated Sandra Day O'Connor, a conservative state court judge from Arizona, to replace Justice Potter Stewart. The only major problem she faced during her Senate testimony was her stance on abortion.

Although O'Connor stated her personal opposition to abortion, pro-life groups questioned her abortion voting record as an Arizona state legislator in the early 1970s. They were singularly unsuccessful, however, in persuading senators to vote against confirmation. Five years later, Reagan offered two more nominations for the high court: Associate Justice William Rehnquist was nominated to be Chief Justice and Antonin Scalia to be an Associate Justice. Though both men held firm antiabortion views, neither nominee was grilled by the senators about abortion.[24]

Reagan's fourth Supreme Court appointment, however, provoked intense lobbying activity from both pro-choice and antiabortion forces. Retiring Justice Powell had provided the decisive fifth vote favoring liberals in many important decisions on social issues such as affirmative action, school prayer, and abortion. The nomination of arch-conservative Robert Bork to fill Powell's vacancy made it very clear that Reagan wanted a justice who would help push his social agenda, especially with respect to abortion. Bork was attacked by many disparate interest groups on the Left, but it was the nominee's statements and writings on abortion and privacy rights that generated the most controversy about his fitness for the high court. Bork was rejected, though primarily because of his views on civil rights rather than abortion. Reagan's final Supreme Court nominee, Anthony Kennedy, did not face such intense scrutiny on abortion, or on any other issue. Unlike Bork, Kennedy attracted only sparse opposition from some women's groups and civil rights activists, since he had never publicly argued against abortion while on the Ninth Circuit Court of Appeals. The National Abortion Rights Action League stayed out of this nomination fight, because it could not document anything negative about Kennedy's record.

In toto, President Reagan appointed three new Associate Justices and elevated Associate Justice William Rehnquist to Chief Justice. George Bush, Reagan's vice president, succeeded to the presidency in 1989 and secured confirmation of two more Associate Justices: One (Clarence Thomas) has been reliably pro-life, though the other (David Souter) unexpectedly took very liberal positions on a range of social questions, including abortion. Though President Clinton was able to make two Supreme Court appointments during his tenure, the Supreme Court today has a 5–4 working conservative majority.

Mary Ann Glendon, a conservative constitutional scholar, argues that *Roe*, by denying any positive legislative role to the states, created the most one-sided abortion policy found anywhere in twenty western democracies. "*Roe v. Wade* and succeeding cases," she observed, ". . . have virtually closed down the state legislative process with respect to abortions prior to viability. Legislative attempts to provide for more information, deliberation, and counseling, more participation by others in the woman's decision-making process, and even protection for the fetus after viability have regularly been struck down."[25] Except for its rulings on publicly funded abortions (see below), the post-*Roe* liberal majority on the Supreme Court yielded little ground to the pro-lifers. The judiciary did not renege on abortion as a woman's constitutional right, refused to acknowledge that the unborn is a "person" in any legal sense, and regularly struck down obstacles designed to prevent women from obtaining abortions. Since *Roe* and *Doe v. Bolton*, its companion case, twenty-three decisions were rendered by the high court in abortion cases through 1994; I estimated that 76 percent of antiabortion restrictions were nullified during the period 1974–88 but that, afterwards, only one of eleven restrictions was invalidated.[26] There was a fundamental shift in the judiciary's pain imposition strategy with respect to pro-choice interests, a direct consequence of the "conservative" Supreme Court majority reconstituted by Presidents Reagan and Bush.

Webster v. Reproductive Health Services (1989) altered the manner of judicial scrutiny of state antiabortion laws. Its immediate effect was to accept a preamble in the challenged Missouri statute that defined life as beginning with conception, intended to prohibit the use of public funds for abortion counseling or the use of public facilities or public employees in the performance of abortions, and to require fetal viability testing prior to abortion. In the long term, while the 5–4 vote in *Webster* did not directly repudiate the constitutional right to abortion established in *Roe*, the strength of that precedent was narrowed considerably because Chief Justice Rehnquist, along with Associate Justices Kennedy and White, abandoned the trimester framework of *Roe*; Associate Justice O'Connor applied her "undue burden" standard to uphold the regulations; and Associate Justice Scalia argued for outright reversal of *Roe*. Because the landmark 1973 ruling had established a "fundamental" right to abortion and thus required "strict scrutiny" of any state or local regulations that prevented or deterred women from obtaining abortions, few laws could overcome that legal hurdle.

Webster was a turning point in abortion jurisprudence and paved the way for the Supreme Court, in *Planned Parenthood of Southeastern Pennsylvania v. Casey* (1992), to approve an array of state antiabortion restrictions that previously had been struck down by the post-*Roe* liberal majority. The Pennsylvania Abortion Control Act required an unmarried woman under eighteen to obtain written consent from at least one parent, or from a judge, and also required a parent to accompany the woman for abortion counseling. After giving her informed consent, the woman had to wait twenty-four hours before getting the abortion. Prior to getting the written consent, doctors had to counsel the woman on the risks of abortion, detail the stages of fetal development, and supply her with a list of facilities that offered alternatives to abortion. Doctors also had to report each abortion performed to the state, including copies of the informed consent and, where appropriate, the parental consent forms; and those documents were to be made available to the public. All these provisions were upheld by the Supreme Court, but not a spousal notification requirement stipulating that a married woman had to certify that she had notified her husband, except under exceptional circumstances.

Casey likely imposed substantial symbolic pain on pro-choice zealots, but in reality those restrictions may have had minimal, if any, impact on a determined women's decision to abort. The amount of opposition generated by these procedural requirements was not commensurate—except in the minds of pro-choice defenders—with the degree of burden actually imposed on women seeking abortions. Indeed, research by Professor Kenneth J. Meier (who has strong pro-choice sympathies) and his associates evaluated twenty-three different antiabortion laws during 1982–92; they found "no evidence that state restrictions on abortions reduced the overall incidence of abortion" and, moreover, concluded that "the post-*Webster* restrictions did not have the immediate effects that pro-choice advocates feared and pro-life supporters anticipated."[27]

Abortion Rights in Canada

The Canadian Supreme Court struck down Canada's existing abortion law in a 5–2 decision, finding Section 251 of the criminal code to be in violation of the Charter of Rights and Freedoms. Five justices, including Chief Justice Dickson, felt that the mandatory procedures of Section 251 caused a delay in obtaining abortions that interfered with a woman's constitutional right to the "security" of her person.[28] Section 7 of the Charter declares that "[e]veryone has the right to life, liberty and security of the person and the right not to be deprived thereof except in accordance with the principles of fundamental justice." Yet two of the five justices who voted to overturn the abortion law argued that if a more timely procedure were enacted by Parliament, it might be acceptable under the Charter.

The Court's decision threw out the existing abortion law, but put nothing in its place. This left the federal government with several unappealing options. It could do nothing, and encourage the provincial governments to regulate abortion based on standards of health and safety. Or the government could pass a "notwithstanding" resolution in the House of Commons pursuant to Section 33 of the 1982 Constitution that would override the Charter of Rights and Freedoms, the source of conflict with the former abortion law.[29] In other words, by simple majority vote the Parliament could reverse *Morgentaler* without having to undertake the complex process of trying to amend the Canadian Constitution. (There is nothing analogous to the "notwithstanding" clause in American federalism or constitutional law.) Finally, the government could attempt to rewrite the law to try to make it compatible with the Charter. No matter what the government did or did not do, it risked angering and alienating millions of voters. With an election expected in less than a year, the Conservatives faced a real political nightmare. But Justice Minister Ray Hnatyshyn immediately dismissed the possibility of overriding the Charter. With respect to governmental action in the near future, the justice minister was vague, promising discussion with the provinces while maintaining a position of leadership to ensure that women's rights were uniformly respected across the country.

Provincial reaction to the Court's edict differed sharply, and the ensuing provincial regulations only accentuated inequalities with respect to women's access to abortion. Some provinces maintained restrictions on services while others liberalized their systems, discrepancies in public policy that stimulated both pro-choice and antiabortion activists. The pro-life movement was especially adamant in pressuring Ottawa to rewrite the law. Toronto's Catholic Cardinal Emmett Carter sent a letter to the prime minister and all MPs urging enactment of a new abortion law that would recognize fetal rights from the moment of conception. Pro-choice groups were also unhappy with the status quo, however, since access to abortion was so unequal across Canada.

Knowing that his Progressive Conservative Party (PC) would face severe divisions if it attempted to formulate an official party position, Prime Minister Mulroney unveiled a strategy that called for a "free vote" (a vote of conscience) in the House of Commons. Technically the vote would be not on legislation but on a resolution to guide the government in writing new legislation. Mulroney was heavily criticized by the opposition parties for a lack of leadership, as well as for unfairly changing the rules of debate in the Parliament.

The motion introduced by the government consisted of two elements. First, it amended the rules for this debate only. Each member could speak only once, and the Speaker was authorized to decide which amendments would be admissible. Second, the motion set out a "main approach" to guide the Commons in drafting abortion legislation. This approach was a compromise between the extreme antiabortion and pro-choice positions. Sponsored by Douglas Lewis, the deputy government House leader, the motion permitted abortion early in pregnancy if one doctor believed it was necessary to protect the physical or mental well-being of the woman. The government stressed that Lewis's proposal did not represent official PC policy, but rather was a device to facilitate debate in the House.

In theory, the "main approach" could be modified to either pro-life or pro-choice extremes by adopting any of the (five) amendments deemed admissible by the Speaker; in reality, the government's strategy was designed to facilitate the defeat of any amendment by an alliance of "moderates" and either pro-life or pro-choice MPs. It was anticipated that the middle-ground position would then be passed by default. This strategy did not succeed, however, although each amendment was defeated, because "militant antiabortionist MPs and advocates of women's choice rose in unison to defeat the [main] resolution."[30] The amendment that came the closest to passing would have imposed severe restrictions on the availability of abortion services;[31] the pro-choice amendments lost overwhelmingly.

Mulroney's strategy did succeed in preventing blame from being focused on his party during the election campaign. Indeed, the prime minister avoided becoming a target for blame himself by failing to vote on any of the motions, as did Liberal Party leader John Turner. But the votes revealed deep cleavages within the Progressive Conservative Party on the abortion issue.[32]

After the vote, Mulroney continued to defend his party from criticism for not taking a stand. "The issue is too subjective and too personal to make a test of party discipline," he argued. The prime minister insisted that only a free vote could settle the abortion question, adding that it would be better to wait until the Supreme Court had heard a second major case relating to the issue.[33] The Joseph Borowski case, brought by a Manitoba antiabortion crusader, asked the Court to declare abortion illegal by declaring that a fetus is a person with constitutional rights. The Court began hearings on the case in October 1988; waiting on the *Borowski* decision had the advantage for the Conservatives, of course, of weakening abortion as an issue in the 1988 election. The Liberals, who were also badly split on the abortion issue, welcomed the respite.[34] Nevertheless, candidates' stances on abortion did become an issue in some ridings, and some candidates sought and won party nominations by mobilizing antiabortion forces.[35] Meanwhile, new provincial regulations passed in the aftermath of the Supreme Court's *Morgentaler* decision tended to reassert restrictions on availability that had existed prior to the decision.[36] After the election, new Justice Minister Douglas Lewis remarked, to no one's surprise, that he was in no hurry to put new abortion legislation on the House's agenda.[37]

The Conservatives made one more attempt to enact a national framework,[38] which was better organized and more oriented toward avoiding a split within the Conservative Party. Prime Minister Mulroney formed a caucus committee of pro-life and pro-choice MPs to forge a compromise, and their work eventually became Bill C-43. It was introduced into the House of Commons on November 18, 1989, and Mulroney made a speech imploring both sides to negotiate, although he also indicated that only PC backbenchers would be allowed a free vote and thus hinted that members of his cabinet were expected to back the government. A parliamentary committee rejected all twenty-four proposed amendments—though only one, from New Democratic Party member Dawn Black, was pro-choice—and sent its unamended bill to the floor. Eleven more amendments were proposed on the floor—again only one, from MP Black, would decriminalize abortion—and all were defeated, whereupon Bill C-43 was barely enacted on May 29, 1990, by a 140–131 vote.

While 83 percent of Progressive Conservatives supported their Government, 88 percent of Liberals and 98 percent of New Democrats were opposed. Statistical analysis of voting on the required procedural votes and the amendments, however, indicated that "[p]artisanship—which exercised the strongest influence at both the beginning and end of the legislative process—was utterly unrelated to MPs' votes on the ten pro-life amendments. Constituency preferences became more important over the course of the consideration of Bill C-43."[39] So it seems that members of Parliament reflected constituency interests as they considered amendments that imposed symbolic pain on abortion proponents; but once they failed, Progressive Conservatives of whatever persuasion unified to defend the government on final passage.

However Bill C-43 was ultimately defeated on a 43–43 tie vote in the Canadian Senate on January 31, 1991. Although Prime Minister Mulroney also permitted a "free vote" in the Senate, "there had been very little pressure exerted on Conservative Senators to toe the party line."[40] This outcome was without precedent in the history of the Canadian Senate, marking the first defeat of a government measure by the upper chamber in thirty years. The division of votes shows that senators appointed by Liberal prime ministers were more unified against Bill C-43 than were senators aligned with the Progressive Conservatives.[41] There were no further attempts by the Mulroney government to re-criminalize abortion, and the new Liberal government elected in 1993 has no political reason to reopen this issue.

Abortion Funding in the United States

When it became apparent that the *Roe* decision could not be quickly overturned, pro-life organizations resorted to other strategies to impose symbolic—as well as substantive—pain on the potential clientele for abortions. They targeted the use of public funds to pay for abortions, mainly the federal-state Medicaid program of medical assistance to the poor, since the vast majority of federally funded abortions were performed under this program.

Three years after *Roe*, pro-life lobbyists were successful in pressuring Congress into passing an amendment to the FY77 Labor-HEW appropriations bill that prohibited the use of Medicaid funds for abortions except when the life of the mother would be endangered if the fetus were carried to term. Sponsored by Representative Henry Hyde (R–IL), the amendment and its later permutations came to be commonly known as the Hyde amendment. Pro-life forces won on the funding issue because they had several strategic advantages that they lacked on the "rights" issue. First, pro-life initiatives could not be bottled up by a hostile committee: The annual nature of the appropriations process ensured that foes of abortion would have an annual vehicle through which they could threaten to generate blame against legislators who opposed their views. It also meant that they had to refight the battle every year; but once antiabortion forces had built a majority, they were able to consistently retain it.[42] Second, antiabortion groups were united, and the expenditure of tax dollars on a procedure that they equated with murder provided a rallying point.

Most important, the Supreme Court quickly sided with pro-life forces with respect to abortion funding by ruling that abortions are not an "entitlement," which the states or federal government are required to subsidize. The three funding decisions of 1977 were the only major judicial victories by pro-life forces between 1973 and 1989. In *Beal v. Doe* (1977), the high court turned aside arguments that the Social Security Act of 1935, as amended, required the states to fund nontherapeutic abortions, and in *Maher v. Roe* (1977) it affirmed that state nonfunding of elective abortions did not violate the Equal Protection Clause of the Fourteenth Amendment. The related case of *Poelker v. Doe* (1977) involved a challenge to restrictive abortion services in a public hospital, but again the Supreme Court sided with local authorities. A direct legal assault against the Hyde amendment was rejected by the Supreme Court in *Harris v. McRae* (1980). By a 5–4 vote the majority upheld as constitutional the congressional ban on Medicaid funding of any abortion for an indigent woman except one necessary to protect her life. Though a Democrat, President Carter tried with no success to placate both sides of the abortion controversy, and he quickly damaged his relations with pro-choice advocates with his cavalier defense of funding restrictions on abortions, saying: "Well, as you know, there are many things in life that are not fair, that wealthy people can afford and poor people can't. But I don't believe that the federal government should take action to try to make these opportunities exactly equal particularly when there is a moral factor involved."[43]

Since its adoption in 1976, some version of the Hyde amendment has been enacted by Congress every year through 2002. But since the amendment does not preclude states from utilizing their own revenues to fund abortions, pro-life groups have pressured state legislatures to adopt rigid abortion funding policies, some of which have been overturned by federal courts as overly restrictive. The fact is, however, that pro-choice advocates have been on the receiving end of symbolic pain imposition by most state governments. As of FY94, the last year when the Alan Guttmacher Institute provided this analysis, only Alaska, Hawaii, Maryland, New York, North Carolina, Oregon, and Washington, plus the District of Columbia, provided nonrestricted funding of abortions, whereas eight more states were under court orders to do so. These jurisdictions accounted for 99.9 percent of the 202,918 publicly funded abortions in FY94, since the other thirty-five states funded a mere 203. Of those states, thirty-two funded abortions in cases of rape, incest, or a threat to the woman's life, while three more states—Iowa, Virginia, and Wisconsin—imposed additional restrictions on publicly funded abortions. The situation has hardly changed today.[44] In states where legislators balked at banning state funding of abortions, antiabortion forces turned to referenda to force their views into law. In the November 1988 election, for example, referenda to disallow state abortion funding passed in Michigan, Colorado, and Arkansas.

A related issue was the use of federal funds to subsidize abortion counseling by family planning clinics. Under Title X of the Family Planning Services and Population Research Act of 1970, grants are made to public and private nonprofit organizations that operate voluntary family planning projects and clinics. Since 1972 there has been an absolute ban on using those grants for abortions, but during that period those clinics could provide abortion information and referrals to women who wanted to consider having an abortion. But in 1987 the Justice Department rendered an interpretation of the law to the effect that any counseling and referrals regarding abortion inevitably *promote* abortion and, therefore, that any grantee organization that offered both abortions and abortion counseling had to keep those two programs entirely separate. The next year the Secretary of Health and Human Services issued new regulations known as the "gag rule," which prohibited abortion counseling altogether on the part of family planning clinics that received Title X grants.

The gag rule continued through the Reagan and Bush administrations, but its constitutionality was challenged in the federal courts on free speech grounds, and in 1991 the Democratic-controlled Congress approved legislation rescinding the rule—but that bill was vetoed by President Bush and an override attempt failed in the House of Representatives. It was a major defeat for the congressional Democratic leadership and their pro-choice allies, a defeat made all the worse when the Supreme Court gave its stamp of approval to the administrative ban in *Rust v. Sullivan* (1991). Chief Justice Rehnquist, joined by Justices Kennedy, Scalia, Souter, and White, held that legislative intent regarding Title X was ambiguous and that, in cases of ambiguous language, the federal judiciary should defer to the executive branch's interpretation of the law. Rehnquist also turned aside arguments that free speech guarantees were violated, saying that "Congress has . . . not denied [organizations receiving federal funds] the right to engage in abortion-related activities. Congress has merely refused to fund such activities . . . and the Secretary has simply required a certain degree of separation from the Title X project . . . ." It was not until 1993, when pro-choice President Clinton assumed office, that the gag rule was rescinded as federal policy.

Abortion Funding in Canada

Funding abortions did not pose a novel political problem for Canada until the issue of abortion *clinics* arose. The umbrella statute that guarantees medical care to Canadians is the Canada Health Act (previously the Medicare Act), but the provinces are the authorities that actually fund the services. Thus, abortions were funded like any other medically necessary service so long as they were performed in hospitals and authorized by the Therapeutic Abortion Committees. In the aftermath of *Morgentaler* there were efforts by provinces to curb abortions through funding limits, but those attempts were challenged in the courts. As Brodie observed: "Perhaps most disconcerting is the potential for provincial governments, whether because of pro-life sentiments or cost-cutting initiatives, to remove abortion from national health insurance, or attempt to carve a regulatory distinction between 'non-therapeutic' and 'therapeutic' abortions—the 'wanted' and the 'needed.'"[45]

British Columbia threatened to withdraw funds for abortions under its medicare plan unless women continued to get approval from a hospital committee. BC's pro-life premier, William Premier Vander Zalm, unveiled a health plan that would pay for only those abortions that were performed in situations that were life-threatening to the mother—cases that were estimated to constitute no more than 1 percent of the total. The 1988 British Columbia cabinet regulation made pursuant to the Medical Service Act proposed making abortions an uninsured service unless performed in a hospital and unless a significant threat to the woman's life existed. But the British Columbia Civil Liberties Association sued, and that regulation was invalidated by the British Columbia Supreme Court.

In 1989 the Nova Scotia legislature passed the Act to Restrict Privatization of Medical Services, which applied to various medical procedures including abortion, making them nonreimbursable by the provincial health program. It was aimed at Dr. Henry Morgentaler, who planned to establish an abortion clinic there—so the Canadian Abortion Rights Action League (CARAL) sued, alleging that this law violated the Canadian Charter of Rights and Freedoms. This case was quite complicated, as lower courts held that CARAL lacked standing to sue. Dr. Morgentaler proceeded to perform clinic abortions, provincial authorities got an injunction restraining him, and the trial of Dr. Morgentaler on charges of performing illegal abortions was eventually reviewed by the Supreme Court of Canada in *R. v. Morgentaler* (1993). The high court simply let stand a ruling by the Nova Scotia Court of Appeal that had nullified the provincial ban on freestanding abortion clinics, signaling that the Supreme Court would not allow provincial authorities to discourage the establishment of non-hospital-based abortion facilities.

That decision did not wholly answer the question of provincial discretion with respect to funding nontherapeutic abortions, however. Yet another lawsuit was brought by Dr. Morgentaler—he had won similar court challenges in Newfoundland, New Brunswick, and Manitoba—against the Liberal government of Prince Edward Island, which reimbursed abortions only when they were performed in hospitals and when a special board deemed the procedure to be medically necessary. Since all physicians on Prince Edward Island had refused to do any abortions, women had to find abortion services on the mainland. If the abortion was performed in a mainland hospital, the physicians' fees were covered, but the patient had to pay those expenses if the abortion was performed in a private clinic. In 1995 the Prince Edward Island Supreme Court agreed with Dr. Morgentaler that the policy was illegal.

Abortion Services in the United States

Roe v. Wade did not require the health care community to provide abortion services in the United States; it simply created a constitutional right for women to choose to have an abortion and the right of doctors and hospitals to offer that service. Thus, hospitals and doctors can comply with *Roe* as the law of the land yet still refuse to perform abortions. Furthermore, there are an array of federal and state "right to conscience" laws that permit health care personnel to refuse to do abortions for religious or moral reasons. As a consequence, more than a quarter century after *Roe*, there exist wide variations in access to abortion services in the United States. And things are not getting any better.

Pro-choice advocates have charged that the mainstream health care community, by abdicating its responsibility to deliver abortion services, has marginalized that medical practice to specialized providers who can be easily identified and targeted by pro-life activists.[46] Had the U.S. health care system responded to the demand for legal abortions, it would have been very difficult for pro-life forces to orchestrate a campaign of harassment against the thousands of hospitals in this country. In 1973, 52 percent of all abortions were performed in hospitals, while the remainder were done in clinics or physicians' offices. But the number of hospital-based abortions rapidly shrank, to just 22 percent in 1980. Moreover, the percentage of the nearly 6,000 U.S. hospitals that provided abortion services peaked at 31 percent in 1976 and has declined ever since; by 1992, only 16 percent of U.S. hospitals provided those services, and collectively they represented only 7 percent of all abortions performed in the United States. Since 1988, 90 percent or more of U.S. abortions have been performed in nonhospital facilities, mainly specialized abortion clinics.[47] Since abortions are relegated to clinics, which are frequently subjected to demonstrations and sometimes violent attacks, both the "stigma" of abortion and the turmoil surrounding the act of getting an abortion involve costs, symbolic, emotional, and sometimes physical.

Abortion clinics grew in number from 789 in 1982 to 889 in 1992 but fell to 869 in 1996, according to the latest statistics by the Alan Guttmacher Institute. Similarly, physicians who perform abortions in their officers numbered 714 in 1982, declined to 636 in 1992, and then dropped even more sharply to 470 by 1996 (although abortions performed in physicians' offices amounted to only 3 percent of the 1996 total). Moreover, while most U.S. counties do not have an abortion provider, this statistic has also risen, from 77 percent in 1978 to 86 percent in 1996. The latest data tell us that 55 percent of metropolitan but 95 percent of nonmetropolitan counties among the approximately 3,000 U.S. counties have no known abortion provider, meaning that women in rural areas may have to travel long distances to locate a provider.[48] One wonders if the antiabortion campaign of harassment is taking its toll on this subculture of abortion clinics and physicians.

Abortion Services in Canada

In the wake of the 1969 parliamentary abortion reforms, medical activists began to take note that the availability of Canadian hospitals with the required Therapeutic Abortion Committee (TAC) was very limited. Data for 1973 compiled by Doctors for Repeal of the Abortion Law (DRAL) determined that 32.9 percent of Canadian hospitals had TACs,[49] which was consistent with the 1977 report by the Committee on the Operation of the Abortion Law, which concluded that "the procedure provided in the criminal code for obtaining therapeutic abortion is in practice illusory for many Canadian women."[50] My replication study for 1986, based on the DRAL methodology, found that 28.4 percent of hospitals had established TACs. In other words, the number of Canadian hospitals with abortion services almost doubled, from 143 in 1970 to 265 in 1974, but then fell slightly to 254 in 1986 before dropping markedly to 191 in 1990. This last figure, based on my own survey of provincial authorities, comes two years after *Morgentaler* and suggests the limited impact of that ruling on the established health care system.[51]

Brodie observed that three distinct abortion delivery systems operated in Canada. Most liberal was Quebec, where nineteen of thirty Canadian abortion clinics were located. Access to abortion services in Ontario and British Columbia improved markedly after the New Democratic Party came to power: British Columbia promulgated regulations under its Health Act to require certain hospitals within each region of that far-flung province to provide abortion services, and Ontario became the only provincial government that fully funded abortions by either hospitals or freestanding clinics. In the other seven provinces "the issue of access has been more problematic, if not moot."[52]

What has happened in Canada—as in the United States—is a decisive turn toward specialized clinics as abortion providers, although abortion clinics emerged in Canada for somewhat different reasons. Abortion clinics in the United States became predominant by default, because hospitals in the U.S. abandoned those services, but in Canada there was a deliberate legal strategy devised by Dr. Henry Morgentaler, first in Quebec and later throughout the country, to shift abortion services from hospitals to his clinics. Thus in 1989 Canadian clinics (mainly those in Quebec) accounted for 8.9 percent of Canadian abortions, but after the Supreme Court struck down as "unworkable" the 1969 abortion code, clinic-based abortions jumped to 21.8 percent in 1990 and again to 29.4 percent in 1992.[53] Data for 1995 (the last year for which there are comparable U.S.–Canadian statistics) show that 33 percent of Canadian abortions were performed in clinics (see table 9-1).

To curb this trend, provincial authorities tried to restrict payments for abortion to hospitals, but Dr. Morgentaler, CARAL, and their civil libertarian allies began a litigation campaign in response. The survival of abortion clinics is related to the flow of public funds for abortions—and, as already noted, Dr. Morgentaler successfully sued Nova Scotia, Prince Edward Island, Newfoundland, New Brunswick, and Manitoba to secure public funds for abortions performed in clinics.

CONCLUSIONS

Processes

The case of abortion shows how much power an independent judiciary has to impose symbolic and substantive losses on society. What had been an emerging policy consensus behind therapeutic abortions was shattered by the U.S. Supreme Court ruling in *Roe v. Wade*, viewed by pro-lifers as an unmitigated defeat, and, similarly, by the Canadian Supreme Court decision invalidating the criminal code on abortion, which left that nation with no abortion law whatsoever. Litigants who want judicial remedies do not seek compromise, and they arrive at the bar of justice armed with biased information and prejudicial arguments to bolster their case.[54] The result is that judicial decrees, unlike the deliberations of a legislative assembly, are typically "zero-sum" policies that eschew centrist positions in favor of the plaintiff or the respondent. The zero-sum quality of judicial decision making is probably heightened in countries with a tradition of judicial activism, a written Bill of Rights, and judges insulated from popular pressures by lifetime tenure. All these attributes characterize the United States, though critics point to the emerging "Americanization" of judicial processes in Canada. If anything, looking ahead, the Canadian judicial system may have greater potential as a loss-imposing institution because nominees for the high court need not be approved by Parliament, whereas nominations to the U.S. Supreme Court must be confirmed by majority vote of the Senate. Senate confirmation hearings offer all sides an opportunity to challenge judicial nominees with respect to their views on sensitive social issues, which affords a measure of accountability in recruiting judges.

In the Canadian House of Commons, the contemporary politics of abortion has consisted mostly of two closely spaced "big bangs," in 1988 and 1989–91. In the U.S. Congress, a closer analogy would be Chinese water torture: Virtually every year there has been some battle—or several battles—on abortion. Abortion fights have complicated everything from the Clinton health care plan (regarding whether abortion should be covered) to foreign aid (and funding for family planning services abroad) to military appropriations (and whether abortions can be performed in military hospitals).

The reasons why the abortion controversy has penetrated the U.S. political process to a greater degree than in Canada are, on the one hand, the weak American two-party system coupled with a decentralized electoral system and, on

the other hand, the existence of stronger interest groups, linked to a weakly regulated system of campaign finance that permits them to be major financial players in national campaigns. Pro-choice advocates have captured the soul of the Democratic Party and channel the lion's share of their campaign contributions to
Democratic candidates, just as Republican congressional and presidential candidates articulate antiabortion views not only because of pro-life backing but also
because of Christian Right votes.[55] Abortion has polarized the American political
parties, and since 1980 the Republican and Democratic national platforms have
included diametrically opposing planks on abortion in order to appeal to their
core constituencies.[56]

Even though the New Democratic Party (NDP) adopted a pro-choice plank as
early as 1971, research on Canadian national elections since 1974 indicates that
"abortion seems to be almost irrelevant"; though the Campaign Life Coalition
and the Canadian Abortion Rights Action League endorsed parliamentary candidates in 1988, neither group had much electoral success. During the height of
the abortion controversy in Canada, in fact, neither the Progressive Conservatives nor the Liberals adopted platform planks, and even the newly organized
Reform Party, though conservative and religious-based, did not impose an abortion litmus test but rather allowed its parliamentary candidates to be guided by
constituency opinion.[57]

The fact that Prime Minister Brian Mulroney allowed the Progressive Conservative caucus to negotiate their differences over abortion suggests that even West-
minister-type parliamentary systems are not immune to intraparty divisions, a circumstance also reflected in the fractured early votes on Bill C-43 in the House of
Commons. It is rare for an MP to break ranks with his party, but the abortion issue
did produce that result in recent Canadian politics. During the 1993 federal election, Ontario Liberal Party officials intervened in several ridings (electoral districts)
to prevent the nomination of pro-life candidates.

It would be difficult if not impossible for a national party organization to meddle
in the local nominating process in the United States, and the decentralized nature
of American political parties guarantees that members of Congress, especially the
House of Representatives, will be responsive to constituency opinion on contentious issues like abortion. Congressional Democrats with pro-life leanings—
even party leaders—have voted with Republicans to enact antiabortion laws, the
most famous example being the Hyde amendment, which bars the use of federal
funds to pay for non–life-threatening abortions for indigent women.[58]

Another striking difference in process between the two countries is the much
greater effort made by abortion opponents in the United States than in Canada
to use the constitutional amendment process to ensure fetal rights. This difference has manifested itself despite constitutional amendment processes that are
extremely daunting in both countries; it reflects both differences in the legislative processes of the two countries and informal characteristics of the constitutional amendment process. In the United States, presidential support is not
required for a constitutional amendment to be pursued in Congress, even if

the prospects for ultimate success are slight. Indeed, pursuit of a pro-life constitutional amendment allows conservative politicians to claim credit with their political base for fighting the good fight despite the fact that it has little chance of succeeding. In Canada, an amendment that does not have the backing of the government will clearly go nowhere, so making it a cause célèbre is not a credible credit-claiming strategy.

In the United States, moreover, constitutional amendments are almost always pursued on an individual, ad hoc basis. In Canada, on the other hand, all but a few constitutional amendments in recent years have been the subject of advanced negotiations between Ottawa and the provinces before legislation is introduced. (Those that involve only a single province face a much lower hurdle for approval.) These amendment "packages" reflect complex intergovernmental deals in which measures that are not given high priority by any of the key actors (Ottawa or the major provinces) are almost certain to be left out. And because these constitutional packages are already controversial, any provision that is likely to increase opposition to the package as a whole is even less likely to win inclusion. Thus, until pro-life forces are able to elect a federal or major provincial government firmly committed to their cause, the constitutional amendment process as a route to advancing their aims is closed.

Outcomes

Perhaps the most intriguing difference in outcomes in the abortion case is that there is no simple national pattern that holds true across all three dimensions of policy: rights, funding, and availability. In both Canada and the United States, decisions by relatively insulated judicial institutions have legalized abortion, but abortion was judged a constitutional "right" by the U.S. Supreme Court, whereas the Canadian Supreme Court defined abortion as a medical necessity. In the U.S., successive legislative challenges at the state level, coupled with politicized Supreme Court appointments, have resulted in a constitutional about-face, whereby states today are allowed to impose restrictions on that "right." Thus far, by contrast, the Supreme Court of Canada has not backtracked on its *Morgentaler* ruling.

More profound policy differences affect the two countries with respect to governmental funding. In the United States, the Supreme Court, Congress, and the majority of state legislatures agree that there is no entitlement to public funding for nontherapeutic abortions. In Canada, on the other hand, governmental funding is available for most abortions, and the Canadian judiciary, in test cases brought by Dr. Morgentaler, uniformly held that no province could withhold funding for abortions done in clinics. This difference probably is due mainly to the Canadian system of "socialized" medicine, which affords government-subsidized health care to all Canadians, as compared with the U.S. Medicaid program, which offers a segregated program of publicly subsidized health care for welfare recipients only.

Since the Canadian Medicare Act requires that provincial authorities insure all medical services, it was but an incremental step for the provincial courts to uphold the right of abortion clinics to receive funding for their services. In the United States, where health care insurance is provided mainly through the private sector—and, moreover, where there is considerable public resistance to government-controlled health care (witness the 1993–94 Clinton health care debacle)—it would have required a fundamental departure for the U.S. Supreme Court to grant poor women an entitlement to publicly funded abortions along with their constitutional "right" to an abortion. The high court has never considered poverty to be a "suspect" category (like race or gender) warranting affirmative action by government, so its rulings upholding congressional and state bans on public funding of nontherapeutic abortions were entirely consistent with American jurisprudence.

The parallels between Canada and the United States are quite striking with respect to the maldistribution of abortion services, the decline in hospital-based providers, and the growth in a specialized abortion clinic delivery system. In these respects, Canada seems to be following in the footsteps of the United States.

Undoubtedly the most striking difference in abortion policy outcomes is the unique position of Canada among western democracies. Since the criminal code provision on abortion was invalidated, Canada has no abortion law; theoretically, one could perform an abortion on a fetus one week from delivery and not be prosecuted. At least *Roe v. Wade* imposed a gestational framework on abortion and, in fact, allowed the states to ban third-trimester abortions, except in dire cases where the mother's life or health was endangered. This opening in the *Roe* decision, along with the reconstituted Supreme Court, has led to legislation by states and Congress (two such bills were vetoed by President Clinton) to prohibit late-term (what opponents call "partial-birth") abortions. To date, there has been no attempt by the Chretien government to deal with the prospect of unregulated late-term abortions.

Explanations

How do we explain these patterns of processes and policy outcomes? Are the explanations to be found in the institutions of the two countries, in their respective socioeconomic contexts, or perhaps in differences in political culture? Elsewhere I addressed this complicated question and declared my verdict: Institutions matter.[59] While I noted instances of "social convergence" between the United States and Canada—notably that both are characterized by moderate public opinion— "the [regime] differences between Canada and the United States are sufficiently great for us to believe that governmental institutions and the party systems that undergird them affect how regimes handle moral conflicts. The Canadian parliamentary system, with its strongly disciplined parties, was able to neutralize the abortion controversy, whereas the American separation-of-powers system, with its loosely organized parties, gave expression to its explosive qualities."[60]

Although parliamentary action on abortion occurred infrequently over the period 1970–90, this issue was more regularly on the judicial agenda, beginning with Dr. Henry Morgentaler's acquittal on criminal charges in Quebec in 1973, his successful appeal to the Supreme Court of Canada in 1975 and subsequent acquittal by a second Quebec jury, and yet a third acquittal by an Ontario jury, which was appealed by the government and set the stage for his landmark 1988 victory before the Canadian Supreme Court. Governments, provincial and federal, were forced to respond to those violations of the criminal code and thus could hardly engage in blame avoidance strategies, since they were being dragged into court by this crusading physician. Once the law was struck down, however, and the Mulroney government failed to recriminalize abortion, the Liberal government after 1993 could safely ignore the issue. Pro-lifers (with the exception of Joe Borowski, who in 1989 litigated before the Supreme Court of Canada that fetal rights were guaranteed by the Charter of Rights and Freedoms, but lost), cannot resort to the judiciary to leverage the political establishment. Besides, Canadian governments of the Left or Right probably have calculated that the pro-life constituency is much weaker than the pro-choice constituency, which is not the case in the United States. One reason is that the evangelical community is much smaller in Canada as compared with the United States (see table 9-1).

In Canada, even the Progressive Conservative government of Prime Minister Brian Mulroney tried not to impose undue symbolic pain on either pro-life or pro-choice forces; but in the United States the shift from a Republican (Reagan and Bush) to a Democratic (Clinton) presidency had a decisive impact on the apportionment of symbolic pain between the two sides. On the other hand, perhaps abortion politicized the executive branch in the United States because "divided government" (where at least one house of Congress is controlled by the opposing party) has been the norm during the past twenty years. Legislative quiescence may be more likely to occur when the executive can control, and thus limit, the policy agenda. Herein lies a significant institutional difference between the Canadian and U.S. systems. Ottawa and Canada's provincial governments have much greater control over legislative agendas, allowing them to avoid taking a stand and leaving the policy status quo intact. Pro-life forces in the U.S. Congress, on the other hand, have used their leverage to hold hostage pieces of legislation sought by their peers unless they incorporated provisions that whittled away at abortion funding and availability.

Ironically, Canada's parliamentary system may also have indirectly contributed to the long legislative stalemate over abortion policy. With respect to the 1991 Senate vote on Bill C-43, Thomas Flanagan has argued that some pro-life senators voted against the bill on the assumption that they would have another opportunity at a later date to vote on a bill more to their liking.[61] Thus they calculated that a tactic of "strategic disagreement" was in their policy interest.[62] But they were wrong, as later governments dodged abortion legislation. Another factor contributing to the staying power of the status quo in both countries, according to Flanagan, is the existence of bicameral legislatures.[63] Moving away from the status quo requires two separate chambers to agree on a specific path of policy change. If the two chambers have different distributions of policy preferences, they may have difficulties in arriving at an agreement for policy change, especially if their median positions are on opposite sides of the status quo. This is surely the case in the United States, where the Senate, regardless of party control, has been more "liberal" on abortion funding as compared with the House of Representatives (despite the fact that the Democrats were the majority from 1973 until the GOP takeover in 1995).

Strategies

Abortion has been a heated political issue in both Canada and the United States. And politicians have responded to this political heat in similar ways—by attempting to avoid it. Blame avoidance has taken a variety of forms. Sometimes governments use the judiciary as a scapegoat to explain why they have not taken action, as when the Mulroney government awaited a ruling in the *Borowski* case before proceeding with its proposal to recriminalize abortion. Blame avoidance strategies may utilize low-profile bodies (e.g., the House Judiciary Committee in the U.S. Congress) to keep the abortion issue off the agenda, so that prominent office-holders do not have to take a public stand on it. Or governments may bundle changes in abortion laws together with a variety of other issues so that they do not have to take a separate stand on abortion, as the Trudeau government did with its 1969 criminal code revisions. The use of "free votes" in Parliament is a maneuver designed to avoid pain imposition by the government while facilitating pain imposition on the part of individual MPs, who face counterpressures from their constituents. At the other extreme, we need to recognize that there are policy advocates who *want* to impose pain on their adversaries. As such, they expand the scope of conflict by forcing their colleagues to openly confront the political costs of pain imposition, as illustrated by the use of legislative antiabortion "riders" (like the Hyde amendment) in the Congress.

Political institutions are an important influence on the strategies used by politicians. The U.S. system of weak parties and checks and balances diffuses responsibility for policy outcomes among all elected officials individually; thus it makes all of them subject to blame-generating pressures from interest groups. Parliamentary systems such as Canada's are normally distinguished by party discipline, which (1) partially shields individual legislators from responsibility, and hence retribution, for collective positions but (2) makes parties, and in particular governing parties, more accountable for their actions. In the case of abortion, however, Canadian parties have been unwilling to accept this accountability, choosing instead to diffuse it among individual members of all parties. While this strategy of allowing "free votes" may serve to "Americanize" the policy process, as individual members become subject to pressures from pro- and antiabortion forces, the reality is that few MPs strayed from party loyalty when voting on Bill C-43.

Apart from the expansive social conflict over abortion, the scope of *institutional* conflict over abortion is great, especially in the United States but also in Canada, owing primarily to venue-switching by the winners or losers in this policy struggle. Here the abortion controversy began with reformers lobbying state legislatures, then shifting to the federal judiciary, where they won a decisive Supreme Court victory. The *Roe* decision caused a backlash in Congress as pro-lifers countermobilized, and the presidency became allied with one side or the other depending upon which party controlled the White House. All the while there was a settled scenario involving federalism, as pro-lifers persuaded states to enact abortion restrictions and pro-choice defenders adopted a litigation strategy to overturn those restrictions in the federal courts. Yet this political tug-of-war became unsettled after 1989, when the Supreme Court issued rulings sympathetic to the pro-life agenda in several cases, causing pro-choice advocates to lobby certain states to codify legalized abortion in the event that the *Roe* precedent is repudiated.

Venue-switching was less convoluted in Canada. The liberalized abortion law that Parliament enacted in 1969 was not subjected to legal challenge—except in Quebec, where the criminal code was deemed unenforceable—until its nullification in 1988 by the Supreme Court. That action shifted the venue to Parliament—but after that body's failure to recriminalize abortion, issues affecting abortion policy implementation shifted again to the provinces, where abortion funding restrictions were imposed, though none survived after a round of appeals to various provincial appellate courts.

GENERALIZABILITY

Since the United States is an anomaly among western democracies with its separation-of-powers system, whereas the Canadian regime is more analogous to Westminister-style parliamentary systems, the lessons drawn from these different settings should have applicability to other countries where abortion has surfaced as a value-focused conflict. Both the U.S. and Canada are anomalies, however, with respect to judicial activism, and we do not expect the high courts of most European countries (except perhaps Germany) to actively set a policy agenda and force political elites to confront the problem of symbolic pain imposition. Where the judiciary is weak, parliamentary rule strong, and political parties centralized and disciplined, one would think that those systems would be more impervious to penetration by pro-life or pro-choice lobbyists. The Canadian system is more hierarchical and based on greater public deference to authority than the American system, so logically those older European societies like England, Sweden, The Netherlands, and France, with even stronger hierarchical structures and mechanisms for channeling popular demands, should be able to impose symbolic pain with relative immunity.

This logic applies despite the fact that France is much more Catholic than the United States or Canada. The other paramount variable, of course, is religion, since the Catholic Church is the mainstay opposition denomination where it chooses to resist the symbolic pain of pro-choice policies. In this regard, therefore, the Quebec experience may be more analogous to France than to English-speaking Canada, let alone the United States, since the Roman Catholic Church in Quebec chose not to aggressively resist abortion liberalization. In the end, institutions trump culture, I believe, because even an assertive Roman Catholic Church would have faced the same institutional barriers that any lobbying group would face in penetrating the decision-making apparatus of a hierarchical regime.

NOTES

1. Longitudinal polling on abortion is summarized by Ruth Ann Strickland in "Abortion: Prochoice versus Prolife," in Raymond Tatalovich and Byron W. Daynes, eds., *Moral Controversies in American Politics* (Armonk, N.Y.: M. E. Sharpe, 1998), pp. 13–18.
2. Lawrence Tribe, *Abortion: The Clash of Absolutes* (New York: W. W. Norton, 1992).
3. Raymond Tatalovich and Byron W. Daynes, "The Lowi Paradigm, Moral Conflict, and Coalition-Building: Pro-Choice versus Pro-Life," *Women and Politics* 13 (1993): 39–66.
4. See the discussion of American and Canadian attitudes toward abortion in Raymond Tatalovich, *The Politics of Abortion in the United States and Canada* (Armonk, N.Y.: M. E. Sharpe, 1997), pp. 109–20
5. Marthe A. Chandler, Elizabeth Adell Cook, Ted G. Jelen, and Clyde Wilcox, "Abortion in the United States and Canada: A Comparative Study of Public Opinion," in Ted G. Jelen and Marthe A. Chandler, eds., *Abortion Politics in the United States and Canada* (Westport, Conn.: Praeger, 1994), p. 140.
6. See Tatalovich, *The Politics of Abortion in the United States and Canada*, 144–66.
7. Lawrence Lader, *Abortion* (Indianapolis, Ind.: Bobbs-Merrill, 1966), p. 87.
8. For the impact of reform agitation on public and medical opinion, see Raymond Tatalovich and Byron W. Daynes, *The Politics of Abortion* (New York: Praeger, 1981), pp. 42–61, 116–23.
9. Tatalovich, *The Politics of Abortion in the United States and Canada*, 100.
10. F. L. Morton, *Morgentaler v Borowski: Abortion, the Charter, and the Courts* (Toronto: McClelland and Stewart, 1992), p. 19.
11. Morton, *Morgentaler v. Borowski*, 26.
12. Janine Brodie, Shelley A. M. Gavigan, and Jane Jenson, *The Politics of Abortion* (Toronto: Oxford University Press, 1992), p. 32.
13. The Committee on the Operation of the Abortion Law reported in 1977 that the procedure for getting a legal abortion was "in practice illusory" for many Canadian women. *Report of the Committee on the Operation of the Abortion Law* (Ottawa: Supply and Services, 1977), p. 141.
14. On Morgentaler's legal battles, see the introduction to Shelagh Day and Stan Persky, eds., *The Supreme Court of Canada Decision on Abortion* (Vancouver: New Star Books, 1988).
15. "Trudeau Rejects Tory Requests to Tighten Up Laws on Abortion," *Globe and Mail* (Toronto), June 10, 1978.
16. Michael Kaufman, "Canadian Doctor Campaigns for National Abortion Clinics," *The New York Times*, December 13, 1982.
17. Tatalovich, *The Politics of Abortion in the United States and Canada*, 65.
18. John T. Noonan, Jr., "Raw Judicial Power," *National Review* (March 2, 1973), p. 261.
19. Cited in "Furor over Abortion—Hotter Than Ever," *U.S. News and World Report*, March 4, 1974, p. 43.
20. Cited in Lauren R. Sass, *Abortion: Freedom of Choice and the Right to Life* (New York: Facts on File, 1978), p. 5.
21. See Eva R. Rubin, *Abortion, Politics and the Courts*, (Westport, Conn.: Greenwood Press), chap. 4, and Robert J. Spitzer, *The Right to Life Movement and Third Party Politics* (Westport., Conn.: Greenwood Press, 1987).

22. See Raymond Tatalovich, "Abortion: Prochoice versus Prolife," in Raymond Tatalovich and Byron W. Daynes, eds., *Social Regulatory Policy: Moral Controversies in American Politics* (Boulder, Colo.: Westview Press, 1988), p. 201.

23. See G. Calvin Mackenzie, "A Test of Fitness for Presidential Appointment?" in Gilbert Y. Steiner, ed., *The Abortion Dispute and the American System*, (Washington, D.C.: Brookings Institution Press, 1983), pp. 47–63.

24. Nadine Cohodas, "Rehnquist, Scalia Headed for Confirmation," *Congressional Quarterly Weekly Report* (August 9, 1986), 1846.

25. Mary Ann Glendon, *Abortion and Divorce in Western Law* (Cambridge, Mass.: Harvard University Press, 1987), p. 34.

26. Tatalovich, *The Politics of Abortion in the United States and Canada*, 66. A listing of all the abortion cases heard by the Supreme Court is found on pp. 67–69.

27. Kenneth J. Meier, Donald P. Haider-Markel, Anthony J. Stanislawski, and Deborah R. McFarlane, "The Impact of State-Level Restrictions on Abortion" *Demography* 33 (August 1996): 310, 311.

28. In his opinion, Dickson cited the findings of the 1977 Committee on the Operation of the Abortion Law that "the average delay between a pregnant woman's first contact with a physician and a subsequent therapeutic abortion was eight weeks." (Day and Persky, *The Supreme Court of Canada Decision on Abortion*, 39).

29. The "Notwithstanding" clause in the Canadian Constitution allows the federal or any provincial government to pass a law notwithstanding the fact that it violates the charter. The law must be reenacted every five years. The federal government has never been used this device.

30. Graham Fraser, "Bid for Abortion Compromise a Tactic That Failed the Tories," *Globe and Mail* (Toronto), July 30, 1988, A5.

31. Gus Mitges's antiabortion amendment called for the prohibition of abortion unless the pregnancy endangered the life of the mother. The amendment was defeated in a 118–105 vote.

32. See Graham Fraser, "McDougall Calls for Choice as House Debates Abortion,"*Globe and Mail* (Toronto), July 28, 1988, A1.

33. Murray Campbell, "Mulroney Plays Down Sales Tax Cost Estimate," *Globe and Mail* (Toronto), October 19, 1988, A9.

34. "It's Time to Face the Abortion Issue" (editorial), Toronto *Star*, November 22, 1988, A20.

35. Ann Rauhala, "74 Antiabortion MPs to Enter House," *Globe and Mail* (Toronto), November 23, 1988, A9.

36. Andre Picard, "One Year after the Abortion Law Struck Down, Little Has Changed," *Globe and Mail* (Toronto), January 28, 1989, A3.

37. Susan Delacourt, "New Justice Minister Not in Any Hurry to Put Abortion Legislation Before House," *Globe and Mail* (Toronto), February 2, 1989, A5.

38. See the discussion in Robert M. Campbell and Leslie A. Pal, "Courts, Politics and Morality: Canada's Abortion Saga," in *The Real Worlds of Canadian Politics*, 2d ed. (Peterborough, Ontario: Broadview Press), pp. 1–51.

39. L. Marvin Overby, Raymond Tatalovich, and Donley T. Studlar, "Party and Free Votes in Canada: Abortion in the House of Commons," *Party Politics* 4 (1998): 381–92.

40. Brodie, Gavigan, and Jenson, *The Politics of Abortion*, 115.

41. Tatalovich, *The Politics of Abortion in the United States and Canada*, 94.

42. See Nadine Cohodas, "Campaign to Overturn Ban on Abortion Funding Begun," *Congressional Quarterly Weekly Report* (August 20, 1983): 1689–93.

43. Quoted in Carll Tucker, "Carter and Abortion," *Saturday Review*, September 17, 1977, p. 64.

44. Terry Sollom, Rachel Benson Gold, and Rebekah Saul, "Public Funding for Contraceptive, Sterilization and Abortion Services, 1994," *Family Planning Perspectives* 28 (July/August, 1996): 172. Currently, two states fund abortions only in cases of life

endangerment; thirty-two do so for life endangerment, rape, and incest; and sixteen provide Medicaid funding for medically necessary abortions.

45. Janine Brodie, "Health versus Rights: Comparative Perspectives on Abortion Policy in Canada and the United States," in Gita Sen and Rachel Snow, eds., *Reproductive Options in the 1990s* (Cambridge, Mass.: Harvard School of Public Health, 1994), p. 134.

46. See Frederick S. Jaffe, Barbara L. Lindheim, and Philip R. Lee, *Abortion Politics: Private Morality and Public Policy* (New York: McGraw-Hill, 1981), chap. 3.

47. These statistics are drawn from Tatalovich, *The Politics of Abortion in the United States and Canada*, 203, 205 and tables 7.1, 7.2.

48. Stanley K. Henshaw, "Abortion Incidence and Services in the United States, 1995–1996," *Family Planning Perspectives* 30 (November/December, 1998): 266, 268–69, and esp. tables 3, 6, and 7.

49. Doctors for Repeal of the Abortion Law, *Survey of Hospital Abortion Committees in Canada* (December 4, 1975), Library of Parliament, Ottawa.

50. *Report of the Committee on the Operation of the Abortion Law*, 141.

51. Tatalovich, *The Politics of Abortion in the United States and Canada*, 207–8 and tables 7.3, 7.4.

52. Brodie, "Health versus Rights," 132.

53. Tatalovich, *The Politics of Aboriton in the United States and Canada*, 203, table 7.1.

54. Jack E. Rossotti, Laura Natelson, and Raymond Tatalovich, "Nonlegal Advice: The Amicus Briefs in *Webster v. Reproductive Health Services*," *Judicature* 81 (November–December 1997): 118–21.

55. Tatalovich, *The Politics of Abortion in the United States and Canada*, 150–64.

56. Byron W. Daynes and Raymond Tatalovich, "Presidential Politics and Abortion, 1972–1988," *Presidential Studies Quarterly* 22 (summer 1992): 545–61.

57. Tatalovich, *The Politics of Abortion in the United States and Canada*, 144,150; quote at 144.

58. Ibid., 99–107.

59. Ibid., 237–38.

60. Ibid., 237.

61. Thomas Flanagan, "The Staying Power of the Legislative Status Quo," *Canadian Journal of Political Science* 31, no. 1 (March 1997): 31–53.

62. On strategic disagreement, see John B. Gilmour, *Strategic Disagreement: Stalemate in American Politics* (Pittsburgh: University of Pittsburgh Press, 1995).

63. Flanagan, "The Staying Power of the Legislative Status Quo," 53.

10

CONCLUSIONS

LESLIE A. PAL AND R. KENT WEAVER

THE EIGHT CASE STUDY CHAPTERS IN THIS BOOK PROVIDE AN EXTENDED
exploration of governmental capacity for loss imposition in public policy along two
major dimensions. The first is a comparative analysis of two types of political institutions: Westminster parliamentary and presidential. While both Canada and the
United States have distinct features that differentiate them from other countries
with the same type of institutions, each represents the key characteristics of their
institutional type. The essential difference, of course, revolves around the differentiation of the executive and the legislature. Since Canada is a parliamentary
regime, Canada's executive sits in the legislature and is in theory responsible to it.
This carries with it a host of institutional consequences, among the most important
of which are party discipline (because if major government legislation is defeated
in the House, the government itself is likely to fall) and clear accountability for public policy and legislation (because of the control that the executive has over the legislative process). As a presidential regime, the United States divides the executive
from the legislature (indeed, more than most regimes of this type). Thus, there is
less party discipline than in a typical parliamentary regime, since the president's political fortunes and those of congressional representatives typically are independent of each other. Accountability is also thereby diffused, since neither the executive branch nor the legislature controls the legislative agenda to the same extent
that a cabinet does in a Westminster parliament.

The other dimension of interest in this book is an analysis of categories of loss imposition. The chapters in the book analyze the capacity of the U.S. and Canadian political systems to impose substantial losses of several types: geographically diffuse losses (pensions and health care), business-oriented losses (tobacco control and telecommunications), geographically concentrated losses (military base closings and nuclear waste disposal), and symbolic losses (abortion and gun control). This research design should allow us to analyze the relative weight of institutions versus type of loss in determining governmental capacity for loss imposition. If one country appears to have a greater capacity for loss imposition across the whole range of policy sectors examined here, it suggests that institutions have a powerful influence on that capacity. If, on the other hand, politicians and political institutions in the two countries generally handle the same type of potential loss imposition initiative in roughly similar ways, with similar outcomes within each sector, it suggests that institutions matter less than policy characteristics in determining capacity for loss imposition.

Each of the case studies in this book also tries to assess the weight of confounding factors, such as policy legacies (the impact of past choices on current decisions), globalization (the greater pressures for change in a smaller economy like Canada's), social structure, and political culture, on outcomes. In this final chapter, we review the findings of the case studies regarding both patterns of outcomes and the causes underlying those patterns and try to arrive at some more general conclusions about how political institutions affect capacity for loss imposition.

VENUES AND PROCESSES

There is little question that loss imposition processes look very different in the two countries, both in terms of the venues in which and the mechanisms through which major decisions are made and the frequency with which loss imposition initiatives appear on the agenda.

Venues and Mechanisms

Loss-imposing actions can take place in several different venues, using different sorts of mechanisms to try to enforce a loss-imposing decision. The most obvious venue is the legislative process. But this can include several different mechanisms, including both ordinary legislation and special forms of procedurally privileged legislative action (notably budget legislation in Canada and omnibus budget legislation in the United States). Another mechanism for loss imposition consists of purely executive (or in Canada, cabinet) orders, which have the procedural advantage of minimal veto points. At the other end of the "barriers to adoption" spectrum are constitutional amendments, which most firmly entrench a loss-imposing decision in policy, but have the disadvantage of much higher hurdles to enactment. Other potential decision-making venues include courts, regulatory

TABLE 10-1
**Primary Institutional Venues for Loss Imposition
(In declining order of importance)**

Policy Sector	U.S.	Canada
Pensions	Legislation Special temporary commission	Legislation Intergovernmental agreement

Health	Legislation (budget)	Legislation (budget)
		Provincial legislation
		Special provincial or
		  sub-provincial hospital
		  boards

Telecommunications	Courts Regulatory commissions	Regulatory commissions Courts
Tobacco control	Courts Legislation Executive order (in re: FDA regulation of tobacco)	Legislation (budget) Courts
Nuclear waste siting	Legislation Courts	
Military base closings	Special temporary commissions	Legislation (budget)
Gun control	Legislation Courts	Legislation
Abortion	Courts State legislation	Courts Federal legislation

bodies, and special temporary bodies (e.g., hospital closure commissions) set up to make specific kinds of decisions.

Table 10-1 lists the major decision-making venues for loss imposition in each country in each case study sector, in declining order of importance. It suggests that loss-imposing actions frequently occur in different institutional venues in the two countries. Somewhat surprisingly, the courts play a major role in loss imposition in both countries; but (less surprisingly) they are more often the dominant loss-imposing institution in the United States than in Canada. Major loss-imposing actions in the case study sectors in Canada frequently take place through procedurally privileged budget legislation rather than regular legislation. The United States tends to rely more heavily on structurally insulated bodies, such as the courts and special temporary commissions.

Executive (or in Canada, cabinet) orders do not figure as major loss-imposition vehicles in most of the cases outlined here, despite their obvious procedural advantage. The reason appears to be that each of these sectors is controversial enough that unilateral executive action has been highly constrained, either through embedding specific provisions in law or by limiting executive discretion in prior legislation. For example, in January 2001 the new president, George W. Bush, used an executive order to ban federal aid to international organizations that promote or perform abortion as a method of family planning, exactly reversing an executive order that Bill Clinton had issued when *he* came into office in January 1993, which itself reversed an earlier ban imposed by the Reagan administration and maintained by the administration of George W. Bush's father.[1] But there was little that these presidents could do to unilaterally change the policies at the core of the abortion controversy in the United States. Limits on executive authority to act unilaterally to impose losses appear in other cases as well, notably in the U.S. Supreme Court ruling that the Food and Drug Administration could not exert regulatory authority over tobacco products without explicit congressional authorization.

Another striking pattern is the frequency with which special legislative procedures for passing budget legislation are used as a vehicle for imposing loss in both countries. This is especially frequent in Canada. While majority governments in Westminster systems can lose votes in the legislature without necessarily being defeated, they do so by indicating that the vote is not a matter of "confidence." There is no such discretion with respect to the government's budget: It is *always* a matter of confidence, and its defeat means that the government has lost the confidence of the House and is defeated as well. Therefore, incorporating a policy proposal (especially a loss-imposing one) in the budget has several advantages. First, since budget-making is typically secret (though much less so in Canada in recent years), the government does not have to consult, or risk alienating, critics. Second, since the budget is a confidence measure, government MPs typically must vote to support it. Third, since the policy proposal is embedded in a highly technical document, the proposal itself may be presented in more technical terms—and, hence, be insulated, to some degree, from attack. Finally, the use of the budget in recent years in Canada as a vehicle for all manner of policy announcements has marshaled the force of the deficit, and of fiscal prudence, behind those announcements. This is what happened, for example, with cuts in health transfers, changes to pensions, and closing military bases.

Budget reconciliation procedures that provide for limited debate and avoid Senate filibusters are also used as a mechanism for loss imposition in the United States. Their usage is not as frequent as in Canada, however (at least in the sectors examined here), nor their success rate as high. Major health care cuts included in budget legislation passed by Congress in 1995, for example, fell victim to President Clinton's veto.[2]

Constitutional amendment also seldom appears as a loss imposition vehicle in the two countries. Abortion is again an exception: Pro-life forces in the United States have tried to pursue a constitutional amendment strategy but so far without success. This is not surprising, given the extremely high hurdles to adoption of constitutional amendments in the U.S.

Agendas

The agenda-setting processes for loss imposition in the two countries also look quite different. Three patterns stand out. First, in the United States, loss-imposition initiatives come onto the "action agenda" of changes given serious consideration by policymakers more often than in Canada. They also originate from a wider variety of sources, because political executives in U.S. have much lower agenda control than in Canada. Second, loss-imposition initiatives in the United States also have a lower success rate in most sectors than in Canada. In a system like that in the United States, with a larger number of veto players, owing to divided government and effective bicameralism, along with shorter election cycles, the capacity of any one player to alter the legislative status quo is significantly less than in a system like Canada's. Hence, in the United States we frequently see more legislative activity and a higher level of open conflict among veto players, resulting in less frequent actual legislative change from the status quo, or at most only marginal changes. In the Canadian case, because of concentrated authority, there is usually less legislative activity within each sector, but greater capacity to change the status quo from time to time. (On the other hand, the Canadian government has also retreated on major initiatives, in areas such as pension reform, abortion, and tobacco taxation.) Third, successful loss imposition initiatives in the United States often generate prolonged political skirmishing and efforts to reverse that decision (e.g., in the cases of abortion and gun control), usually with little actual policy change. Government agenda control in Canada generally prevents skirmishing to reverse loss-imposing actions.

OUTCOMES

Despite very different decision-making processes and venues, the chapters in our book frequently detail very similar outcomes. Indeed, considering the case studies as a whole, the theoretical loss-imposing advantages of the Canadian Westminster type of system appear more modest in practice. This pattern is evident in table 10-2, which provides very rough estimates of governmental success in each of the policy sectors, and in some cases more differentiated measures of loss imposition in particular subsectors or time periods. Loss imposition is measured on a rough scale of one to five diamonds, with a filled (darkened) diamond representing greater success at loss imposition. Thus "no filled diamonds" represents virtually no losses whatsoever; one filled diamond, losses that are very narrow in incidence or scope or amount essentially to a "slap on the wrist"; three diamonds, losses that are substantial but not overwhelming; and five filled diamonds, losses that are truly catastrophic for a particular constituency. While the Canada and U.S. columns are intended to provide measures of absolute success at loss imposition, the middle column shows relative success at imposing losses, recognizing that two countries can attain similar outcomes in a sector with relatively high (telecommunications) or low (nuclear waste siting) levels of loss imposition.

Several patterns stand out in table 10-2. The first and most obvious one is that neither country imposed losses of a truly catastrophic nature (five filled diamonds) in any sector, which is perhaps not surprising in two countries that have elected governments and strong protections in terms of procedural rights. (Note that in the telecommunications case, losses are scored as originally perceived by participants, but those losses turned out to be lower in practice.) A second pattern is that loss imposition policy outcomes more frequently look similar within sectors across

TABLE 10-2
Relative and Absolute Loss-Imposition Outcomes across Cases

	U.S.	Relative Capacity	Canada
Public Pension Reform			
Retrenchment, 1977–83	◆◆◆◇◇	— —|— — — — — — — — — —	◆◇◇◇◇
Retrenchment, 1984–2000	◆◇◇◇◇	— — — — — — — — —|— — —	◆◆◆◇◇
Increasing payroll taxes, 1977–83	◆◆◆◇◇	— —|— — — — — — — — — —	◇◇◇◇◇
Increasing payroll taxes, 1984–2000	◇◇◇◇◇	— — — — — — — — — — —|—	◆◆◆◇◇
Restructuring	◇◇◇◇◇	— — — — — — — — —·|— —	◆◇◇◇◇
Health Care for the Elderly			
Cutting benefits and eligibility	◆◇◇◇◇	— — — — — —|— — — — —·	◆◇◇◇◇
Increasing user charges	◇◇◇◇◇	— — — — — — —|— — — — —·	◇◇◇◇◇
Cutting reimbursement to providers	◆◆◇◇◇	— — — — — — — —|— — — —	◆◆◆◇◇
Limiting capital expenditures for providers	◇◇◇◇◇	— — — — — — — — — —·|— —·	◆◆◇◇◇
Closing facilities	◇◇◇◇◇	— — — — — — — — — —·|— —·	◆◆◇◇◇
Tobacco Control			
Advertising restrictions	◆◆◇◇◇	— — — — — — — — — —·|—·	◆◆◆◇◇
Warning labels	◆◇◇◇◇	— — — — — — — — — — —·|—·	◆◆◆◆◇
Taxation/Pricing, 1980–93	◆◆◇◇◇	— — — — — — — — — — —·|—·	◆◆◆◆◇
Taxation/Pricing, 1994–2000	◆◆◆◇◇	— — — — — — —·|— — — — —·	◆◆◆◇◇
Telecommunications Deregulation			
Terminal equipment	◆◆◆◆◇	— — — — — —·|— — — — —·	◆◆◆◆◇
Long distance services entry	◆◆◆◆◇	— — — — — —·|— — — — —·	◆◆◆◆◇
Nuclear Waste Siting			
	◆◇◇◇◇	— — — —·|— — — — — —·	◇◇◇◇◇
Military Base Closings			
1977–87	◇◇◇◇◇	— — — — — — — —·|— — — —·	◆◇◇◇◇
1988–95	◆◆◆◇◇	— — — — — — —·|— — — — —·	◆◆◆◇◇
1997–2000	◇◇◇◇◇	— — — — — — —·|— — — — —·	◆◇◇◇◇
Gun Control			
Types of guns allowed	◆◇◇◇◇	— — — — — — — — — — —|—	◆◆◆◆◇
Owner licensing	◇◇◇◇◇	— — — — — — — — — — —|—	◆◆◆◆◇
Use and storage	◇◇◇◇◇	— — — — — — — — —·|— —·	◆◆◆◇◇
Abortion			
Entrenching abortion rights	◆◆◆◇◇	— — — —|— — — — — — — —	◆◆◇◇◇
Financing abortion services	◆◇◇◇◇	— — — — — — — — — — —|—	◆◆◆◆◇
Limiting access	◆◆◇◇◇	— — — — — — —·|— — — — —·	◆◆◇◇◇

◆ and ◇ are described in text.

countries than they do within countries across sectors. Moreover, within individual sectors, there frequently is no consistent ranking with respect to Canada–U.S. differences in capacity to impose losses in specific subsectors or over time.

The Canadian system does show evidence of greater loss imposition capacity in several cases. Gun control and tobacco regulation, both cases wherein a concentrated interest trying to block loss imposition confronts a relatively diffuse interest in favor, are the clearest examples. With the 1995 Firearms Act, Canada has one of the toughest gun control regimes in the world, governing ownership, type, and use. In the United States, virtually every significant attempt at gun control on the national level has been stymied, weakened, or reversed. Canada has also imposed substantially stronger warning labels on tobacco products and somewhat tougher taxation and advertising restriction regimes. This suggests that there is much truth to the conventional wisdom that the U.S. system does advantage large concentrated interests when they face no powerful opponent that can either (1) face off against them in the political arena or (2) shift venues to a more favorable site, like the courts.

Loss imposition with respect to health care exhibits a more complex pattern but some important Canadian advantages, as Carolyn Tuohy's chapter demonstrates in detail and table 10-2 shows in summary form. Health care offers numerous ways to impose losses, from cutting benefits and eligibility for recipients or raising user charges or payroll taxes to imposing losses on providers, reducing capital availability for new technologies, or rationalizing facilities (which may impose costs on both providers and recipients). These options can to some extent substitute for one another: doing more of one lowers the fiscal pressure to do more of another. In both countries, the federal government has avoided politically suicidal direct assaults on health care benefits and eligibility as they affect the elderly. Nevertheless, there were modest cuts of an indirect (and thus blame-obfuscating) nature in both countries. In Canada, these took the form of longer waiting lists for some procedures and selective hospital closures. As will be discussed further below, however, hospital closures—the most visible form of loss imposition—were decided by provincial governments, or by specialized bodies created by the provinces. In the United States, indirect benefit cuts took the form of new reimbursement systems that encouraged health care providers to provide fewer services. Similarly, neither government was willing to impose major increases in user charges by increasing (or, in the Canadian case, imposing) payroll taxes, or by increasing copayments or deductibles for elderly recipients of health care services. The major exception to that rule—the Medicare Catastrophic Coverage Act of 1988 in the United States—was quickly rescinded after a storm of protest from seniors.

In both countries, there was heavy reliance on cutbacks to providers (for example, by cutting reimbursement rates or capping provider incomes). Although providers are a more concentrated set of potential opponents to loss imposition than patients, patients are far more numerous; when forced to choose between imposing highly visible losses on elderly patients or on providers, policymakers in both countries have almost always opted for the latter. Because of the absence of a centralized hospital budget-setting process in the more fragmented United States health care sector, there was no equivalent to the hospital rationalization process that occurred in many Canadian provinces. Similarly, Canada's health care financing system has facilitated greater control over capital expenditures on medical technology. In each of these areas, however, the rapid growth of managed care providers in the United States may be shifting leverage away from providers toward funders of health care.

Military base closings show a mixed picture. In both countries, there were long periods of impasse followed by a significant burst of success. Ultimately, the Canadian government was more successful in closing bases than its American counterpart, though it started from a much smaller number of bases.

In other sectors examined in this volume, the two countries show similar outcomes in loss imposition. The clearest example was in Rabe's chapter on high-level nuclear waste. In this case the United States Congress acted more decisively than the Canadian parliament, choosing to impose on Nevada the loss of becoming a single storage site for the entire country. However, opponents have been able to use the courts and other mechanisms to resist this loss so effectively that little has been done. In the Canadian case, by contrast, there has been policy paralysis as the issue has been studied interminably by federal agencies and commissions. The ironic result is that outcomes in the two systems are almost identical.

Weaver makes a similar point regarding the Canadian capacity to deal with pension restructuring and retrenchment. Canada was more successful in imposing losses on pensioners by increasing contribution rates in the 1990s, owing in part to the capacity to push an intergovernmental deal through parliamentary institutions, and perhaps also to the fact that Canadian Pension Plan (CPP) payroll taxes began from much lower levels than in the United States, since the U.S. had raised its payroll tax rates much earlier. Outcomes with regard to benefit eligibility, retrenchment, and program restructuring were more ambiguous in the two countries. Retrenchment initiatives came onto the American agenda more frequently and from a wider variety of sources than in Canada until the medium-term solvency of Social Security was restored in 1983, but there was virtually no action after that point. Canadian politicians backed down on some significant retrenchment initiatives (e.g., partial deindexation of Old Age Security under the first Mulroney government and the Seniors Benefit under Chrétien), while succeeding in others. Canada's record on restructuring shows modestly greater movement than in the U.S., particularly with respect to moving to collective investments in equity markets. But this was largely due to the fact that it encountered less resistance to change (i.e., the change was not seen by any major group as loss imposition), rather than to a greater capacity to impose losses. In recent years, proponents of privatization have had far more success in putting that issue on the agenda in the U.S. than in Canada, but no success in getting their proposals turned into law. The pensions case as a whole does not demonstrate the marked Canadian superiority in loss imposition that was evident in our first group of cases.

Tatalovich's chapter also displays substantial ambiguity in the capacity of governments to impose losses with respect to the financing and availability of abortion services and the right to them. In this instance, it was court decisions in the United States (*Roe v. Wade* in 1973) and Canada (*Morgentaler* in 1988) that imposed dramatic symbolic losses on pro-life (antiabortion) proponents by invalidating legislation that restricted access to abortion. Legislative attempts by the Mulroney government in 1989–91 to impose a new abortion regime failed, despite a high concentration of power in the executive. In the United States, abortion bills come in a constant stream, and the abortion issue has polarized American politics. In this respect, the greater permeability of the American system has permitted the issue to stay on the national agenda, whereas after 1993 the Liberal government has used its parliamentary power to keep the issue *off* the agenda. The Canadian system of Medicare has allowed the courts to strike down any attempts to restrict abortion financing, while in the United States the funding system has allowed congressional and state bans on public funding of nontherapeutic abortions. The two countries are quite similar in terms of geographical differentials in limitations on the availability of abortion services, a form of loss imposition on pro-choice groups.

Overall, the evidence suggests some very mixed patterns of policy outcomes. Canadian political institutions do appear to offer some important advantages with respect to loss imposition that show up, to varying degrees, in table 10-2 in several sectors—indeed, in one of each of the four types of losses examined here: geographically diffuse (health care), business-oriented (tobacco control), geographically concentrated (military bases), and symbolic (gun control). But the similarity between Canadian and U.S. outcomes within the remaining individual sectors is at least equally striking.

INSTITUTIONAL DIFFERENCES

Chapter 1 introduced a rich array of hypotheses about the effects of political institutions on loss imposition. These hypotheses, and a summary of what the evidence in the case studies suggests about them, are summarized in table 10-3. Clearly the evidence provides support for many of these expectations, but the effects are often subtle and contingent rather than strong and universal.

Presidential vs. Westminster Parliamentary System

Our primary expectation was that the Westminster Canadian system would exhibit a greater capacity to impose losses than the United States presidential system, primarily but not exclusively because of (1) the concentration of authority in the executive and (2) greater party discipline. As noted above, four of our policy cases supported this hypothesis to varying degrees.

The strongest confirmation came with gun control. Gun control in Canada is stronger not because Americans reject gun control per se; there are many examples of state legislation, and opinion polls show a continuing shift toward support for more stringent controls, especially after a string of shootings in 1999. Indeed, some of the worst American gun-related massacres were the stimuli for gun control efforts in *both* countries, but these efforts succeeded more frequently north of

TABLE 10-3
Summary of Hypotheses and Research Findings on Political Institutions

Theoretical Expectation	U.S.–Canada Application	Research Findings
Presidential vs. Westminster Parliamentary System		
Combination of greater party discipline and concentration of power in Westminster system creates greater capacity for loss imposition than in separation-of-powers system, all other things being equal	Canadian federal government will be more capable of imposing losses on powerful interests than its U.S. counterpart	Party discipline in the Canadian House is a critical channel that enhances loss imposition capacity in Canada, giving interests less leeway for lobbying and working through individual politicians, except on rare "free" votes. When the Canadian government does take loss-imposing actions, it frequently does so as part of the federal budget, which undergoes limited debate and is always a party-line vote. Controversial measures can be partially buried in these big packages. There are some parallels in the U.S., but the typically much longer debate, multiple veto points, and weak party discipline make the budget a much less effective vehicle for loss-imposing actions in the United States. U.S. institutions give interests (e.g., in gun control) greater capacity to withstand surges in public opinion until an issue returns to low salience
Westminster party systems increase risk of reversal of loss-imposing actions when party in control of government changes	Canada is more likely to impose and later reverse losses on groups linked to a particular party when party control of the House changes than when legislative chamber control shifts in the U.S.	Change in party control of the legislature plays a weak role in leading to reversal of losses in Canada.
Concentration of accountability in Westminster systems partially offsets their advantages in loss imposition, especially as an election nears	Canada-U.S. differential in loss imposition capacity will be greatest immediately after elections; governments in both countries have diminished loss-imposition capacity as election nears	Governments in Canada frequently time initiatives for post-election period, but they do not always succeed (e.g., 1984–85 Old Age Security cuts). Government's heightened agenda control in Canada does give it greater capacity to keep divisive issues like abortion off the agenda

TABLE 10-3
Summary of Hypotheses and Research Findings on Political Institutions *(continued)*

Minority government in Westminster system lowers capacity for loss imposition	Governmental capacity for loss imposition in Canada will be lower than usual in periods of divided government	No data available
Divided government imposes further veto points and further weakens capacity of separation-of-powers system to impose losses over organized opposition	Governmental capacity for loss imposition in U.S. will be especially low in periods of divided government	Limited evidence suggests that tendency to gridlock in U.S. is strong even during rare periods of united government, but divided government may strengthen it further

Effective Bicameralism

Effective bicameralism provides additional veto points, making loss-imposing changes from the status quo less likely	Weaker check from Canadian Senate makes Canadian federal government more capable of imposing losses on powerful interests than its U.S. counterpart, especially in loss imposition concentrated on less populous provinces/states	Canadian Senate occasionally does act to prevent movement away from default position (e.g., on abortion), but plays much less active role in blocking change than its U.S. counterpart
Supermajority requirements in legislative chamber stifle loss-imposing initiatives and lead to increasing advantage for status quo policies	Supermajority requirements in U.S. Senate stifle loss imposition initiatives	Senate voting rules inhibit loss imposition in gun control, nuclear waste siting, abortion

Electoral Cycles

Longer electoral cycles provide greater window for loss imposition by government	Loss imposition in both U.S. and Canada will be concentrated immediately after elections; longer electoral cycles in Canada create greater capacity for loss imposition	Shorter electoral cycles in U.S. do undercut loss imposition capacity in some cases (e.g., gun control). But in both the tobacco and pension cases the potentially beneficial effects of the longer Canadian electoral cycle (generally four years for the House of Commons versus two years for the House of Representatives and one-third of the Senate in U.S.) are offset in some cases by the fact that Canadian federal politicians also pay more attention to provincial elections (especially in Quebec) and potential Quebec sovereignty referenda when making calculations about whether to take loss-imposing actions

TABLE 10-3
Summary of Hypotheses and Research Findings on Political Institutions *(continued)*

Courts

Nonelected judges will play a substantial role in loss-imposing actions because they do not fear electoral retribution	Lower capacity of U.S. executive and legislative institutions will be partially offset by more activist courts in U.S., but differential will decline in post-Charter era in Canada	The courts and nonelected judges play a very strong role in taking many of the strongest loss-imposing actions (e.g., on abortion and tobacco control) in *both* the U.S. and Canada. They serve as arbiters who cannot easily be overruled, sometimes reinforcing and sometimes overturning the status quo

Federalism

Political competition effects: Loss imposition is especially unlikely in cases where jurisdiction is subnational and potential loss sufferers can take valued activities elsewhere	May occur in either country	Not found in these cases because most involve substantial federal jurisdiction.
Passing-the-buck effects: (1) Where national government sets broad program parameters and shares funding responsibility with states/provinces, it may be able to force the latter to take blame for loss imposition, but (2) where jurisdiction is unclear, both federal and provincial/state governments may shirk from taking loss-imposing actions	May occur in either country; depends on jurisdictional structure in a particular policy sector	First type of passing-the-buck effect does occur in health care sector, especially in Canada.
Joint decision traps: Where loss-imposing actions require approval of both federal and provincial governments, capacity for loss imposition diminishes	Higher incidence of joint federal/provincial decision-making mechanisms in Canada will undercut loss imposition capacity more there	Joint decision traps appear most important in pensions, where they delayed but ultimately did not prevent payroll tax increases
Emulation effects: Where a state or provincial government takes a loss-imposing action and diffuse benefits become more obvious, other states or federal government may follow its lead	May occur in either country	Evidence limited by predominant federal jurisdiction in most policy sectors examined here, but evident in tobacco litigation in the United States. Collective investment in Canada Pension Plan also drew from Quebec experience

the border than south of it. As outlined in chapter 8, the number of national-level gun control initiatives in the United States exceeded Canada's, but such initiatives were more successful in Canada. The key reason is institutional and is consistent with the conventional wisdom concerning the Westminster system: Once cabinets were persuaded to initiate legislation, there was very little that anyone could do to stop them. To this must be added the clear jurisdiction that Ottawa has over guns through the criminal code and the regulatory powers tht flow from that jurisdiction. Opposition was evident in Canada as well, but it was stared down by the government, often by conveying the centrality of the legislation to the government's agenda (a way of implying that this was a confidence vote).

Institutional differences also play an important role in the greater capacity in Canada to impose losses that are evident in chapter 3 on health cuts and chapter 5 on tobacco control. Chapter 3 shows how cuts to health care funding were carried on the back of fiscal constraint. Despite clear control of the health care system coupled with cabinet authority, no Canadian government in the first two decades of Medicare would take the risk of imposing funding cuts. The fiscal pressures of the 1990s drove both levels of government to make cuts, and federal cuts gave the provinces a blame-avoiding excuse to make their own reductions. But Canada's single-payer health care financing system facilitated imposing losses on providers much more than the fragmented U.S. health care financing system—as did a federal system that facilitated "passing the buck" to the provinces to avoid blame.

Chapter 5 by Studlar on tobacco regulation echoes Tuohy (chapter 3) in arguing that Canada's greater regulatory effectiveness in imposing concentrated losses on the tobacco industry was due to the absence of the multiple veto points that impeded such initiatives in the United States. All serious regulatory and tax initiatives on tobacco in the U.S. have come from the executive branch or independent agencies, and Congress has consistently resisted them.

These cases both show, to varying degrees, a superior capacity on the part of the Canadian Westminster style system to impose losses. This capacity seems to vary over time and circumstances, however. Other chapters suggest that this theoretical capacity may be quite weak in practice, often because political will is lacking. With respect to high-level nuclear waste, Rabe argues in chapter 7 that the modestly greater capacity of the United States to impose losses in this area may be due to superior federal jurisdictional power in the environmental field coupled with the dynamics of the congressional system, in which localism frequently trumps party. These characteristics provided incentives to search out a single repository for a substance produced throughout the United States—"ganging up," as it were, on a single jurisdiction with very few elected representatives.

Westminster parliamentary institutions can also aid in loss imposition by constraining the ability of those who have lost from a policy decision to seek its reconsideration. Thus, while Tatalovich (in chapter 9) makes the case that outcomes on the abortion issue are varied, not exhibiting any one clear pattern, he argues forcefully that the parliamentary system in Canada did permit politicians, once loss was imposed on pro-life groups, to keep the issue off the legislative agenda in a way that was not possible in the United States.

Institutional differences between Canada and the U.S. are less important in other sectors, however, in part because the United States has developed mechanisms to work around institutional gridlock and in part because concentration of accountability in Canada frequently erodes politicians' willingness (if not their capacity) to impose losses. In the case of military base closings, for example, the United States seemed paralyzed throughout most of the 1970s and the 1980s despite the seeming necessity of cuts, but then in 1988 Congress devised the BRAC method and succeeded in selecting over 500 bases for closure or realignment. The "all or nothing" method ingeniously circumvented the extreme localism of base-closing decisions and allowed congressional representatives to oppose if they wished, safe in the knowledge that their opposition would not impede necessary action. The Canadian cabinet faced similar problems throughout the 1970s and 1980s with respect to closing bases, in large part because of the greater salience of regionalism and the important economic role of military bases in depressed parts of the country. Protests were remarkably effective in stalling the putative power of the cabinet, to the point that by 1992 the government was considering implementing a BRAC-like mechanism of its own. But the newly elected Liberals in 1993 flexed their full institutional muscle and announced major cuts in their first two budgets in 1994 and 1995. In this case, the cabinet's power was mobilized through a budgetary process that insisted that base closings were essential in order to deal with a fiscal crisis. In short, institutional capacity for loss imposition in Canada was strong, but it was utilized only when accompanied by political will, a blame-reducing budget procedure, the scapegoat of a budget crisis, and the longer political horizon available immediately after an election.

Our conclusion, therefore, with respect to the impact of concentration of executive authority and greater party discipline in the Westminster system must be cautious: These institutional features certainly have the potential to facilitate loss impositon given the right circumstances—such as political will (perhaps induced by some "crisis," or a large parliamentary majority) or clear constitutional jurisdiction. The gun control case and military base closings after 1993 illustrate this well. Even in these two "strong" cases, however, both the governing party caucus as an "internal opposition" and regional interests had considerable power to constrain loss imposition by cabinet. The abortion case shows the influence of caucus as well—though, as we note below, the defeat of Bill C-43 was due more to a rare display of effective bicameralism. In other instances of success, such as health cuts and some aspects of pensions, the advantages of the Westminster system had to be amplified by putative fiscal pressures or carried through as part of a budget process.

The United States presidential system has for the most part lived up to its theoretical predictions a bit more robustly than the Westminster system has: While the U.S. did display significant capacity for loss imposition in some eases, it was often fairly anemic. It was not that the United States system was incapable of imposing losses; it clearly has done so in military base closings, telecommunications deregulation, aspects of pensions and health care cuts, and, more ambiguously, in the case of nuclear waste siting. However, those impositions frequently required extraordinary circumstances, such as bipartisan agreement (e.g., gun control), or extraordinary mechanisms (e.g., the 1983 Social Security cuts and the BRAC). The multiple veto points and absence of strong party discipline in the United States system mean that there is a strong bias toward the status quo, while the permeability of the U.S. system permits much greater (if frequently fruitless) legislative lobbying and activity. Multiple veto points can have a critical impact on loss imposition in cases like gun control and tobacco control, where government initiatives are frequently fueled by waves of public revulsion against the industry (tobacco) or tragic shootings (guns). In Canada, governments have on several occasions acted in response to such waves of public sentiment, whereas in the U.S. the industries were able to stall and wait until public interest had declined, thereby avoiding loss-imposing actions. With respect to the potential for policy "flip-flops"—reversals of loss-imposing actions upon change of party control of the executive and/or legislature—the evidence in these case studies does not suggest that this is a serious or frequent problem in either country.

Overall, the findings from the case studies in this book make a case for reasonably robust institutional effects. But the effect of institutions is also contingent on other factors. In the case of Westminster parliamentary systems like Canada's, the central tendency—absent other factors—is concentration of authority and the institutional capacity to impose losses. If reinforcing variables are present—playing to Quebec, in the case of gun control; the absence of seats in western Canada, insofar as military base closings were concerned; and budgetary pressures, with respect to pensions and health care—politicians can be strongly reinforced to impose losses if they are so inclined. In the American case, the systemic tendency to loss diffusion is so strong that even an almost perfect alignment of factors that would reinforce loss imposition sometimes is not enough to alter policy outcomes (nuclear waste disposal).

Even these cautious conclusions about the effects of presidential/Westminster institutional differences should be interpreted carefully, moreover, because they are based on governing experience during a time period—roughly, 1980–2002, when minority government (which would be expected to weaken loss imposition capacity) was entirely absent in Ottawa. Moreover, in the period since 1993, the Liberal Party—like Margaret Thatcher in the U.K. for most of her time in office—faced such a weak and divided opposition that concentration of accountability was a much weakened barrier to loss imposition.

In the U.S., on the other hand, unified party control of the presidency and Congress (which would be expected to strengthen loss-imposing capacity) was present for only a little over two years (1993–94 under Clinton, three months under George W. Bush in 2001) during this period. And the first of those periods of united government featured a president elected with a plurality of the popular vote and narrow control of Congress, while George W. Bush did not even win a plurality of the popular vote. Overall, we cannot state definitively that the modest differences observed in institutional capacity are the result of the nature of the presidential and Westminster systems per se rather than of differences between their respective weak (divided, separation-of-powers government) and strong (majority, Westminster government with fragmented opposition) manifestations.

Effective Bicameralism

Effective bicameralism is another important source of the multiple veto points that characterize the United States system. While in principle the Canadian Senate is coequal to the House of Commons, in practice the fact that its members are appointed by the party in power and hence are almost as constrained by party discipline as are MPs means that only in rare instances (usually soon after a change in party control of the House, before the new prime minister has been able to fill enough Senate vacancies to give him or her a majority in the appointed chamber) does the Senate contradict the House. In the United States, of course, senators are separately elected for a six-year term and are less constrained by party discipline. To this must be added procedural rules that permit individual senators to effectively block legislation on the floor through filibusters that require a supermajority to overcome, along with seniority rules that give senators positions on and chairmanships of influential committees relevant to their regional interests.

The evidence from our chapters clearly upholds the theoretical expectation that the Canadian Senate is anemic in the extreme. Whereas in the United States the Senate is a key platform for various opponents of loss imposition, in Canada it is a negligible one. Of course, in a few cases such as abortion, the government found itself surprised that its own party members in the Senate turned against the government's legislation. As Tatalovich points out, this may have been due less to party disloyalty than to miscalculation. In other cases, such as gun control in the case of Bill C-68, Canadian Conservative senators broke ranks with their own party and helped the government's legislation along. The Canadian Senate played no role in pension reform, nuclear waste siting, tobacco control (Senator Kenny's bill on tobacco taxes was summarily defeated on a procedural motion in the House), telecommunications deregulation, health cuts, or military base closings.

The contrast with the United States could not be sharper. Party control in the House of Representatives and the U.S. Senate is looser than in the House of Commons, and so both chambers of the U.S. Congress have been important platforms from which interests opposed to a shift in the status quo have been able to exercise a veto. The American system is permeable enough that many more legislative proposals come forward to upset the status quo than is characteristic of Canada; abortion and gun control are good examples. It is simply harder to keep public issues off the agenda or completely out of sight in the United States. At the same time, the multiple hurdles that bills must clear on the way to enactment give numerous opportunities for American legislators to block bills that might impose losses.

The tobacco and military base closing cases also illustrate how American bicameralism helps geographically concentrated interests defend themselves. In both cases, the politics of localism meant that it was very difficult to impose losses through the legislative process in the U.S.; congressional reperesentatives and senators would fight for their constituents. Even though the Canadian Senate is supposed to be regionally representative, it provides no real opportunities for regionally affected groups to mount a defensive campaign against the executive.

Electoral Cycles

Opponents of loss imposition can try to punish, or threaten to punish, loss-imposing politicians at the ballot box. In theory, the longer an electoral cycle, the greater the opportunity for politicians to impose losses early in the cycle in the hopes that voters will forget their pain over time. The Canadian electoral cycle is generally four years in length and can be as long as five years. The election cycle is two years for the United States House of Representatives, six years for the Senate (on a staggered basis), and four years for the presidency. Our expectation was that shorter electoral cycles in the United States, combined with almost constant campaigning and hence constant pressure to raise funds and respond to constituents, would inhibit loss imposition. Possibly counteracting the longer electoral cycle in Canada is the possibility that politicians in Ottawa will be more sensitive to provincial elections because of nonsynchronized federal and provincial electoral cycles, and because of the importance of Quebec elections and referenda, whenever they are held. In the American case, the predicted hypersensitivity to the electoral cycle might be partially counterbalanced by the poor prospects faced by challengers in the vast majority of House districts.

The case studies generally suggest that longer electoral cycles do provide at least a modest advantage with respect to loss imposition. Canadian politicians, of course, keep their eye on the polls, and issues *are* debated in electoral campaigns. Moreover, loss-imposing initiatives frequently have been presented shortly after federal elections in a number of sectors in Canada, including health care, pensions, military base closings, and abortion. Nonsynchronized federal and provincial elections in Canada weaken some of the felicitous effects on governmental loss imposition capacity created by Canada's longer federal electoral cycle, but only on issues of high regional salience, especially respecting Quebec. Studlar points out in chapter 5 that there is no evidence of tobacco being an issue in federal election campaigns, but it was important in the 1994 Quebec provincial election, when the federal Liberals tried to help their beleaguered provincial cousins as they faced the voters. Weaver points out in chapter 2 that the Liberals were constrained in dealing quickly with pension reform in the same period owing to fears of a Parti Québécois victory in the 1994 Quebec provincial election and another referendum in 1995, as well as the 1997 federal election.

In the United States, short election cycles appear to have constrained politicians' willingness to impose losses as well as the timing of loss-imposing initiatives. But a short cycle per se may be less important than liberal campaign financing laws in the U.S. Campaign financing laws had an impact on the tobacco issue, for example, and reflected deeper institutional differences between the two countries. With virtually unlimited capacity to funnel money to potential supporters, U.S. tobacco interests were able to shore up the support they needed in Congress and use that institution as a bulwark against regulation and taxation. In Canada, stricter laws prohibit extensive financing of individual candidates. In any case, MPs have so little capacity to influence legislation that it would make little sense. Tatalovich makes the same point in chapter 9 with respect to abortion, as does Pal (in chapter 8) with respect to gun control: The weak campaign finance regime in the U.S. allows large interest groups, highly mobilized around symbolic issues, to funnel huge amounts of money into election campaigns.

Courts

Courts are important to loss imposition in two key ways. First, because superior judges (in the U.S., all federal judges and many state judges) are more insulated from voter retribution than politicians are, they can conceivably undertake more unpopular decisions and thereby impose losses. Second, because they can overturn decisions made in the other branches of government, they encourage opponents as well as proponents of loss imposition to try to achieve their goals through litigation. The Canadian situation is interesting, because adoption of the Charter of Rights and Freedoms in 1982 vastly expanded the potential scope of judicial review. Nevertheless, we might expect the courts to play a larger role in policymaking in the United States, because courts have generally been more deferential to legislatures in Canada.

One of the key findings of this study is the very substantial role of the courts in imposing and constraining loss imposition. And as noted in table 10-1, courts play a more important role in the United States. The role of the courts is highly variable across sectors, however. Tatalovich's chapter on abortion reveals some interesting dynamics of venue-switching with respect to courts. In both countries, pro-choice advocates became impatient with legislative attempts to relax abortion laws in the 1960s and went to the courts. Canada did not have a constitutional Charter of Rights at the time, and so Canadian litigation addressed the nuances of criminal law, whereas the U.S. arrived at a decision about fundamental rights in *Roe v. Wade* in 1973. The *Roe* decision led to a convoluted game wherein pro-life forces would lobby state governments to restrict the scope of the law, while pro-choice forces would fight those restrictions in the courts. In the Canadian case, the court was more uniformly pro-choice in its decisions, and the Canadian mechanism for health care funding made all provincial attempts to restrict abortion funding unsuccessful.

Tatalovich's chapter 9 also highlights the importance of courts in the general policy process in both countries. In the United States, the Supreme Court is more explicitly political in the sense that appointments are widely understood to have important ideological consequences and have to be confirmed by a majority vote in the Senate. The Court has swung through liberal and conservative phases and has engaged in loss impositions that would be difficult for elected politicians to accomplish. In Canada, there has been more debate recently about the ideological nature of Supreme Court decisions, but appointments to the bench are still made by the cabinet.

Courts played an important role in several of the cases discussed in this book, but a minimal role in others. In the cases of gun control, tobacco regulation, abortion, and (in the U.S. only) nuclear waste siting they were front and center. With respect to military base closings, opponents of the closure of the Philadelphia Naval Shipyards in 1991 took unusual steps to argue their case before the courts. In a typical example of venue-shifting, they tried in those cases and others to get the courts to agree that the BRAC procedure was unconstitutional. But this was unusual. In the abortion and gun control cases, the potential for litigation has hinged on alleged human rights violations. In the case of the successful tobacco suit, and the attempt to extend it to the firearms industry, it seems to be a case of trying to stretch concepts of product liability and negligence to cover a health and safety issue. The negligible role of the courts in the other sectors, such as pensions and health care, may have to do with governments having (or being perceived to have) clearer jurisdiction to manage and implement those programs and, thereby, impose losses if necessary.

The greater role of the courts in the United States is subject to two interpretations. The first is that if the courts in the United States were less activist, government would truly be paralyzed, with very limited capacity to impose losses. A contrasting interpretation is that given the weak capacity of the U.S. Congress to take on a loss-imposing role, that set of activities, which is likely to arise in any society, tends to flow to the "venue of least resistance." In the United States, with its tradition of adversarial legalism and relatively open and active courts, the political path of least resistance frequently leads up the courthouse steps. Thus, less activist courts in the United States, according to this understanding, would not necessarily lead to policy paralysis; rather, it might lead to the selection of another decision-making venue, or back to the legislature. Relying heavily on court-imposed loss imposition, however, is likely to lead to different outcomes than loss imposition imposed by legislatures. Because judges do not have to be re-elected, they are much more likely to rely on abstract principle and less likely to engage in compensation strategies for loss imposition. Hence, different loss-imposing venues in Canada and the U.S. are likely to lead to outcomes that are significantly different across the two countries in their incidence and scope if not in their overall magnitude.

Federalism

The introductory chapter noted that federalism may have several quite distinctive effects on loss imposition, ranging from a competitive "race to the bottom" to emulation effects, whereby successful loss imposition in one jurisdiction that proves popular with voters will be copied by others. As a result, theoretical expectations about the impact of federalism on loss imposition can be quite ambiguous.

Our case studies were selected to emphasize sectors wherein the federal government is a major if not dominant player, so it is not surprising that they show limited evidence of a race to the bottom. But many of the other hypothesized effects of federalism *do* appear. Weaver's chapter on pensions, for example, argues that high procedural barriers to loss imposition were evident in the CPP/QPP because of its decision-making structure. However, he also notes that these federal arrangements allowed for quick action once a near-consensus on change among federal and provincial government executives was reached. One type of "passing the buck"—the national government compelling state or provincial governments to undertake loss-imposing actions for which the latter are likely to take most of the blame—is visible mostly in the health care sector. Reasons why this effect appears to be limited in practice are discussed in more detail in the "strategies" section below.

The gun control, abortion, and tobacco cases represent cases where *venue-shifting* is evident. In the abortion case in both countries, losses were imposed at the national level, and opponents rapidly shifted to the subnational level, where there was still some jurisdictional leverage. They enjoyed limited success in the United States but failed in Canada, where the courts repeatedly struck down provincial attempts at restricting abortion access or funding. In the case of tobacco controls, a weak regulatory system and low taxes were imposed at the national level in the United States, so supporters of controls shifted their attention to the state level, where they enjoyed significant successes. It was those successes that led to emulation in trying to get states to pass more significant gun control legislation, and indeed to adopt a similar litigation strategy against gun manufacturers. The twist in the Canadian experience with gun control is that losses were imposed at the national level, and so opponents of loss, rather than proponents, sought support from the provinces—primarily the western provinces—which were in noncompliance vis-à-vis implementing the new law, and from appeals to the court.

The institutional impact of federalism is sometimes hard to separate from the political impact of regionalism, which is discussed later in this chapter. Both countries are federations, but their institutional arrangements channel regional political forces in different ways. In the American case, regional interests are expressed directly in national institutions, primarily through the Senate. In Canada, though the Senate was designed to do much the same thing, it lacks any credibility as a forum for regional representation. That role has, instead, been absorbed by the provinces, and is one ingredient in the Canadian practice of executive federalism (direct negotiations between federal and provincial political executives). In some instances the federal government's capacity to impose losses (e.g., gun control) was impeded or compromised by the need to negotiate with the provinces. In other cases, such as increases in contribution rates for the CPP/QPP, federal-provincial agreements reached behind closed doors provided a powerful impetus to policy decisions.

Indeed, American states rarely act in concert in the way that Canadian provinces do. In Canada, there are a host of mechanisms to facilitate provincial coordination in making policy proposals to Ottawa; recent demands for increased health care funding are a prime example. American states can and do deviate from or resist federal policies, but despite the existence of coordinating bodies like the National Governors Association, their actions tend to be disaggregated and only loosely coordinated. This is clear with respect to abortion rights: States have collectively succeeded in rolling back some rights and services, but they have done so for their own reasons and not as part of a coordinated response. A partial exception is the case of tobacco, where it was state attorneys general, with their own electoral base, who drove the legal settlement with the companies.

TYPES OF LOSS

What is most striking in looking at individual policy sectors is how similar the politics—and frequently the outcomes—are on both sides of the Canada–U.S. border. We began with several expectations about the politics of imposing different types of losses, and how those might play out in terms of cross-border differences in outcomes. For example, the high salience of regional cleavages in Canada might make it especially responsive to geographically concentrated protests and representations. The United States was expected to provide more opportunities than Canada for business to resist loss imposition, partly because of the greater permeability of congressional institutions and partly because of the wider array of institutional "venues" to which those seeking to avoid losses can appeal. And losses that are primarily symbolic or value-based, because they are more resistant to pragmatic trade-offs (e.g., grandfathering or some form of compensation), might be particularly hard to impose in the United States, where multiple veto points tend to favor the policy status quo and groups can use those veto points to prevent policy change.

Our theoretical expectation that (1) it would be more difficult for governments to impose geographically concentrated losses than geographically diffuse ones, and (2) this would be especially true in Canada, were only weakly supported. In the end, both countries had about as much success in closing military bases as they did in cutting pensions and health care costs. (Of course, the Americans had to devise a new mechanism to avoid blame in closing military bases, whereas the Canadians took advantage of a fiscal crisis and an extremely weak parliamentary opposition after 1993.) Both countries failed miserably at nuclear waste siting, Canada slightly more so. Our cases did not include sectors where specific regional grievances in Canada are especially salient (e.g., language in Quebec, energy in western Canada, employment and fisheries in the Atlantic provinces). But in those sectors, we would expect that differences in issue salience between the two countries would make it difficult to draw any generalizable conclusions.

Our expectation that imposing losses on business would be more difficult in the U.S. than in Canada was only partially supported. Both tobacco control and telecommunications deregulation demonstrate that imposing losses on business interests is indeed difficult but far from impossible. The Canadian government was more successful in imposing losses in the tobacco case but not telecommunications. Overall, outcomes seem to depend less on some abstract power that business wields in a capitalist economy than on the institutional and political configurations faced by these interests within their specific sector and their linkage to other salient issues, and in the institutional venue opportunities confronting business interests and their opponents. For example, tobacco interests in Canada were best able to resist and even turn back control measures when they could bundle their issue with a cluster of others more salient to Ottawa. As long as it was a matter of health, they usually lost. When they could tie tobacco to law and order, treatment of Aboriginals, and Quebec, as they did during the smuggling episodes in the mid-1990s, they had a chance—particularly during an election year. In the United States, tobacco interests were aided by their geographical concentration and the existence of election campaign financing laws that allowed them to spend large amounts of money on political supporters in Congress. Significant losses were eventually imposed on tobacco interests in the U.S. as well, although it was primarily through a litigation strategy spearheaded by the states—a venue opportunity more available in the U.S. than in Canada.

Two symbolic issues, abortion and gun control, also provide mixed support for our expectations that losses of this type might be especially hard to impose in the United States. This proved to be true in the case of gun control, in abortion only with regard to financing. Rather than generalizing across cases of value-oriented losses, it seems more appropriate to note that Canada showed greater capacity for loss imposition (1) where interest organizations were primarily on one side of a divide rather than two interests were organized against one another, as in the abortion case, and (2) where policy is made primarily in legislatures rather than courts.

Overall, our four-fold typology of loss impositions proved more useful as a device to spark thinking about the tasks and strategies needed to impose losses in a particular sector than in explaining governmental capacity for loss imposition. The two cases within each category of loss imposition generally showed only limited similarities in success of loss imposition (table 10-2). Within the value-oriented and business-oriented categories, there was as much variation between the two cases as we saw across categories of losses.

CONFOUNDING VARIABLES

As we pointed out in the introduction to this volume, our attempts in the previous pages to arrive at conclusions about governmental and institutional capacities to impose losses assume that we can draw a direct causal line from institutional arrangements through institutional capacity for loss imposition to outcomes. Differences in outcomes, however, may in fact be the result of other, confounding variables that are overlooked or underplayed in this simple causal model. We highlighted five such categories of variables in our introduction—policy legacies, globalization, emulation, cleavage structures, and political culture and ideas—and asked authors to address them explicitly or implicitly as they worked through their cases. We outline the expected and actual impact of these variables in table 10-4.

"Policy legacies" simply refers to the fact that government decisions today are made against the backdrop and effect of government decisions made yesterday or years ago. As one moves down a decision path, therefore, it becomes harder and harder to simply reverse direction, and less possible to avoid incorporating some aspects or inheritances of those past decisions into current ones. Legacies of this type can come in the form of institutional decision-making mechanisms or specific program features; we saw strong evidence in some of the cases for the impact of legacies of both these types. In the health care for the elderly and pensions cases, for example, crucial decisions were made in both countries in the 1950s and 1960s regarding how services and benefits would be structured and how governments and the private sector would come to decisions about future program changes. In chapter 3 Tuohy points out that in the case of health care for the elderly, the two systems are closer than is often thought, but that nonetheless the broader systems are fundamentally different in that the United States decided early on to distinguish between public and private financing in terms of population groups, while in Canada that distinction was decided on the basis of services. Retrenchment and loss-imposition strategies in the 1990s were powerfully affected by these legacies. Weaver's chapter on pensions points out that the United States system dominated by Social Security (a contributory system financed by payroll taxes), with a small role for the means-tested Supplementary Security Income, created a set of policy challenges and political opportunities for loss imposition substantially different from the three-tiered Canadian system combining universal benefits through Old Age Security, an income-tested benefit through the Guaranteed Income Supplement, and an earnings-related one through the Canada Pension Plan.

Legacies were also evident in other sectors. In the case of gun control, Canadian efforts to impose losses through the Firearms Act were considerably easier because of earlier legislative initiatives to license firearms and impose a regulatory regime based on criminal law. American abortion politics was powerfully affected by the Supreme Court's 1973 decision in *Roe v. Wade*. In the nuclear waste siting case, the failure of regulators to put a disposal regime in place before initial plant licensing, relying instead on the hope of some future technological fix, meant that when the problem was finally addressed, it was of enormous dimensions. Even in those cases where policy legacies were clearly critical, however, important institutional effects were often at play as well.

The impact of globalization in terms of loss imposition is that we might expect the more vulnerable polity—in this case—Canada's, to be more acutely pressured by global forces tending toward integration and harmonization of standards, as well as greater mobility of people and capital. This greater vulnerability might lead to instances of more vigorous loss imposition, since the more vulnerable the polity and economy, the less choice government has in responding to these forces. The United States, because of its size, might be able to afford to ignore these pressures, at least temporarily.

The evidence in our cases for a globalization effect, however, is slim. As noted in the introductory chapter, the cases selected for examination here excluded sectors where the pressures for policy harmonization are most direct, so they may not accurately reflect the strength of such pressures. In our cases, globalization effects may have been evident indirectly in the health care, pensions, and military base closing cases through the fiscal pressures that the Canadian federal government found itself facing and to which it responded with sudden alacrity after 1993. There were also some spillover effects in the cases of tobacco (smuggling between Canada and the United States) and gun control. But there is no strong evidence that Canada, apart from its fiscal exposure to international financial markets, faced disproportionate

TABLE 10-4
Summary of Hypotheses and Research Findings on Confounding Variables

Theoretical Expectation	U.S.–Canada Application	Research Findings
Policy Legacies		
Policies in place that (1) facilitate use of blame-avoiding strategies by governments and (2) put in place "action-forcing mechanisms" will lead to more loss imposition	Country- and sector-specific policy legacies will overwhelm effects of Canada–U.S. institutional differences with respect to governmental capacity and policy outcomes	Policy feedbacks, and in particular whether current policies facilitate blame-avoiding strategies and provide action-forcing mechanisms, play an important role in determining outcomes in both countries, but they interact with rather than overwhelm institutional differences
Globalization		
Global economic integration (1) makes it more costly to impose losses on mobile capital and (2) shields domestic social interests from the costs imposed by global trends	Governments in both countries will have weak leverage to impose losses on business or to compensate domestic losers from economic integration, but greater trade dependence means that this will be especially true in Canada	Trans-border pressures pose some constraints on governmental action (e.g., the potential for cigarette smuggling lowers the capacity to raise cigarette taxes in Canada), but these pressures are generally not determinative in the cases examined here
Smaller countries will increasingly find it difficult to pursue policies that deviate from those of their major trading partners	Canadian decisions that impose greater losses on powerful domestic interests than in the U.S. may be the result less of strong political institutions than of stronger pressures for harmonization	Limited evidence of direct pressures for policy harmonization, but this may be the result of case selection. Possible evidence of indirect pressures for lower social expenditures through pressures to limit taxes and lower budget deficits

TABLE 10-4
Summary of Hypotheses and Research Findings on Confounding Variables *(continued)*

Emulation

Countries emulate policies in other countries—especially neighboring or "peer" countries—that appear to be successful

As a result of emulation, especially on the Canadian side, Canada–U.S. policies will tend toward convergence that masks institutional differences

Policymakers in Canada are more aware of policy proposals and outcomes in the U.S. than vice versa, but the process is more often one of lesson-drawing and adaptation to domestic environment than of direct emulation

Cleavage Structures

Loss imposition initiatives that exacerbate sensitive social cleavages will be more difficult to accomplish

Strength and sensitivity of regional cleavages in Canada will make imposing region-specific losses more difficult than in the U.S., especially where Quebec is involved

Region-specific loss imposition in Canada does sometimes pose obstacles, even in unexpected sectors (e.g., tobacco control), but there do not appear to be systematic cross-national differences in capacity to impose region-specific losses. However, aboriginal issues also pose unexpected obstacles in some cases (tobacco, nuclear waste, gun control) in Canada

Political Culture and Ideas

Loss imposition initiatives that can be portrayed by opponents as inconsistent with dominant national values will have more trouble getting on agenda and winning adoption than those that are, or are seen as, consistent

Stronger resistance in U.S. to taxation and direct governmental intervention provides more resources to U.S. interests resisting those sorts of loss imposition mechanisms than in Canada

Opponents of loss imposition can draw on anti-tax sentiment among the American public and (especially) Republican politicians to block initiatives that involve higher taxes in cases such as pension reform and tobacco control. Group rights (e.g., for aboriginal peoples and women) play a larger role in Canada than the U.S.

pressures to respond to globalization or integration and trade with the United States. Canadian policy and policy dynamics around abortion, gun control, pensions, health, tobacco, and nuclear waste have been quite distinct from those in the United States, and there is no good reason to assume that they will converge any time soon. The determining factors here seem to be policy legacies and institutional arrangements.

With respect to emulation effects, as expected, Canadian policymakers seem to be more aware of developments to their south than vice versa. But that does not mean that the mechanisms and policies chosen were the same. School shootings in the U.S., for example, seem to have had a greater effect in Canada than in the United States. Canadian policymakers were aware of the success of base-closing commissions in facilitating cutbacks in defense infrastructure in the United States, but ultimately decided to use a more direct process for instituting their own cuts. And Canadian policymakers were certainly aware of U.S. debates on whether to collectively invest Social Security funds in equities (as well as of Quebec's experience in doing so), but they were able to move forward on the issue while the U.S. was not. Rather than being a matter of direct policy emulation, then, this process is perhaps better characterized as one of lesson-drawing and adaptation in light of domestic policy inheritances and political realities.

"Cleavage structures" refer to the structure of social divisions and social organization in the two countries, primarily revolving around region and language, which may raise the cost of imposing losses in one country (where such divisions are salient), but not in the other. In the Canadian case, of course, language is much more salient as a cleavage and it increasingly tends to be synonymous with the place and role of Quebec, reinforcing the regional dimension in Canadian politics. Overall, regional cleavages appear to have had a greater salience in Canada than in the United States, despite the American adage that "all politics is local." The base closings issue clearly shows both the sharper salience of regionalism in the Canadian political system and the special role of the Quebec-versus-Rest-of-Canada dimension. Any closures that affected Quebec were dealt with more gingerly by the government because of the implications for national unity. The closures of western bases were, by contrast, dealt with expeditiously because the region had historically been anti-Liberal and because, by happy circumstance, key bases were in opposition ridings. Nonetheless, PEI was able to mobilize compensation from Ottawa, possibly on the strength of the argument that eastern regions and provinces were especially vulnerable.

Obviously regionalism and localism are important in America, but with fifty states, a much more regionally dispersed population, and no convergence of territory and language, there is no American equivalent of Quebec. The "Quebec factor" was important in all the Canadian cases except telecommunications and nuclear waste disposal and had no parallel in the United States. Making an appeal to regional grievance (especially Quebec grievance) was most often used as a tool by those trying to avoid or reverse losses by enlisting additional allies on a regional basis. But there were exceptions: Gun control was powerfully driven by the Lépine massacre *and* by Quebec public opinion, which was highly supportive of tighter regulations.

Our final category of confounding variables is political culture and ideas. The stereotypical differences between Canada and the United States are, of course, an allegedly greater support for both social order and governmental intervention in Canada, less resistance to taxation, and perhaps a less strident culture of "individual rights." Here the argument is that under these conditions, Canadian governments may find it easier to impose losses because the public is generally more supportive of strong governmental action, so that differences in outcomes that might at first glance appear to be caused by institutional differences between the two countries in fact have cultural or ideological roots.

There were indeed some sharp differences in policy discourse between the two countries, though not always in the expected direction. Women's rights, for example, as a collective or group right were invisible in the United States debate over gun control but quite important in Canadian discussions. The same was true with respect to aboriginal rights, which were salient in the Canadian gun control debate but not in the American one. The ideological capacity to argue, with some plausibility, a "right to bear arms" in the United States is simply absent in the Canadian gun control case.

Tax aversion did seem to play a role in the United States pensions debate, but not a significant one in Canada. But of greater importance, we would argue, is that political culture did not appear in any of our cases to be a determining factor in policy outcomes. Gun control, apart from the differences mentioned above, is argued in very similar terms in the United States as in Canada. The same is true with respect to abortion. These were the policy fields most susceptible to cultural or ideational factors, because they represented symbolic loss imposition; there were no major differences in the other policy fields. This suggests that cultural differences between the two countries, while they exist, are sometimes exaggerated as an influence on policy when compared with institutional factors. It also suggests the possibility of greater convergence on core values of government, individual rights, and markets. Our point is twofold. First, even under conditions of ideological or cultural convergence, some differences will remain, and these will affect policy and loss imposition. But second, "convergence" refers only to averages or means. There can still be substantial differences within each political community around the average—differences, moreover, that are quite similar in their patterns, but that get reflected differently in policy outcomes because of different institutional configurations. As Pal argued in chapter 8 on gun control, it is clear that American public opinion (or political culture) is just as divided over gun control as is Canada's, but American gun control opponents have had considerable institutional resources at their disposal to stop the yearly tide of gun control measures that are introduced in Congress.

STRATEGIES

Most politicians will be reluctant most of the time, irrespective of institutional system or policy type, to impose losses, for fear of antagonizing voters, supporters, regions, or classes. In keeping with this reluctance, politicians will usually try to reduce hide the losses they impose, or reduce their impact, by using strategies that manipulate procedures, perceptions, and payoffs so as to achieve their policy objectives while minimizing blame and political retribution. The case studies richly illustrate the diversity of strategies used by politicians and other interested parties to reconcile their political and policy interests. Table 10-5 provides a very rough summary of the principal strategies used by proponents and opponents of loss imposition in the two countries, in approximately declining order of importance, in each case.

Three primary patterns emerge from the table. First, the strategies used by loss imposers and loss avoiders within each sector are generally quite similar across countries. Second, the case studies also clearly show that opportunities and payoffs for using specific loss imposition strategies differ strongly across sectors: Sectoral characteristics (for example, whether losses are geographically concentrated or dispersed) are a much better predictor of the strategic options that will be employed than country. Third, where the two countries do differ in the strategies employed within a single sector, these differences appear to be strongly affected both by the structure of their respective political institutions and by the legacy of past policy choices in that sector.

Strategies to Facilitate Loss Imposition

MANIPULATING PROCEDURES

The introductory chapter for this volume outlines several ways in which politicians and their allies can manipulate procedures so as to facilitate loss imposition: *insulation* (delegating loss imposition to other institutions, such as commissions or courts), *passing the buck* (setting out the broad parameters of losses to be imposed while forcing other political actors to make the detailed choices), and *agenda limitation*.

Our cases showed instances of all of these techniques. The BRAC method and the attempt to replicate it in Canada in the early 1990s clearly combined aspects of all three techniques: Legislators were implicated in setting up the process and defining its overall objectives, but they could point to another, independent body as the source of detailed recommendations, and the ratification process limited the agenda so as to prevent those recommendations from either being overturned outright or suffering the "death of a thousand nicks." As noted in the discussion of decision-making venues that opened this chapter, utilizing special budget procedures that insulate decision makers and limit the agenda are used in both countries—although more frequently and with greater success in Canada. The courts clearly serve as insulated decision-making venues with respect to abortion in both countries—though as much by accident as by design. Both countries rely extensively as well on "experts" to guide decision making. Reliance on experts is an unavoidable feature of policymaking in complex political systems over complex issues, but it is clear that politicians often seek to insulate themselves from criticism by turning issues over to experts and thereby casting the decision-making process as technical rather than political. Nuclear waste siting in both countries, though to a greater extent in Canada, has reflected this dynamic.

Passing the buck was used in relatively few cases other than base closings in the U.S.—perhaps most notably in the case of health care retrenchment in Canada. The reason is that it requires an institutional structure that simultaneously allows politicians to (1) set the overall parameters for losses, (2) delegate responsibility to another body for setting out the details of those losses, and (3) credibly avoid culpability for imposing those losses. In areas where the national government has clear jurisdiction, such as military bases in both countries or guns in Canada, it is difficult if not impossible to blame other political actors. In areas like health care in the Canadian case, on the other hand, Ottawa could make cuts in transfers to the provinces, which would then in turn have to impose those losses directly on citizens through cuts to the provincial health system. Indeed, the failure of Congress to renew the base-closing mechanism (or fast-track trade negotiation authority) in the United States after 1995 in the wake of extremely high mistrust between President Clinton and the Republican congressional majority shows just how fragile such mechanisms are likely to be in the United States. Congress is reluctant to create such mechanisms with "presumed perpetuity," so they are very vulnerable to falling by the wayside when they come up for renewal, especially if those insulated bodies or procedures have resulted in unpopular actions, or if Congress and the president are of different parties.[3]

MANIPULATING PERCEPTIONS

The introductory chapter also suggested that potential loss imposers may try to alter *perceptions* by employing such strategies as *obfuscation* (hiding losses in technical language), *finding a scapegoat, circling the wagons* (trying to achieve an all-party consensus before an initiative is announced), or *redefining the issue* (changing the way an issue is perceived so as to enlist new allies). The pensions case is a good example of decisions such as changes in benefit formulas being couched in obscure, highly technical terms. The same was true with respect to cuts to health benefits for the elderly in the United States.

Circling the wagons occurred in several cases, but its utility as a technique for avoiding blame is probably limited. It requires normally competitive political actors to collude in presenting a united front, and thereby a fait accompli. The best instance of this technique was in the case of pensions in Canada, where the federal and provincial governments agreed on revisions to CPP/QPP and carried them forward. The steadfast congressional support for a single nuclear waste site in the United States might also be seen as an example of this technique. The scapegoating technique was evident in virtually every case. Loss-imposing politicians continuously underscored their reluctance to impose pain by pointing to various factors that made the pain unavoidable: court decisions in the case of abortion), a fiscal crisis (pensions, health, military base closings), or civil disorder (tobacco smuggling). A classic illustration was President Clinton's acceptance "with reluctance" of the 1995 base-closing commission's recommendations. Clinton denounced those recommendations as "an outrage," but noted that he had to accept all or nothing and that "the overwhelming national security interest in reducing our base structure in line with the personnel reductions already taken" compelled him to go along."[4]

TABLE 10-5
Strategic Choices Utilized by Loss Imposers and Loss Avoiders (In declining order of importance)

Policy Sector	Loss-Imposing Strategies		Loss-Avoiding Strategies	
	U.S.	Canada	U.S.	Canada
Pensions	• Insulation and agenda limitation (through use of omnibus budget legislation) • Obfuscation (through highly technical changes to benefits) • Insulation and circling the wagons (through 1982–83 special commission) • Exemption (of current retirees from cutbacks) • Concentration (of cutbacks on upper-income recipients) • Scapegoating (fiscal and demographic crises)	• Insulation and agenda limitation (through use of budget legislation) • Obfuscation (through highly technical changes to benefits) • Insulation and circling the wagons (through federal-provincial negotiations) • Exemption (of current retirees from cutbacks) • Concentration (of cutbacks on upper-income recipients) • Scapegoating (fiscal and demographic crises)	• Concentrating blame	• Concentrating blame
Health	• Obfuscation • Insulation and agenda limitation (through use of omnibus budget legislation) • Scapegoating (fiscal crisis and providers)	• Insulation and agenda limitation (through use of budget legislation) • Obfuscation • Passing the buck (to provinces and special sub-provincial boards) • Scapegoating (fiscal crisis and providers)	• Redefine the issue (as cutting health care so as to finance tax cuts for the wealthy)	• Redefine the issue (as national government arrogance, and in Ontario as minority language rights)
Telecommunications	• Insulation (through use of regulatory commissions and courts)	• Insulation (through use of regulatory commissions and courts)	• Venue-shifting (to courts)	• Venue-shifting (to cabinet)
Tobacco control	• Redefining the issue (as one of corporate misconduct)	• Redefining the issue (as one of corporate misconduct)	• Redefining the issue (as one of excessive taxation)	• Redefining the issue (of tobacco taxation as a regional and law-and-order issue)

TABLE 10-5
Strategic Choices Utilized by Loss Imposers and Loss Avoiders
(In declining order of importance) *(continued)*

Policy Sector	Loss-Imposing Strategies		Loss-Avoiding Strategies	
	U.S.	Canada	U.S.	Canada
Nuclear waste siting	• Passing the buck (to technical bodies charged with identifying sites) • Concentration (of costs on Nevada)	• Insulation (by passing the buck to expert bodies)	• Venue-shifting (to courts) • Redefining the issue (as risk of transporting waste to final storage site)	
Military base closings	• Passing the buck, insulation, and agenda limitation (through special commissions and procedures for ratifying their decisions)	• Insulation and agenda limitation (through use of budget legislation)	• Redefining the issue (as regional grievance) • Venue-shifting (to the courts) • Concentrating blame • Cutting off the camel's nose (by arguing that allowing some base closings would open the way to additional ones)	• Redefining the issue (as regional grievance) • Concentrating blame • Cutting off the camel's nose (by arguing that allowing some base closings would open the way to additional ones)
Gun control	• Redefining the issue (as one of safety) • Venue-shifting (to state legislatures and courts)	• Redefining the issue (as one of safety and violence against women)	• Venue-shifting (to courts) • Redefining the issue (as one of safety from crime)	• Venue-shifting (to provincial implementers) • Redefining the issue (as one of regional grievance and aboriginal rights)
Abortion	• Insulation (through delegation to courts)	• Insulation (through delegation to courts)	• Venue-shifting (to Congress and state legislatures) • Redefining the issue (as one of fetal rights) • Cutting off the camel's nose (by resisting any compromise on abortion restrictions) • Concentrating blame	• Venue-shifting (to Parliament, provincial legislatures, and hospital abortion committees) • Redefining the issue (as one of fetal rights)

MANIPULATING PAYOFFS

We noted four broad strategies for manipulating payoffs in order to facilitate loss imposition: *dispersion* (spreading losses so as to reduce their incidence), *compensation* (partial offsetting of losses), *exemption* (removing troublesome subcategories of losers), and *concentration* (deliberately targeting losses on groups that are least able to resist or least likely to be viewed sympathetically by others). All four strategies were richly documented in the case studies.

Dispersion involves either spreading the loss over a larger group in order to reduce the individual incidence of that loss or spreading the losses over time, perhaps by phasing them in. Dispersion over a large group was not a prominent feature of our cases. The simultaneous closure of several military bases and the imposition of loss on health groups in the tobacco case were the clearest illustrations. Somewhat surprisingly, politicians did not shrink from targeting losses as much as might have been expected. In the pensions case, for example, cuts were concentrated on high-income earners and immigrants. The cases of gun control (in Canada only) and nuclear waste siting (in the U.S. only) showed politicians to be quite willing to focus pain on specific groups. In other words, concentration techniques seemed to be preferred to dispersion techniques, with the exception of dispersion over time. Losses in the gun control and pensions cases, for example, were softened by gradually phasing them in. This was often complemented by exemption strategies such as the grandfathering of current pension beneficiaries or current owners of guns. Compensation techniques were also evident in two cases—tobacco and military base closings—quite possibly because of the impact of these losses on regional economies.

Some patterns emerged from the cases. For example, compensatory techniques are of limited use, though not impossible of application, in symbolic or value-based losses. Gun control, while a highly emotive issue, also lends itself to a wide range of policy instruments and interventions covering gun owners, equipment, and use. Abortion, on the other hand, while it is distinguished by a range of possible interventions with respect to funding and services, is less malleable, because an abortion is all or nothing. As well, compensatory techniques tended to be used in our cases in instances were the loss being imposed (closing a military base or cutting tobacco funding to arts groups) removed a current benefit that could plausibly be seen to be a key factor in the support or sustenance of a group or a region.

Strategies to Avoid or Reverse Loss Imposition

Like loss-imposing strategies, strategies to avoid or reverse losses can be divided into three broad categories: manipulating *procedures*, to increase the height and/or number of hurdles to loss imposition; manipulating *perceptions*, to increase the efficacy of blame-generating efforts against those who imposed losses or acquiesced in them; and manipulating *payoffs*, so that losses are lessened or made bearable for your own group (and possibly others).

Some strategies to avoid losses are simply the reverse of strategies to impose losses. There is one important difference between loss-imposing and loss-avoiding strategies, however. In most loss-imposition scenarios, it is politicians who are considering a policy proposal that will impose losses on some group or constituency who make the first move. They are aware in advance, therefore, of who might be affected and how they might respond; hence, they will likely build some loss-imposition strategies into their proposals at the outset. In this respect, those seeking to avoid losses (or to reverse a loss once it has been imposed) will likely be responding simultaneously to both the loss imposition and to some strategies that have been embedded in it to blunt opposition. We need to keep this in mind—because, in principle, a loss-imposing proposal that is packaged with a sufficient array of compensating or targeting strategies may not generate much visible opposition at all.

MANIPULATING PROCEDURES

In the introductory chapter, we identified venue-shifting (trying to shift policy decision making to more favorable venues) and maximizing accountability (trying to ensure that decisions in existing venues will be taken in an open manner, so as to facilitate blame-generating) as key strategies of this type. The case studies suggest that venue-shifting is a preeminent loss-avoiding strategy. There are several reasons for this. It is always better to try to stop a policy decision before it has gone into effect and become the new "default position"; venue-shifting can often accomplish this. Moreover, elections may be far off and incumbents solidly entrenched, so threatening dire electoral consequences to loss imposers may be an empty threat. Under these circumstances, potential losers have to harness institutional power that is equal to or at least close to that of the politicians imposing the loss.

Courts emerged in our case studies as a key alternative venue, wherein potential losers can argue their case and, with luck, get a decision that supports them and turns back the loss. We saw this in the cases on tobacco in Canada, where companies went to court and won in 1995; in telecommunications, where companies on both sides of the border unsuccessfully sought relief in the courts; in gun control and abortion; and with respect to military base closings and nuclear waste siting in the United States. Another instance of venue-shifting involves losing at one level of government in a federal system but then trying to enlist support from state or provincial governments; this pattern was clearest in the gun control and abortion cases. Jurisdictional divisions in both countries mean that substantial rearguard actions can be fought at the other level of government. We should note that in Canada, this venue-shifting to the provincial level with regard to gun control and abortion was unsuccessful, largely because those efforts were then stymied by court decisions that upheld the original policy decision.

Manipulating procedures to maximize accountability is less evident in these case studies, although for somewhat different reasons in the two countries. In the United States, standard operating procedures already in place in the legislative process focus a high degree of accountability on individual politicians. In this hyperaccountable system, there frequently is not much that opponents of loss imposition initiatives can do to increase accountability further. In the Canadian system, on the other hand, legislators are shielded from individual blame by party discipline, but they may nevertheless face blame and electoral retribution for supporting those party positions. The governing party normally has such a high degree of control over decision-making procedures, however, that those who are trying to resist loss imposition rarely have the leverage to force a parliamentary "free vote" or other change in order to maximize accountability for individual politicians.

MANIPULATING PERCEPTIONS

Forces trying to avoid losses may also try to manipulate perceptions in order to meet their objectives. Several strategies are available, including *concentrating blame* for the loss imposition on those politicians who are most vulnerable and making those cuts seem unnecessary or capricious, and *redefining the issue* in ways that are disadvantageous to the loss imposers (e.g., by widening the scope of groups that perceive themselves as losers in order to build broader alliances). Our cases show that concentrating blame is particularly useful in cases like Social Security reform in the U.S., where elections are frequent, simple negative messages (e.g., on the risk of privatization) can be broadcast, and legislators are not protected from voters' wrath by claims that "party discipline made me do it" The wide-open and decentralized system of campaign finance in the U.S. also facilitates concentrating blame in issues such as abortion and gun control.

Redefinition of the issue was used even more frequently in the telecommunications case, where existing quasi-monopolies tried to argue that deregulation would negatively affect consumers and the integrity of a universal system. Opponents of nuclear waste disposal in Nevada focused on the potential hazards from terrorists and the possibility of accidents when transporting wastes from and across many other states. In the case of gun control, the National Rifle Association has perennially rejected defining the issue in terms of safety in favor of rights, and abortion foes have struggled to define the issue in terms of the life of the fetus rather than the rights of the mother. As noted earlier, increased efforts to redefine issues in terms of violated rights and a growing litigiousness around rights in both countries (although in Canada this has a group rights dimension as well) are closely connected with a strategy of venue-shifting the issue to the courts in hopes of a favorable decision.

MANIPULATING PAYOFFS

As noted earlier, strategies that involve manipulating payoffs may not be workable in all loss-imposition cases, particularly ones involving rights or symbolic losses. We did see, however, that loss imposers frequently use strategies such as compensation, phased implementation of losses, and exemption to reduce opposition. We saw in the military base closing cases that losing communities would often demand financial compensation or the relocation of other government offices.

Arguing that the government's strategy was the camel's nose was most notable in the gun control and military base closing cases. In the case of military base closings, affected communities in Canada tried to coalesce to maximize their opposition, but with limited success once Ottawa was determined to make cuts. And as pro-choice forces have moved into a defensive posture in the United States, they too have generally resisted any compromise on abortion rights issues (e.g., with respect to parental notification and restrictions on certain types of late-term abortion procedures). The frequency of "camel's nose" strategies in the abortion and gun control policy sectors reflects the rights-based nature of policy discourse in those sectors and the intensity of polarization among policy activists.

In the introductory chapter, we raised the question of whether certain types of strategies of loss avoidance might be more typical of one political system than the other. Based on the empirical cases in this book, we can offer several observations. First, it would appear that venue-shifting is a more widely available and utilized strategy in the United States, simply because of the greater variety and leverage of veto points throughout the system. Since the Charter of Rights and Freedoms was introduced in Canada in 1982 there has been an increase in venue-shifting to the courts there, but there is no parallel in Canada to being able to play off executive against legislature, legislative chamber against legislative chamber, regulatory agencies against legislature and the executive, and so on. All this supports our conclusion that loss imposition in the United States tends to be more challenging because there are more avenues for loss avoidance. Loss avoiders in Canada do have alternative venues, but fewer of them. Moreover, when they do exercise some pressure on the party caucus, for example, it tends to get suppressed by party solidarity, owing to the Westminster system.

Second, the shorter electoral cycle combined with looser campaign financing legislation makes electoral threats by loss avoiders more plausible in the United States than in Canada. Third, it would seem that opportunities to redefine the issue may be somewhat greater in the United States. In part this is because of greater diversity of media and interest groups, but it is also because there is a greater availability of venues in which to make a case. In Canada, policy debate tends to be largely limited to positions taken by the handful of political parties—and especially by the governing party. In the United States, there is a greater possibility of finding a champion for a point of view that is not mainstream. In addition, and equally important, the specific sorts of redefinition that are possible in a country depend heavily on the dominant values and cleavages in that society. In the United States, redefinitions of an issue that appeal to individual rights are most likely to find fertile ground, while in Canada appeals to group rights and to regional grievances are more likely to strike a chord with potential allies.

CONCLUSIONS

Loss imposition is a key challenge for any democratic system, given that most of those who will suffer a loss will resist it, and in political terms they have the right and often the capacity to organize their resistance through various means. The evidence presented in this book suggests that institutional arrangements have a major impact on where (i.e., in which institutional venues) loss imposition occurs, a strong impact on the strategies that potential loss imposers and loss avoiders use, and significant but uneven impacts on the capacity to impose losses and thus on policy outcomes. Loss imposition tends to be somewhat easier in the context of the concentrated powers of a Westminster system than in the American presidential-style system, while the U.S. system tends to provide greater institutional leverage for loss avoiders, or, indeed, for any group that wishes to sustain the policy status quo against alternatives. Viewed another way, the Canadian system has some substantial democratic deficits when compared with political institutions in the United States. The Canadian system does indeed concentrate much power in the governing party and increasingly in the office of the prime minister—when he chooses to exercise it.[5] The United States allows many voices to be heard, and its system tends to generate more gridlock and paralysis than the Canadian one, especially when it comes to imposing losses on well-organized groups with lots of resources.

These institutional effects are far from constituting consistent "advantages" and "disadvantages" across all or nearly all cases, however. They are better understood, rather, as institutional "risks" and "opportunities" that take a well-defined form only through their interaction with other factors, such as policy legacies, cleavage structures, and other institutional differences (e.g., federalism, the role of the courts, and the nuances of legislative procedure). That this is so should not be surprising: Institutional effects are never entirely unidirectional, and in some cases (e.g., federalism) they are extremely complex. In addition, the capacity of loss imposers and loss avoiders to employ strategies such as redefining an issue depend heavily on how other groups, less directly affected, perceive the issue, which may in turn depend on whether they themselves harbor regional grievances or have strong identifications with specific individual or group rights.

Moreover, the cases suggest that the politics and outcomes within sectors, across countries, are more alike than politics and outcomes across sectors, within countries. This, too, should not be surprising. In two countries with broadly similar cultures and sets of interests, at similar levels of economic development, the types of interests that mobilize around a particular issue are also likely to be broadly similar as well. Neither system is likely to even consider options that impose catastrophic losses on well-organized groups. Thus, while interests in the two countries are working within different institutional systems and pulling different institutional levers to attain their goals, marginal adjustments to the status quo rather than fundamental changes to the policy in place are the norm in both countries.

NOTES

1. Robin Toner, "Opponents of Abortions Cheer New Administration, *New York Times*, January 23, 2001, A16, and Frank Bruni, "Bush Acts to Halt Overseas Spending Tied to Abortion," *New York Times*, January 23, 2001, A1.
2. See R. Kent Weaver, "Deficits and Devolution in the 104th Congress," *Publius: The Journal of Federalism* (summer 1996): 45–87.
3. Helen Dewar, "Behind the About Face on Base Closings," *Washington Post*, July 16, 1997, A17.
4. Otto Kreisher, "Reluctant Clinton OKs Base Closings," *San Diego Union-Tribune*, July 14, 1995, A1.
5. Donald Savoie, *Governing from the Centre* (Toronto: University of Toronto Press, 1999).

CONTRIBUTORS

Lilly J. Goren is chair and assistant professor in the Department of Political Science at the College of St. Catherine in St. Paul, Minn. She holds a Ph.D. in political science from Boston College. Her book on base closures, *Not in My District: The Politics of Military Base Closings*, is forthcoming from Peter Lang Publishing. She and P. Whitney Lackenbauer collaborated on *The Comparative Politics of Military Base Closures* (University of Maine Press, 2000).

P. Whitney Lackenbauer is a doctoral candidate in history and a research associate with the Centre for Military and Strategic Studies at the University of Calgary. His previous publications have examined the social and political impacts of military facilities on communities, aboriginal–military relations, and Northern sovereignty and security.

Leslie A. Pal is professor and director at the School of Public Policy and Administration at Carleton University. His research interests include social policy, human rights, interest group politics, and, more recently, information technology and international governance. He also writes and lectures extensively on the techniques and challenges of policy analysis. His publications include several edited volumes of *How Ottawa Spends* (Oxford University Press), coauthorship of *Parameters of Power: Canada's Political Institutions* (Nelson, 2002), and *Beyond Policy Analysis: Public Issue Management in Turbulent Times* (Nelson, 2001).

Barry Rabe is professor of environmental policy in the School of Natural Resources and Environment, professor of public policy in the Gerald R. Ford School of Public Policy at the University of Michigan, and director of the university's new Program in the Environment. Previous publications include *Beyond NIMBY: Hazardous Waste Siting in Canada and the United States* (Brookings Institution Press, 1994). He recently completed a book on subnational approaches to greenhouse gas reduction.

Andrew Rich is an assistant professor of political science at Wake Forest University. His research examines the role of experts and ideas in American policymaking. He is completing a book about the proliferation of think tanks and the politicization of expertise in the United States.

Richard Schultz is professor of political science at McGill University and the former director of the McGill Centre for the Study of Regulated Industries. His main research interests are in policy development processes in the communications sectors. He was coeditor of *Changing the Rules: Canadian Regulatory Regimes and Institutions* (University of Toronto Press, 1999). His current project is "Contested Networks: The Politics of Telecommunications Restructuring in Canada, 1976–1993."

Donley T. Studlar is Eberly Family Distinguished Professor of Political Science at West Virginia University. His research interests include comparative electoral systems in Europe and Canada, comparative public policy, and women and politics. His recent books include *Tobacco Control: Comparative Politics in the United States and Canada* (Broadview Press, 2002), and *Great Britain: Decline or Renewal?* (Westview Press, 2002).

Raymond Tatalovich is professor of political science at Loyola University in Chicago. He received his Ph.D. at the University of Chicago. His institutional area is the American presidency and his policy focus is moral conflicts. He has written *Nativism Reborn? The Official English Language Movement and the American States* (University Press of Kentucky, 1995), *The Politics of Abortion in the United States and Canada* (M. E. Sharpe, 1997), and, with T. Alexander Smith, *Cultures at War: Moral Conflicts in Canada, the United States, and Europe* (Broadview Press, forthcoming).

Carolyn Tuohy is professor of political science at the University of Toronto, and is currently vice president for policy development and associate provost of the University of Toronto. She holds a B.A. from the University of Toronto and an M.A. and Ph.D. in political science from Yale University. Her area of research and teaching interest is comparative public policy with an emphasis on social policy. Her most recent book is *Accidental Logics: The Dynamics of Change in the Health Care Arena in the United States, Britain and Canada* (Oxford University Press, 1999). She is also the author of *Policy and Politics in Canada:*

Institutionalized Ambivalence (Temple University Press, 1992). In addition, she is the author of numerous journal articles and book chapters in the areas of health and social policy, professional regulation, and comparative approaches in public policy.

R. Kent Weaver is professor of public policy and government at Georgetown University and a senior fellow in governance studies at the Brookings Institution. His major fields of interest are American and comparative social policy, comparative political institutions, and the politics of expertise. He is the author, most recently, of *Ending Welfare As We Know It* (Brookings Institution Press, 2000). He was coauthor and coeditor of *Do Institutions Matter? Government Capabilities in the U.S. and Abroad* (Brookings Institution Press, 1993). He is currently completing a book on what the United States can learn from the experiences of other advanced industrial countries with regard to reforming public pension systems.

INDEX